ARMORED BEARS, VOLUME TWO

ARMORED BEARS, VOLUME TWO

THE GERMAN 3RD PANZER DIVISION IN WORLD WAR II

VETERANS OF THE 3RD PANZER DIVISION

STACKPOLE
BOOKS

Published by
STACKPOLE BOOKS
5067 Ritter Road
Mechanicsburg, PA 17055
www.stackpolebooks.com

10   9   8   7   6   5   4   3   2   1

ISBN 978-0-8117-1171-5

The Library of Congress has catalogued the first volume as follows:

Geschichte der 3. Panzer-Division, Berlin-Brandenburg, 1935–1945. English
   Armored Bears : the German 3rd Panzer Division in World War II. Vol. 1 / Veterans of the 3rd Panzer Division.
      p. cm.
   Originally published: Geschichte der 3. Panzer-Division, Berlin-Brandenburg, 1935–1945. 1967.
   ISBN 978-0-8117-1170-8
   1. Germany. Heer. Panzer-Division, 3.   2. World War, 1939–1945—Tank warfare.   3. World War, 1939–1945—Campaigns—Eastern Front.   4. World War, 1939–1945—Regimental histories—Germany.   I. Traditionsverband der Ehemaligen Dritten Panzer-Division.   II. Title.   III. Title: German 3rd Panzer Division in World War II.
   D757.563rd .G47 2012
   940.54'1343—dc23
                                                   2012033432

CONTENTS

CHAPTER 1

From the Tim to the Donez: The Fighting for Kharkov in Spring 1942

On 3 March 1942, the *3. Panzer-Division* received orders to move into the sector of the *6. Armee* around Kharkov. It was directed for the division to be temporarily attached to the *LI. Armee-Korps*. Its future missions were still uncertain. The Soviet field armies had exploited the winter in the south, just as they had in the center of the front, to launch their offensive against *Heeresgruppe Süd*. The enemy's plans were to drive the German divisions from the industrial area of the Donez. In the process, they had succeeded in driving a wedge into the German front at Isjum. They had crossed the river along a frontage of ninety kilometers and had advanced to within twenty kilometers of Dnejpropetrowsk. The enemy salient, which extended far to the west, practically invited a continuation of the attack, which would then endanger the city of Kharkov.

During the last days of February, the division had dispatched a battle group—or *Kampfgruppe*—under the new commander of *Schützen-Regiment 394*, *Oberst* Chales de Beaulieu, in the direction of Kharkov. At the time, de Beaulieu's battle group was the only completely motorized formation of the division. It had been made so by detachments from other troop elements of the division. It consisted of the headquarters of *Schützen-Regiment 394*, *Bataillon Wellmann* (consisting of *ad hoc* units formed from both of the division's rifle regiments), *Pionier-Bataillon 39*, the *III./Artillerie-Regiment 75*, and the heavy infantry gun company of *Schützen-Regiment 394*. In addition, there was a company of tanks, with about ten to twelve operational fighting vehicles.

The companies and batteries moved out from Kursk on 20 February. Their route led them through Obojan, Bjelgorod, and Mikojanowka. As a result of the continuing cold and the high snowdrifts, the march turned out to be more than difficult and was delayed accordingly. The battle group did not arrive in Kharkov until 4 March. After a few days of rest, *Oberst* de Beaulieu's forces had to move into the area south of Tshugujew. The Soviets had broken through the positions of the *44. Infanterie-Division* there and had to be pushed back by means of a counterattack. The riflemen, engineers, and cannoneers of the division attacked after a short preparation. It was possible for them to advance from Andrejewka to Schebelinka and eject the enemy forces there.

The main body of the division was still in the area around Kursk—up to 120 kilometers apart— and prepared for the movement. An advance party under the command of *Oberst* Westhoven was assembled. On 6 March, it started moving through heavy snowdrifts from its former quarters in the direction of Kharkov. Two days later, *Generalmajor* Breith had orders issued for the movement of the main body of the division.

The battle staff of the division moved the next day via Obojan and Bjelgorod to Kharkov. At Kharkov, Breith initially reported in to the commander in chief of *Heeresgruppe Süd*, *Generalfeldmarschall* von Bock. He then went on to report to the commander in chief of the *6. Armee*, *General der Panzertruppen* Paulus, who had once been the commander of *Aufklärungs-Abteilung 3* in Berlin-Stahnsdorf.

Paulus briefed Breith on the overall situation. The Soviets had been attacking the *LI. Armee-Korps* ever since 8 March with two to three infantry divisions and one armor division. They had penetrated into the corps' front. For the time being, the *3. Panzer-Division* was to remain a reserve of the field army. It could only be employed on express orders from the field-army group.

There was no pause for *Kampfgruppe de Beaulieu*, however. It received orders to return to Kharkov. It took an entire day to disengage the companies from the enemy. The units brought about 100 Russian prisoners back with them. That night, the orders of the battle group were changed, and it was reinserted into the lines of the *44. Infanterie-Division* in the Liman–Andrejewka sector.

At this stage, the division could not be considered a full-fledged fighting force. Only some headquarters elements and combat formations had arrived in Kharkov. *Major* Frank was there with an advance party of the armored regiment. On 12 March, it was able to take receipt of the forty new *Panzer III's* that *Leutnant* Stigler and his detail had picked up in Worosha. The only intact tank company was already being employed outside of Kharkov under *Hauptmann* Markowski. At 0930 hours on 10 March, the division had radioed the regimental headquarters in Orel:

> For employment south of Kharkov, *Panzer-Regiment 6* sends 32 tank crews to Kharkov as soon as possible for new issued *Panzer III's*. They are to be picked up in Orel by transport aircraft of the headquarters of the *6. Armee*. *Oberst* Munzel is to request expedited release of those crews from the Headquarters of the *2. Panzer-Armee*. Commander of *Panzer-Regiment 6* and his headquarters to move to Kharkov to the *3. Panzer-Division* location. Ongoing missions in Orel to be supervised by *Oberstleutnant* Schmidt-Ott.

Oberst Munzel, who was still employed in infantry operations at Iwanowka, had to turn over his command to *Hauptmann* von Prittwitz. He returned to Orel and made arrangements for the return of the elements of his regiment that were still in outposts around the city. They started moving toward Kharkov on 10 March, in some cases in horse-drawn transport. All tanks and vehicles in need of repair were loaded on trains at Kursk, to be sent to Prague for repair.

On 11 March, the division received orders from the field army to assume command of the

"Garrison City" of Kharkov
Unterbrinungsraum = Quartering area of individual troop elements

sector manned by the *294. Infanterie-Division*. Fortunately, the commanding general of the *XVII. Armee-Korps*, *General der Infanterie* Hollidt, had discussed this possibility with Breith, so that the division headquarters was familiar with the situation there. The headquarters was moved to Neprokriyaja on 12 March, where the command post of the Saxon infantry division of *Generalleutnant* Gabcke was located.

The situation there was anything but clear and straightforward. The Soviets had been attacking with superior numbers at Rogatschewka against the battle groups of *Oberst* Winkler and *Oberst* Mikosch for days on end. They were also attacking at Ternowaja, where the companies of *Major* Pape's motorcycle infantry battalion were just arriving in the face of bitter cold. The Soviets had broken into the positions of the infantry division with their strong forces and were advancing from the north to the south along the west bank of the Donez. Effective 12 March, *Infanterie-Regiment 429* (of the *168. Infanterie-Division*) was attached to Breith's forces, but only the 3rd Battalion was immediately available. The battalion was brought forward to Fedorowka to pass the withdrawing forces of the Saxon infantry division through the lines. In the midst of all the confusion, orders were received from the corps that the division headquarters was to move to Lipzy. It was to supervise the arrival and staging of the remaining battalions of *Infanterie-Regiment 429* and *Kampfgruppe de*

Beaulieu there. For the time being, *Kampfgruppe Mikosch* was attached to the *3. Panzer-Division*. It was not clear what the overall intent was until the headquarters of the *6. Armee* provided clarification.

The command elements of the *3. Panzer-Division* moved to Lipzy on 13 March. They were able to get *Kampfgruppe de Beaulieu* released form the sector of the *44. Infanterie-Division* and moved back to Kharkov, where the elements arrived early in the morning. Since the enemy was active everywhere and was attacking at Rogatschewka and Fedorowka at the same time, the battle group was employed again by 1400 hours, marching in the direction of Nepokritaja. *Oberst* de Beaulieu received orders to not only hold up the Russians but to also take back the Babka River line.

The division rear command post was located near the corps command post in Kharkov East. Together with his brigade headquarters, *Oberst* Westhoven assumed responsibility for the forces located in the eastern part of the city as the *Verteidigungsstab Ost* (Defense Headquarters East). During the day, the 1st Company of the signals battalion and Bridging Section 1 arrived from the division, with the latter element employed in the construction of positions in the eastern part of the city. The highest level of alert was imposed on the forces within the city.

The fourteenth of March saw the temperatures dip to -20 (-4 Fahrenheit), after it had snowed during the night. The weather conditions delayed the movements of *Kampfgruppe de Beaulieu*. The enemy continuously attempted to disrupt the movements by sorties launched by individual aircraft. The battle group staged during the morning hours and attacked the enemy from Nepokritaja as soon as the sun rose. After a short artillery preparation, the riflemen made good progress, supported by the tanks of *Hauptmann* Markowski. They were able to retake Rogatschewka. The Russians pulled back over

the high ground, where they were once more taken under fire by the German guns. The Soviets lost a battery that consisted of three captured German light howitzers, one antitank gun, and three light fighting vehicles.

While the battle group established an all-round defense around the village located on a rise, *Hauptmann* Markowski's tanks successfully mounted an attack against Hill 211.8 in the afternoon. Once again, a battery was taken and two tanks, including one T-34, were destroyed. It was the first visible sign of success for the division after days of painful losses.

Kradschützen-Bataillon 3, which was employed in the sector of *Kampfgruppe Mikosch*, was then subjected to continuous enemy attacks in the area around Ternowaja. There was not a single house in which to warm up, and it was impossible to dig into the frozen ground. Manning a sector of some two or three kilometers, the battalion turned back all attacks, in some cases by means of immediate counterattacks conducted by small groups. *Hauptmann* von Cochenhausen performed magnificently. Cases of frostbite increased. The battalion was soon at the end of its strength, after having suffered eleven dead and forty-seven wounded, including five officers, in the course of three days.

Fortunately, forces from the division started arriving in Kharkov. *Oberst* Munzel arrived with seventeen tanks and took over command of his regiment again. That same afternoon, *Major* Frank was sent to Nepokritaja with twenty-one tanks to reinforce *Kampfgruppe de Beaulieu*. The crews for the tanks had been flown in by *Ju 52's* from Kursk. After the arrival of the personnel and the receipt of the forty *Panzer III's*, the regiment was able to form three companies, which were led by *Leutnant* Rodenhauser, *Leutnant* Rühl, and *Leutnant* Bodig.

Oberst de Beaulieu's battle group in Rogatschewka received orders on Sunday, 15 March—*Heldengedenktag*[1]—to immediately continue its

---

1. "Heroes' Commemoration Day," a holiday introduced by the National Socialists in 1934 to commemorate war dead, with an increased emphasis on the heroic nature of those deaths.

advance so as to create the prerequisites necessary for the planned future attack on Bairak. The riflemen moved out again, even though it had been some time since they had eaten something warm. The persistent snowdrifts made it impossible for supply elements to move forward. The field messes, in addition to the fuel trucks, were still far to the rear. The forces in Kharkov could only be supplied from the air. After the tanks had received their fuel in that manner, they moved out at 1145 hours, soon penetrating the initial enemy positions. The attack made good progress and the tanks and riflemen remained on the heels of the Soviets. Dragunowka was taken and the attack continued east in the direction of Krupjewacha. The enemy had established defenses in front of that village and defended stubbornly. Friendly losses increased. *Hauptmann* Bachmann, the company commander of the *11./ Schützen-Regiment 394*, was killed in the attack on the village. But the riflemen and cannoneers did not give up. The Russians were ejected from their defensive positions and Krupjewacha was assaulted.

The Soviets were aware of the importance of that village. Their artillery fired ceaselessly on the German positions, which were exposed like targets on a range. It was not possible to silence the enemy batteries. The forward observer of the 9th Battery, *Leutnant* Sporns, was able to place a few well-aimed salvoes on the enemy guns, but the enemy did not give up his efforts, either that night or the next day. The situation remained unchanged, and the casualties mounted in all sectors. *Kradschützen-Battalion 3* was at the end of its strength. The last remaining men had nothing left in them. While the German forces continued to shrink, the division intelligence section that day estimated that the division was facing a minimum of four rifle divisions and one tank brigade. During the evening of 15 March, the field army ordered that the operations to take Boljschaja-Babka be continued. All companies that were not absolutely essential at the front were employed to clear snow. But it continued to snow, and it turned into a Sisyphean effort, which had no end.

The Soviets took the initiative in the sector of *Kampfgruppe de Beaulieu*. Disregarding casualties, they continuously attacked the weakened battalion's positions starting on the morning of 16 March and were able to temporarily penetrate into the lines. The few tanks on hand had to be constantly employed to eject the Russians that had penetrated. Against all expectations, their efforts worked, with the exception of Krupjewacha, where the enemy was already so strong that it took hours before *Major* Frank's fighting vehicles could clean up the situation there.

Oberst de Beaulieu rendered a situation report to *Generalmajor* Breith at noon. It was decided to pull the friendly forces back to the Babka during the night, before they were completely cut off. It was high time, since the enemy's artillery fires started increasing. The white-clad Russian soldiers attacked the German strongpoints with their battle cry of "Urräh!" and succeeded in going around *Major* Wellmann's battalion, which had expended almost all of its ammunition. The companies had to disengage form the enemy at 1745 hours, pulling back behind the Babka.

Oberst Mikosch's battle group at Fedorowka was subjected to the same heavy fighting. The commander of the divisional engineers, *Major* Petzsch, was badly wounded in the fighting and died the next day of his wounds. The German lines were stretched to the breaking point. *Hauptmann* Markowski's tanks were sent to support the motorcycle infantry battalion. In the process, his men were able to take Hill 226.3.

The enemy was very active that night, pressing hard on *Oberst* de Beaulieu's withdrawing forces. He was able to retake Dragunowka. The friendly forces also suffered at the hands of the continuous enemy artillery fire. Despite that, the companies put up an energetic defense and even launched immediate counterattacks. The Russians then started to employ the Red Air Force, against which the German ground forces were practically defenseless.

The division employed the *I./Infanterie-Regiment 429*, which had arrived the previous night, along the Babka. It was at that location that the Soviets were conducting a dangerous attack against the thin German lines. The motorcycle infantry battalion was completely exhausted. The *ad hoc* assault company of *Leutnant* Störck was quickly sent out from Kharkov to reinforce the motorcycle infantry at Ternowaja. Likewise, the tank company of *Leutnant* Rühl, which had previously been employed in the local defense of Kharkov, was moved out. The tank company attacked into the woods north of Ternowaja. It was able to eject the enemy there, but then the tanks had to stop in the face of newly arriving strong enemy forces. Prisoners stated that the Russians were planning to attack the next day. The headquarters of the 6. *Armee* ordered a friendly attack with tanks against Bolsch-Babka.

The eighteenth of March saw a change in the weather. It turned somewhat warmer, and there was a light snowfall. During the previous night, the enemy had remained quiet. An advance by *Hauptmann* Markowski's tank company against Petschanoje had registered success. The company returned to the division command post at 0940 hours, but it was sent south in the direction of Bolsch-Babka at 1200 hours to attack again. The company entered the village towards evening, accomplishing its mission. *Leutnant* Rühl's tanks, entering the woods north of Ternowaja again, determined that there was no longer any enemy forces there. In a surprising turn of events, the enemy had pulled back. His casualties over the previous few days may have been too high, with the result that he did not continue his attack that day.

The group of enemy forces arrayed in front of the division sector on 18 March was as follows (north to south): 1st Guards Rifle Division; 81st, 227th, and 169th Rifle Divisions; 34th Motorized Brigade; 226th and 124th Rifle Divisions; and the 14th and 10th Tank Brigades. Despite being significantly outnumbered in men and materiel, the relatively weak forces of the 3. *Panzer-Division* were not defeated. The division attempted a few reorganizations that day, with the intent of pulling the rifle and engineer elements out of the line and leaving only the tank companies in prepared positions.

The twentieth of March saw brilliantly clear winter weather. The snowfall had stopped and the temperature sank to -31 [-23.8 Fahrenheit]. Friendly aircraft were seen in the skies. They dove on the enemy aircraft that had been attacking the division's positions at Petschanoje since early morning. The hard fighting was still not over by evening. The Soviets entered the village once, only to be ejected a short while later by *Leutnant* Rühl's tanks. A few hours later, the situation was reversed. The fighting raged back and forth, until the enemy was finally able to occupy half the village. The seesaw struggles for individual farmsteads and houses produced a lot of casualties for the forces. *Feldwebel* Dreger, a brave noncommissioned officer from the *1./ Schützen-Regiment 3*, was killed during one such raid.

The command element of the division moved back to Kharkov. *Major* Petzsch (*Pionier-Bataillon 39*) and *Leutnant Freiherr* von Thüna (*Panzer-Regiment 6*) were buried. The grief for the dead was not lessened by the announcement in the Armed Forces Daily Report: "Infantry elements, supported by tanks, inflicted considerable losses on the Russians during the defense east of Kharkov and achieved local successes."

General der Panzertruppen Paulus arrived at the division command post on 21 March and discussed the planned attack for 24 March with *Generalmajor* Breith and *Oberstleutnant i.G.* Pomtow. The division commander informed Paulus of the critical tank situation. The commander in chief replied that he would personally ensure that the 3. *Panzer-Division* received new tanks and that the 23. *Panzer-Division*, recently activated in France, would most likely arrive soon. Both of the general officers then rode to the front and received reports in Wesseloje from *Major* Ziervogel, whose reconnaissance battalion had been in action there since 18 March, and in Ternowaja from *Oberst* Friebe and *Oberst* Gruner.

Elements of the *294. Infanterie-Division*, as well as *Kampfgruppe de Beaulieu*, continued to have to repel enemy attacks. There was also bitter fighting for Petschanoje and Dragunowka. German reconnaissance aircraft reported large enemy movements and the approach of a cavalry corps. Despite that more than difficult situation, the sector commanders all received instructions to release all non-essential forces for an attack by the *3. Panzer-Division* on Bairak.

The division was attached to the *XVII. Armee-Korps* of *General der Infanterie* Hollidt, although it was considered a reserve of the *6. Armee*. Planning efforts for the attack to take back the banks of the Donez continued at a whirlwind pace. The command posts were abuzz with conferences, telephone conversations, reports, and "paper wars" of all types, while the troops in the front lines continued to fend off strong enemy attacks, which were especially intense around Isbitzkoje. The *294. Infanterie-Division*, which had shared that intense fighting and heavy casualties with the *3. Panzer-Division* for some days, experienced a tragic event that day. Its command post received a direct hit from a bomb, killing the division commander, *Generalleutnant* Gabcke, as well as his operations officer. *Oberst* Block assumed acting command of the division from Saxony.

On 23 March, the division moved its various headquarters elements and forces closer to the front. The command post was established in Wesseloje-Lipzy, with the command staff setting up a forward command post in Ternowaja. In the course of the day, the *III./Infanterie-Regiment 375* (*221. Infanterie-Division*) was attached to the division and brought into sector at Ternowaja; the *III./Infanterie-Regiment 530* (*299. Infanterie-Division*) was also attached and sent to Rasskye-Tischki. *Oberst* Munzel's *Panzer-Regiment 6* moved to Wesseloje. *General der Infanterie* Hollidt appeared at the command post in the afternoon in order to discuss final details.

The enemy did not remain inactive on that clear and sunny winter day, either. He attacked Isbitzkoje with about 1,200 men, and the village was encircled for a while. In addition, there was a threatening thrust towards the positions of the motorcycle infantry battalion. The heavy and continuous enemy artillery fires made movements along the Wesseloje–Ternowaja road difficult. The division finished its reorganization for the attack during the night. With the arbitrarily assembled formations, it meant a considerable risk, even if it intended to finally take the initiative from the enemy in the Kharkov sector.

The southern battle group was under the command of *Oberst* Gruner, the commander of *Infanterie-Regiment 419* (*125. Infanterie-Division*). To accomplish his mission, he had been given two battalions from *Infanterie-Regiment 226* (*79. Infanterie-Division*), one battalion from his regiment, one battalion from *Infanterie-Regiment 530*, and a detachment of five tanks. *Oberst* Munzel commanded the northern battle group with his armored regiment headquarters. In addition to elements of his regiment, he had the *III./Infanterie-Regiment 375* and the *II./Schützen-Regiment 3*. *Oberstleutnant* Dr. Weissenbruch had divided the divisional artillery into two groups and directed them to support the two battle groups. The first wave of Munzel's forces was formed by *Kampfgruppe von Pape*, which consisted of *Kradschützen-Bataillon 1*, *Aufklärungs-Abteilung 1*, the assault company of *Leutnant* Störck, and four tanks from the armored regiment. Pape's forces were staged in the Ternowaja–Isbitzkoje area. Munzel directed the *I./Infanterie-Regiment 530* to replace the thinly manned forces at Isbitzkoje.

Using the final moments of darkness, the last assembly areas were occupied. Only the fighting vehicles experienced any difficulties. Due to the ice, they were unable to move out of Wesseloje until 0430 hours. Correspondingly, the attack was postponed until 0615 hours. The enemy, who apparently was unaware of those movements, turned active in the Isbitzkoje area, encircling the area at first light. The defenders were able to hold off the enemy from the burning houses of the village.

The German attack started at 0630 hours on 24 March. The enemy was surprised by the concentrated power of the blow and only offered stubborn resistance in front of *Kampfgruppe Gruner*. The Russians had dug in splendidly in the woods and literally defended to the last round. Despite that, the infantrymen and engineers were able to penetrate the enemy's positions and advance through the lanes in the woods to the east. After a short, sharp fight, the village of Bairak on the eastern side of the woods was taken. That meant that the day's objective at that location was already taken by 1100 hours.

At the same time, *Kampfgruppe de Beaulieu*, still attached to the *294. Infanterie-Division*, moved out from the south. Its lefthand battalion, the *III./Infanterie-Regiment 429*, broke into the Russian trench system on Hill 211.8 after overcoming tough resistance and finally took the hill in the southern sector of the wooded terrain. The battle group established contact with the *3. Panzer-Division* there. At the same time, the battle-tested companies of *Schützen-Regiment 394* took the localities of Dragunowka and Krupjewacha, showing that despite all the setbacks and losses of the recent past, there was still enough combat power on hand.

The armored battle group of *Major* Frank moved east along bad routes. It was not stopped until the Soviets started taking the fighting vehicles under direct fire with artillery and antiaircraft guns that had been positioned in the woods west of Roshedsnoje. The tanks succeeded in destroying the enemy forces and entering the locality. All of a sudden, enemy fighting vehicles appeared: KV-I's and T-34's. A short duel developed, with the German tanks emerging victorious. Unfortunately, the tanks could not advance any farther, since they had expended all of their ammunition and fuel and the terrain was not suited for armor. Around 1750 hours, the elements of *Oberst* Munzel's armored regiment employed at Roshedsnoje set up an all-round defense; their day's objective had been taken.

The center battle group of *Oberst* Gruner remained hot on the heels of the enemy. After his battalions had assembled in Bairak and reorganized, they continued the attack east at 1530 hours. The Soviets put up an especially stiff defense along the edge of the woods. They then yielded to the German infantry, which started an immediate pursuit, reaching the large village of Wiknina by 1700 hours. As a result of those successes by the division's forces and those attached to it, the intermediate Soviet position between the Babka and the Donez had been reached.

The attack was continued the next morning. The tank companies reached the main road that ran from the northeast towards the Donez. The tankers of the armored regiment succeeded in breaking the enemy's resistance along the road and establishing a foothold in the western portion of Rubeshnoje along the Donez. The commander in chief of the Soviet forces, Marshal Timoschenko had been there the previous day, where he had inspected the positions. While the German forces claimed the western and southern portions of the locality, the Soviets remained in the northern portion of the long "road" village. They put up a stiff defense around the church, and the German companies had a tough time of it.

The tank companies were ordered through Bairak to the south to support *Kampfgruppe Gruner* in its attack on Star.-Ssaltow. The enemy exploited that situation by immediately launching a counterattack at Rubeshnoje. The situation of the riflemen grew ever more precarious by the hour, since the Soviets also started employing heavy tanks. The western part of the village had to be evacuated. *Major* Boehm's *II./Schützen-Regiment 3* and *Major* von Prittwitz's *III./Infanterie-Regiment 375* pulled back to the west. The leader of the battle group, *Oberst* Munzel, was wounded and had to be evacuated by tank.

The battle group immediately pursued the riflemen and infantry and took the village of Bugrowka in an advance from the north. *Major* Boehm was wounded in the fighting, but he was able to remain with his battalion.

The enemy had gone over to the offensive all along that sector of the front. Ski battalions were attacking from the east and rifle companies from the north. Tanks were constantly being brought forward from the east. The Soviets attacked ceaselessly and with support from the Red Air Force. The *III./Infanterie-Regiment 530* lost "Windmill" Hill and, in the end, also had to give up Wiknina.

The division command had only an ill-defined picture of what was going on. It gained the impression that the friendly forces in the north had been battered and were pulling back in the face of superior numbers of a pursuing enemy. For that reason, the commander of the *3. Schützen-Brigade* received orders to assume command of the northern sector, stop the retrograde movement of the German forces and establish a defensive line. *Oberst* Westhoven decide to move with his headquarters into Bairak, which was on dominant high ground. Over the next few days and weeks, that locality would become a focal point of the fighting. It was constantly under fire and the objective of many attacks. When the brigade headquarters arrived in Bairak, there was not a single German soldier left in the locality. It had to be assumed that the Russians could appear at any moment.

The first forces that the brigade commander encountered were the infantry of *Major* von Prittwitz's *III./Infanterie-Regiment 375*, which were moving back along the road three kilometers north of Bairak. They were stopped, and despite the cold and their exhaustion, they had to set up defensive positions along both sides of the road on Hill 203.4, a key terrain feature. Later on, the commander of the *III./Infanterie-Regiment 530* reported into Bairak with the exhausted remnants of his battalion. Even though the locality was almost defenseless, orders were issued that with the exception of guards all were to receive warm food and rest for at least two hours in heated huts. The men then had to go out again into the snow and cold to occupy defensive positions.

A heavy weight fell from the brigade commander's shoulders when he returned to the locality shortly before darkness after an inspection tour and found the *II./Schützen-Regiment 3* there. The battalion, being held in good order by its wounded commander, provided the brigade commander with strong reinforcement.

Kampfgruppe Gruner, which wanted to continue the attack at 1000 hours, had to wait until the tanks arrived early in the afternoon, before it could complete its preparations. The tanks companies, which were to form the main effort, had already suffered a lot of losses. The fighting vehicles rolled across the icy road from Bairak to the south, moved through the woods east of Krupjewacha and approached Star.-Ssaltow from the north. They remained bogged down in enemy defensive fires well before the outskirts of the locality, with the result that *Major* Frank had to give orders to pull back to Bairak that evening, where his forces reinforced the hard-pressed *Kampfgruppe Westhoven*. Only the riflemen of *Major* Wellmann's *I./Schützen-Regiment 3* had been able to follow the tanks to some extent. They advanced to Hill 177.5, two kilometers outside of Star.-Ssaltow and set up defensive positions there. They held the position, despite all of the efforts of the enemy to take it back. By establishing a position there, Wellmann's battalion became a bulwark of the division. The effort to force the enemy back across the Donez had failed and heavy casualties had been taken. It had been a black day for the division.

General der Panzertruppen Paulus and *General der Infanterie* Hollidt had been at the division command post in the morning, where they were convinced of the difficulty of the situation. In the process, there were disagreements between the commanding general and *Generalmajor* Breith concerning the leadership of the division. Those arguments would continue the next day as well, when the situation was also very serious. Despite the misty and rainy weather, with the first snow beginning to melt, the Soviets were attempting to batter down the German positions. The division's attached and organic formations defended with exemplary courage and, wherever possible, moved out in immediate counterattacks as well. For instance, the *III./Infanterie-Regiment 530* attempted to retake Wiknina with the help of a few tanks. But the Russians beat the Germans to the punch and forced the German grenadiers back to the west with their T-34's. Even a counterattack by *Leutnant* Rühl's tank company at Bugrowka did not change anything with regard to the dangerous situation. The German tanks were inferior to the T-34's, since they were only capable of penetrating the Soviet armor at 400 meters or less.[2] The main gun rounds of the T-34's, on the other hand, could penetrate the German armor at distances up to 1,000 meters.

The division reorganized once more and placed most of the divisional artillery and the remaining operational tanks under the control of the rifle brigade. After *Stukas* and artillery had temporarily paralyzed the enemy batteries, the *II./Schützen-Regiment 3* and *Hauptmann* Markowski's tanks were finally able to take Bugrowka and eliminate a threatening salient, even though it was at the cost of painful numbers of casualties. The divisional artillery lost two brave officers in that round of fighting. The commander of the 1st Battery, *Oberleutnant* von Studnitz, and his battery officer, *Leutnant* Kölle, were killed on that day.

While the crisis was temporarily overcome in the sector of *Kampfgruppe Westhoven*, the enemy renewed his attacks against the sectors around Dragunowka and Krupjewacha. *Bataillon Wellmann* acted like a breakwater along that frontage and made it possible for *Oberst* Gruner's companies to set up defensive positions. Despite that, Russian cavalry were able to press as far forward as the messengers of the command post of *Kampfgruppe de Beaulieu* and a gun platoon that was defending nearby. *Oberst* de Beaulieu's command post was threatened for hours.

The night of 26–27 March was colder and clearer. It brought good prerequisites for an air attack. The enemy once again had the advantage and bombed the command post in Wesseloje several time during the morning. When it started to turn light, he concentrated his bombing runs against Bairak, while at the same time launching an armored assault on Wiknina. Fortunately, the ground attack was identified in time. When the Russian fighting vehicles started steamrolling their way against the German positions, *Stukas* were on hand to scatter them.

That caused the situation around Wiknina to settle down somewhat. The German formations could then concentrate on improving their positions. At Bairak, however, Soviet fifty-two-ton tanks pressed against the positions of *Kampfgruppe Westhoven*, whose command post was hit by a main-gun round. The Soviets tanks broke through after the *Flak* had been eliminated in the sector of the *III./Infanterie-Regiment 375* and turned west along the road. The few available tanks placed themselves in the way of the vastly superior Soviet KV-I's. *Hauptmann* Markowski was wounded. That night, after the Soviets withdrew their tanks, *Kampfgruppe Westhoven* launched an immediate counterattack. The enemy was ejected from the positions he had won and was forced back to his original line of departure.

There were intense engagements resulting in heavy casualties during the day in the sector of *Oberst* Gruner's battle group. The Soviets had emplaced large amounts of artillery in the Werchnij–Ssaltow area, which were causing even more casualties to the already battered companies. It was impossible to bring supplies and replacements forward. As a result of the slow thaw, the roads and trails had been transformed into an indescribable condition. It was barely possible for vehicles, horses, or humans to move forward. It required a physical strength that the forces in the field were no longer capable of.

During the night, the Soviets brought up more forces. They started firing with all calibers, including Stalin organs, very early—it had just turned 0300 hours—along the division's front.

---

2. The *Panzer III Ausf. J/L* with the 5-cm L/60 main gun is being referred to here.

There was a monstrous noise. The last few huts and hovels went up in smoke and flames; there were soon gigantic clouds of smoke above the woods. Even the snow had lost its color.

Oberst Westhoven's battle group on the left had to defend with everything it had. *Hauptmann* Haspel's *II./Schützen-Regiment 394*, which had been brought forward from Kharkov, defended stubbornly from the ruin of Bugrowka and brought the enemy advance to a standstill. *Oberfeldwebel* Arndt of the 5th Company of the rifle regiment allowed the Russian tanks to overrun his men twice, only to fire on the following Soviet infantry, cutting them down. He was in large part responsible for the success of the defensive effort that day. He was later awarded the German Cross in Gold and given a battlefield promotion to *Leutnant*.

Nonetheless, the left wing of the battle group had to pull back. For the second time in as many days, it had to pull back to Hill 203.4. The men of *Major* Prittwitz's *III./Infanterie-Regiment 375* were not capable of doing more than that. The artillery and the available antitank guns fired until the barrels glowed. But the point arrived when the battery commanders had to report: "No more ammunition!" The commander of the 8th Battery, *Oberleutnant* Kormann, was mortally wounded while defending against an attack on Wiknina.

Kampfgruppe Gruner was also caught up in the maelstrom of events on 28 March; on that day, it lost more than 100 officers and men. The losses in officers and combat-experienced noncommissioned officers was significant. *Feldwebel* were leading companies and *Gefreite* platoons.

It was hardly possible to relieve forces in the front lines. The division no longer had any appreciable reserves, with the exception of *Hauptmann* von der Heyden-Rynsch's *I./Schützen-Regiment 394*, which started moving forward with its three companies from Kharkov at 0500 hours. The men had to force a route through the snow and morass to Ternowaja. From there, they were immediately sent farther forward. The battalion, which had five fighting vehicles attached to it, was sent to *Major* Ziervogel's battle group. *Leutnant* Störck's assault company was relieved by a rifle company under *Oberleutnant* Hagenguth and sent back to Ternowaja as a ready reserve. The *III./Infanterie-Regiment 375*, which was at the end of its strength, was also relieved from its positions and sent to Wesseloje.

The division had lost so much blood in the previous few days that it could barely be considered a major formation any more. The commanding general, *General der Infanterie* Hollidt, personally brought the news that afternoon, that the division would soon be pulled out of the line.

Heavy artillery hammered into the German positions during the night, which had turned cold again. On top of that, there was a howling snowstorm, which covered all of the roads and trails in the blink of an eye. Right at 0300 hours, the enemy batteries ceased firing. In its place in the whistling wind was the thunder of tank engines and the harsh cries of attacking riflemen. The Soviet III Guards Cavalry Corps had moved out to conduct a breakthrough attack. Its objective was the road between Bairak and Bugrowka.

Within half an hour, stubborn fighting developed along the outskirts of both of those villages. The riflemen, engineers, and antitank elements had long since picked up carbines, pistols, and hand grenades to make the enemy's purchase as expensive as possible. *Oberleutnant* Hagenguth's company, which did not have time to man its defenses, was smashed at Bugrowka. The Russian fighting vehicles steamrolled their way towards Bairak and entered the northern portion of the village. *Oberst* Westhoven, whose command post was under direct fire from the tank main guns, organized the defense and rallied his soldiers to an immediate counterattack.

Major Frank advanced into the enemy ranks with the few tanks he had available. The Russians were so surprised by that action, that they were unable to put up a disciplined defense. In the space of a few minutes, seven Russian tanks were knocked out and another two damaged. At that point, the Soviet riflemen weakened and started pulling back from everywhere in Bairak.

By the time it turned daylight, a defensive success had been achieved, which was directly attributable to the efforts of all of the soldiers involved.

Oberst Westhoven had his signals officer, *Leutnant* Schwarzenberger, send the following message to the division at 0715 hours: "Attack on Bairak turned back. Immediate counterattack to retake Gorochowatka initiated." The hard-hit battalions of the battle group collected themselves and, exploiting the success, were able to take back all of the positions that had been lost. The Russians had suffered such heavy casualties in front of Westhoven's positions that they no longer attacked that day. On 30 March, the Armed Forces Daily Report announced, in part: "Intense attacks by the enemy in the area of the Donez east of Kharkov were turned back in stubborn fighting and nine tanks were destroyed in the process."

The situation did not change the next day. The Soviets did not repeat their effort to break through. In place of an attack, however, there was continuous barrage fire by artillery across the entire sector that was as bad as anything that had been experienced in the First World War. Large casualties were taken among the forces as a result of those fires. *Kampfgruppe Gruner* was hit the worst. The *Oberst* reported that he could calculate to the day when he would be the sole person left in his position. In the afternoon, the Soviets attempted to feel their way forward around Bugrowka with rifle elements, but they were turned back.

Even though there was no large-scale fighting at the moment, the losses of the previous few days had been so large that the friendly strength was small and growing smaller and it would no longer be adequate to deal with another major enemy attack. *Generalmajor* Breith personally went to the corps headquarters again and again to ask to either have the division relieved or new forces brought forward so that it could continue to accomplish its mission. He received no answer, however.

The overwhelming numbers of the Russian field forces were demonstrated once again on the last day of the month. The enemy's artillery fires continued without interruption and brought additional casualties. No enemy tanks were seen on that day, however. In their place, there were attacks by rifle companies against the strongpoint defenses of the division. The largest attacks were conducted during the night, but they were all turned back by 0500 hours. The enemy then renewed his efforts to break through along the right wing and *Major* Ziervogel's sector. Even though the Russians had to withdraw with a bloody nose, there was no hiding the fact that the German forces were getting weaker defensively by the day.

The Soviets brought up new forces on 31 March. For instance, formations of the Soviet 3rd Rifle Division appeared in the sector of *Oberst* Gruner's battle group. Men from *Schützen-Regiment 394* took in prisoners for the first time from the 13th Rifle Division. The "Ivans" confirmed that new motorized elements were approaching. The enemy situation from north to south along the frontage of the *3. Panzer-Division* was as follows: 3rd Rifle Division, 1 Guards Rifle Division, 32nd Cavalry Division, 5th Guards Cavalry Division, 6th Guards Cavalry Division, 13th Rifle Division, 10th Tank Brigade, and 6th Guards Tank brigade.

In the face of that situation, it had the appearance of a bad joke when the field army directed that the division was to be fully combat capable again by 22 April. *Generalmajor* Breith wrote the following in his personal diary: "April Fool's!" Up to that point, there had been no noticeable increase in reserves or ammunition, despite many requests. The exception was the Wuertemberg *23. Panzer-Division*, which had just arrived from France and was still to the rear. On 31 March, its commander, *Generalmajor Freiherr* von Boineburg-Lengsfeld, went to the command post of the *3. Panzer-Division* to establish contact with the headquarters of the division and *Generalmajor* Breith.

The first of April saw no change in the situation. The Soviets placed barrage fire along the entire sector, starting in the early morning hours. Around 0730 hours, the Russian riflemen rose from their trenches and penetrated into the German positions, despite a snowstorm. The enemy succeeded in reaching Wiknina. Tanks were brought forward to launch an immediate counterattack, and the Russians were ejected form the village by noon. Two hours later, the village was the objective of another enemy attack, which had "Windmill" Hill as its focal point. Once again, the German fighting vehicles were able to drive back the Russian riflemen. The constant attacks and counterattacks and the uninterrupted artillery fire on the strongpoints tore at the physical and psychological strength of the soldiers. The battalions of both *Infanterie-Regiment 429* and *Infanterie-Regiment 530* were at the end of their tether; the men only performed their duties apathetically.

The division established an urgent telephone connection with the corps. *Generalmajor* Breith reported in no uncertain terms concerning the combat situation. He also made recommendations for the continued operations of the division, as well as a request for the most urgent of supply needs. The division commander requested that *Infanterie-Regiment 429* be relieved by other forces and that additional forces be brought forward to Hill 188.1, in addition to more artillery and engineers.

The general's urgent request garnered some success. But it was also high time that something be done. The Soviets attacked again during the night and retook "Windmill" Hill. A *coup de main* attempted against Wiknina was turned back. During that action, the men of the *3./Schützen-Regiment 394*, who had just recently arrived, distinguished themselves. The company defended the edge of the woods west of the village, and all enemy attacks there failed. In the course of the day, the *I./Schützen-Regiment 128* of the *23. Panzer-Division*, as well as a heavy howitzer battery, were brought forward into the sector. The weather that day was dreary and rainy, with the snow starting to thaw again. Movements were delayed because of that.

That afternoon, *General der Infanterie* Hollidt visited the division command post. In detailed discussions with the division commander and the operations officer, the commanding general agreed to new lines for *Kampfgruppe Gruner*. The battalions were to withdraw from Wiknina and occupy positions farther west. The fighting that day had cost the battle group 187 men, of which 144 had to be operated on by doctors. Those numbers demonstrate the harshness of the fighting.

The elements of the *3. Schützen-Brigade* employed at Wiknina evacuated their positions in the snow during the night and moved to the west. *Oberst* Westhoven established a new command post in a log cabin at the point of the patch of woods west of Bairak. The Soviets immediately pursued. As a result of their actions, they were able to ambush the rearguard company at 0300 hours and take the small village southwest of Wiknina.

The battalions established new positions for the defense on Hill 183. The Russians also placed constant artillery fires on the new sector. *Infanterie-Regiment 226* suffered heavy casualties and lost almost 50 percent of its combat power in the space of a few hours. An immediate counterattack launched to the south against Kut was unable to achieve its objective, because the forces employed were insufficient. The companies were pulled in tighter and tighter around Hill 183, which dominated the entire sector.

A company of tanks and a company of riflemen were sent to *Hauptmann* Haspel in Bairak. With those reinforcements, the riflemen of the *II./Schützen-Regiment 394* were able to launch an immediate counterattack that night against the northern outskirts of Kut and eject the enemy from the village one more time. The Soviets also kept busy and attacked the positions of *Kampfgruppe Gruner* with two battalions at 0300 hours and again at 0500 hours. The advance was turned back, although both sides suffered heavy losses. After that last round of fighting, *Infanterie-Regiment 226* had a trench strength of only 240 men. *Oberst* Gruner, whose health had worsened over the previous few days, had to be relieved in command that day by *Oberst* Wittkopf.

The weather changed again on 4 April. There was snow mixed with rain; it did not clear up until the afternoon. While the soldiers had moaned about the cold and the snow only a few days previously, they started to curse the wet and the rain and thought anxiously about the coming mud season in the spring. This time, however, the softened earth proved to be an ally of the Germans. When a few combat patrols felt their way forward to Wiknina early in the morning, they found the village clear of the enemy. As a result of the overly saturated ground, the Russians had evacuated the village. The situation calmed down a bit on 5 April, although the artillery continued to howl in as it had previously, especially churning up the ground around Bairak. For the first time in quite a while, deserters appeared in front of the German positions. They had been assigned to the 169th Rifle Division, which had been facing the *3. Panzer-Division* for the last fourteen days.

Without express orders from higher headquarters, the *3. Panzer-Division* then decided to reconnoiter fallback positions and, if possible, to improve them. *Oberst* Mikosch was given that mission and approached his assignment with enthusiasm and energy. The corps had announced that a relief-in-place of the division was not under consideration. Despite that, the first formation of the division was pulled out of the line that day. *Major* Wellmann's *I./Schützen-Regiment 3*, which had previously fought with *Kampfgruppe de Beaulieu*, turned over its sector to elements of the *294. Infanterie-Division*. Along with the riflemen, the *2./Pionier-Bataillon 39* left its positions around Nepokritaja. The exhausted companies left their positions and were transported to Kharkov.

The movement of Wellmann's battalion was completed on 6 April. A few hours later, the headquarters of *Schützen-Regiment 394*, which had been in action without interruption for weeks, also departed for Kharkov. *Oberst* Chales de Beaulieu transferred command to *Oberstleut-*

nant Zimmermann. The general situation along the front quieted down somewhat. The enemy stopped attacking; only the artillery continued to place constant fires on the German positions. Fortunately, the tireless sections of the division support command under *Major* Feldhuß made it possible to bring ammunition forward. For the first time in quite some time, the divisional artillery was able to fire for longer periods that day. The heavy howitzer battery had all three of its guns in positions and engaged the Russian artillery at Roshedsnoje with visible success.

The next day saw radiant weather, which also brought with it a resurgence of enemy air activity. The enemy's aerial attacks focused mostly on Bairak. The tank battalion's fuel dump went up in flames. There were no major engagements, however. Patrols determined that the Russians were digging in everywhere and withdrawing forces from their positions. It was later determined that the enemy was regrouping his divisions.

But there were also changes happening on the German side as well. The advance parties of a Slovakian artillery regiment arrived and established contact with *Oberstleutnant* Dr. Weissenbruch. The Slovakian regiment with its total of six batteries was to relieve the divisional artillery. That signaled an increase in the rumors that the *3. Panzer-Division* was finally going to be pulled out of the line.

The division still had not received any word to that effect. The division intelligence officer, *Oberleutnant* von dem Knesebeck, had other worries. Russian deserters from the 6th Tank Brigade reported during interrogation that new forces wee arriving along the Donez Front. Just in the Rubeshnoje area alone, some twenty tanks had arrived that day, including several T-34's. In addition, heavy artillery was also closing up. Of course, that put a damper on hopes for any possible relief.

On 9 April, it seemed as though spring had finally arrived. The sun shone down from a blue heaven and there was no fighting anywhere. The air warmed up and industrious souls were on the lookout for spring snowflakes. Unfortunately, the warming of the ground and the melting of the snow brought with it morass and muck. Movement for the supply columns became torture. It was almost regarded as a miracle when five guns from the Slovakian artillery regiment suddenly appeared in Ternowaja. The first two batteries had been directed to move forward during the coming night to relieve batteries of the divisional artillery.

The second pleasant surprise of the day was an order from the corps: "The *3. Panzer-Division* will be systematically withdrawn from its positions, platoon-by-platoon, and be prepared for other employment." The orders for the relief were issued. According to them, the battle groups of *Major* Ziervogel and *Hauptmann* Haspel were to be relieved by *Oberst* Gruner's *Infanterie-Regiment 429*. The companies of Gruner's regiment arrived that same 9 April and assumed the positions of the two battalions over the next twenty-four hours. Orders were issued for the relief of *Major* Pape's motorcycle infantry battalion and *Oberst* Dr. Weissenbruch's artillery regiment on 10 April.

It goes without saying that the regrouping of the forces did not happen all at once or that some were without incident. The Russians also had their part to contribute. The tank and rifle companies still had to defend against incoming artillery—albeit not so intense as once was the case—and combat patrols. The last few elements of the division were to remain in that sector for almost three weeks and did not return to Kharkov until the beginning of May.

The division headquarters moved to Kharkov on 10 April for the purposes of conducting a battlefield reconstitution. *Oberst* Westhoven assumed command of the remaining forces in the area between the Babka and the Donez. Besides forces from the *3. Panzer-Division*, these included two battalions from the *23. Panzer-Division*, *Infanterie-Regiment 226* and *429*, and artillery elements, including the Slovakian batteries. His command post was in Wesseloje. *Oberleutnant* von dem Knesebeck's intelligence section was attached to the *3. Schützen-Brigade*.

The resupplying of those elements was extraordinarily difficult, since the trucks were getting continuously stuck in the mud and muck. The horse-drawn columns lost many horses, since they likewise got stuck and perished.

Generalmajor Breith held discussions with the quartermaster of the *6. Armee*, *Oberst i.G.* Pamberg, and the commander of the *23. Panzer-Division*, *Generalmajor Freiherr* von Boineburg-Lengsfeld, on 10 April. The next day, he went to Poltawa and reported to the commander in chief of the field-army group, *Generalfeldmarschall* von Bock, and the commander in chief of the *6. Armee*, *General der Panzertruppen* Paulus. On 13 April, Breith climbed about a courier aircraft with his liaison officer, *Leutnant* Liebrecht, that took them via Baranowitschi to Lötzen in East Prussia. They then moved by vehicle to Rastenburg and the *Wolfsschanze*, Hitler's headquarters. Breith was received by the chief of the General Staff, *Generaloberst* Halder, and personally reported to Hitler at 1400 hours, who presented him with the well-deserved Oak Leaves to the Knight's Cross. After being dismissed, Breith spoke with the quartermaster of the army, *General* Wagner, with regard to the reconstitution of the division.

For most of the division, the month of April was a relatively "quiet" time. After the different formations gradually disengaged from the enemy, they made it back to Kharkov, which functioned as the division's "garrison city" for the immediate future. Kharkov was the capital of the Ukrainian Socialist republic and the fourth-largest city in the Soviet Union, with its 600,000 populace. Kharkov was a relatively new city; it was not founded until 1654 as an outpost against the Tatars. The city developed into the most important city of the Ukraine, despite having changed hands several times. In the nineteenth century, it became a trade and industrial center. In 1917 it was occupied by the Bolsheviks; a year later, temporarily by the German Army. In 1919 it was occupied by the Bolsheviks again, followed by the White Army. In 1920 it finally became the capital of the Ukraine. In 1923 the city had only 310,000 inhabitants; twenty years later, that figured had doubled, a proof for the booming growth of the city. Around the "Red Square" in the center of the city were gigantic business and administrative buildings that had an almost American character about them.

Life in the big city in 1942 had a completely civilian aspect to it. The coffee houses and movie theaters were open, the theaters and cabarets performed, and the young women went for walks on Sundays with their colorful scarves and outfits. The soldiers could almost forget that there was fighting raging a few kilometers east of the city. The rear-area services of the division had been there since March. The fighting forces from the front gradually arrived as well.

Oberst Westhoven, who assumed acting command of the division while *Generalmajor* Breith was away, established his headquarters in the northwestern portion of the city of 13 April. The headquarters commandant, *Oberleutnant* Weidlich, had arranged everything well. For instance, the division map point of *Oberleutnant* Paulisch was able to print 10,000 handbills in Russian a few days later. Near the command post were the quarters of the headquarters of the armored regiment, the division logistics section, the field-replacement battalion, the 1st Company of the signals battalion, and the 1st Maintenance Company.

Schützen-Regiment 3 and *Aufklärungs-Abteilung 1* were quartered in the western part of the city, while the remaining divisional elements were in the eastern portion, on the far side of the Kharkov and Lopenj Rivers. The battalions were frequently widely separated. Only the elements of the division support command were collected together in one spot north of the city in an effort to assure a seamless resupply of the division.

Through the end of March and the beginning of April, the companies in Kharkov had to spend time shoveling snow, clearing the supply routes or improving defensive positions. At the end of April,

the snow was gone and a brilliant spring sky arced over the Ukraine. The "alert" companies were disbanded, with those assigned to them returning to their parent units. Eventually, the regiments and battalions began to look like their former selves. Replacements had also arrived from the homeland, whose officers and enlisted personnel had to be assigned to the respective formations. For instance, the armor regiment received 68 noncommissioned officers and enlisted personnel and the *II./Schützen-Regiment 394* received 2 officers and 109 enlisted personnel. It was imperative at that point to mold the long-time soldiers and the new ones into cohesive units. In addition to combat training and drills, there was also classroom instruction, terrain exercises and gunnery.

The maintenance companies and sections had their hands full in an effort to get the weapons, vehicles and equipment back into serviceable condition. The vehicles that could not be repaired at the front were loaded on trains and sent to Prague. Just the bridging section alone turned in twenty-five trucks, one staff car, and eleven motorcycles during the period from 26 March to 25 April. New weapons and vehicles made it from the homeland to the division. The armored regiment received thirty *Panzer III's* and six *Panzer IV's*. The artillery regiment also received new guns, with the result that the division was able to "recover" in terms of its armaments. Life was returning to the division.

On 27 April, work started in the boiler works. *Oberfeldwebel* Noscynski and *Schirrmeister* Braus supervised the work of the fitters, welders and painters. The new tanks were driven into the gigantic halls of the factory.

Once again, the armored regiment had three strong battalions. *Major* Frank and *Major* Ziervogel were each given command of one. *Aufklärungs-Abteilung 1* was deactivated and consolidated with *Major* Pape's *Kradschützen-Bataillon 3*.[3] Succeeding Major Frank in

---

3. This was true across the board for most reconnaissance battalions in 1942. They were deactivated and consolidated with the division motorcycle infantry battalions. In 1943, the process was reversed, with the motorcycle infantry battalions being reorganized and redesignated as armored reconnaissance battalions.

command of *Panzerjäger-Abteilung 521* was *Major* Streger. The divisional artillery was able to field three battalions again as well. The battalions were organized as follows: The 1st Battalion with the 2nd, 3rd, and 7th Batteries; the 2nd Battalion with the 4th, 5th, and 8th Batteries; and the 3rd Battalion with the 1st, 6th, and 9th Batteries. The *I./Schützen-Regiment 3* was reorganized as an *SPW* battalion; it received forty-six *SPW's*. The *6./Flak-Regiment 59* and *Beobachtungs-Batterie 327* were also welcome additions to the division's forces.

There was even some time to engage in more "civilian" activities. Movies, variety shows, and theater performances were offered. In addition, the division music played concerts at the local plazas. Soldier homes were opened and, more importantly, leave trains started rolling towards the homeland. The first train departed on 16 April and not a week passed after that that did not see soldiers of the division on their way home. The following members of the division were awarded the German Cross in Gold for bravery in the face of the enemy in the recent past: *Oberleutnant* Mente (*Schützen-Regiment 3*), *Leutnant* Schiller (*Schützen-Regiment 394*), and *Oberfeldwebel* Wacker (*Panzer-Regiment 6*). Another source of welcome news for the soldiers was the fact that the capital of Berlin officially "sponsored" the division on 8 May 1942.

On 24 April, the armored regiment was torn out of its "rear-area existence" by an alert. The Soviets had driven a wedge into the German front about 120 kilometers south of Kharkov, which was to be eliminated by a simultaneous attack by the *1. Panzer-Armee* from the south and the *6. Armee* from the north. To that end, the field army had ordered an advance by the *23. Panzer-Division*, the *71. Infanterie-Division*, and *Panzer-Regiment 6*. But during the preparations for that operation, the German command became aware of other offensive designs of the enemy. The Soviets wanted to exploit their strategically favorable situation by taking Kharkov again by means of a pincers attack and rolling up the entire German front in the Donez industrial area.

The Red Air Force opened the new offensive on 5 May with rolling bombing attacks on the German positions between the Donez and the Babka west of Woltschansk. But bombs also fell on Kharkov and the approach routes and alerted the formations located there. No one realized the great danger, until the Soviets moved out on the morning of 12 May for a major blow. By concentrating extremely strong forces, the Red Army broke through the German positions, ripped open the front, and pressed irresistibly from east to west directly towards Kharkov.

The division, back under the command of *Generalmajor* Breith, who had returned from leave on 7 May, was telephonically notified that it was to be committed. At 2000 hours, *Oberst* Westhoven called all available commanders together for a conference. At the meeting, the officers discovered that the Soviets had already taken Nepokrytaja, some twenty kilometers east of Kharkov. The field army thereupon ordered a counterattack to interdict the dangerous penetration. It was directed for the *23. Panzer-Division* to attack Star.-Ssaltow from the south on 13 May, while the available infantry forces were to stand by in the Michailowka area.

The *3. Panzer-Division* was to immediately attach a strong battle group to the *23. Panzer-Division*, all the while continuing to guarantee the defense of Kharkov. In order to accomplish the latter mission, *Schützen-Regiment 394* was initially employed, but it was practically without vehicles, since most had been sent away for overhaul. *Oberstleutnant* Zimmermann was entrusted with command of the regiment, since *Oberst* Chales de Beaulieu was on leave. The companies left their quarters by 2400 hours and occupied the positions that had already been reconnoitered along the edge of the city. *Hauptmann Freiherr* von der Heyden-Rynsch's 1st Battalion was employed on the left with the 2nd Battalion on the right. *Major* Peschke, the commander of the division's replacement battalion, was given command of that battalion, since the actual commander, *Major* Haspel, was also on leave. Both battalions were given one light howitzer and several antitank guns in support. The 2nd Company of the divisional engineers assumed the mission of guarding the bridges north of Kharkov. *Oberstleutnant* Schmidt-Ott was given command of the reinforced motorized battle group of the division. His forces consisted of the *III./Panzer-Regiment 6* (*Major* Ziervogel), the *I./Schützen-Regiment 3* (*Major* Wellmann), the *3./Pionier-Bataillon 39*, and the *1./Artillerie-Regiment 75*. The battle group received orders to be prepared to move out over the next few days.

What was the overall situation? Both sides wanted to restore movement to the front after the stalemate of the winter. As early as 5 April, Hitler had already issued general directives for the continuation of the war. In part, he stated: "The objective of the main operation . . . is to take the Caucasus Front by decisively beating and destroying the Russian forces that are located in the area around Woronesch to the south, the west and, possibly, the north of the Don."

The employment of the envisioned German forces—most of the armored formations—was to take place from the area south of Orel, that is, around Kharkov. At the same time, Marshal Timoschenko, the commander in chief of the Soviet field armies, prepared an offensive in the Kharkov area, which was to eject the German divisions from the Ukraine after the city had been captured. The Red Army had beaten the Germans to the punch with its major offensive west and south of Kharkov. The northern attack arm tore open thirty kilometers of German front that day. The enemy was advancing on Kharkov with eighteen rifle divisions, two cavalry divisions, and ten tank brigades. The Saxon *294. Infanterie-Division* was not up to the task of holding up those overwhelming forces and had evacuated its positions on the high ground east of Nepokrytaja. The Russians pursued and were able to take Hill 198.5, as well as the once hotly contested villages of Krupjewacha, Dragunowka and Bairak. The Slovakian artillery regiment in position there was lost. By evening of the first day of the attack, the Soviets were along the

Babka. There were no German forces between that river and the city of Kharkov. A few battle groups held out behind the enemy lines, including *Oberst* Gruner with elements of *Infanterie-Regiment 429* and a few guns in Ternowaja. The *297. Infanterie-Division* was able to hold out in Bolsch.-Babka, despite the enemy's overwhelming numbers.

At 0730 hours on 12 May, the *LI. Armee-Korps*, under its new commanding general, *Generalleutnant* von Seydlitz-Kurzbach, alerted the *23. Panzer-Division*, which was positioned east of Kharkov, to advance from the south into the flanks of the enemy forces that had broken through and drive them back across the Donez. The *3. Panzer-Division* was directed to support the effort through *Kampfgruppe Schmidt-Ott*. The battle group left the city at 0600 hours on 13 May and moved to the northeast. Around 0930 hours, the designated assembly area at Kutusowka was reached. The first casualties were sustained, since Russian aircraft bombed and strafed the motorized columns. It did not take long before Soviet artillery fire was also received. A few minutes after that, the first T-34's were reported along the left flank. While a tank company screened off to the left, the battle group moved out at 1130 hours to attack Nepokrytaja.

Oberstleutnant Schmidt-Ott moved with the lead elements of his battalions. The Russian artillery continued to send in its rounds with undiminished ferocity. As the command vehicle exited a patch of woods, it received a direct hit. The regimental signals officer, *Leutnant* Goetze, and the radio sergeant, *Unteroffizier* Rothe, were killed instantly. The driver, *Feldwebel* Burgmüller, was badly wounded, while *Oberstleutnant* Schmidt-Ott was only slightly wounded. The tanks were engaged at the time and did not notice the loss of the command vehicle. *Major* Ziervogel's *III./Panzer-Regiment 6* churned its way through the impacting artillery and moved east across high ground and through defiles and woods. *Major* Wellmann's *I./Schützen-Regiment 3* moved forward more

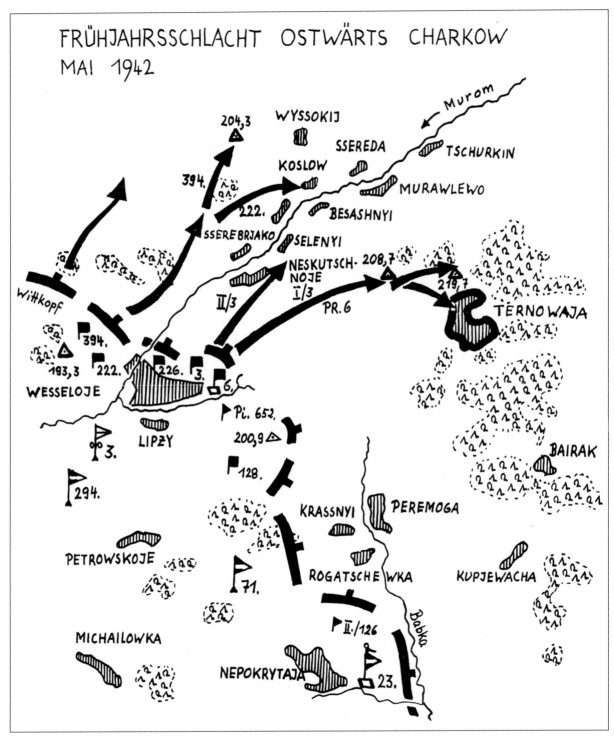

Fighting in the spring east of Kharkov, May 1942

slowly, since enemy fighting vehicles and rifle-men were appearing everywhere.

The wounded *Oberstleutnant* Schmidt-Ott was finally discovered by the regimental adjutant, *Leutnant Freiherr* von Funck, and taken to a division command post in a *SPW*. The commander rendered a report and then returned to the front to be with his forces. By then, it had turned dark. The commander encountered only soldiers from a Saxon infantry regiment under *Oberst* von Aulock,[4] who stated that friendly tanks were already to the east. Schmidt-Ott continued east in his staff car, which was accompanied by two motorcycle messengers, and suddenly found himself in the middle of advancing Russians. *Gefreiter* Jessen had the presence of mind to advance against the Soviets, thus allowing the others to "jump into the bushes." Hours later, they all arrived at Major Ziervogel's command post, exhausted but intact. The tanks moved back during the darkness from the high ground they had reached west of Nepokrytaja in order to avoid the heavy artillery fire. During the heavy fighting that day, the battle group succeeded in knocking out or damaging twenty-three enemy tanks.

It was 0945 hours when the reinforced battle group moved out to attack again. While the riflemen screened to the west, the tanks advanced on Nepokrytaja from the south. The enemy was surprised and did not compose himself with sufficient forces to offer resistance until in the village proper. By 1230 hours, the village was firmly in German hands. Unfortunately, it did not prove possible to advance across the bridges to the ridgeline on the far side, since the crossing points had been destroyed. The battle group set up an all-round defense in Nepokrytaja. *Generalmajor* Breith ordered elements of the divisional engineers forward to build a bridge. Despite enemy artillery fire, the bridge was finished by 1800 hours.

The friendly attack, conducted with equal intensity by both the tanks and the riflemen, was a complete success. The enemy was driven from the dominant high ground through close combat. The German formations set up for the defense. Schmidt-Ott's battle group was relieved over the next few hours by elements of the *23. Panzer-Division*, that arrived at Nepokrytaja via Petschanoje. The motorcycle infantry battalion of the *23. Panzer-Division*, *Kradschützen-Bataillon 23*, was attached to Schmidt-Ott's forces.

A short while later, the entire *23. Panzer-Division* was subordinated to *Generalmajor* Breith, who had received orders from the corps to advance north with both divisions to attack the enemy in the flank at Wesseloje.[5] The enemy continued to remain in a gap in the front, which had resulted from the scattering of the *294. Infanterie-Division*. Russian tanks and riflemen were in the flanks of *Kampfgruppe Schmidt-Ott*, which had established a thin screening line to the west. The corps inserted the *71. Infanterie-Division* along the Babka between the *297. Infanterie-Division* and the *23. Panzer-Division*, so as to free up the regiments of the armored division for the planned attack north. The *23. Panzer-Division* occupied Nepokrytaja. Schmidt-Ott's forces moved farther west in the morning at 0700 hours, although Soviet artillery fire made the movements difficult.

The *23. Panzer-Division* moved out of Nepokrytaja punctually with *Oberstleutnant* von Heydebreck's *I./Panzer-Regiment 201* and *Hauptmann* Neubeck's *I./Schützen-Regiment 126*. Enemy tanks that approached were destroyed and Hill 194.5 assaulted in hard fighting. Since a continued movement north was being made difficult by numerous defiles and deep marshes, von Heydebreck turned west on his own initiative and wound up in the rear of the enemy positions on Hill 214.3. His forces

---

4. Andreas von Aulock was the commander of *Infanterie-Regiment 226* of the *79. Infanterie-Division*. He went on to acting command of that division while still an *Oberst*. He was the 551st recipient of the Oak Leaves to the Knight's Cross in the German Armed Forces, and he became famous for his stubborn defense of the port of St. Malo during the fighting in Normandy in 1944.

5. This constellation of forces, which also later included the *71. Infanterie-Division*, was unofficially known as *Korpsgruppe Breith*.

destroyed sixteen guns, seven tanks, and eleven antitank guns of the surprised enemy. That cleared the way north. Around 1600 hours, the high ground south of Wesseloje was reached.

On the other hand, things were difficult for *Kampfgruppe Schmidt-Ott*. Enemy artillery had been firing on his assembly area. That was followed by an attack with tanks. His forces had to pull back, although they were able to knock out five attacking KV-I's in the process. It was not until 1100 hours that the battle group was able to move out offensively again. It was reinforced by *Oberleutnant* Büschen's tank company in time for the attack and had more than forty tanks at its disposal. In the face of tough resistance, the attack only made slow progress. *Leutnant* Rofenhauser and *Ingenieur* Bärwinkel were wounded. In the end, however, the lead fighting vehicles were able to establish contact with *Panzer-Regiment 201* at Hill 214.3.

Schmidt-Ott turned north in the direction of Wesseloje with his companies. The Russian resistance stiffened, and the advance eventually bogged down just south of the locality. *Panzer-Regiment 201* made better progress under its new commander, *Oberstleutnant* Soltmann, and reached Hill 200.9 east of Wesseloje with its 2nd Battalion, which was under the acting command of *Oberleutnant* Fechner, an officer formerly assigned to *Panzer-Regiment 6*. Some success had been achieved, even if the day's objective had not been taken.

Generalmajor Breith, who was visited that day by *General der Panzertruppen* Paulus and *Generalmajor* Schmundt, Hitler's senior adjutant, intended to have the *23. Panzer-Division* prepare to advance east during the night, while *Kampfgruppe Schmidt-Ott* continued its attack north. Schmidt-Ott's preparations were complete around 0200 hours. This time, Schmidt-Ott decided to go at Wesseloje from the east, as opposed to from the south. The Russian artillery identified the maneuver in time, however, and was able to set several German fighting vehicles alight before the attack even started. Nevertheless, tanks, motorcycle infantry, and *SPW's*

started pushing slowly forward towards the Russian positions, which were fortified with antitank guns. By surprise, the men of *Krad-schützen-Bataillon 23* discovered an undamaged bridge over the Murom. The motorcycle infantry crossed immediately and found themselves in the rear of the Russians. It was then time for *Major* Wellmann and his *I./Schützen-Regiment 3*. The riflemen advanced on the locality through the bottomland and entered the outskirts, the enemy fleeing. The fighting vehicles, which were following, were able to knock out one KV-I and four T-34's. Wesseloje was firmly in the hands of the battle group.

During their flight, the Soviets had set the former German rations point on fire, but the soldiers were able to save "whatever there was to save." That was followed by a terrible mishap. A *Stuka* group that had not been informed of the swift capture of the locality dropped its bombs on the already devastated houses. Fortunately, the casualties were not high. The battle group took the high ground north of the locality that afternoon and forced the enemy to finally start pulling back along Murom Valley.

The *23. Panzer-Division*, which had moved out to the east, fought its way toward Ternowaja against stiff resistance. *Oberleutnant* Fechner and his tank battalion were finally able to relieve *Oberst* Gruner and his men, who had been cut off for days. But the pleasure was short lived. The Russians soon attacked again with strong forces and encircled Ternowaja for the second time. Not only was *Infanterie-Regiment 419* in the small "pocket" at that point but also the *II./Panzer-Regiment 201* and the *I./Schützen-Regiment 126*.

Generalmajor Breith ordered *Kampfgruppe Schmidt-Ott* to attack northeast the next day, while the encircled forces in Ternowaja broke out to the northwest. Both forces were to link up in Murom Valley and cut off the Russians east of Wesseloje, before continuing the attack. The *23. Panzer-Division* was in no position, however, to participate in the operation. The Soviets had been attacking Hill 200.9 since the early-morning hours, which was being held by elements of *Schützen-Regiment 128*, *Pionier-Bataillon 652* (a corps asset), and *9./Panzer-Regiment 201*. To support those hard-pressed forces, the encircled *II./Panzer-Regiment 201* was directed to break out of Ternowaja to the southwest. That battalion's attack bogged down in its first attempt, however, with the loss of thirteen tanks.

Oberstleutnant Schmidt-Ott knew nothing of that when he moved out at 0700 hours on 17 May from Wesseloje and into Murom Valley. Enemy resistance was unusually slight and Neskutschnoje was taken by around 1000 hours, along with 720 prisoners. Enemy artillery west of the locality did not move, and it had to be eliminated. In the process, the battle group expended its ammunition and was no longer able to advance. In the afternoon, orders to withdraw were received, since enemy armored attacks against the *23. Panzer-Division* had increased and it was feared he would achieve a penetration. The battle group went back to Wesseloje, where *Leutnant* Becker arrived during the night with an additional fifteen *Panzer III's*. That allowed the battalion to regroup.

The formations of the *3. Panzer-Division* that had been committed in front of Kharkov did not receive any rest during this period, either. On 13 May, *Oberstleutnant* Zimmermann's *Schützen-Regiment 394* established blocking positions; on 15 May, it was attached to the *294. Infanterie-Division*. *Kampfgruppe Zimmermann* consisted of Zimmermann's regiment, the *1./Flak-Regiment 12* and the *5./Artillerie-Regiment 294*. *Hauptmann Freiherr* von der Heyden-Rynsch's *I./Schützen-Regiment 394* was designated as the ready reserve of the *XVIII. Armee-Korps* and remained in Bolsch Prochody. The regiment's 2nd Battalion took up screening positions around Mal. Prochody. The battle group moved on to Lipzy the next day and guarded the road to Kharkov there. The *I./Schützen-Regiment 394* occupied Hill 193.3 during the evening of that same day, after it had been taken a few hours earlier by *Infanterie-Regiment 222* (from *75. Infanterie-Division*). With the exception of in-coming artillery, the battle group had not had any enemy contact.

The heavy defensive fighting around Kharkov made it impossible for the *6. Armee* to start the planned offensive in the south to cut off the Soviet formations west of the Donez in the Isjum area. In view of the situation, the field-army group had ordered that only *Generaloberst* von Kleist's *1. Panzer-Armee*, in conjunction with elements of the *17. Armee*, was to launch the offensive. The *1. Panzer-Armee* started its offensive on 17 May, which later was entered into the history books as the "Battle for Kharkov." Two days after the start of the offensive, the southern group, consisting of the *XXXXIV.* and *LII. Armee-Korps*, retook Isjum, while the *III. Armee-Korps (mot.)* of *General der Kavallerie* von Mackensen took the hills north of Barwenkowo. The armored forces then turned west to support the advance of the *XI. Armee-Korps* and the Romanian VI Corps. On 21 May, the lead elements of the *14.* and *16. Panzer-Divisionen* reached the Bratai.

The planned counterattack on Hill 226 on 18 May by *Korpsgruppe Breith* had to be called off, since the enemy reinforced his elements during the night and attacked with massed forces against the positions of the *23. Panzer-Division* and the *71. Infanterie-Division*. The fighting was especially hard around Hill 200.9, where the *23. Panzer-Division* suffered heavy casualties. Then enemy armored advances—with fifty to sixty fighting vehicles—were directed against *Generalmajor* von Hartmann's *71. Infanterie-Division* at Nepokrytaja. Fortunately, that attack could be stopped before it reached the German positions by means of the brave actions of *Sturzkampfgeschwader 77* (77th Dive-Bomber Wing).

Kampfgruppe Schmidt-Ott was reinforced with four 8.8-centimeter *Flak* and was temporarily designated the corps reserve in Wesseloje. But when the situation worsened around noon, the battle group was attached to the *71. Infanterie-Division*. The division operations officer, *Oberstleutnant i.G.* Schütz, personally briefed the battle group. The movement to the new area of operations was difficult, since it had very hot for days on end. The columns were constantly covered in sand and dust. That not only encrusted the weapons and equipment, but also any exposed portions of the human body.

Kampfgruppe von Aulock assumed the guard mission at Wesseloje. His forces consisted of *Infanterie-Regiment 226*, the *II./Schützen-Regiment 3*, a battery from *Artillerie-Regiment 75*, a tank company, and one company from *Kradschützen-Bataillon 3*. *Kampfgruppe Zimmermann*, positioned farther to the north, was attacked several times that hot day by Russian rifle formations. The worst fighting took place in front of the positions of *Major* Pintschovius's *Infanterie-Regiment 222* and *Hauptmann Freiherr* von der Heyden-Rynsch's *II./Schützen-Regiment 394*. All of the attacks were successfully repelled.

During the continuous fighting of the previous few days, the individual formations of *Korpsgruppe Breith* were constantly being sent back and forth. Breith's forces enjoyed considerable success: 142 tanks, 77 guns, 50 antitank guns, and 31 mortars destroyed; 3,820 prisoners taken. The constant movements were effected by the shifting focal points of the enemy attacks and, unfortunately, the poor leadership in some places, which did not coordinate with one another. For example, during the night of 18–19 May, *Oberstleutnant* Schmidt-Ott received two completely different orders at the same time: one directed him to support the *71. Infanterie-Division*, and the second one to march immediately to the sector of the *23. Panzer-Division*, which was once more engaged in heavy defensive fighting.

On that sunny summery day, *Generalmajor* Breith and the division headquarters departed the sector. They were summoned back to Kharkov to assume a command along the southern portion of the field army's front. The *6. Armee* desired to transition to the attack in order to link up with the *1. Panzer-Armee*, which had already been attacking north for two days.

Oberst Westhoven assumed command of all of the divisional elements that were attached to the *23. Panzer-Division*. He assembled his forces at Wesseloje. It was intended to launch a large attack on Ternowaja from there on 20 May in order to finally relieve the formations encircled there. For that operation, Westhoven was not only given command of the divisional elements—*Kampfgruppe Schmidt-Ott* and the *II./Schützen-Regiment 3*—but also forces attached to him from the *23. Panzer-Division*. These included *Kradschützen-Bataillon 23* and the *II./Artillerie-Regiment 128*.

The twentieth of May once again saw hot and sunny weather. The battalions prepared for operations at Wesseloje and in Murom Valley. But before the German artillery could start its preparation, Russian tanks started approaching Wesseloje. *Major* Ziervogel's *III./Panzer-Regiment 6* took up the fight, and it succeeded in knocking out six T-34's. At that point, *Stukas* howled above the heads of the riflemen and the tank drivers and then dove on the Russian positions. Exploiting the situation, the ground forces started moving out at 1055 hours. Since the Soviets were affected by the hammer blows of the *Stukas* and the tanks, the German forces gained ground rapidly, soon passing Neskutschnoje to the south and continuing east. *Kampfgruppe Schmidt-Ott* assaulted Hill 208.7 and then briefly halted to refuel and rearm. By then, the riflemen also arrived. *Major* Wellmann's *I./Schützen-Regiment 3* followed the tanks, while the 2nd Battalion of the rifle regiment (*Major* Boehm) entered Neskutschnoje at noon and occupied it. The fighting for the village took hours before the Russians gave up. In that fighting, the adjutant of the 1st Battalion of the rifle regiment, *Leutnant* Jobst, especially distinguished himself. *Oberstleutnant* Zimmermann's battle group, advancing to the left, also closed up to that area by noon. The battle group lost several officers that day to wounds, including *Hauptmann Freiherr* von der Heyden-Rynsch, *Oberleutnant* Dürrholz, *Oberarzt* Dr. Evers, and *Leutnant* Bollenhagen from the *I./Schützen-Regiment 394* alone. *Oberleutnant* Dittmer assumed acting command of the battalion.

Kampfgruppe Schmidt-Ott was in the center of the attack that afternoon that was directed to the east. By evening, it had taken Hill 219.7, just outside of Ternowaja. Unfortunately, it was not possible that day to relieve the encircled forces of *Oberst* Gruner. The enemy fired without pause on the German columns, with the result that the battle group had to pull back again during the night. The rifle battalions screened in Murom Valley. *Kampfgruppe Zimmermann* was located on Hill 204.3 that evening. The *III./ Infanterie-Regiment 183 (62. Infanterie-Division)* was brought forward to reinforce it.

The Soviets defended stubbornly. Their artillery plastered all movement with fire. The commander of the *III./Panzer-Regiment 6, Major* Ziervogel, was badly wounded. The brave officer died a short while later at the main clearing station.

Oberst Westhoven consolidated the battle groups of *Oberstleutnant* Zimmermann and *Oberst* Wittkopf. After being attacked from the air, the German formations moved out at 0930 hours. The Russians appeared to finally be giving in. They evacuated the positions they had defended so bravely and pulled back to the northwest. The armored regiment thrust forward in a narrow wedge towards Hill 219.7 and then moved on to Ternowaja in a single bound. The lead tanks reached the initial outposts of the encircled men at 1005 hours. *Oberstleutnant* Schmidt-Ott, who was with the lead elements, later received the Knight's Cross in October for the bold raid. *Oberleutnant* Fechner and *Oberleutnant* Schewe of *Panzer-Regiment 201*, but once assigned to *Panzer-Regiment 6*, were the first to greet their former tanker comrades.

Schmidt-Ott had one tank company each screen to the north and to the south. A column of forty trucks was then shunted into Ternowaja in order to evacuate the 350 wounded men of *Oberst* Gruner and *Oberst* Soltmann. The encircled men were truly at the end of their strength; they had literally starved over the previous few days, receiving only 125 grams (4.4 ounces) of hardtack and 200 grams (7 ounces) of canned vegetables.

The rifle battalions remained along the Murom to screen the operation. While doing that, *Kampfgruppe Zimmermann* gained ground to the northeast, after *Infanterie-Regiment 222* had taken Koslow. In the course of the day, the enemy also evacuated his positions there and pulled back. German combat aircraft were constantly in the air and unquestionably dominated the air space. When the breakthrough attempts of the Red Army east of Kharkov failed, the attacks by the Soviet 6th, 9th, and 57th Armies to the south of Kharkov were also called off. The Russian offensive in the southern portion of the sector was over. It was then the turn of the armies of *Generalfeldmarschall* von Bock's field-army group.

The evacuation of the wounded in Ternowaja was concluded during the night of 21–22 May. The German formations there pulled back, protected by *Panzer-Regiment 6*, and occupied positions farther west. Toward noon, orders arrived directing that the entire battle group be withdrawn. *Oberst* von Aulock's *Infanterie-Regiment 221 (294. Infanterie-Division)* was to assume the sector. The remaining formations of the *3. Panzer-Division* continued to be under the command of *Oberst* Westhoven. The companies of *Schützen-Regiment 394*, which had heretofore been employed up front, were pulled back closer to Wesseloje in the course of the day, where they relieved elements of the *23. Panzer-Division*. The regiment took up positions along the eastern outskirts of Wesseloje as far as the northern portion of Peremoga.

Kampfgruppe Schmidt-Ott, which had been called back to Kharkov, used the next day to rest and regroup. The line elements of the regiment were given to *Major* Frank to command, while *Oberstleutnant* Schmidt-Ott assumed charge of the rest. But the desired peace and quiet did not come. The battle group received warning orders, and it started marching south by noon.

Ever since 21 May, *Generalmajor* Breith and the division headquarters had been employed along the southern sector of the *6. Armee. General der Panzertruppen* Paulus had given him the mission of forming an ad hoc corps equivalent, consisting of the *44. Infanterie-Division*, the *3. Panzer-Division*, and the *23. Panzer-Division*. It was to screen the front off the field army to the east while simultaneously attacking south. To that end, *Korpsgruppe Breith* reported to *General der Artillerie* Heitz's *VIII. Armee-Korps*. But the overall situation changed the next day, when the lead elements of the *III. Armee-Korps (mot.)* of *General der Kavallerie* von Mackensen had pushed closer to Balakleja. The Saxon *14. Panzer-Division*, under the command of *Generalmajor* Kühn, who had received the Knight's Cross as the commander of the *3. Panzer-Brigade* in 1940, took Bairak during the afternoon of 22 May and reached the southern banks of the Donez. The *44. Infanterie-Division* was along the northern banks. That meant that the ring around the two Soviet field armies south of Kharkov had been closed.

Korpsgruppe Breith joined the fighting from the approach march. Up to that point, only formations of the *44. Infanterie-Division* and the *I./Panzer-Regiment 201* of *Oberstleutnant* von Heydebreck were available to Breith. Breith's attack started at 0230 hours on 23 May from Balakleja. Initially, the enemy put up stubborn resistance, only to then pull back into the pocket to the west. Von Heydebreck's tank battalion established contact with the *14. Panzer-Division* at 0830 hours and gained ground to the south later on, where the lead elements of *Generalleutnant* Hube's *16. Panzer-Division* were already approaching. Not all of the Russians showed signs of defeat, especially when they were masterfully supported by antitank and antiaircraft guns. The losses sustained by von Heydebreck's tank battalion were heavy, and he did not receive reinforcements until that afternoon. *Oberleutnant* Meister's *3./Kradschützen-Bataillon 3* was attached, as was a battery of *Flak*. *Kampfgruppe von Heydebreck* resumed the attack and gained considerable ground to the south of Schebelinka.

During the night before Pentecost Sunday, 23–24 May, *Oberst* Westhoven and his headquarters arrived at the location of *Korpsgruppe Breith*. His forces had been marching since 1100 hours the previous day and had moved via Tschugujew, Brakowo, and Mospanowo. Westhoven collocated his command post there. *Oberstleutnant* Schmidt-Ott's tank companies were not too far away. Those formations of the *3. Panzer-Division* did not have any opportunity to participate offensively in the pocket battle. Their mission was to prevent breakout attempts by the enemy over the next few days, as well as route reconnaissance, the building of bridges and the collection of prisoners.

The weather was not typical for the season. The skies were cloudy, the wind cool and rain showers saturated the Ukrainian soil several times. During the night, the *23. Panzer-Division* started crossing the Donez at Andrejewka. After all the motorized elements were on the south bank in the morning, *Panzer-Regiment 201* started its attack. The tanks, supported by *Schützen-Regiment 128* and *Kradschützen-Bataillon 23*, advanced west, broke the initial enemy resistance and drove on Schebelinka. The *44. Infanterie-Division* on the left joined the attack and closed on Glasunowka.

German fighting vehicles also approached from the south. They were the tanks of *Oberst Graf* von Strachwitz, the commander of *Panzer-Regiment 2* of the *16. Panzer-Division*. Strachwitz would go on to become one of the most famous armor commanders of the war. Elements of von Heydebreck's *1./Panzer-Regiment 201* established contact with the *16. Panzer-Division* on Hill 208.5, east of Schebelinka. The battalion then pressed past the village to the south and took Kisselij, while *Kradschützen-Bataillon 23* turned off to the southwest. *Oberleutnant* Meister's *4./Kradschützen-Bataillon 3*, the lead element of the *3. Panzer-Division*, occupied Hill 204.5 west of Schebelinka. Elements of *Kampfgruppe Schmidt-Ott* were inserted between the *23. Panzer-Division* and the right wing of the *44. Infanterie-Division*. Its mission was to maintain contact between the two divisions while oriented to the east. In the process, it established contact with *Pionier-Bataillon 16* (*16. Panzer-Division*) and helped seal the pocket.

The enemy was also active and attacked from west to east with all forces available along the extended flank of the *16. Panzer-Division*. *Schützen-Regiment 128* turned south in an effort to hit the Russians in the flank. Its efforts soon took effect. By evening, *Korpsgruppe Breith* had taken in 5,000 prisoners.

The attack south on Pentecost Monday soon collapsed in the face of enemy armor. The Soviets continued to try to break through from the west to the east. The *23. Panzer-Division* did not resume its attack until the afternoon, after it had been reinforced by its own fighting vehicles. The thrust ended successfully with the capture of a hill east of Maichailowka. The *16. Panzer-Division* was able to stabilize its front and then start advancing west towards Krutojarko with two battle groups.

Since the Soviets repeated their efforts to break out, *Kampfgruppe Westhoven* was sent across the Donez. It was directed to clear the terrain that the *23. Panzer-Division* had taken and support the *III. Armee-Korps (mot.)*. The *60. Infanterie-Division (mot.)* and the *1. Gebirgs-Division* (1st Mountain Division) were enduring strong attacks. The battle group started its approach march at 0300 hours on 26 May and set up in the Ponowka area around 0900 hours. The commander in chief of the field-army group, *Generalfeldmarschall* von Bock, made a surprise visit to get oriented on the situation. The battle group moved another sixty kilometers south that afternoon and was employed at Uspenka. In the course of the next two days, the rifle companies were able to bring in around 1,000 prisoners.

Reporting directly to *Korpsgruppe Breith*, *Oberleutnant* Meister's light *SPW* company, the *4./Kradschützen-Bataillon 3*, received the mission to reconnoiter south through the pocket and establish contact with a Hungarian division advancing there. The company encountered re-

sistance several times in the pocket, but it was also able to break it each time. The men thought they had found the Hungarians at Belikon, when a column of regimental size appeared in front of them, but it turned out to be Soviets. The company immediately attacked the marching infantry in the flank in an inverted wedge with thirty-two light *SPW's* and took 600 prisoners. Fleeing elements were pursued by *Oberfeldwebel* Hess's platoon and also captured. The platoon then encountered T-34's, but it was able to evade them. That operation by the recently formed 4th Company, whose soldiers came from the former reconnaissance battalion, was a decisive day for armored reconnaissance, since it proved that information had to be gained though fighting and the reequipping of the motorcycle companies with light *SPW's* had been the proper decision.

Generalfeldmarschall von Bock and *General der Panzertruppen* Paulus visited *Generalmajor* Breith's command post in Andrejewka on 26 May. Breith reported that the *23. Panzer-Division* had entered Michailowka that morning and had established contact with the lead elements of the Romanian VI Corps, which was approaching from the west. That division turned its armored regiment east at noon to help the *60. Infanterie-Division (mot.)* again. It reached the Bereka in the afternoon; Romanian forces were already on the southern banks. The enemy put down his arms, after he was ceaselessly attacked by the *Luftwaffe* and had suffered considerable casualties. On 27 May alone, the *23. Panzer-Division* counted more than 47,000 prisoners.

The situation changed again during the night. The Soviets succeeded once again in attacking along the Bereka. It was not until 0445 hours that *Oberst* Soltmann's *Panzer-Regiment 201* was able to turn south and eject the Russians. *Major* Wellmann's *I./Schützen-Regiment 3* participated in that operation. Around 0900 hours, the Bereka River line had been taken for the second and final time.

At that point, the Soviets in Bereka Valley started surrendering. The terrain was saturated with the ruins of a defeated army. Dead soldiers and horses and blown-apart guns and vehicles were scattered in the fields and woods. A horrific image. *Korpsgruppe Breith* was able to report the taking of 55,000 prisoners that day, as well as capturing 410 guns, 99 tanks, 2,100 motorized vehicles, and 2,000 horses.

While the fighting came to a conclusion in that sector, it continued to rage farther east. It was the turn of the *14. Panzer-Division* to need help. *Kampfgruppe Westhoven* was sent in that direction. But as the riflemen entered the area around Assejewka, the fighting was already over. Once again, the *Stukas* had smashed the Russian formations.

The operations officer of the division, *Oberst i.G.* Pomtow, returned to the front from his homeland leave during this period. *Oberstleutnant i.G.* Franz had performed the duties of division operations officer during the weeks of his absence. *Oberst* de Beaulieu, the commander of *Schützen-Regiment 394*, also returned from the homeland.

The "Battle for Kharkov" was over. Although *Kampfgruppe Westhoven* was needed by the *14. Panzer-Division* on 28 May for a clearing operation at Orlihojarski, the remaining formations of *Korpsgruppe Breith* assembled. By noon, the *44. Infanterie-Division* was released from its attachment. That evening, orders arrived for the *3.* and *23. Panzer-Divisionen* to move back to Kharkov. *Kampfgruppe Westhoven* headed north around 0400 hours on 29 May.

The skies were initially dreary, but the weather soon cleared up and the forces of the *3. Panzer-Division* that had been employed in these operations—*Panzer-Regiment 6*, the *I./Schützen-Regiment 3*, the *I./Artillerie-Regiment 75*, *Kradschützen-Bataillon 3*, and the *1./Pionier-Bataillon 39*—were soon rolling out of the railhead at Andrejewka to the north. The return journey on the single-track line was not a pleasure by any stretch of the imagination—the trains had to stop several times—but it did not matter to the soldiers. The soldiers had the feeling of being victors again. (It turned out to be the last great pocket battle that the German Army won.)

The Soviet 6th, 9th, and 57th Armies no longer existed. The following Red Army formations had been wiped out: the 14th Guards Rifle Division; the 41st, 47th, 99th, 103rd, 106th, 160th, 210th, 248th, 253rd, 260th, 270th, 317th, 333rd, 335th, 337th, 341st, 351st, 393rd, and 411th Rifle Divisions; two motorized brigades; the 26th, 28th, 34th, 38th, 49th, 60th, 62nd, 64th, and 70th Cavalry Divisions; the 5th Guards Tank Brigade; and the 6th, 7th, 15th, 36th, 37th, 38th, 48th, 64th, 67th, 121st, 131st, 198th, and 199th Tank Brigades. The commanders in chief of the 6th and 57th Armies (Lieutenant Generals Gorodnjanski and Podlas) had been killed.

The Armed Forces Daily report for 30 May 1942 announced, in part: "The number of prisoners has climbed to 240,000. The bloody losses of the enemy are immense. The number of captured or combat-destroyed materiel numbers 1,249 armored fighting vehicles, 2,026 field pieces, 538 aircraft, and uncounted quantities of other weapons and equipment."

While the three attack armies of Marshal Timoschenko were being defeated south of Kharkov, other formations of the *3. Panzer-Division* continued to be engaged with elements of the Red Army at and around Wesseloje. During the previous week, the two battalions of *Schützen-Regiment 394* and their attached elements had engaged in heavy fighting in the sector of *Oberst* Block's *294. Infanterie-Division*. The Soviets attempted to tear open the German front once again with their tanks and riflemen.

During an engagement on 23 May east of Hill 200.9, the commander of the *II./Schützen-Regiment 394*, *Major* Peschke, was wounded twice in the space of a few hours. *Oberleutnant* Maske assumed acting command of the battalion. *Leutnant* Arndt was also wounded, but he continued to command his 5th Company, which happened to be in the middle of the heaviest fighting. The enemy attacks grew stronger the next day. In the course of the fighting, the Russians succeeded in penetrating along the battalion boundaries and advancing as far as Wesseloje. Close combat flared up everywhere. The few antitank guns were unable to put the Russian fighting vehicles out of commission. Fortunately, the *2./Flak-Regiment 19* was there with its four 8.8-centimeter *Flak*, knocking out six T-34's. Despite that, the companies had to pull back to reverse slope positions on Hill 200.9. The acting commanders of the 6th and 7th Companies, *Leutnant* Hartwig and *Oberleutnant* Maske, were wounded. *Leutnant* Gress and, later, *Leutnant* von Wedel assumed command and continued the fighting. In the afternoon, *Major* Haspel returned and assumed powerful command of his battalion, which had suffered eleven dead and forty-seven wounded in the recent fighting.

Over the course of the next two days, the Russians did not launch any attacks. Combat patrols determined that the enemy to the front was digging in. On 27 May, the *I./Schützen-Regiment 394* observed that the enemy was pulling back. Patrols sent forward found the initial foxholes empty. Since the 2nd Battalion of the regiment could not observe any retrograde actions on the part of the Russians, two large combat patrols were sent out on the morning of 28 May to the east of Hill 200.9. They came from the 5th and 6th Companies. *Unteroffizier* Strucken of the 5th Company, a battle-tested noncommissioned officer, entered the patch of woods northeast of the hill, rolled up the enemy positions with hand grenades, and took one officer and thirty-five enlisted men prisoner. That had been the rearguard of the enemy regiment that had already started pulling back unobserved.

After the two patrols returned, the battalion established two squad-sized combat outposts on both sides of the road to Ternowaja. In the afternoon, on order of the regiment, a reinforced platoon under *Feldwebel* Letzas from the 7th Company established another combat outpost on Hill 207.2, three kilometers to the front. The platoon was able to establish its positions without enemy interference. The combat outposts of the battalion established contact with one another on 30 May and to their left-and right-hand neighbors. A platoon from the *4./Pionier-Bataillon*

294 (*294. Infanterie-Division*) was sent to reinforce them. The systematic clearing of Hill 200.9, which had been hotly contested only a few days previously, yielded 9 machine guns, 2 mortars, 6 antitank rifles, 137 rifles, 400 hand grenades, 150 Molotov cocktails, and 30,000 rounds of rifle ammunition. About 100 dead were counted. After the Russian 632nd Rifle Regiment continued to pull back some more, *Schützen-Regiment 394* went about improving some of its positions. *Hauptmann* Roll's 1st Company was pulled out of the line to form a reserve. A platoon under *Leutnant* Wallraff from the 6th Company relieved Feldwebel Letzas and his men on Hill 207.2 on 30 May. The companies all went about improving and strengthening their positions.

On the other hand, the Soviets did not give up their terrain without a fight. They started working their way forward to Hill 207.2 on 1 June and were able to surround it on three sides. At that point, *Leutnant* Gress's 6th Company was moved forward. When the enemy attacked the hill the next day, the regiment ordered it evacuated. The riflemen were practically exhausted, since they could not move around the hill during daylight hours and had to endure the oppressive summer heat. The company moved back during the night of 3 June. The enemy pursued and immediately occupied the hill. The regimental infantry gun platoons of Geiger, Peters, and Minzlaff engaged the Russian positions during the course of the hot summer days. Otherwise, the situation remained unchanged.

Major Freiherr von Türckheim, the commander of *Panzerjäger-Abteilung 543*, arrived at the command post of *Schützen-Regiment 394* on 3 June and brought information that the regiment would be pulled out of the line during the night of 4–5 June. It would move to Kharkov, where the division was assembling. Von Türckheim assumed acting command of the regiment. *Oberstleutnant* Zimmermann returned to Kharkov, where the *I./Schützen-Regiment 3* had also returned from the southern portion of the field-army sector.

During the preparations for the relief of the regiment, the *294. Infanterie-Division* ordered another large raiding party to disguise the movements. Despite objections from *Major* von Türckheim, the division insisted upon it. The operations was conducted by *Leutnant* Möller's 1st Company, which moved out to the east around 2130 hours after a short but intense artillery preparation by the guns of *Hauptmann* Kersten's 3rd Battalion of artillery and the fires from the combined infantry guns under the command of *Oberleutnant* Peters (acting commander of the 9th Company). The Russians pulled back, but no prisoners were taken (the objective of the raid). At that point, *Leutnant* Möller decided on his own initiative to advance as far as Hill 207.2. Although the enemy was surprised, he put up an energetic defense. The raiding party was able to take one prisoner, but it lost one dead and two wounded.

By then, elements of *Oberst* Pilling's *Infanterie-Regiment 513* were on hand, relieving the 2nd Battalion of the rifle regiment in its positions by 2230 hours. In all, thirty-one noncommissioned officers and enlisted personnel were killed in the area around Wesseloje; five officers and eighty-three enlisted had been wounded. The 1st Battalion, which was still awaiting the return of the 1st Company, did not leave its trenches until around midnight. A telephone team from the regiment remained behind, since the relieving infantry regiment did not have one. *Major Freiherr* von Türckheim reported the completed relief telephonically to *Generalmajor* Breith around 0100 hours. *Oberst* Block, the acting commander of the *294. Infanterie-Division*, said good-bye to the regiment in a general order that read, in part: "I would like to express my thanks and recognition to the brave regiment, while at the same time lowering my sword in honor of the sacrifices the regiment had to make. May the regiment continue to enjoy a rich bounty of professional success!"

On that 5 June 1942, the *3. Panzer-Division* was once again completely assembled in Kharkov. The formations and troop elements reoccupied their former quarters. Normal duties were resumed. Once the officers and men had washed away the muck of the last round of fighting, they were informed they would soon be conducting combat training, gunnery etc. Some elements were reorganized. Newly arrived replacements were sent to the companies. The *II./Schützen-Regiment 394*, for instance, received fifteen noncommissioned officers and ninety-two enlisted personnel. The low numbers of vehicles started to improve, after the first new vehicles arrived from Prague on 9 June. *Major* Feldhuß's supply companies of the division support command would bring in 600 vehicles of all different types from Prague over the coming month. The tanks received new camouflage paint: gray, brown, gray. The division operated at full speed, since it was directed to be combat operational again by 15 June.

Of course, there was still some time for rest and relaxation. Visits to the movie house, the theaters and the variety shows were on the daily itinerary. Coffee houses and soldier homes were opened and art competitions conducted. The division chaplains held services and proxy marriages conducted (for instance, *Gefreiter* Rohmann of the *7./Schützen-Regiment 394*). Awards were also presented, in addition to a number of other activities. On 30 May 1942, four members of the division were presented with the German Cross in Gold: *Major* Frank (*II./Panzer-Regiment 6*); *Major* Peschke (*II./Schützen-Regiment 394*); *Leutnant* Arndt (*5./Schützen-Regiment 394*); and *Oberfeldwebel* Pfeiffer (*1./Schützen-Regiment 3*). One week later, two other commanders received the same award: *Major* Wellmann and *Hauptmann Freiherr* von der Heyden-Rynsch.

Shortly after returning from the south, *Generalmajor* reported to the headquarters of the *XXXX. Armee-Korps (mot.)* of *General der Panzertruppen* Stumme, since the *3. Panzer-Division* was attached to it. He received instructions for the focus of the division's training as well as a briefing on the planned summer offensive. The division had until 15 June to be ready to move. A second conference was held on 8 June. The commanders of the *3. Panzer-Division*, the *23. Panzer-Division*, and the *29. Infanterie-Division (mot.)* were present and discovered that the *XXXX. Armee-Korps (mot.)*, together with the *VIII. Armee-Korps*, was to move from the Kharkov–Woltschansk area to the northeast in the direction of Woronesch to link up with the forces of the *4. Panzer-Armee*. The operation was to commence once the code word Wilhelm was received. On 12 June, advance parties conducted initial route reconnaissance in the area defined by Nepokrytaja–Pissarewka–Woltschansk.

The division was reorganized. On 20 June, *Oberst Freiherr* von Liebenstein, the former chief of staff of the *2. Panzer-Armee* became the new commander of *Panzer-Regiment 6*. The regiment had two line tank battalions, which were led by *Oberleutnant* (later *Hauptmann*) Rohrbeck and *Major* Frank. The 3rd Battalion remained intact as a training battalion without fighting vehicles. *Oberstleutnant* Schmidt-Ott was transferred to another duty position. The two rifle regiments remained organizationally unchanged, with each having two battalions. They both received a 10th Company, however, which was a *Flak* battery. *Panzerjäger-Abteilung 521* was taken away from the division. The divisional artillery retained three battalions. *Panzer-*

jäger-Abteilung 543 and *Pionier-Bataillon 39* each retained their three line companies. *Major* Groeneveld assumed command of the divisional engineers. Since the division's own lift capacity would not be ready in time for the planned operation, *Kraftwagen-Transport-Abteilung z.b.V. 578* was attached to it temporarily. *Krad-schützen-Bataillon 3* was reinforced with a signals platoon and two companies from the former *Aufklärungs-Abteilung 1*. Its new organization increased its combat power and also enabled it to conduct wide-ranging reconnaissance. The battalion was organized as follows:

- Headquarters with signals platoon
- 1st Company: Armored Car Company (Wheeled)
- 2nd Company: Light Motorcycle Infantry Company
- 3rd Company: Light Motorcycle Infantry Company
- 4th Company: Light Motorcycle Infantry Company
- 5th Company (Heavy): Heavy company with one engineer platoon, one antitank platoon and one light infantry-gun platoon.

When movement orders were received on 20 June, everyone knew that the new offensive was around the corner. But no one knew at the time that the offensive would take the *3. Panzer-Division* to the gates of Asia . . .

The winter of 1941–42: Maloarchangelsk, southeast of Kiev.

Main street in Kursk in February 1942.

Oberst Chales de Beaulieu, the new commander of *Schützen-Regiment 394*, shovels out his staff car. At left: *Major* Petzsch, the commander of *Pionier-Bataillon 39*.

Major Kersten, the commander of the *III./Artillerie-Regiment 75*.

The officer corps of *Schützen-Regiment 394* in Kharkov in the spring of 1942 (sitting, from left to right): *Oberleutnant* Wagner, *Hauptmann* Stein, *Major* Haspel, *Oberst* de Beaulieu, and *Hauptmann* Heyden-Rynsch.

At the division headquarters in Kursk (from left to right): *Hauptmann (Ing.)* Reim, *Hauptmann* Dorrong, *Hauptmann i.G.* Barth, Siegling (civilian official), *Oberstarzt* Dr. Zinsser, and *Major* Feldhuß.

Oberfeldwebel Ernst Kruse, platoon leader in the *7./Schützen-Regiment 3*.

Major Ziervogel, the commander of *Aufklärungs-Abteilung (mot.) 1*, with his adjutant *Oberleutnant* Finckenstein.

Oberstleutnant Schmidt-Ott, the commander of *Panzer-Regiment 6*. For his achievements in the spring fighting around Kharkov, he was awarded the Knight's Cross.

CHAPTER 2

From the Donez to the Don: The Summer Offensive of 1942

It was intended for the summer offensive to proceed in four sequenced phases. Initially, the two northern field armies south of Kursk were to break through the Soviet front and cross the Don at Woronesch. In the second phase, the enemy forces east of the *6. Armee* in the area around Woltschansk were to be destroyed. To do that, the *4. Panzer-Armee* had to swing south at the Don. In the process, it was also necessary to take the banks of the Don and all of the bridgeheads leading south and east. The third phase was conducted by two groups of forces: *Heeresgruppe B* with the *6. Armee* and the *4. Panzer-Armee* and *Heeresgruppe A* with the *17. Armee* and the *1. Panzer-Armee*. Both were to advance across the Don and eliminate the transportation hub and industrial center of Stalingrad in a gigantic pincers movement. After the third phase had been completed, it was planned to reorganize the field armies and then advance into the Caucasus on a line running from Batum to Baku, that is, roughly from the Black Sea to the Caspian Sea.

After the fighting in the spring around Kharkov had ended, the operational plans above were to be realized. On 1 June 1942, Hitler arrived for the last time at the headquarters of the field-army group in Poltava to discuss the operations.

Before the major offensive was to start, *General der Panzertruppen* Paulus's *6. Armee* had to take the area around Woltschansk so as to create the prerequisites for its corps to launch the later attacks. Since the enemy was completely on the defense at the end of May and beginning of June, the field army succeeded in completing *Unternehmen Friederici* (Operation Fredericus) quickly. The *22. Panzer-Division*, which had been brought up from the Crimea, advanced from the south and linked up southeast of Woltschansk with the *305. Infanterie-Division*, which was coming from the north. After cleaning up the pocket, the Soviets left behind 20,000 prisoners, 100 guns, and 150 tanks.

The *6. Armee* then occupied its designated assembly areas for *Unternehmen Blau* (Operation Blue) for the first phase of the German summer offensive (from left to right):

- *VIII. Armee-Korps* (*General der Artillerie* Heitz): *375.*, *389.*, and *113. Infanterie-Divisionen*
- *XXIX. Armee-Korps* (*General der Infanterie* von Obstfelder): *336.* and *75. Infanterie-Divisionen*
- *XXXX. Armee-Korps (mot.)* (*General der Panzertruppen* Stumme): *29. Infanterie-Division (mot.)* and the *3.* and *23. Panzer-Divisionen*
- *XVII. Armee-Korps* (*General der Infanterie* Hollidt): *384.* and *97. Infanterie-Divisionen*
- *LI. Armee-Korps* (*General der Artillerie* von Seydlitz-Kurzbach): *44.*, *297.*, *294.*, and *305. Infanterie-Divisionen*

Unternehmen Blau was divided into three phases. In the first phase, the *6. Armee* was to take the Oskol between Stary-Oskol and the Donez and, if possible, establish a bridgehead at Wolokonowka. The second phase involved the encirclement of the Russian forces between the Oskol and the Don. The third phase envisioned a general thrust to the south. While the forces closed up for that operation and received their final orders, an event occurred that placed the execution of the entire operation in question.

The operations officer of the *23. Panzer-Division, Major i.G.* Reichel, was shot down between the lines in his Fieseler *Storch* on 19 June. The General Staff officer had all of the plans for *Unternehmen Blau* with him. Patrols that were immediately sent out could only find the remains of the officer and his pilot. The secret files were missing. The Soviets had captured them. The Soviets were unable to correctly analyze everything, however. The Russian command centers were able to determine that an attack on Woronesch was going to be launched, but that the offensive would then be directed toward Moscow. Because of that, the Soviets concentrated strong forces around Woronesch.

Hitler wanted to set an example. The commanding general and the chief of staff of the *XXXX. Armee-Korps (mot.)*, as well as the commander of the *23. Panzer-Division*, were relieved irrespective of the impending fighting and court-martialed. Although they were given "house arrest," they were soon back in command positions.

General der Panzertruppen Freiherr Geyr von Schweppenburg was summoned from the homeland and appointed as the new commanding general of the *XXXX. Armee-Korps (mot.)* on 28 June. *Oberstleutnant i.G.* Wagener, who had been the operations officer of the *3. Panzer-Armee*, became the chief of staff. Neither of the officers was familiar with the attack plans and had to familiarize themselves with the situation over the course of a few days. After conferring with *Oberst* Westhoven, who was leading the first attack wave, *Generalmajor* Breith recommended changing the attack plans. He wanted to employ the division farther to the south instead of behind the *23. Panzer-Division*. Schweppenburg agreed and successfully argued for the change to the field army commander.

On 5 July, the Army High Command ordered the redesignation of *Schützen* formations to *Panzergrenadier*.[1] In addition, all subordinate formations of the division were also redesignated to receive the prefix *Panzer* in front of

---

1. The redesignation did not change the organization of the formations, with only a portion of any given *Panzergrenadier* regiment being fully armored or equipped with *SPW's*.

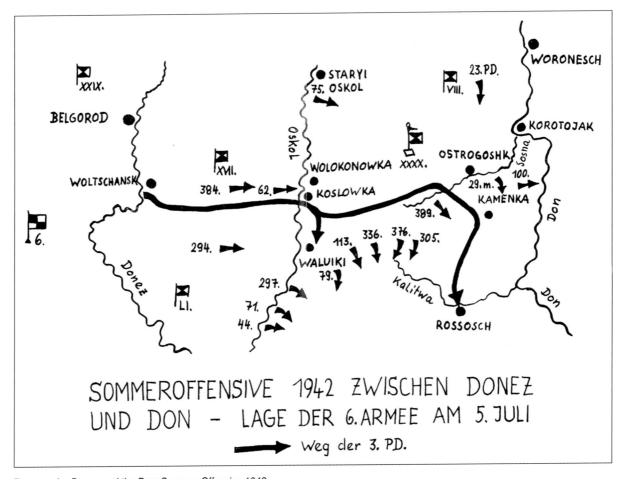

SOMMEROFFENSIVE 1942 ZWISCHEN DONEZ
UND DON – LAGE DER 6. ARMEE AM 5. JULI
→ Weg der 3. PD.

Between the Donez and the Don: Summer Offensive 1942
Situation of the *6. Armee* on 5 July
Weg der 3. PD = Movements of the *3. Panzer-Division*

their previous designations, if not already present—e.g., *Panzer-Artillerie-Regiment 75, Panzer-Pionier-Bataillon 39,* and *Panzer-Nachrichten-Abteilung 39.*[2]

The advance parties of the division left Kharkov on 20 June to the northeast. The battalions followed a short while later. Despite the constant rainfall of the previous few days, the roads were in a passable condition. The movement took the formations through the villages that had been burned down during the winter fighting. Nepokrytaja was crossed; at Rubeshnoje, the formations crossed the eighty-meter-wide Donez. A few thought about their comrades, who were at their eternal resting spots there. That same evening, the division command post was established at Ilmenj, a small, tidy village on the east bank of the Donez, about ten kilometers southwest of Woltschansk. The armored regiment headquarters and its 2nd Battalion set up camp there. The battalion had three companies with a total of 49 officers and 533 enlisted

---

2. An exception being *Kradschützen-Bataillon 3*, which remained unchanged. On 9 July, orders were also issued redesignating the former motorized corps into armored corps (*Panzer-Korps*).

personnel. There were eighty-nine tanks on the books. The next few days were not marked by any fighting. Instead, there was terrain orientation, maintenance and similar items on the training schedule. The engineers sent out route reconnaissance parties, as well as mine-clearing details, to make sure all the approach routes were open. One column from *Panzergrenadier-Regiment 3*, for instance, ran into a minefield on 25 June to the southwest of Bairak. Later on, it was determined that they had been German mines that had been there since January. In the course of clearing mines in the Peremoga area on 29 June, Bridging Section 1 suffered three wounded.

On 26 June, the *XXXX. Armee-Korps (mot.)* issued orders to attack the next day. A few hours later, that order was rescinded, since there was a downpour in the Woltschansk area that afternoon. All of the roads and trails were transformed into muck and mud in short order. The division in its staging area had been barely affected by the weather. Since the next day featured brilliant sunshine, the officers and enlisted personnel expected the attack order to be reissued. The attack was delayed again, however, since the rainfall had caused too much damage elsewhere.

On 29 June, attack orders were issued for the next day. The attack was to occur in the sector of the *XVII. Armee-Korps. Kampfgruppe Westhoven* was to move out in the first wave. It consisted of the *II./Panzer-Regiment 6, Panzergrenadier-Regiment 3*, the *I./Panzer-Artillerie-Regiment 75*, the *1./Panzer-Pionier-Bataillon 39*, and one battery of *Flak. Kampfgruppe de Beaulieu* followed in the second wave and had been directed to cross the Donez to the east during the night at 0200 hours. *Generalmajor* Breith went to the command post of the *XVII. Armee-Korps* that afternoon to coordinate the employment with the *79.* and *113. Infanterie-Divisionen.* The multitude of events, orders, reorganizations, and movements led to the fact that none of the officers and men were aware that the actual summer offensive had started several days previously, when the *2. Armee* and the *4. Panzer-Armee* had moved out.

Stukas opened the attack on Soviet field positions at 0245 hours on 30 June. The infantry regiments arose from their trenches at the same time, exploited the fires and took the first enemy positions. The Russians were surprised and pulled back. Later on, after the enemy had recovered and the ground fog had cleared, he launched immediate counterattacks with tanks. The resistance in front of the *336. Infanterie-Division* and the *100. Jäger-Division* proved to be especially tough. The *23. Panzer-Division* also had difficulties advancing and bogged down in some instances in Russian minefields and tank fire.

The *XVII. Armee-Korps* had employed the *79. Infanterie-Division* on the right and the *113. Infanterie-Division* on the left. Both of the divisions were able to take the initial enemy positions in a rapid jump forward. The *3. Panzer-Division* moved out with *Kampfgruppe Westhoven* at 0715 hours. The fighting vehicles of the armored regiment were in front, followed by the mechanized infantry. The attack rolled through Busowaja on its way towards Rublenoje. The minefields turned out to be a problem there as well and delayed progress. After the battle group had taken Rublenoje, it started to receive heavy antiaircraft-gun fire. Heavy enemy tanks that were positioned farther to the rear engaged the attacking companies. A rifle attack from the southeast threatened the open flank of the armored battalion.

The division command post moved to Rublenoje around 1100 hours, since it was impossible to establish radio contact. *Generalmajor* Breith ordered *Kampfgruppe de Beaulieu* and *Kampfgruppe Pape* forward. The motorcycle infantry, reinforced by a company of tanks and a battery of artillery, reached the area around Bussowaja. *Panzergrenadier-Regiment 394*, which had crossed the Donez by 0600 hours, followed more slowly and did not reach that area until the onset of darkness due to numerous roadway difficulties and traffic jams.

Kampfgruppe Westhoven remained on the attack. The Russian fighting vehicles started pulling back. Westhoven's forces attacked Hill 225.4 after the *II./Panzergrenadier-Regiment 3* had closed up. The Soviets were well dug in there and wanted to prevent the high ground from being lost with all the means at their disposal, including Stalin organs. They were ejected, however, and pulled back to the east. The battle group pursued and made it as far as Borissowka in a single bound. Unfortunately, the bridge there was blown up. The engineers that were sent forward could not put up a new bridge until three hours later.

The corps recognized by the afternoon that the enemy could no longer be decisively defeated on the near side of the Oskol. The infantry divisions and the *23. Panzer-Division* had taken heavy casualties and had not made it much beyond initial success. The corps therefore requested that the *3. Panzer-Division* be allowed to cross the Oskol in the neighboring sector and to bring up the *29. Infanterie-Division (mot.)*, which had been held in reserve previously, behind the *3. Panzer-Division*. The armored division from Berlin and Brandenburg had met all expectations up to that point, with the result that Schweppenburg noted in his personal diaries: "The good, old, iron 3rd has smashed its way through completely!"

At 1600 hours, *Generalmajor* Breith received orders to advance on the Oskol to the east instead of the north and to establish a bridgehead there. *Oberst* Ullrich's *Artillerie-Regiment 70* and the corps engineer battalion would be attached to the division for that purpose. The storms that commenced in the afternoon delayed the continuation of the attack until the night. The soldiers, on the other hand, were happy to have the storm, since the day had been extraordinarily hot.

Major Frank's *II./Panzer-Regiment 6*, moving as the spearhead of *Kampfgruppe Westhoven*, reached the Oskol at 0430 hours, after having moved out during the night. The first two fighting vehicles, under the command of *Leutnant*

Steindamm, crossed the bridge at Oskolitscha without being opposed. Then the bridge flew into the air. The mechanized infantry closed up and both battalions of *Panzergrenadier-Regiment 3* waded through the shallow water, establishing a bridgehead. Although the Russians then conducted immediate counterattacks, they were all turned back. Luftwaffe elements also joined the fray. The Stukas and fighters dove on the Soviet tanks, before they could join the fight.

Bridging Section 1 was ordered forward. Despite being bombed by the Russians, the engineers unloaded their equipment and started building a sixteen-ton bridge over the thirty-eight-meter-wide river. They finished their work at 1600 hours. That allowed the entire division to work its way forward to the river, including the division command post. The enemy aircraft repeatedly bombed the approaching columns and caused losses, among them some in *Panzer-Nachrichten-Abteilung 39*. While all of the attacks on the east bank of the Oskol could be turned back, there was still stubborn fighting on both flanks of the division west of the river. *Kradschützen-Bataillon 3* had to defend against Russian tanks several times and was only able to emerge victorious with difficulty. At 1630 hours, *Major* Frank conducted an attack with twenty fighting vehicles south of Gruschewka. *Oberleutnant* Sauvant became the first officer killed in the new offensive.

The *XXXX. Armee-Korps (mot.)* then exploited the success of the *3. Panzer-Division*. The *23. Panzer-Division*, which had only thirty-five operational tanks after taking its heavy losses, was stopped in its sector and ordered behind the *3. Panzer-Division*. That meant that the *Schwerpunkt* of the attack had switched to the right ring. Since the *336. Infanterie-Division* reached the Oskol at Jutanowka at the same time, the corps intended to continue its offensive directly east. The headquarters of the *6. Armee*, however, directed the corps to pivot north and establish contact with the *4. Panzer-Armee*.

On 2 July, the *3. Panzer-Division* received orders to keep the bridgehead open for the following divisions and guard the corps' attack. *Oberstleutnant* Zimmermann's battalions had been able to expand the bridgehead as far as Hills 187.2 and 202.1 the previous evening. While doing that, however, the *II./Panzergrenadier-Regiment 3* was hit by surprise by five T-34's. Fortunately, *Stukas* were in the air, and they were able to knock out four of the tanks by dive bombing them. *Panzergrenadier-Regiment 394* was called forward to relieve the battalions committed up front. The mechanized infantry arrived at the right time. The Russians weren't throwing in the towel and were attempting to reduce the German bridgehead. To the west of the Oskol, the Russians were launching continuous attacks from the south against the thin outpost lines, which were starting to weaken.

The *II./Panzergrenadier-Regiment 394* was in a defile four kilometers west of Oskolino, when T-34's started rolling against its southern flank. The 5th and 7th Companies were earmarked for an immediate counterattack. Artillery and *Flak* were also moved forward and joined the firefight. The companies of Hagenguth and *Oberleutnant* Koblitz then attacked. The enemy was ejected, Jablonowa cleared and the northern outskirts of Pogromez reached. Eleven T-34's littered the route and one hundred twenty-three prisoners taken. The mechanized infantry suffered two dead, as did Bridging Section 1. *Major* Pape's *Kradschützen-Bataillon 3* completed the defensive victory: The enemy pulled away from the southern flank of the division and evacuated the western bank of the Oskol.

Enemy aircraft attempted to destroy the engineer bridge and the corduroy road during the day and into the night. Nonetheless, the first attack objective of the corps had been reached, with the Oskol being crossed and the boundary between the Soviet 21st and 28th Armies ripped open.

The morning of 3 July indicated another clear day. The corps advanced north the first few hours. Shortly thereafter, a radio message was received from the *6. Armee*: "The *Führer* wants to know which elements can move on Waluiki!" Even before the corps could answer, directives

came for the *3. Panzer-Division* to immediately send a formation towards that objective, thus enabling the formations of the *XVII. Armee-Korps* to have an easier crossing over the Oskol.

The *3. Panzer-Division* gave the mission to *Kampfgruppe Westhoven*, which this time consisted of the *II./Panzer-Regiment 6*, the *I./ Panzergrenadier-Regiment 3*, the *4./Panzer-Artillerie-Regiment 75*, a battery of *Flak*, and a company of engineers.

The screening mission for the bridge site, which was constantly being attacked by enemy aircraft, was taken over by *Kampfgruppe de Beaulieu*, which consisted of *Panzergrenadier-Regiment 394*, the *II./Panzergrenadier-Regiment 3*, *Panzerjäger-Abteilung 543*, and the rest of the *II./Panzer-Regiment 6*. The battle group conducted reconnaissance to the north as far as Wolokonowka, which had already been evacuated by the Soviets. Around 1800 hours, the division received corps orders stating it would be relieved in the bridgehead during the night by the *336. Infanterie-Division*, thus freeing it up for farther advance to the north. The division established an advance guard under *Major* Pape in the evening hours. At 2230 hours, *Kampfgruppe Westhoven* received orders to call off its continued advance south and assemble in the Pokrowka area by noon.

The approach march and the staging for the planned attack on 4 July was conducted on the open meadows. In some instances, the villages had already been shot up and no longer offered any concealment. *Sonderführer* Demidow was used as the temporary local military commander in every larger village that the division crossed through. He had to conduct the initial discussions with the local civilians, write out the first certificates, and redirect the refugees.

During the night, the corps established contact with elements of the Hungarian 2nd Army at Skorodmoje through the *23. Panzer-Division*. By doing so, it closed a pocket around the Russians east of Stary Oskol. In the end, 40,000 prisoners were taken there. By then, the corps had received a new mission. Around noon, the

3. Panzer-Division received an order "from the saddle" that was typical for armored formations: "Corps turns right. Attack objectives: *3. Panzer-Division* = Nikolajewka; *29. Infanterie-Division (mot.)* = Ostrogoshk; *23. Panzer-Division* = Korotojak. Establish bridgeheads!"

Once again, the main mission of the corps was to protect the southern flank of the *4. Panzer-Armee*, which had already reached Woronesch but had encountered unexpectedly strong resistance there. The movements of the *3. Panzer-Division* were relatively rapid. They led through villages that had heretofore not seen a single German soldier. A lot of cattle was seen on the roads, and the farmers appeared to have been shielded from the war up to that point.

Kampfgruppe Pape was in the lead as the advance guard. The enemy was quickly ejected from Wesseloje. The Russians formations were pulling back rapidly everywhere. The many destroyed bridges over the small creeks posed an occasional obstacle. The division covered between 80 and 100 kilometers and reached Ssaldatka with its advance guard as it started to turn dark and cool. *Kampfgruppe Westhoven* secured in the Prilepy–Werch. Sossna area, and *Kampfgruppe de Beaulieu* was located around Dubki.

The mission for the division on 5 July: Advance on Werch. Olschan to establish bridgeheads over the Tichaja-Sossna to protect the southern flank of the *XXXX. Armee-Korps (mot.)*. On that day, there were huge gaps along the corps frontage, since its lefthand divisions were still advancing to the northeast. The division used the morning hours of that hot day to refuel and bring up supplies. *Major* Pape's advance guard was the first element ready to move. Around 1100 hours, the motorcycle infantry battalion, *Pionier-Bataillon 635* (a field-army asset temporarily attached to the *3. Panzer-Division*), a tank company, a *Flak* battery, and a light artillery battery left their assembly areas and started advancing again. It had started to rain again, which turned the few good roads into seas of mud. Many vehicles got stuck or slid off the roads. *Kampfgruppe Westhoven* waited in Ssaldatka for a bridge to be built, while *Kampfgruppe de Beaulieu* remained in Dubki. It was not ordered forward until the following night.

The advance guard, which started following the division commander's battle staff at 1630 hours, moved across the softened roads to the northeast. In the area around Krakow, it turned to the southeast, only to then return to the original direction of march later on. The localities of Afanassjewka and Repenskoje were passed through. The vehicles were near the river when the clocks showed 1700 hours. Nowoje Olschan was attacked. The battle group advanced into the town from two sides, quickly unhinging the last pockets of resistance and taking 800 prisoners. In addition, eight freight trains were captured, some of them loaded with brand-new T-34's. Unfortunately, the bridge could not be used. A heavy enemy tank had broken through while fleeing and was located in the water, along with wooden portions of the bridge.

Although the corps had received orders to assemble and not cross any farther than the Tichaja Sossna that day, the *6. Armee* sent our orders a few hours later (Order: Operations Section, No. 2583 SECRET) to advance south to the Kalitwa River. The field army was still hoping to eliminate the enemy west of the Don. But this was the enemy of 1942 and not of 1941. His withdrawal was deliberate. Whereas the Red Army of 1941 had stubbornly held on to outflanked positions, the enemy at this point pulled back without leaving heavy weapons behind. Sometimes, he did so without even fighting. The Soviet command had learned to use space as part of its defense.

At 0400 hours on 6 July, the engineers starting building a sixteen-ton span across the long wooden bridge over the Tichnaja Sossna. It was not until noon, when the construction was complete, that the division could contemplate continuing its advance. The supreme command had waited a long time for that, and the question had already arrived from the *Führer* headquarters: "Why is the *3. Panzer-Division* behind the infantry divisions?"

At 1000 hours, *Major* Pape's advance guard started moving in the direction of Kamenka. The advance guard moved across flooded meadowlands. The civilian populace had posted itself at the entrances to the villages. In contrast to the populace of middle Russia, the women wore garishly colored dresses and bright blouses and headscarves. The route led farther through blooming meadows and the slopes of hills, where the grass and flowers were aromatic. The first fields full of sunflowers appeared, but there were no woods to be seen anywhere. A fine coating of dust and sand formed on the soldiers and the vehicles.

Little was seen of the enemy. Usually, it was cavalry, that withdrew whenever the lead elements approached. At 1400 hours, *Major* Pape and his men were at the Kamenka rail station. The building had been attacked a few minutes previously by German aircraft and was still burning. The rail line was blown up by the engineers. The village was quickly occupied, and the advance guard was able to rest for a few minutes. All of a sudden, three T-34's appeared, against which the 5-centimeter antitank guns that had been brought along were powerless. But before the light howitzers that were with the lead company could be brought forward, the enemy tanks disappeared.

Oberst Westhoven and his battle group closed up and reached the area around Karenkowo. Around 1700 hours, orders arrived stating that the division was to continue advancing in the direction of Rossosch. *Kampfgruppe Westhoven*, with the *I./Panzergrenadier-Regiment 3* in the lead, started moving south around 1900 hours. *Major* Pape and his forces followed solely behind. That day, *Kampfgruppe de Beaulieu* had also crossed the Tichaja-Sossna. Because of a lack of fuel, the *II./Panzer-Regiment 6* was stranded and did not participate in the continued march.

Despite the late hour, *Kampfgruppe Westhoven* continued marching south. The enemy, who was pulling back, was hardly in a position to offer much resistance. Since the *SPW's*, staff cars and motorcycles were moving at full throttle, they were constantly running into the retrograde movements of Russian formations. Just before nightfall, the mechanized infantry succeeded in capturing fourteen Russian guns. In the darkness, there were numerous skirmishes with cavalry that belonged to the 5th and 6th Guards Cavalry Divisions.

A short rest was ordered around midnight, before the advance was continued under the starry skies. At 0230 hours, the road to Rossosch was reached by the formations. The engines roared, and the vehicles continued south. *Oberleutnant* Busch's 1st Company of the mechanized infantry was in the lead, followed by the battalion headquarters, the 2nd Company (*Oberleutnant* Bremer), and a battery of artillery. At first light, the first impoverished houses of Rossosch were reached. Krakowka, a translator, fetched a farmer from one of the huts and interrogated him. It turned out that the Soviets had built a bridge capable of holding tanks just a few days previously.

Major Wellmann committed his companies. The mechanized infantry raced the final kilometers through the sleeping village. The *SPW's* of the 1st Company rolled past a sports field, where a few liaison aircraft were parked. They pressed on without stopping. A military facility off to the left, with guards at the gates, was ignored. The Russian soldiers were so surprised that they did not even think about firing.

Oberleutnant Busch advanced towards the first bridge, overran the guard force and established his men on the south banks of the Kalitwa. The command vehicle, following behind, was stopped by the Russians. A radio operator by the name of Tenning had the presence of mind to jump out of the *SPW* and knock the rifle out of the hands of the first Russian he encountered. He then took the Russian's comrades prisoner. By then, the 1st Company had established a bridgehead. The vehicles were positioned in the gardens near the bridge, with the mechanized infantry setting up, ready to engage, behind bushes and vegetation.

The fighting of the 1st Battalion was not yet over, however. The first bridge had been taken, but then there was a second . . . a third . . . a fourth . . . and a fifth. All were taken! A large number of prisoners were taken. In the process, *Feldwebel* Neumann's platoon particularly distinguished itself. The 1st Battalion scored a major success that morning, but six comrades also paid for that success with their lives. Two other men were badly wounded, while twelve were slightly wounded.

It was 0430 hours. The city of Rossosch, with its 20,000 citizens, was in German hands.

Later on, *Major* Wellmann was recognized for his bold actions by promotion to *Oberstleutnant* ahead of his peers and the presentation of the Knight's Cross.

But that did not mean the fighting was over. The enemy launched immediate counterattacks. The sounds of machine guns and carbines whistled through the city from every corner. The companies that followed had to work their way forward, street-by-street. *Generalmajor* Breith followed closely behind the brigade headquarters with his battle staff. He entered the city at 0500 hours and found himself and his battle staff in the middle of a Russian tank attack.

The Russian fighting vehicles had appeared out of nowhere. In the din the street fighting, in the crackling sound of burning houses and above the noise of the German vehicles, no one had noticed them. It was as though the city of Rossosch had magically conjured them up. The T-34's moved wildly through the streets, firing with their main guns and machine guns in all directions. They rammed into *SPW's* and overran trucks and motorcycles. It was a mess. The mechanized infantry were powerless against the fighting vehicles. Although the antitank elements had quickly emplaced their guns behind trees and the corners of houses, they had either been overrun before they could fire a round or the tanks themselves had long since moved on. The Russian fighting vehicles created a passageway from the northwestern portion of the city to the Kalitwa by means of their fires. Grotesque situa-

tions emerged. For instance, the *SPW* of *Obergefreiter* Drews of the *1./Panzergrenadier-Regiment 3* was screening a bridge at the outskirts of the city. It was discovered there by a T-34. The *SPW* moved to the closest house to conceal itself. The tank followed it. The *SPW* continued moving around the house, continuously followed by the T-34, until the Russian tank grew tired of the game.

The division battle staff was not spared, either. *Oberleutnant* Doerner's staff car was crushed under the tracks of a tank. The division intelligence officer, *Oberleutnant* von dem Knesebeck, was just barely able to escape the same fate at the hands of a T-34. A 5-centimeter antitank gun had unlimbered right next to the staff car of the division operations officer, *Oberstleutnant i.G.* Pomtow. The gunner remained cold-blooded and took up aim, knocking a track off of the vehicle.

Finally, the artillery and *Flak* arrived. The first 8.8-centimeter *Flak* went into position on the main street and placed a round into the belly of a KV-I from a distance of thirty meters. Batteries from the divisional artillery rolled up. Unfortunately, the ammunition sections weren't with them yet. As a result, the Soviet tanks had to regroup and strike back. In the process, they were able to blow two light field howitzers to bits and damage a third. There were four T-34's that were fighting like madmen. Finally, the ammunition showed up. The first fighting vehicle was set alight and the second one flew into the air. The 6th Battery was able to destroy the remaining two. *Oberleutnant* Treppe, a platoon leader in the *4./Panzergrenadier-Regiment 3*, was able to eliminate another T-34 by means of a Teller mine.

The fighting for Rossosch was still not over, but the engagement with the tanks represented its climax. There were still Soviet riflemen in various parts of the city. The *II./Panzergrenadier-Regiment 3* assaulted the military garrison, while the 1st Battalion of the regiment took the veterinary school. Marshal Timoschenko had been there the previous day. As a result of the rapid possession of the city and the formation of the bridgeheads, the Soviet leadership was unable to prevent a few Russian aircraft from approaching the airfield, where they were treated to a "reception" by the *Flak* posted there. When one of the aircraft was shot down, a senior administrator for a Soviet field army was captured. He had been directed to set up a rations point at Rossosch.

At 0800 hours, *Kampfgruppe de Beaulieu* received orders to move up to Rossosch. *Panzergrenadier-Regiment 394* moved into the burning city with its attached tanks and artillery by 1030 hours. Still mounted up, the regiment was immediately dispatched across the bridges to relieve the battalions of *Oberstleutnant* Zimmermann's *Panzergrenadier-Regiment 3*. Because it turned out that the area as far as Jessavlowka was clear of the enemy, the 5th and 6th Companies of *Panzergrenadier-Regiment 394* were employed at noon in clearing the terrain and the villages. By then, *Kampfgruppe Westhoven* had expanded the bridgeheads as far as Artemowka and Teschernischewka.

The *II./Panzer-Regiment 6* had also advanced as well and was moving south. There was a tropical heat in the flat, broad terrain. The air shimmered in front of the eyes of the drivers. All of a sudden, there was a crashing sound between the vehicles. Tanks, moving at speed, appeared a few hundred meters in front of the lead company. The German tanks immediately opened fire. The companies to the rear attempted to envelop, but the T-34's were maneuvered cleverly. They did not allow themselves to be engaged at close range, but they also used every opportunity to conduct immediate counterattacks. Since the Soviets were moving in packs, they continuously baited the German tanks, with the fighting devolving to piecemeal actions. The German losses increased, especially in the companies of *Oberleutnant* Paulus and *Oberleutnant* Voigts. A few of the German tanks had expended all of their ammunition or were running low on fuel and had to evacuate the battlefield.

The effort to make a rapid advance by *Major* Frank's *II./Panzer-Regiment 6* had failed. The enemy, consisting of forces from three recently introduced tank brigades, pursued and entered the outpost lines of *Oberleutnant* Busch's *1./Panzergrenadier-Regiment 3* for a while. Fortunately, the artillery was able to prevent a breakthrough. The situation remained critical.

The attack south planned by the division for 1700 hours did not take place due to the appearance of the enemy tank battalions. Later on, it was called off completely. To reinforce the two battle groups up front, *Oberst* Ullrich's *Artillerie-Regiment 70* was brought forward in support. It was in position by nightfall. During the evening, the division battle staff returned to Rossosch and set up in the northern part of the city.

On that 7 July, *Kampfgruppe Pape* was able to score a success for itself. The motorcycle infantry advanced from Rossosch to the northwest in the direction of Olchowatka. They succeeded in scattering the enemy's rearguards and establishing a bridgehead over the Kalitwa. In spite of repeated Russian immediate counterattacks, the battalion was able to hold its position until the first formations of the *23. Panzer-Division* arrived.

When the hot day came to a close, there was a rainstorm, which was greeted by all as a way to cool off. The division had achieved tremendous success that day but, in the end, it stalemated in the face of the enemy tanks. The night was used to assemble, regroup, bring reinforcements forward, and rearm. In Rossosch proper, the division established prisoner, weapons and materiel collection points. For the first time, there was American equipment among the spoils of war, including an especially large number of trucks. That was the result of the Lend-Lease Agreement that had been signed during the winter, with which the United States delivered military equipment to the Soviet Union. *Sonderführer* Demidow was once again named the local administrative commander, and he was assisted in his efforts by six soldiers: Henninger, Holtz, Wolodja, Julius, Hornejus, and Schalk.

During the night of 7–8 July, the *6. Armee* was located in the area between the Oskol and the Don with all of its divisions. The *3. Panzer-Division* was on the field army's extreme left wing, deep in the enemy's rear. Behind it were the *23. Panzer-Division*, the *29. Infanterie-Division (mot.)*, and the *100. leichte Division*. They were between Swoboda and Ostrogoschk, to the west of the Don. The infantry divisions were fighting in the northwest and were pressing across a broad front to the south. Since the field army had not received any specific directives from the field-army group, it ordered its formations to close up on 8 July.

At the same time, the Russian high command had ordered its field armies on both sides of the Don to pull back in the face of the German forces and only conduct energetic resistance with rearguards. The Red Army was aware of the German intent and was pulling all of its formations back in the direction of Stalingrad and the Caucasus, where it intended to establish a defense.

The enemy in the sector to the front of the *3. Panzer-Division* had been reinforced. As it turned light, the refueled vehicles of the *II./Panzer-Regiment 6* moved out form their assembly areas and headed south. But shortly after moving out, an enemy force of up to twelve fighting vehicles was identified in the vicinity of the village of Ukrainez. *Major* Frank thereupon ordered his battalion to pivot west in order to envelop the village from the rear. While the tanks churned their way through the high corn, they could not tell that they were being continuously observed by T-34's, which soon threw down the gauntlet. Once again, a time-consuming and casualty-intensive engagement for both sides ensued. Although seventeen enemy fighting vehicles eventually went up in smoke and flames, the German tank companies suffered greater losses. As a result, the battalion broke off the engagement.

Despite the setback, the division made efforts to continue the advance. An assault-gun battalion was attached to it. It was sent forward across the Kalitwa, as were two platoons of *Panzer-*

jäger-Abteilung 543. They arrived at the right moment, since enemy tanks appeared on the west flank of the division, which started attacking and pushing back the combat outposts with exemplary *élan*. It was not possible to take back Ukrainez until the afternoon and all available forces had been concentrated. That at least established a jumping-off point for the next day. *Generalmajor* Breith noted in his diary: "Difficult, unsatisfying day!"

The corps radioed that it wanted the division to continue pursuing the enemy to the south. The division moved out at 0345 hours with *Kampfgruppe Westhoven*. The objective for the battle group was Budjaki. At Worischilewka, the route was blocked by an antitank-gun belt. Artillery had to be called forward to clear a path. The movement then continued. The next resistance was encountered at Budjaki proper. The enemy had emplaced a heavy howitzer battery there. After the enemy was ejected, the battle group fought its way to the open terrain. From that point forward, the tanks, *SPW's*, and motorcycles could move south rapidly.

The movement continued through Ssofiewka and Wassiljewka and ended in the afternoon at Michailowka. A halt was necessary by the fact that fuel and ammunition had to be brought forward. The division had driven a deep wedge into the enemy with the *II./Panzer-Regiment 6* and *Panzergrenadier-Regiment 3*. By doing so, however, the flanks were threatened especially since the advance could only be conducted on two roads.

There were strong Russian forces to the west and northwest of the division, and they were trying to fight their way to the east. Several Soviet formations were moving towards Schramowka to the rear of the lead group in the hopes of using the cover of the high ground to allow them to ex-filtrate east through the many defiles. *Major* Haspel's *II./Panzergrenadier-Regiment 394* was the closest to those dangerous forces, and it was directed to eject the enemy before he succeeded in cutting off the division's trains and rear-area columns.

Haspel's 6th Company was the first unit committed. The mechanized infantry moved into a depression east of the village, where they broke light resistance, reached Hill 211.3 and ejected the enemy. *Oberleutnant* Koblitz's 7th Company then entered the fray. It pivoted towards Schramowka proper and combed though the village, while the 5th Company assumed a flank guard mission to the east. The mechanized infantry were able to hold up four enemy fighting vehicles, but the crews were able to blow them up before the infantry could get to them. A fifth tank was captured undamaged. *Major* Haspel and *Gefreiter* Thiele had leapt up on the tank and taken the crew prisoner.

That did not mean the end to the fight, however. Nine T-34's appeared. They were the same tanks that had been committed against the advance guard of the division a few hours earlier. The Russian group succeeded in advancing past Schramowka to the northeast and shooting up a supply column. *Hauptmann* Hein, the leader of the transportation section, was killed. *Oberleutnant* Pollmann's 6th Company, reinforced by infantry guns and antitank guns, was then pivoted in the direction of Leskowyi to attack the Soviets positioned there and eject them from the avenue of advance. Heavy *Flak* supported the thrust, which finally succeeded in scattering the enemy. Remaining behind were 130 Russians, 3 more tanks, and a large quantity of small arms. The road had been cleared, and the division could continue its attack south without disruption.

By then, it was the afternoon. The counterattack of the Soviet 110th Tank Brigade had delayed the division's advance. *Kampfgruppe Westhoven* marched along the road that led directly east. The *SPW* companies, in the lead, were able to get as far as Golaja, when they ran into Russian columns that were headed from west to east. *Oberst* Westhoven ordered his forces to halt, since a night attack into the unknown with exhausted troops did not seem advisable. *Major* Pape's *Kradschützen-Bataillon 3* reached the whistle stop at Passenowo and set

up an all-round defense there. The battle staff of the division also moved to that location, where it spent the night. *Kampfgruppe de Beaulieu*, along with most of the artillery, reached the area around Michailowka.

The night was short. As soon as it started to turn first light, the first companies of *Panzergrenadier-Regiment 3* moved out. It was 0400 hours. The mechanized infantry moved through the long "street" village of Golaja and then rattled south towards the Bogutschar in their *SPW's*. The enemy barely showed himself and, when he was encountered, he evacuated the provisional positions. Moving quickly, the battalions took the bridge at the northwest entrance to Smaglejewka. In short order, they occupied the village and established a bridgehead.

Then orders reached the division that created a completely different situation. According to the orders, the *XXXX. Panzer-Korps* was to pivot sharply to the east with the objective of taking Meschkoff. To that end, the division was to form a powerful attack group to conduct that mission. *Oberst* Chales de Beaulieu was at the division command post early in the morning to be briefed. A battle group was formed with the following elements: the *II./Panzer-Regiment 6*, the *II./Panzergrenadier-Regiment 394*, *Pionier-Bataillon 635*, *Panzerjäger-Abteilung 670*, the *II./Panzer-Artillerie-Regiment 75*, *Beobachtungs-Abteilung 28*, and a platoon from *Panzerjäger-Abteilung 543*. The lead element of the battle group, the tank battalion, started moving out at 0700 hours. The mechanized infantry followed around 0900 hours. The advance moved fairly rapidly through Golaja and Smaglejewka. The bridge there did not sustain the weight of the fighting vehicles for very long and was soon non-trafficable for tracked vehicles. The engineers were busy with improving the structure and were able to make it trafficable again by 1100 hours.

Once the improvements were effected, the *II./Panzer-Regiment 6* crossed the Bogutschar, followed closely by the *II./Panzergrenadier-Regiment 394*. They then turned in the direction of Kolessnikowka. Unfortunately, the column began to stretch out, with the result that the last of the mechanized infantry did not cross the river until around 1600 hours. *Major* Frank's fighting vehicles continued rolling southeast, however, and got as far as Kolessnikowka after some disruptions by tank obstacles and air attacks. From there, they could see the advance guard of the *23. Panzer-Division*, which was marching along the parallel road to the west.

Kampfgruppe Westhoven remained that day in the area it had taken in the morning. The soldiers of *Oberstleutnant* Zimmermann's *Panzergrenadier-Regiment 3* and *Hauptmann* Kersten's 3rd Battalion of artillery were exhausted from the difficult marches and the severe heat. The motorcycle infantry battalion was brought forward to the south bank of the Bogutschar in the afternoon. The elements of the division farther to the rear once again ran into the danger of being overrun by Russian forces attempting to break through. *Hauptmann* von der Heyden-Rynsch's *I./Panzergrenadier-Regiment 394* participated in some sharp engagements against enemy tank and rifle forces in the process of protecting those elements.

Early in the afternoon, the division's communications center received new orders by radio. According to them, the division was to send a battle group to the northeast. The *6. Armee* had ordered the corps at 1315 hours to establish a bridgehead on the east bank of the Don at Bogutschar. At that point, the *XXXX. Panzer-Korps* was moving in three divergent directions. The *23. Panzer-Division* and *Kampfgruppe de Beaulieu* were headed due south in the direction of Millerowo, the *29. Infanterie-Division (mot.)* was moving southeast toward Meschkoff and the *3. Panzer-Division* was being directed northeast.

In the course of those movements, the rear area remained unprotected. The divergent columns, the broad frontages and the open flanks that resulted made it impossible for the division to keep the rear area under control. Since there were scattered Russians everywhere, thee was a constant danger for the supply elements that

were following. In the course of the day, the roads were blocked several times, since the Soviet formations were attempting to break through to the Don. The supply elements brought their trucks forward in convoys. The commanding general of the *XXXX. Panzer-Korps* was only able to visit his individual divisions by means of a Fieseler *Storch*.

At 2000 hours on 10 July, *Oberst* Westhoven received orders to advance along the Bogutschar at first light as far as the Don. He was to cross the river there and cut off the retreat route for the enemy forces. Westhoven and his staff immediately started preparations for the operation. Just as the battalions that had been earmarked for the operation got ready to move out on 11 July, the operation was called off.

During the night, the *VIII. Armee-Korps* and the *XXXX. Panzer-Korps* were allocated to the *4. Panzer-Armee*. That field army had been rolling south from the area around Woronesch for twenty-four hours. *Generaloberst* Hoth's *4. Panzer-Armee* had received orders to advance as quickly as possible to the southeast to make it impossible for the enemy to retreat across the Don in front of the *1. Panzer-Armee*. The new field-army headquarters instructed the *XXXX. Panzer-Korps* to drop all individual operations and advance in the direction of the lower Don with concentrated forces.

The corps first had to assemble its forces. The *3. Panzer-Division* was directed to assemble its forces along the Losowaja south of Meschkoff. *Kampfgruppe de Beaulieu*, which was already advancing in the direction of Meschkoff, reached the area southwest of the city in the course of a very hot day, with temperatures rising up to 40 degrees [104 Fahrenheit]. The battle group set up around Schapiloff. *Panzergrenadier-Regiment 394* spread out in a wide arc to protect the approaching division from the east and south. *Kampfgruppe Westhoven* moved slowly to the southeast.

The movement in the almost unbearable heat were very difficult, since the fine sand coated everything in a thick layer. The pretty countryside made up for that somewhat. The vehicles rolled through fragrant meadows and waving fields of grain, across blooming hillocks, past small lakes and through idyllic woods of pine. There were no large tracts of woods or mountains to limit the view. The people there were also different than the previously encountered types. The first Caucasians and Cossacks appeared. On that 11 July, the soldiers of the *3. Panzer-Division* saw camels for the first time. They really were in a foreign environment.

The German columns encountered large columns of Russian soldiers again and again. Most of them were without weapons. They were trying to find some way to the east. The motorcycle infantry battalion, reinforced by a company from *Panzerjäger-Abteilung 670* and a platoon of *Flak* from the divisional artillery, encountered one such column west of Lasowyje. The number of prisoners climbed by the hour. It proved impossible to guard the growing mass of men. They were simply shown the way to the rear. With the few people available, it was impossible to verify whether those groups actually continued heading to the rear or attempted to continue fleeing east. There were soldiers of all ethnic groups: Russians, Ruthenians, Caucasians, Mongolians, Tartars, Cossacks, and others.

The next day was Sunday, the kind of Sunday that made you want to go for a ride back home. But the division was unable to enjoy it very much. The advance was to continue. As early as 0200 hours, the battle groups of the Obersten Westhoven and de Beaulieu started moving on the roads to the southwest. Since the roads were relatively good and the heat did not yet lay thick on the countryside, the movement proceeded fairly rapidly. Just before 0800 hours, the lead elements—*Kradschützen-Bataillon 3* and the *I./Panzergrenadier-Regiment 394*—were outside of the large village of Djegtewa, where the Losawaja emptied into the Kalitwa. *Artillerie-Regiment 70* had covered the advancing columns in a series of bounds.

Hauptmann von der Heyden-Rynsch's *I./Panzergrenadier-Regiment 394* turned off the movement route to the west and cleared Djegtewa in short order. The battalion occupied positions to guard the marching division to the west. Enemy forces that temporarily appeared were driven off. *Major* Pape's motorcycle infantry battalion, still the lead element, was a few kilometers further south in Balabanowka, a small, tidy village. The soldiers discovered later on that the village had been occupied by German settlers until 1941, when they were evacuated.

The advance of the division continued relentlessly. There was no time to be worried about the protection of the rearward lines of communications. There was only one word: Advance! In every village that was crossed, a squad of mechanized infantry remained behind to wait for the following columns and then be relieved by them. But because the distances grew ever greater by the hour and groups of Russian continued to appear, *Major* Boehm's *II./Panzergrenadier-Regiment 3* remained in the area around Djegtewa–Balabanowka.

The road then paralleled the banks of the Kalitwa. If there hadn't been a war, you could almost think you were on a vacation trip. A young officer from the 6th Battery of the division artillery wrote in his diary:

There were often images of incomparable beauty. The vehicles created a pathway through grass plants that, in some cases, had shot up as tall as a man. All types of blooming flowers in lavish profusion. One type that we frequently encountered remains in my memory: Calices of tender yellow or pale rose peaked out of green leafy tendrils, delicately swishing back and forth like the bells of a Chinese temple. In between were the blue islands of mulleins, the buttercups and the stars of innumerable other blooms. Their fragrance, of an almost intoxicating flavor, filled the quivering white heat of the summer's day. It was like a magical garden from a distant planet, undisturbed by war and untouchable by humans. The countryside stretched on to the horizon in swells, with an occasionally gently rising comely hill. And when the sun went down, you saw colors—nothing else. Trees were seldom seen . . .

The peaceful Sunday was soon over for the advance guard. When the lead elements of *Krad-schützen-Bataillon 3* approached the small village of Kriworoshje, where the road took to a sharp turn to the east, it encountered enemy resistance. It was thought that it could be broken quickly, but the Russians turned out to be the stronger ones that time. The motorcycle infantry and the antitank elements bogged down and had to wait for the arrival of the mechanized infantry. Once they were there, the enemy was finally ejected. *Kampfgruppe de Beaulieu* turned southwest, reaching Jekaterinowka and establishing a bridgehead on the west bank of the Kalitwa. The *6./Panzergrenadier-Regiment 394* screened to the west, while the other two companies combed the nearby huts. After the battle group crossed, it continued in the direction of the Lower Donez.

Major Pape's reinforced *Kradschützen-Bataillon 3* attacked in the direction of Korbin–Archipoff along the road on the ridgeline. To its left, *Major* Haspel's *II./Panzergrenadier-Regiment 394* marched along the valley road in the direction of Jerofejew along with the *3./Panzer-Artillerie-Regiment 75*. It slowly turned dark, and since hardly any of the officers had maps, the movement slowed considerably. It was only by asking local peasants that it was possible to reach the area just north of Kurnakowo–Lipowskaja by 2200 hours. By doing so, the lead elements of the *3. Panzer-Division* were boring like arrows into the frontage of the Soviets. Fires lit up to all sides; signal flares hissed into the air; machine guns hammered away; and tank engines thundered in the distance. *Kampf-gruppe de Beaulieu* found itself around midnight on that Sunday far in front of the remaining formations of the corps. The formations of *Oberst* Westhoven that were following—the *II./Panzer-Regiment 6*, the *I./Panzergrenadier-Regiment 3*,

and the main body of *Panzer-Artillerie-Regiment 75*—remained on the east bank of the Kalitwa. The *II./Panzergrenadier-Regiment 3* secured the road that the division wanted to advance upon.

On 10 July, the headquarters of *Oberst Frei-herr* von Liebenstein's *Panzer-Regiment 6* and well as *Hauptmann* Rohrbeck's 1st Battalion departed Kharkov. They were still well behind the rest of the division. The supply elements had caught up, however. The engineers, some of whom were still in the rear busy with the construction of bridges, linked up with the combat forces that day. Coming from Smaglejewka, Bridging Section 1 arrived in Balabanowka, after road marching some 212 kilometers. The columns had been attacked several times by Russian aircraft and had sustained considerable losses.

The division battle staff had crossed the Kalitwa and set up in Antonowka. The division intelligence officer determined that the *3. Panzer-Division* was in the Soviet rear area as the result of its bold advance. The enemy forces had started to break up and were attempting to escape to the east.

At first light, *Kampfgruppe de Beaulieu* resumed its advance south. The *II./Panzer-grenadier-Regiment 394* advanced through Kolitwenez Creek Valley, which was framed by minor hills. The village of Kurnakowo-Lipowskaja was clear of the enemy and crossed quickly. Slight enemy resistance was encountered at the entrances to the next few villages that were on the road. In general, they were small rearguards. The lead company moved through the village at high speed each time and left it to the companies that followed to clear it with dismounted elements. The motorcycle infantry battalion attacked to the right of the mechanized infantry across the high ground. The *I./Panzergrenadier-Regiment 394* screened the advance to the west. The batteries of *Oberst* Ullrich's *Artillerie-Regiment 70* were split up among the columns.

The first major resistance was encountered in a depression south of Nisowki. While the

7./Panzergrenadier-Regiment 394 held down the enemy, the rest of the battalion advanced and reached Jerofejew shortly after 0900 hours. A halt was ordered to secure the rearward lines of communications, have the supply and rations trains brought forward and perform maintenance on the overworked vehicles. The 6th Company of the mechanized infantry regiment and the artillery batteries were charged with securing the rest area. The engineers established contact with the motorcycle infantry at Kamenew.

The leaden oppressiveness of the summer heat laid itself once again over the land. The sun streamed from a clear blue sky, as if it wanted to make up for what the horrific winter had done. But the enemy remained industrious. The formations that were still west of the division continued to attempt to break through to the east. Marshal Timoschenko had ordered his forces to no longer conduct delaying actions. Instead, they were to regroup behind the Don.

Since the German armored divisions were much too weak to monitor all of the conquered areas, it was unavoidable that thousands of Russians were able to get across the Don. Although the Army High Command had directed that the *4. Panzer-Division* was to advance as quickly as possible to the south to block the enemy's retreat route, good intentions do not make up for a lack of forces.

The *3. Panzer-Division* was not spared in the efforts of the Soviets to break out. The west flank of the division was threatened all day long. The Russians even launched attacks with tanks against *Kampfgruppe Westhoven*. *Major* Boehm's *II./Panzergrenadier-Regiment 3* had to turn back several energetic immediate counterattacks by the enemy at Jakaterinowka. In the process, the enemy continuously committed his air force as well. The situation grew worse for the mechanized infantry as a result of the low-level attacks, reaching a climax in the afternoon. In

an effort to relieve those forces, the division, whose command post was in Antonowka, established a battle group under the command of *Major* Böttge, the commander of *Panzer-Nachrichten-Abteilung 39*. The battle group, consisting of a platoon of Flak, two antitank guns and a company from *Lehr-Regiment "Brandenburg,"*[3] set off for the north, but it did not have to be committed.

Oberleutnant Koblitz's *7./Panzergrenadier-Regiment 394*, which screened the west flank of the lead battle group, attacked the enemy forces on the high ground in the afternoon. After a sharp fight, the enemy evacuated his positions and left behind 300 prisoners. The battlefield was littered with 70 dead. The number of prisoners taken and equipment captured for the regiment that day totaled 452 prisoners, 123 carbines, 29 submachine guns, 11 mortars, 6 machine guns, 11 trucks, 2 tractors, and 17 *panje* carts.

Generalmajor Mack's *23. Panzer-Division*, advancing to the rear on the right, was attacked by Russian tanks. The enemy attempted to tear open the front of the division with 120 fighting vehicles in an effort to avoid encirclement. In the end, the *23. Panzer-Division* was able to knock out 28 enemy tanks, but its advance also stalled outside of Millerowo.

At 1800 hours, the corps ordered the *3. Panzer-Division* to attack in the direction of the Donez, where bridgeheads were to be established. *Generalmajor* Breith was not enthused with the order and pointed out to the corps that the division was currently defending. If another attack were conducted, the flanks would be lengthened still. In addition, an attack would require more infantry than the division had. The corps remained firm. Correspondingly, *Kampfgruppe de Beaulieu* received orders forty minutes later to move out. The two battalions of *Panzergrenadier-Regiment 394* were to form the nucleus of the attack, while *Kradschützen-Bataillon 3* screened the flanks.

---

3. The Brandenburgers were a commando force that originally reported to the Intelligence Directorate of the Armed Forces High Command. Continuously expanded during the war, the formations eventually evolved into a formation of division size, which eventually became *Panzergrenadier-Division "Brandenburg"* (September 1944) and was employed conventionally.

After a short preparation and a corresponding artillery preparation, the 2nd battalion of mechanized infantry moved out with its lead elements at 1930 hours from Jerefejew. The movement made relatively rapid progress until the onset of darkness, when there were difficulties negotiating the road network. Since there were few maps available, there were unexpected encounters with creeks, depressions, and defiles. It was long past midnight when the first company reached Gussew. It did not appear advisable to continue advancing in the direction of the city of Nishnij-Brochin. The battalion set up an all-round defense for the remainder of the night.

The German forces had been advancing ceaselessly for two weeks. They had covered great distance and were at the end of their physical capabilities. The enemy had never offered battle; instead, he had pulled back. For that reason, the German advance encountered thin air. The Army High Command and, even more emphatically, Hitler, insisted that the *4. Panzer-Armee* continue its march south to encircle the Soviets who, by that time, had already escaped to the east. The *6. Armee* swung to the southeast and found itself advancing toward the bend in the Don and Kalatsch. The commander in chief of *Heeresgruppe Süd*, *Generalfeldmarschall* von Bock, stated that he could no longer accept responsibility for the excessive demands placed on the forces. Hitler relieved him of command and replaced him with *Generaloberst Freiherr* von Weichs.

Ever since the early-morning hours of 13 July, *Major* Pape's motorcycle infantry battalion served as the advance guard for the advance south, attempting to leapfrog past the enemy cavalry and armored formations that were conducting a fighting delay. The lead company continuously encountered completely surprised Soviet rearguards and supply elements, which barely put up any resistance and, in most cases, could be captured intact.

Late in the afternoon, an enemy reconnaissance aircraft was shot down near Piechakoff by the concentrated employment of all available machine guns and rifles. As it turned dark, the day's objective was reached. The battalion turned west to encircle the enemy pulling back from the north by taking the villages east of Millerowo.

The 2nd Company of the motorcycle infantry received the mission to take Karpowo-Russkiy and to screen from there for the night. There were no signs of life in the extended "street" village, which ran about two kilometers long from east to west along the edge of a marshy creek bottomland. It was already dark when the motorcycle infantry entered the village. They noticed Russian tracked vehicles fleeing to the south. The onset of night did not allow for any reconnaissance of the surroundings. In a hurried move, the platoon leaders were given positions based on the map in order to establish a gap-prone and thin security line along the ridgeline to the north. The battalion was in a similar situation with its remaining units farther to the east.

Since the company was supposed to receive reinforcements in the form of tanks during the night, the onset of engine and track noises coming from the northeast shortly after midnight were held to be coming from the promised reinforcements. But two or three tanks then rolled quickly through the dusty village and halted right in front of the provisional company command post. The tankers in the turrets were hanging out of the hatches. In the dust and the pale moonlight, the silhouette of the lead fighting vehicle was not clearly identifiable. For a few seconds, the company commander and the men of his headquarters section were uncertain whether they had friends or foes in front of them. There moments of intense uncertainty. All of a sudden, a signal flare shot vertically into the sky and, almost at the same time, the words *Idi szuda* rang out from the tank commander to the frozen German soldiers. Both sides knew what was up by then. The Russians disappeared into the turrets of their tanks in the blink of an eye, followed by tracer rounds whipping through the darkness. The only available antitank gun was screening at the outskirts of the village. But the unexpected situation in the middle of the village was also unsettling for the Russians. Before anyone was in a position to approach the tanks with a bundled charge, the enemy fighting vehicles pulled back and took off quickly.

By then, however, the sound of tracked vehicles had increased in the eastern portion of the village. Accompanied by riflemen, the tanks were attempting to cross the marshy creek bottomland to get to the south. Sharp fighting ensued with the Soviet infantry, which had run into the strong-points established by the motorcycle infantry. The Soviets thought they were facing a cohesive front. The enemy, who appeared to have been without adequate stocks of fuel and ammunition for some days and who also believed he was already encircled, left behind his vehicles and entered the village in an effort to escape to the south. In the confusion, it took some time to sort out what was happening. Contact with the battalion headquarters had been lost. The platoons had set up their defenses tied into the houses of the village. By first light, however, some order had been restored. Although the strong-points were widely dispersed, the defensive positions were strong and suited for engaging the fleeing Soviets. In the morning haze along the creek bed, sixteen T-34's were able to cross the narrow waterway and escape to the south. They had little ammunition, but their armor protected them from the 5-centimeter antitank gun doing any harm. The Russians were forced to leave behind numerous trucks, a few light guns and a large amount of light weapons and pieces of equipment. A few of the tanks got stuck in the bottomland. One of them fired into the village from time to time, thus providing the withdrawing infantry with some cover. It was not until the afternoon, when contact was reestablished with the battalion headquarters, that the enemy tank was destroyed by a light howitzer that was brought forward and fired over open sights.

The battalion headquarters and the remaining companies had also been involved in sharp defensive engagements a few kilometers farther to the east. It wasn't possible to more or less reestablish the thin security line until 14 July. Fortunately, friendly losses were relatively small.

But that did not mean that the situation was no longer fluid. Millerowo still had not been taken, and from Karpowo-Russkiy, one could observe the fighting involving the *23. Panzer-Division* through binoculars.

The following night was another extremely critical one for the 2nd Company. Although the defensive positions could be improved, the left wing was still hanging in the air and there were unmistakable gaps between the platoons. The friendly forces to the right were two kilometers away in their positions.

Under the cover of darkness, an enemy cavalry troop—apparently the lead element of the regiment following—succeeded in entering the western portion of Karpowo-Russkiy from the north along a narrow pathway. Initially, the movements of the troop were not noticed. The unexpected neighing of horses alerted the guards in the village. When the white signal flares illuminated the main road, the chaos of the previous night returned. Murderous machine-gun fire slammed into the surprised troop and yielded a rich harvest. A short while later, the regiment that was following joined the fray with all of the forces at its disposal. Another night fight development, with all of the attributes of that type of combat. This time, the battalion was able to assist with the light *SPW's* of *Oberfeldwebel* Hess. At first light, coming from the east, the *SPW* Company attacked the cavalry formations by surprise in the flank and decided the unequal struggle for the German side with the aid of artillery. The day resulted in a large number of spoils of war in the form of weapons and materiel, as well as the capture of quite a few prisoners.

That signaled the end of a small episode on the periphery of the larger events. While the success may not seem to have been so great at first glance, the low number of forces was able to inflict considerable casualties on the enemy, hold up the enemy's weakened elements, and gain some time.

At 0245 hours on 14 July, *Oberst* de Beaulieu moved out his battle group. The *II./Panzergrenadier-Regiment 394* was the lead element; an hour later, it entered Nishnij-Brochin. The enemy offered little resistance and was soon ejected. The 5th Company of the mechanized infantry screened to the west, the 8th to the south, the 6th to the east, and the 7th to the north. The 3rd Battery of the divisional artillery, which was incorporated up front into the battle group, took up firing positions along the southern edge of the city. The Soviets did not bother the German forces. The mechanized infantry observed Russian columns moving east to the south of the city. Because of the bad fuel situation, it was not possible to disrupt those movements except for the occasional firing of the battery.

The division closed up slowly, as the western flank grew ever longer. The 3rd Company of the division engineers received orders to advance on the Rostow–Moscow railway line and to blow up a stretch of track. It was intended to disrupt the continuous troop transports of the Red Army through that operation. The company left its quartering area at 1050 hours with six *SPW's*, moved through the outpost lines of the mechanized infantry and advanced into no-man's-land. Russians were only infrequently seen and, if so, then they were stragglers. After moving six kilometers, the railway line could be seen in a valley. The engineers moved via the depressions and snuck up on the railway line. All of a sudden, there was a T-34 in front of the men. *Oberleutnant* Brandt, the company commander, ordered his driver to move out at full speed. He raced toward the tank in his *SPW*, dismounted his vehicle in front of the steel monster, and flung a charge into an open hatch. It was then time to get out of there as quickly as possible. Enemy fighting vehicles also appeared on the far side of the high ground as well. The railway line was behind them. One train after another was stacked up. The engineers were able to approach to within 300 meters of the tracks without being observed. But the Soviets then grew attentive and covered the company with fire, forcing the *SPW's* to veer off.

Oberleutnant Brandt attempted another approach. Two *SPW's* covered the other ones, which were headed straight for the tracks. Enemy rounds screamed in from everywhere. The *SPW's* continued their movement, undeterred. Using a freight train for cover, *Feldwebel* Gerhard, *Feldwebel* Knopke, and *Gefreiter* Paatz moved up to the tracks. The vehicle commanders jumped down, along with *Obergefreiter* Lübeck, *Gefreiter* Doehring, *Gefreiter* Kalies, *Gefreiter* Schmidt, and *Pionier* Malucha. The men ran along the tracks, accompanied by the rattle of Russian machine guns, and blew them up in three places along a stretch of 100 meters. As the last charge detonated, all of them remounted their vehicles and took off. On their movement back, the engineers ran into a few Russian stragglers in a cornfield and took eleven prisoners. After two and one half hours, they reached the German combat outposts. The commanding general soon sent a radio message: "Special praise and thanks to *Oberleutnant* Brandt and his brave engineers for their magnificent performance!"

General Geyr von Schweppenburg arrived at the division command post late in the afternoon with his adjutant, *Oberstleutnant* Momm, to be briefed on the situation. The commander in chief of *Luftflotte 4* (4th Tactical Air Force), *Generaloberst Freiherr* von Richtofen, landed a short while later in his Fieseler *Storch*. The *Luftwaffe* general officer insisted that the *3. Panzer-Division* attempt to take the area around Gruzineff, so that the *Luftwaffe* could establish an airfield there.

That mission was later successfully accomplished by a hastily assembled battle group under the command of *Hauptmann* von dem Heyden-Rynsch. In all, there were considerable casualties that day, especially among some *Flak* elements, which were overrun by surprise by a pack of enemy tanks.

The enemy did not let the intense heat stop him from repeatedly attempting to break out to the east. Since the outpost lines of the division were much too thin, the Soviets even succeeded in blocking the roadway for periods of time. *Kradschützen-Bataillon 3* was responsible for a sector of ten kilometers all by itself. It was only through the help of the *8./Panzer-Regiment 6*, which arrived in the nick of time, that an attacking enemy battle group could be scattered. In the process of that engagement, the German tanks destroyed seven enemy tanks and two Stalin organs. The assistant to the division intelligence officer, *Leutnant Graf* zu Dohna, ran into an enemy column in his staff car. That did not shake him. He jumped out of the vehicle with *Sonderführer* Kalnin and *Unteroffizier* Krause and took forty prisoners after an exchange of fire. In the evening, the road was once more blocked, with the result that the commanding general could not go back and had to spend the night at the division command post.

The night was cool, but the morning brought with it a clear, blue sky, and it turned hot again. The situation in general did not change that day. The enemy—in all, elements of forty rifle divisions—attempted to break through the German front one more time. The effects of the advance of the armored divisions of the *1. Panzer-Armee* started to be felt. The *14.* and *22. Panzer-Divisionen* had already reached the area southwest of Millerowo. The *XXXX. Panzer-Korps* had established an extended front oriented to the west in order to interdict the withdrawing Russian formations.

The *3. Panzer-Division*, which could finally establish contact with the *23. Panzer-Division* coming from the north on 15 July, had to fend off continuous attacks at Nisowki. The Soviets attacked repeatedly with tanks and pressed against the positions of *Kradschützen-Bataillon 3* and the other formations holding there again and again. *Leutnant* Becker's *8./Panzer-Regiment 6* was able to create some breathing space by knocking out several T-34's. A second hot spot remained the bridgehead at Jakatirnowka. *Major* Boehm's *II./Panzergrenadier-Regiment 3* was able to maintain its positions only after the last remaining company clerk had picked up a rifle. The third threatened sector of the front was at Gratschi, where *Oberst* de Beaulieu was in charge.

That day, the division regrouped. *Oberst* Westhoven was given the northern sector. Reporting to him were the *II./Panzergrenadier-Regiment 3*, the *II./Panzer-Regiment 6*, two batteries from *Panzer-Artillerie-Regiment 75*, and one company each from *Panzer-Pionier-Bataillon 39* and *Lehr-Regiment "Brandenburg." Oberst* de Beaulieu was in charge of the central sector of the front with *Kradschützen-Bataillon 3* and the *I./Panzergrenadier-Regiment 394*. The *I./Panzergrenadier-Regiment 3* and the *II./Panzergrenadier-Regiment 394* were in the south around Nishnij-Brochin under the command of *Oberstleutnant* Zimmermann. All of the formations sent out combat patrols, if they were not involved in defensive fighting. *Oberst Freiherr* von Liebenstein arrived in Djegtewa with the rest of the armored regiment—some sixty fighting vehicles—and was a welcome sight. Coordination with the *Luftwaffe* was discussed anew, when the commanding general of the *VIII. Flieger-Korps*, *Generalleutnant* Fiebig, arrived at the division's location.

The situation in the air had died down somewhat. The Russian pilots hardly contributed to the ground fighting any more. Most of the Red Air Force presence was reconnaissance aircraft. On the other hand, the enemy's rifle formations did not give up their efforts to break out. Starting early in the morning, the enemy pressed against the battle groups of both *Oberst* de Beaulieu and *Oberst* Westhoven on both sides of Nisowki. *Generalmajor* Breith and *Oberst* Westhoven directed the employment of their battalions from the "General's Hill," a piece of high ground at Blagoweschtschewskij, which could only hold their positions after the commitment of the last of the division's reserves. The number of prisoners brought in climbed by the hour. But that did not mean that the fighting was over. *Major* Frank's *II./Panzer-Regiment 6* fought a sharp engagement that afternoon with Soviet tanks, antitank guns, and antiaircraft guns.

But it seemed that the situation was changing. Early in the morning, contact was initially established with the *14. Panzer-Division*, which was coming from the west. Around 0800 hours, the *5./Panzergrenadier-Regiment 394* reported establishing contact with the *22. Panzer-Division*, which was advancing from the northwest to the south. Contact was maintained in the course of the day by strong reconnaissance efforts by tanks and *SPW's*. The Russian forces gradually disengaged from the area around Nishnij-Brochin. Friendly patrols barely encountered the enemy. Unfortunately, it proved impossible for the *3. Panzer-Division* to pursue to withdrawing enemy due to totally insufficient fuel allocations, which amounted to approximately thirty kilometers a day.

That evening, the division intelligence officer reported the totals of the prisoners collected and the spoils of war captured to date (from 29 June to 16 July): 11,944 prisoners; 137 tanks; 2 armored cars; 92 artillery pieces; 10 Stalin organs; 32 antiaircraft guns; 61 antitank guns; 58 mortars; 106 antitank rifles; 344 trucks; and 309 tractors. Thirteen aircraft had been shot down, while one was destroyed on the ground and one captured. In addition, 1 armored train and 15 transport trains had been set alight.

The defensive fighting of the recent past drew to a close. Despite all of the efforts, deprivations, and casualties, the *3. Panzer-Division* had been able to hold its sector of seventy kilometers. On 17 July, another hot day, there were hardly any enemy forces of note in front of the division's positions. It was only in the sector of *Kampfgruppe Zimmermann* that a Russian column was observed in the vicinity of Nishnij-Brochin. The *10./Panzer-Regiment 6* and mounted mechanized infantrymen of the *7./Panzergrenadier-Regiment 394* moved out against it. The Soviets were scattered and left behind 328 prisoners, 2 guns, 3 antitank guns, several light infantry weapons, and 15 *panje* wagons.

Contact with the neighboring divisions was improved. The *6./Panzergrenadier-Regiment 394*

pushed forward to Forschstadt on the Donez, where the lead elements of the *14. Panzer-Division* had fought their way forward. The *22. Panzer-Division* dispatched a liaison officer to the headquarters of *Kampfgruppe Zimmermann*. *Panzergrenadier-Regiment "Großdeutschland"* arrived from the north, marched past the east flank of the *3. Panzer-Division*, and stopped even with its lead elements. That afternoon, medical aircraft evacuated the first wounded. The vehicles of the two medical companies were constantly on the go, taking the wounded to the landing strips of the *Ju-52's*.

On 18 July, *Generalmajor* Breith released a general order in which he addressed the topic of the successes of the division again. The number of prisoners had climbed to 18,872. The division commander wrote:

I am using this opportunity to express my thanks and recognition to all of the members of the division and the attached corps troops, especially those of Artillerie-Regiment 70, for their extremely high levels of devotion to duty. . . . That which was achieved through exemplary cooperation of all arms enable me to express the hope that in the future, as it has always been in the past, that every member of the division will give his all in the further course of operations so as to contribute his part in bringing them to a successful conclusion . . .

Rain marked the eighteenth of July. Streets, roads, and the places the soldiers were staying formed a porridge of mud. The division could not move and not only because of the muck. There was also a lack of fuel. The *4. Panzer-Armee* had redirected all fuel to the *XXXXVIII. Panzer-Korps*, which was already moving south through Bokowskaja. For the time being, the *XXXX. Panzer-Korps*, whose command post was in Bablanowka, was held back with its *3.* and *23. Panzer-Divisionen*.

The commander in chief of the *4. Panzer-Armee*, *Generaloberst* Hoth, arrived at the division command post in the morning. It was initially intended for the division to contribute to the encirclement of the enemy forces that were still north of Rostow. Then there was a change: To the Caucasus! Advance parties of the division moved southeast into the area around Tazinskaja to reconnoiter approach routes, roads and bridges. The formations used the time to assemble their units and maintain their vehicles and equipment. The movement order for the advance guard of the division arrived in the evening. The march objective was Konstantinowskaja on the Don.

On the morning of 20 July, *Oberst* Westhoven left the quartering area with the first march serial of he division. His advance guard consisted of the headquarters of *Panzergrenadier-Brigade 3*, the *I./Panzergrenadier-Regiment 3*, the *3./Pionier-Bataillon 635*, and the *III./Panzer-Artillerie-Regiment 75*. The day burned hot across the entire land. The SPW's, prime movers, staff cars, and motorcycles rattled through fertile fields that stretched for kilometers, where tomatoes, watermelons, grains, corn and sunflowers bloomed. Extensive ridgelines were crossed, and the vehicles churned their way through deep depressions and creeks. The ground, grown hard by the heat, allowed rapid movement. Small villages were crossed, most of which were in the deep river valley floors. Shrubs and flowers grew there that were not to be seen in the steppes. The houses and huts were all inviting. They were surrounded by hedges and gardens, and the inhabitants were friendly and welcoming. The march went on, kilometer after kilometer.

The advance guard moved south rapidly, since there was no enemy to be seen. The batteries and companies then reached the plains that led to the Don. Konstantinowskaja was in front of the formations. The soldiers initiated a *coup de main* in the direction of the bridge, and they were greeted by heavy artillery from the far side. The Russian artillery placed heavy fires on the approach route and the entire area around the bridge site. The bridge itself was completely destroyed. The advance guard established security along the river and set up an all-round defense for the night.

The remaining elements of the division formed up and moved out late in the afternoon of the hot summer's day. *Oberst* Ullrich followed with *Artillerie-Regiment 70* and the division headquarters as the second march serial. It moved out in the direction of Marjeff-Prozilowski at 1600 hours. Transport squadrons of the *Luftwaffe* flew in eighty-eight cubic meters of fuel at the same time. The remainder of the division started out at 0400 hours on 21 July to cover the long distance to the Don.

Oberst Westhoven was still arrayed along the river with his battalions. The enemy resistance was as tough on 21 July as it had been the day before. A crossing would probably only be possible, if all of the artillery were employed. The commanding general, Schweppenburg, was also up front. He ordered the division to move to Nikolajewskaja. *Major* Richter had conducted a bold raid there with *Kradschützen-Bataillon 23* of the *23. Panzer-Division*. It had assaulted the large bridge over the Don there and established a bridgehead. Since the *23. Panzer-Division* was still far to the rear as the result of shortages of fuel, Westhoven's advance guard was quickly brought forward to that location.

Oberst Westhoven assumed command of the bridgehead and subordinated *Kradschützen-Bataillon 23* to his forces. *Kradschützen-Bataillon 3* and *Panzer-Pionier-Bataillon 39* were dispatched forward to the crossing site to reinforce Westhoven's original advance guard. *Major* Groeneveld, the commander of the divisional engineers, was given the mission of overseeing all engineer-related tasks. The Soviets recognized their setback and attempted to offset the capture of the bridge and the rapid building of a pontoon bridge by means of continuous attacks. The engines of enemy aircraft were constantly thundering in the skies above. A few difficult situations arose, since there were no antiaircraft defenses of any type.

After marching 180 kilometers, the main body of the *3. Panzer-Division* slowly approached the

Don flood plains. *Kampfgruppe Ullrich* was in the lead. The division headquarters followed and later occupied quarters in Ssaweljeff. The village seemed almost like an oasis. In addition to its inviting houses, there were fertile gardens. *Oberst* de Beaulieu led the next two battle groups: Group One under *Oberstleutnant* Zimmermann consisted of the *II./Panzergrenadier-Regiment 3*, the *I./Panzer-Artillerie-Regiment 75*, and the *1.* and *2./Panzerjäger-Abteilung 543*; *Major* Haspel's Group Two had *Panzergrenadier-Regiment 394*, the *II.* and *IV./Panzer-Artillerie-Regiment 75*, the *2./Panzerjäger-Abteilung 543*,[4] and the *3./ Panzer-Pionier-Bataillon 39*, along with the division's bridging sections. *Oberst Freiherr* Liebenstein led the rest of the division, including *Panzer-Regiment 6* and the attached *Panzer-jäger-Abteilung 670*. That group of forces had had to remain behind in the old divisional area until it could finish refueling.

The movements did not always proceed flawlessly, since the columns frequently bottlenecked at creek- and river-crossing sites. The open nature of the terrain permitted the companies to advance parallel to one another, but as soon as a waterway was encountered, all of the columns had to merge together again. Since the *23. Panzer-Division*, the *16. Panzer-Division*, and the *29. Infanterie-Division (mot.)* all had the same direction of march, that was reason all by itself for time-consuming delays caused by the intermingling of columns.

Generalmajor Breith traveled the remaining thirteen kilometers to the Don and into the bridgehead from Ssaweljeff. That same evening, he received orders from the corps not to wait for his division to close up. He was to attack the next day and take the Ssal River line. Only *Kradschützen-Bataillon 23* was to remain in the bridgehead. The corps engineers were attached to the *3. Panzer-Division* to facilitate the advance by improving the military bridges at Nikolajewskaja and guarding them.

On 22 July, the *XXXX. Panzer-Korps* brought five bridging sections forward. They attempted to build a bridge over the 150-meter-wide river, despite incessant air attacks. The engineers first had the elements of Westhoven's advance guard cross over to the south bank. The crossings proceeded in fits and starts, since Russian aircraft attacked again and again and caused damage and casualties. After the sixth bridging section arrived, the crossing could be sped up. The bridge was completely serviceable by 2000 hours. Since the *XXXXVIII. Panzer-Korps* on the left had not yet crossed the river, the *3. Panzer-Division* became the first division of the *4. Panzer-Armee* to force the mighty river.

---

4. The 2nd Company of the antitank battalion was already identified as being in Group One. It may be assumed that at least one of the companies of the battalion was in this group, although it is impossible to determine which one.

Departure from Kharkov at the start of the 1942 summer offensive. The vehicle of *Hauptmann* Wagner of *Schützen-Regiment 394* bears the tactical insignia of the division as well as the unit insignia. The oversized "G" is a holdover from the previous year, when the division was part of *Panzergruppe Guderian*.

Forming up on 30 June 1942.

Church in Rossosch. The city was taken in a *coup de main* by the *I./Schützen-Regiment 3*.

Riflemen wade through a tributary of the Oskol at Waluiki.

The dividing line between Europe and Asia is reached.

Oberleutnant Tank, the commander of the *6./Schützen-Regiment 3*.

Typical village encountered during the advance towards the Kalmuck Steppe in the summer of 1942.

One of two experimental antitank guns assigned to *Panzerjäger-Abteilung 521* in the fall of 1941. The *10.5 cm K gepanzerte Selbstfahrlafette* was outfitted with a 10.5-centimeter main gun on a highly modified *Panzer IV* chassis. This is probably the only surviving gun, since the other one was involved in an accident. It was completely destroyed after catching on fire and its basic load of ammunition blew up. The weapons system was ultimately not adopted for frontline service, primarily because of power-to-weight issues. The surviving vehicle, nicknamed the *dicker Max* ("Fat Max"), continued to see active frontline service until 1943.

The divisional engineers erect a sixteen-ton bridge composed of several segments.

A quad 2-centimeter *Flak* on a prime mover during the advance. The trailer behind the half-track was for ammunition.

Another view of the same vehicle in position. Note the "kill" rings on the barrels.

The *1./Schützen-Regiment 3* takes Pjatigorsk.

A new mode of transportation is tested.

CHAPTER 3

From the Don to the Terek: The Advance to the Caucasus

The summery and hot month of July came to a close. Despite all of the setbacks during the winter, the German Army had achieved new success over the previous four weeks and once again shown that its soldiers were capable of accomplishing great deeds. The area between the Donez and the Don was taken in a short period, with the entire southern wing of the Soviet Armed Forces forced to retreat.

The *6. Armee* of *General der Panzertruppen* Paulus pivoted east toward the great bend in the Don with the *XIV. Panzer-Korps* and other formations and then, later on, toward Stalingrad. Three other field armies were moving in the last week of July along the lower course of the Don to advance into the Caucasus. The advance guard and the first battalions of the main body of the *3. Panzer-Division* were on the south bank of the river, as other formations to the west pushed over it as well. On the evening of 25 July, the forces were arrayed as follows, from left to right: the *4. Panzer-Armee* (*Generaloberst* Hoth); the *1. Panzer-Armee* (*Generaloberst* von Kleist); and the *17. Armee* (*Generaloberst* Ruoff). Reporting to these field armies were the Romanian VI Army Corps, the *XXXXVIII. Panzer-Korps*, the *XXXX. Panzer-Korps*, the *III. Panzer-Korps*, the *LVII. Panzer-Korps*, the *LII. Armee-Korps*, the *XXXXIV. Armee-Korps*, and the *XXXXIX. Gebirgs-Korps*. Up to that point, only *General der Panzertruppen Freiherr* Geyr von Schweppenburg's *XXXX. Panzer-Korps* and *General der Panzertruppen* Kirchner's *LVII. Panzer-Korps* had been able to establish bridgeheads, with von Schweppenburg's forces at Nikolajewskaja and Kirchner's forces at Rostow.

On 23 July, Hitler released Directive No. 45 for the continuation of Operation Braunschweig. It stated, in part:

1. The next mission for *Heeresgruppe A* is to encircle the enemy forces that escaped across the Don in the area south and south-east of Rostow and destroy them.

To that end, large motorized formations are to be employed from the bridgeheads . . . in a generally southwesterly direction, towards Tichorezk; infantry, light infantry and mountain divisions are to be employed across the Don in the Rostow area. In addition, the mission to interdict the Tichorezk–Stalingrad railway line with advanced forces remains . . .

2. After eliminating the group of enemy forces south of the Don, the most important mission of *Heeresgruppe A* is to take the entire east coast of the Black Sea in its possession . . .

3. At the same time, a group of forces consisting primarily of motorized formations is to be formed to take the area around Grossnij, while maintaining a flank guard to the east, and, with some of its elements, to block the Ossetian and Grusinian military roads, if possible, along the passes. Following that, the area around Baku is to be taken after an advance along the Caspian Sea.

That long-range objective would also become the objective of the *3. Panzer-Division* later on and determine its fate from that day forward. Directive No. 45 was one of the most far-reaching and fateful decisions Hitler made. The Supreme Commander of the Armed Forces had ignored the objections of his advisors and, in contrast to previous directives, had ordered that the German Army was to achieve two operational-objectives at the same time in the summer of 1942. The German field armies would fail in those objectives, ushering in a shift in fortunes on the Eastern Front.

In contrast, the Red Army had learned from its strategic mistakes of the past year. It also had access to the geared-up armament capacity of the gigantic Soviet Empire and American help. When *Heeresgruppe A* prepared to advance into the Caucasus, it encountered a better-prepared Soviet leadership. On 28 July, Marshal Budjonny assumed command of all of the forces in the southern area. Reporting to him were the Southern Front of Lieutenant General Malinowski on the lower course of the Don, the North Caucasus Front under his own command and the Transcaucasus Front under General Tjulenjew.

During the night of 22–23 July, the Red Air Force attacked the bridges and crossing points at Nikolajewskaja in waves. Despite that, most of the *I./Panzergrenadier-Regiment 3* was able to cross by first light. *Oberstleutnant* Wellmann received orders to advance via Piroshok and Malyi-Lessnoj towards the Ssal as the advance guard of *Kampfgruppe Westhoven*. He left the bridgehead at 0500 hours with the elements that had already crossed—the *I./Panzergrenadier-Regiment 3*, two batteries of the *III./Panzer-Artillerie-Regiment 75*, the *1./Panzerjäger-Abteilung 670*, *Panzer-Pionier-Bataillon 39*, and a light battery of *Flak*—and advanced across the open countryside to the southwest. At first, there were some slowdowns for the march because of the poor road network in the area around the marshy floodplains. That was followed by a zone of green meadows that stretched far and wide.

In a single move, *Oberstleutnant* Wellmann reached the Ssal at Orlowka, forty kilometers away. *Oberleutnant* Bigon's *2./Panzergrenadier-Regiment 3*, in the lead, was able to take intact the bridge at Kalinowskij in a *coup de main*, thus forming the first bridgehead along the Ssal. Seventy Red Army soldiers were taken prisoner.

In the morning, the division had closed up further and, starting at 1030 hours, crossed the remaining elements of *Kampfgruppe Westhoven* (*Kradschützen-Bataillon 3*). Movements were then stopped for some time, since Soviet aircraft succeeded in the evening in destroying the bridge for several hours. At the moment, there were no fighter defenses available, since all fighter groups were in support of the *6. Armee*. Although corps engineers, as well as field-army engineer assets that were brought forward, were busy, it took four hours before any further crossing was possible. *Kampfgruppe de Beaulieu*, which had arrived by then, had to spend the time on the north bank of the river.

The first day along the Ssal did not involve any enemy contact for the forces there. The only thing that could be seen were Russian aircraft flying high above the Cossack villages on their way to the Don. The night also passed quietly. The patrols sent out in the morning, which ranged out to distances of forty kilometers, brought back two camels with them. In the afternoon, rain showers transformed the routes into muck. By then, *Leutnant* Jobst, the adjutant of the *I./Panzergrenadier-Regiment 3*, had established a prisoner collection point in the vicinity of the bridge.

The division was along the Don and started crossing *Panzergrenadier-Regiment 394* at 0330 hours, after the corps engineers had made the bridge, which had been damaged in many places, trafficable again. The division command post moved to Dubenzowskaja, south of the Don. The Red Air Force did not give up on its efforts, and it succeeded once again at 1130 hours in damaging the bridge. Forty-eight pontoons sank in the waters of the Don. Crossing was continued, but only in ferries, and it cost valuable time.

The *I./Panzergrenadier-Regiment 394* screened the bridge to the west and *Kradschützen-Bataillon 3* to the east. *Kradschützen-Bataillon 23* was attacked by surprise by enemy forces coming from Morosoff and pushed back. *Generalmajor* Breith ordered an immediate counterattack. The motorcycle infantry battalion was only able to eject the enemy and retake Morosoff after it had committed all of its companies. It was determined all along the front that the Soviets were reinforcing their elements, presumably to launch an offensive against the bridgehead.

The *3. Panzer-Division* found itself in an unenviable position, since it had lost physical contact with its forward elements because of the loss of the bridge and no ammunition or fuel could be brought forward. Although the engineers had built three ferries, only one was large enough to carry three trucks at a time. The other two were smaller. It was no small achievement to cross the main body of the divisional artillery, a tank company, and the *II./Panzergrenadier-Regiment 394* in the course of the day.

On 25 July, the bridgehead was finally firmly established. The enemy attacked the positions of *Kradschützen-Bataillon 23* with American-built tanks at 0400 hours. The advance could be turned back. The air superiority of the *Luftwaffe* began to be felt. *Luftflotte 4* had moved fighters north of the Don during the morning. They immediately scrambled whenever enemy aircraft appeared in the skies.

The division received orders that day to close up to the Ssal and prepare to advance along the Proletarskaja–Stalingrad railway line. The *23. Panzer-Division* assumed responsibility for the bridgehead so as to be able to launch an attack east to allow the *29. Infanterie-Division (mot.)* to cross the Don at Zymljanskaja. In the afternoon, it was possible to use the engineer bridge again, after all of the reserves of equipment had been committed. That enabled the main body of *Panzer-Regiment 6* to cross the river that day. The *II./Panzergrenadier-Regiment 3*, which was still screening at Konstantinowskaja, was finally sent forward to the division.

The Russians seemed to be weakening. The *II./Panzergrenadier-Regiment 394* reinforced *Kradschützen-Bataillon 23* in continuing its attack south of Morosoff. The *10./Panzer-Regiment 6* also supported in the attack on Bolschowkaja, which ended in success. Seven hundred prisoners were taken, and fifteen Russian tanks remained burnt-out in the marshy meadows. At the same time, *Oberst* Westhoven had conducted an attack west with the *I./Panzergrenadier-Regiment 394* and *Kradschützen-Bataillon 3*, which also succeeded in ejecting the enemy. The batteries from *Artillerie-Regiment 70*, which were in direct support, contributed greatly to the success.

The rain on 25 July had muddied the roadways in the bridgehead to such an extent that all thoughts of continuing the fighting had to be temporarily postponed. When the next day dawned, however, the sun promised radiant weather. The commanding general was at the division command post at 0800 hours to be briefed by *Generalmajor* Breith. It was directed that the division initiate an attack on Proletarskaja.

The division started its advance, after all of its forces, with the exception of the *II./Panzergrenadier-Regiment 3*, had crossed the river by noon and the west flank had finally been cleared of the enemy. *Kampfgruppe Westhoven*, consisting primarily of the main body of the *I./Panzergrenadier-Regiment 394* and *Kradschützen-Bataillon 3*, moved in the direction of Orlowka, while *Oberst Freiherr* von Liebenstein and the *II./Panzer-Regiment 6* turned in the direction of Nessmejanowka. Both of the battle groups moved through a broad, sandy and marshy valley floor, which transitioned into a desolate salt steppe. The only thing that could be seen was sparse patches of withered grass and occasional wild horses and donkeys without owners. The small, yellow clay huts of the black-haired Kalmucks disappeared under the thick dust of the tropical heat. The companies of the armored regiment reached the Ssal in the afternoon and were able to occupy Nessmejanowka. The Russian artillery fire significantly disrupted friendly movements. Among others, the commander of the *6./Panzer-Regiment 6* was badly wounded. The enemy did not fall back until the tanks appeared. *Oberstleutnant* Wellmann's mechanized infantry were able to establish contact with the tanks of *Oberst Freiherr* von Liebenstein.

The Soviets took up the initiative the following morning and advanced against the bridge at Orlowka at 0300 hours. A defensive perimeter was quickly established by the forces available. Engineers were positioned next to cannoneers, *Flak* gunners next to truck drivers and mess personnel next to mechanized infantry. *Oberstleutnant* Wellmann had some antitank elements move forward. *Hauptmann* Kersten, the commander of the 3rd Battalion of the divisional artillery, directed the few guns that were ready to fire. The Russian attack soon collapsed in the face of the German fires. The enemy left behind forty prisoners.

Westhoven's and Liebenstein's battle groups became firmly established along the river. As a result, the division command post was brought forward to Nessmejanowka during the morning. The *II./Panzergrenadier-Regiment 394* was brought forward from the Don and employed in a guard mission oriented to the west at Kalininskij. The elements of Westhoven's battle group already employed there, including the *I./Panzergrenadier-Regiment 3*, were relieved. Starting at noon, the division gradually had all of its forces move to the south bank of the Ssal. *Artillerie-Regiment 70* was sent forward to the location of the armor regiment. Preparations for the attack, which had been ordered for the following morning at 0230 hours, were made at a feverish pace.

During the night, the Soviets attempted to break out to the east across the Ssal. Artillery fire, including that from Stalin organs, rained down on the outposts of the armor regiment at Markowskij starting at 0100 hours. Temporary penetrations were ironed out. Two hours later, the enemy repeated his attack against Nessmejanowka. The enemy was able to penetrate into the village, where his surprise appearance inspired a wild firefight. The security elements of the division headquarters had to go after the Russians with cold steel. After two hours of man-to-man fighting, the situation was cleared up. The headquarters platoon suffered one dead and seven wounded.

In accordance with orders, the advance continued at 0230 hours. *Leutnant* Becker's *8./ Panzer-Regiment 6* was the spearhead of the division in its drive south. Russian formations were not identified until after thirty kilometers had been covered; they were ejected from their positions. The resistance was slight and without unified command. By 0730 hours, the two battle groups of Westhoven and Liebenstein had taken 500 prisoners. The mechanized infantry brigade reached Budennowskaja, while the armored regiment advanced as far as the area around Gantschukoff.

The sun was high in the sky again and gave rise to a tropical heat across the barren land. After moving eighty-five kilometers, the battle groups halted to allow the division and the supply columns to close up. The command staff of the division crossed the Ssal around 0900 hours and arrived in Budennowskaja a short while later. The corps ordered the destruction of the Proletarskaja–Orlowskaja rail line. By then, the field army had directed the corps to prevent the enemy withdrawing north of the Manytsch in escaping to Proletarskaja. Correspondingly, the *3. Panzer-Division* was stopped in its direction of march and turned so that its front was oriented west. The division flank was nearly ninety kilometers long and was protected by *Panzergrenadier-Regiment 394*. In the evening, its 1st Battalion turned back intense enemy attacks at Nowij Sadkowskij and, in the process, captured six artillery pieces. It was directed for a battle group to move forward during the night and blow up the Proletarskaja–Orlowskaja rail line.

The *4. Panzer-Armee* radioed orders to the corps at 0640 hours on 29 July that the *3.* and *23. Panzer-Divisionen* were to advance along the rail line. The *3. Panzer-Division* was directed to take Proletarskaja.

The division attacked on 29 July with two battle groups. *Oberst Freiherr* von Liebenstein moved out at 0930 hours with the *II./Panzer-Regiment 6* and elements of *Artillerie-Regiment 70* from Gantschukoff. Liebenstein's mission was to get to the area around Donskoj, roughly half way between Orlowskaja and Proletarskaja. The armored regiment's 1st and 4th Companies formed the spearhead and initially headed east, only to turn south later on. Starting at 1030 hours, *Oberst* Westhoven moved out with the main body of the mechanized infantry brigade and the 1st Battalion of the armored regiment. The battle group moved out from Budennowskaja and moved via Mokraja-Jelmuta and Ssuchata-Jelmuta on the road to Proletarskaja. The battalions advanced quickly. The obstacles to be overcome that day were the sand and the dust. There was a short halt when the bridge over Elmut Creek, north of Proletarskaja, turned out to be unusable. The engineers arrived quickly and built temporary bridges. The advance continued.

Major Frank's *II./Panzer-Regiment 6* was already in Donskoj at 1330 hours. *Leutnant* Becker's 8th Company was turned in the direction of the railway line to blow it up. The company completed its mission a few minutes later. Since the Soviets were sending a lot of rail transportation along the important line, the German fighting vehicles started engaging in "target practice." In all, nine locomotives, a transport train with grain, a hospital train, and a train loaded with components for an electrical plant were secured. On its way there and back, the company also shot up five trucks and scattered any Russian forces it encountered.

Stukas flew over *Kampfgruppe Westhoven* and dove on Proletarskaja, which soon started to burn. By then, the advance guard of the mechanized infantry brigade was already at the outskirts of the city, approaching form the north. The artillery was unable to keep up and hung behind. *Oberst* Westhoven ordered an attack on Proletarskaja from the approach march. Individual pockets of resistance were broken up by aggressive actions. The enemy was surprised one more time and had no time to organize his defenses. The mechanized infantry of *Panzergrenadier-Regiment 3* entered the city. *Oberfeldwebel* Kruse, a platoon leader in the regiment's 3rd Company, once again distinguished himself

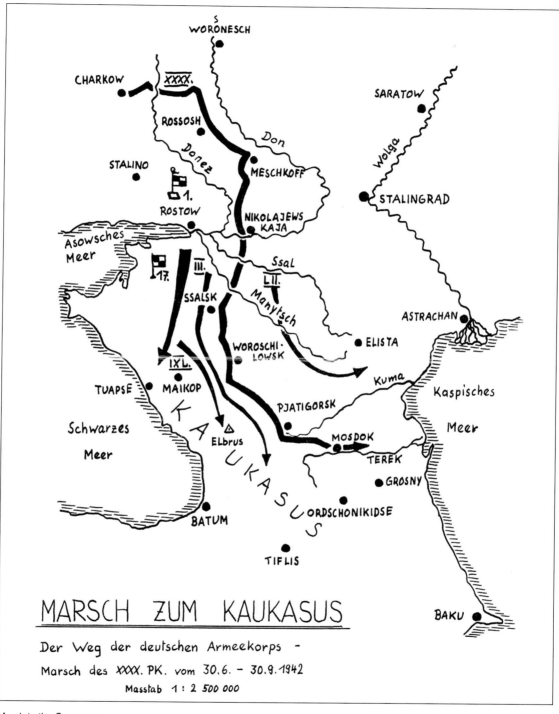

MARSCH ZUM KAUKASUS

Der Weg der deutschen Armeekorps –
Marsch des XXXX. PK. vom 30.6. – 30.9.1942
Masstab 1 : 2 500 000

March to the Caucasus
The Movements of the Army Corps
March of the *XXXX. Panzer-Korps* from 30 June to 30 September 1942
Schwarzes Meer = Black Sea; *Asowisches Meer* = Asovian Sea; *Kaspisches Meer* = Caspian Sea; *Masstab* = Scale.

through his bravery, as he had so often in the past. He assaulted at the point of his soldiers, thus enabling the rapid movement forward of the 1st Battalion. For his deeds, he was later awarded the Knight's Cross.

Around 1500 hours, *Panzergrenadier-Regiment 3* took the city. It was not until then that the enemy started to react cohesively, employing elements at different locations in the defense. *Hauptmann* Rohrbeck's *I./Panzer-Regiment 6*, which was brought forward, provided the mechanized infantry the additional firepower they needed. Once the engineers arrived, the assault was continued in the direction of the bridges over the Karytscheplak. *Oberleutnant* Brandt's 3rd Company of engineers charged the structures. The engineers, supported by the mechanized infantry of *Major* Boehm's 2nd Battalion, succeeded in crossing the railway bridge. The road bridge was blown up by the Soviets, however. With the taking of the bridge, the enemy forces in Proletarskaja were finally defeated.

Generaloberst Hoth, the commander in chief of the *4. Panzer-Armee*, congratulated the division on its success with the following: "Bravo, *3. Panzer-Division*! I'm happy to recognize you for the dashing success today!"

In its official report, the Armed Force High Command stated:

> Motorized forces assaulted and took the city of Proletarskaja to the south of the Ssal River on 30 July, interdicting the last major railway connection between the Caucasus and the rest of the Soviet Union at several places. In do so, an armored division from Brandenburg particularly distinguished itself!

German radio stations added to the official announcement with this supplementation:

> One armor division had covered more than 1,000 kilometers since 30 June. Mechanized infantry took the city of Proletarskaja without waiting for the arrival of the artillery, which was still closing up.

Kampfgruppe Westhoven was not allowed to rest on its laurels, however. The engineers started reconnoitering crossing points over the many tributaries of the Manytsch or creating new ones. The division's bridging section had already started constructing a bridge 2.5 kilometers east of Proletarskaja across the Tscheirak during the afternoon of 29 July. It was a sixteen-ton span. *Panzer-Pionier-Bataillon 39* and *Pionier-Bataillon 52* (a separate engineer battalion and field-army asset) worked on the destroyed road bridge in Proletarskaja, which proved to be a difficult undertaking. In addition to blowing up the bridge, the Soviets had also torn up the embankment for a length of 100 meters, resulting in the roadway being flooded. The issues with the rebuilding of the bridge were finally solved by modification of the engineer bridge, the construction of a reinforced support for the beams on the shores and an elevation of the embankment by means of sandbags.

A company from the *II./Lehr-Regiment "Brandenburg"* arrived in the division's sector. The effort to take the Manytsch Reservoir in a coup de main by the battalion failed due to the alertness of the enemy. One of the battalion's *Leutnants* succeeded in crossing the pedestrian bridge on the northern end of the reservoir and entering the guardhouse, which was captured. By doing so, he prevented the demolition of that portion of the bridge, which would have been of importance for the success of the rest of the mission. Later on, the officer received the Knight's Cross for his actions.

In the course of the day, *Oberst* Westhoven's mechanized infantry brigade had pushed its combat outposts all the way to the north banks of the southern arm of the Manytsch. *Panzer-Pionier-Bataillon 39* reconnoitered along the multi-branched river. *Leutnant* Moewis of the 3rd Company found a potential crossing point over the second tributary of the river. Additional elements of the engineer battalion found two additional potential crossing points on 30 July, which were suitable for crossing by assault craft and floats. The Manytsch was no river in a traditional sense. Instead, it was a continuous chain of lakes of up to two kilometers in width.

In order to support the efforts of the mechanized infantry brigade to cross the river south of Proletarskaja, the division commander decided to attempt an additional crossing at Burgusstenskij. *Oberleutnant* Deichen's *2./Kradschützen-Bataillon 3*, supported by engineers, was able to cross to the other bank starting at 1100 hours. Success was achieved, but it had to be expanded. The *II./Panzergrenadier-Regiment 394*, which was still far to the rear, was ordered forward to Burgusstenskij. The 1st Company of that regiment was left behind in its old positions to await the closing up of the *23. Panzer-Division* and *Infanterie-Division (mot.) "Großdeutschland."*

Oberstleutnant Zimmermann was placed in charge of operations around Burgusstenskij. *Major* Haspel's *II./Panzergrenadier-Regiment 394* arrived over the next few hours. His 5th Company was the first one put across by the engineers. Most of the vehicles had to remain behind due to an absence of ferries; only motorcycles and light staff cars could be taken across. The crossing of the 1,200-meter-wide river was not as easy as it appeared; despite the shallow water, the waves were relatively high.

By then, the *2./Kradschützen-Bataillon 3* had moved three kilometers west in the direction of Perwomaiskaja. The motorcycle infantry first encountered enemy forces in the form of cavalry in the area around Krasny-Manytsch. Because it took so long to cross forces on that 30 July, no more mechanized infantry companies were crossed that day. They assembled along the banks, where a battalion of artillery had also closed up and gone into position.

The *II./Panzer-Regiment 6*, which was considerably further to the east, protected the flanks of the division along the railway line. Its companies were positioned all by themselves along the broad plain. The countryside was desolate and empty, with only the occasional locality showing itself. Despite all of the security measures and obstacles, a Russian armored train appeared by surprise along the remaining intact piece of track.

Oberfeldwebel Sorge's platoon from the 7th Company was immediately sent after it. After a short engagement, his fighting vehicles brought the train to a standstill, and it started to burn.

As the day drew to a close, the *3. Panzer-Division* had solidified its position along the Manytsch.

At first light on 31 July, *Kampfgruppe Zimmermann* crossed the river with the remaining companies of the *II./Panzergrenadier-Regiment 394*. This time, the crossing went more quickly, since the engineers had constructed larger ferries during the night. On the other hand, the enemy pressure against the bridgehead had increased. The *2./Kradschützen-Bataillon 3* was even encountering motorized elements, but the Soviets were still continuing to fight without unified command. Most of the forces were scattered elements, which wanted to withdraw from the Rostow area to the east or south.

Since the water level of the Manytsch sank more and more over the course of the day, the heavy vehicles could not be crossed. Fortunately, all of the field messes made it into the bridgehead. But without its vehicles, the mechanized infantrymen were immobilized. Correspondingly, the battle group could not execute its original mission and advance south to facilitate the establishment of a bridgehead at Proletarskaja by the mechanized infantry brigade.

The *3. Panzergrenadier-Brigade* then prepared to cross the Manytsch to the south. The divisional artillery, together with *Artillerie-Regiment 70* and attached *Nebelwerfer* batteries, reconnoitered firing positions for the attack, which was to be executed during the night. In the course of the day, the *II./Panzer-Regiment 6* was also pushed forward into the area around Proletarskaja.

When the clocks struck twelve, all batteries of the supporting artillery opened fire all at once. The fight for the Manytsch crossing had started! While the rounds were still landing on the positions of the NKVD and the regular forces of the 19th Rifle Division, the engineers pushed their nineteen assault craft into the water. Men from the *II./Panzergrenadier-Regiment 3*, the divisional engineers and the engineer platoon of the motorcycle infantry battalion climbed into the small watercraft and moved across the broad reservoir in the dark of night.

Oberleutnant Tank's *6./Panzergrenadier-Regiment 3* was the first unit to land on the far shore, where it heard the whistling of enemy rounds as it landed. The mechanized infantry had to assault the Russian positions directly from the boats, and close combat ensued. The second crossing of the assault craft did not proceed as smoothly. Many of the boats sprung leaks and needed a lot of time to cross. Two boats were sunk after being hit. Finally, the men of the 3rd and 7th Companies, under the command of *Oberleutnant* Vormann, were crossed.

It was high time, since there was no more time left for a third crossing attempt. The Soviet artillery had identified the German attack zone and hammered down on all of the approaching boats. Friendly artillery fire support was missing during the first few minutes, since all of the forward observers had been killed when crossing over, except for one. Only *Leutnant* Buchmann of the 9th Battery was able to establish radio contact with his unit. The battery started firing with everything it had. That morning, the divisional artillery fired a total of 1,200 rounds.

The fighting by the infantry of the *II./Panzergrenadier-Regiment 3* was all the more tough due to the fact that the NKVD soldiers would not surrender and fought with a wild doggedness. *Major* Boehm was mortally wounded. His adjutant also went with him, as did a number of other officers and enlisted personnel. *Oberleutnant* Tank then rallied the remaining men of the battalion. The twenty-six-year-old officer assumed command and assaulted the Russian positions at the head of the mechanized infantry. When they started to run out of ammunition, the men fixed bayonets and charged with the German battle cry of "Hurra!" on their lips. The Soviets started wavering. The men entered the Soviet trench lines and wrested one position after the other from the enemy.

But then heavy defensive fires from Manytshstroj and the reservoir prevented the brave mechanized infantry from advancing any further. The motorcycle infantry battalion had relieved the company from *Lehr-Regiment "Brandenburg"* on both sides of the reservoir, and was pinning the enemy in his bunkers on the south bank. Of special concern there were the enemy snipers, who initially prevented every effort to work the forces forward.

Finally, *Oberleutnant* Meister's *3./Kradschützen-Bataillon 3*, supported anew by concentrated artillery fires, was able to assault across the embankment and eliminate the enemy snipers. The company had suffered bitter losses as a result of headshots at the hands of the snipers. But the embankment had been taken and the far bank of the Manytsch taken. It occurred at just the right time to bring some relief to the mechanized infantry of *Oberleutnant* Tank, who were attacking from the other side in the direction of Manytschstroj. The mechanized infantry and the motorcycle infantry linked up—dirty and exhausted but happy after the successful fighting—at the outskirts of the Manytschstroj along the far side of the river.

The 2nd Battalion of *Panzergrenadier-Regiment 3* had suffered thirty-six dead that morning. It was a high price to pay, even for such a great success. For his role, the fallen *Major* Boehm was posthumously entered into the Army Honor Roll; *Oberleutnant* Tank would later receive the Knight's Cross.

In spite of the ongoing enemy fire, *Oberst* Westhoven issued orders to *Oberleutnant* Brandt, the commander of the *3./Panzer-Pionier-Bataillon 39*, to start building a bridge. At 0915 hours, the 3rd Company started assembling the supports. Just one hour later, the first portion of the bridge was complete; by 1115 hours, the construction was ended. The work in finishing the bridge—29.3 meters long and capable of twenty tons—was made even more difficult by the fact that enemy fires of all calibers were constantly being placed on it. Casualties were unavoidable, and *Leutnant* Moewis died a soldier's death as the result of a mine explosion. A second difficulty was the marshy approach route. Forty cannoneers from the 4th Battalion of the divisional artillery were employed to build a corduroy road. It was not possible to release traffic for the already completed bridge until around 1930 hours.

The day brought with it storms and a cloudy sky, with the result that neither air force had the opportunity to intervene in the ground fighting. That day, the total casualties for *Panzergrenadier-Regiment 3* were forty-eight dead and eighty-three wounded. The Russian forces started pulling back to the south, leaving behind about 1,000 prisoners in German hands. That evening, the division established a pursuit force under *Oberstleutnant Freiherr* von Liebenstein, consisting of the *II./Panzer-Regiment 6*, *Kradschützen-Bataillon 3*, a battery from the divisional artillery, a battery of *Nebelwerfer*, a battery of 8.8-centimter *Flak*, and one company from *Pionier-Bataillon 52*.

With the crossing of the river, the soldiers of the division were in Asia. Geographically, the south bank of the Manytsch belonged to another continent.

There were strong storms during the night, but the morning brought with it radiant sunshine. The Russians attempted to attack in the twilight, but they were turned back by the *II./Panzer-Regiment 6*. In the process, nine enemy tanks and one gun were destroyed. *Major* Pape's pursuit detachment left the bridgehead at 0245 hours and advanced in a single move along the railway line to Salsk. Pape's tanks, *SPW's*, and motorcycles swung to the south and reached the village of Sandata along the Bol. Jegorlyk in blazing heat. The companies advanced up to the bridge and were able to take it in a *coup de main*. The Soviets engaged the approaching column with artillery, but they were unable to prevent the establishment of a bridgehead.

Kampfgruppe von Liebenstein, consisting of the *II./Panzer-Regiment 6*, the *I./Panzergrenadier-Regiment 3*, two companies of engineers, and three batteries of artillery, followed the pursuit

detachment to Salsk. The main body of the division remained in Proletarskaja, however, in order to hold the bridge against any possible enemy attacks and to secure the advance of the division. Unfortunately, not all of the forces could move, since the fuel sections of the rear-area services had simply not been able to make it forward. That day, the division moved its command post to Salsk.

The *XXXX. Panzer-Korps*, to which the *3. Panzer-Division* was still attached, was allocated to *Generaloberst* Kleist's *1. Panzer-Armee* effective 1 August. The *4. Panzer-Armee* turned east and north with its remaining corps to take Stalingrad. The *XXXX. Panzer-Korps* was on its own. Its main mission: take Grosny. It was also given a secondary mission of protecting the entire east flank of the *1. Panzer-Armee*.

The objective for the *3. Panzer-Division* on Sunday, 2 August, was Woroschilowsk, 200 kilometers distant. The division formed two advance guards. *Kampfgruppe Pape*, which was attached to the *I./Panzer-Regiment 6* that day, advanced south. The companies marched through tracts of land that were practically devoid of humans. One could observe far across the fields and grazing lands. There were hardly any changes in elevation on which one could orient. The vehicle commanders in the tanks and *SPW's* simply moved in accordance with the compass.

Kampfgruppe von Liebenstein headed out from Salsk at 0700 hours. The battle group moved via Sandata, Iku Tuktum, Farm 2, Nishnije Burul, and Koleshniko towards Pregradnoje. There was hardly anything to be seen of the enemy. Around 1400 hours, enemy aircraft attacked the columns in the area of Nishnije Burul and caused a few casualties with their bombs. Shortly after 1630 hours, the *8./Panzer-Regiment 6* arrived in Pregradnoje. The city was taken by the German forces without a fight. The only spoils of war were sixty prisoners and four mortars. The remaining Russian forces that had been there took off in flight to the south.

The command staff of the division arrived in the locality at the same time as the battle group.

It looked as though everything had died. The Russians rarely came out of their huts. But the Cossacks soon gained trust in the German soldiers and greeted them as liberators. The women shook the hands of the *Landser*, constantly making the sign of the cross. Without being asked, they brought out bread, milk and eggs.

The forces had covered 130 kilometers on that hot day. By then, however, almost all the fuel had been used up. Only *Kampfgruppe Pape* was able to advance along the sandy road to the southeast and reach Besopassnoje. By doing so, Pape's men were far ahead of any other German units. Clouds of dust could also be seen off to the right of the division. They were coming from the *13. Panzer-Division* of the neighboring *III. Panzer-Korps*. Under *Oberst* Westhoven, the rest of the division, with the exception of the *II./Panzergrenadier-Regiment 394*, moved from Proletarskaja to Salsk on 2 August, where it bedded down for the night. The mechanized infantry battalion remained in the bridgehead along the Manytsch for another two days to wait for other troop elements to close up. The patrols sent out by the battalion continued to encounter scattered Russian units and stragglers, all of which surrendered apathetically. On 2 August alone, the battalion took 557 prisoners.

The night of 2–3 August passed quietly, but enemy aircraft were in the skies early in the morning. They were observation aircraft. The division was able to continue its advance around 0700 hours with all of its battle groups. *Major* Pape and the advance guard departed Besopassnoje and headed due south toward Donskoje. *Kampfgruppe von Liebenstein* left Pregradnoje in the direction of Besopassnoje. It was there at 0830 hours that contact was established with the lead element of the *23. Panzer-Division*, which was responsible for screening to the east from that point forward.

The companies and batteries of the division moved deeper into the broad expanse of land, kilometer by kilometer. In its broad expanse and unique beauty, it was the image of Asia. The impressions left behind were diverse. A member of the division headquarters wrote the following to his loved ones back home:

> Pregradnoje a large, extended and rambling locality. Villages of several thousand people are not uncommon. Gigantic herds of livestock approach us, magnificent cattle and sheep. The best of purebred horses, always in groups of several hundred. The people are true nomads. They wind their way from one grazing area to the next, with bag and baggage, primitive trailers, transportable watering holes for the livestock, water canisters etc. The harvested grain is spread out in long rows, just like we do with the potatoes, a few tons each time. Huge quantities of sunflower seeds are also stacked in the same manner. There are large scooping buckets at each of the lakes . . . the steppes have become fruitful soil. An intoxicating view. The plains transition into rolling countryside. . . . The many spots along the slopes reveal themselves to be grazing livestock when you look a bit closer. There is one village after the other. The localities leave a tidy and nice impression. There are lavish gardens around each farmstead. . . .

And this from a soldier in *Panzergrenadier-Regiment 3*:

> The continued advance led us through the Kalmuck Steppes. . . . We snuck up to a village and the patrol leader radioed in that enemy tanks had moved up to the edge of the locality. A short while later, laughing, we were able to determine that the "tanks" were camels. Over the next few days, we frequently saw dromedaries and camels. . . . The terrain turned more mountainous and the sun hotter. The armored vehicles had a hard time crawling up the mountains in those temperatures . . .

Finally, a cannoneer from the divisional artillery:

The terrain started to change its appearance. Mountains that climbed to 800 and 1,000 meters began to appear. Most were barren and had a yellowish brown color. Surrounded by clouds of dust, gigantic herds of cattle headed in that direction. . . . The steppes and grazing lands transitioned to expansive fields of grain. The localities came across as more tidy and well maintained. In place of the usual thatched roofs, red roof tiles appeared more and more often between the trunks of deciduous trees. . . . Groups of prisoners trotted past us with no weapons and no guards. They frequently waved or greeted in a friendly manner. . . . Camels wandered about leisurely with smug faces and a Habsburg-like lower lip. They reminded us once more that this area formed the frontier between Europe and Asia . . .

The companies of *Kradschützen-Bataillon 3* moving out ahead encountered slight enemy resistance outside of Donskoje. It was quickly broken. They then advanced through a small creek valley to Moskowskaja and then Pelagiada. Tanks were surprised to discover a long transport train at the Pelagiada rail station. The locomotive was still under steam. The fighting vehicles immediately headed in that direction. The Russian guards fled head over heels. The tankers were astonished when they counted up the spoils: two KV-I's, one T-34, one Mark II, three BT-60's, and two howitzers.

Long columns of refugees moved along the sides of the roads. Some of the carts were pulled by camels. The people looked at the German soldiers in a friendly manner; the war was over for them. They could return to the villages or cities from which the Red Army had evacuated them.

The closer the advance guard got to the city of Woroschilowsk, the more apparent the signs of war became. Bomber and *Stuka* wings of *Luftflotte 4* had hit the Russian road network and strong-points. Freight trains were burning on the open track and there, where the city had to be located, were undulating and thick masses of smoke above the high ground. All of a sudden, the tanks and motorcycles halted. They were greeted with an unforgettable sight: on the far side of a deep valley was Woroschilowsk, the former Stawropol, embedded on the crest of a mountain, surrounded by trees in full bloom. Then the engines began to howl. The vehicles moved down the serpentine, past gardens with apricots and plums and, once at the bottom, started back up the mountain.

The lead elements of *Kampfgruppe Pape* were at the outskirts of Woroschilowsk at 1345 hours. No one knew where the enemy was. There were flames shooting high everywhere. There was nothing to be seen of the civilian populace. *Major* Pape issued a short order: "Attack!" The men of *Kradschützen-Bataillon 3* and the *I./Panzer-Regiment 6* advanced down the streets. In the lead were the fighting vehicles of *Oberleutnant Graf* von Kageneck's 4th Company, followed by motorcycle infantry. By then, the *2./Panzer-Regiment 6* was also attacking from the northeast. There was only sporadic resistance. Surprisingly, the Soviets pulled back into the center of the city. But the streets there were so full of columns that they could offer no disciplined resistance there. The companies fanned out and advanced to the far side of the city. *Hauptmann* Rohrbeck's tank battalion secured a fuel and oil storage point at the airfield, and the motorcycle infantry captured a supply dump with 5.5 million pounds of wheat. The Soviets were so surprised by the capture of the city that Russian aircraft continued to attempt to land over and over again. The mechanized infantry succeeded in shooting down a large aircraft with four engines. The accompanying *Flak* shot down an additional seven aircraft. By 1500 hours, Woroschilowsk was firmly in the hands of the division.

Generalmajor Breith, who was with the command staff right behind the advance guard, entered the city. The division command post was set up at the large and modern sports field. The motorcycle infantry screened the outskirts of the city. For the time being, it was not possible to consider continuing the advance, since there was no fuel available.

Kampfgruppe von Liebenstein remained toward the rear in Pelagiada and guarded the route of advance, focusing toward the west. *Oberst* Ullrich arrived with the main bodies of the two artillery regiments—*Artillerie-Regiment 70* and *Panzer-Artillerie-Regiment 75*—in Woroschilowsk in the afternoon. The artillery was followed by the mechanized infantry. The *I./Panzergrenadier-Regiment 3* assumed responsibility for guarding the large grain silos and the mental institution.

The city showed a lot of signs of war. Individual houses had been burned to the ground or badly damaged. The railway station was in flames. The corpses of soldiers and civilians and the remains of horses, all of which had fallen victim to the air strikes, had to be removed. Many of the buildings displayed posters portraying German soldiers as criminals and plunderers and exhorting the populace to fight the occupiers. Life returned to normal slowly. The people started coming out of their hiding places. They greeted our men and provided them with goods and services.

Generaloberst Kleist, the commander in chief of the *1. Panzer-Armee*, dispatched a radio message: "Thanks and recognition to the admirable forces and the dynamic leadership!" The Armed Forces Daily Report announced the next day: "The industrial city of Woroschilowsk was taken today after intense house-to-house fighting!"

The corps issued orders for the division to remain in the city on 4 August and await the arrival of the rearward elements. The soldiers, who were not involved with guard or patrol activities, had the opportunity to view the pretty city. The division commander appointed *Sonderführer* Demidow as the local area administrative commander. All of the businesses had been completely plundered. The local populace had taken everything that hadn't been nailed down. But the division also enjoyed a large amount of spoils. The fuel situation improved as a result of the capture of the Russian fuel dump. Reconnaissance to all sides conducted by *Kradschützen-Bataillon 3* and *Panzergrenadier-Regiment 3* revealed that enemy columns were moving southeast along the western flank. To the east, however, no enemy forces were detected.

Panzergrenadier-Regiment 394 and the *III./Panzer-Artillerie-Regiment 75*, which had heretofore remained in the bridgehead on the Manytsch, were ordered forward the evening of 4 August after it was determined the fuel situation up front was acceptable. Up to that point, the formations had had hardly any fuel and were restricted to security duties along the river crossing points. They had had hardly any enemy contact, but there were always Russian deserters. Through 4 August, the mechanized infantry regiment reported the following spoils: 1,004 prisoners, 6 machine guns, 15 mortars, 83 carbines, and assorted small arms.

Oberst Westhoven moved with the mechanized infantry regiment, the artillery battalion, and *Panzerjäger-Abteilung 543* at 0330 hours on 5 August from the quartering areas along the Manytsch. For the time being, the *II./Panzergrenadier-Regiment 3* remained behind. The march serial rapidly reached Pregadnoje, where enemy artillery fire temporarily slowed down the movement. The march serial then continued its movement and reached Woroschilowsk around 1500 hours, where Westhoven's forces were employed in screening the city of 90,000 people.

Oberst Freiherr von Liebenstein's battle group, consisting of *Panzer-Regiment 6*, the *I./Panzergrenadier-Regiment 3*, the *I./Panzer-Artillerie-Regiment 75*, *Pionier-Bataillon 52*, and the *I./Werfer-Regiment 52*, had sent reinforced combat outposts forward to protect the avenue of advance to all sides. Reconnaissance was conducted early in the afternoon, to include as far as Tatarskoje, to the south of Woroschilowsk, after the advance guard had moved out in the direction of the Kuban.

Major Pape started moving south with his formations at 0300 hours. *Oberleutnant Graf von Kageneck's 4./Panzer-Regiment 6* was in the lead again, followed by the *I./Panzergrenadier-Regiment 3*. Also with Pape's advance guard were *Kradschützen-Bataillon 3*, the *I./Panzer-Artillerie-Regiment 75*, *Panzer-Pionier-Bataillon 39*, the *10./Artillerie-Regiment 70*, and a supply section. The movement proceeded relatively rapidly and moved via Barssukowskaja in the direction of Njewinnomyskaja on the Kuma River.

The terrain gradually grew higher. The road turned along many curves going uphill. The countryside was reminiscent of the mountains and woods of Thuringia. The mountainous beauty also brought difficulties with it for a motorized force. The vehicles were barely capable of performing in the face of the heat, dust, and overuse. The *4./Panzer-Regiment 6* had only six fighting vehicles that could keep the pace. When the advance guard approached Njewinnomyskaja, it received Russian artillery fire. The Soviets had established a well-prepared position with gun pits along the southern slopes of the Kuma.

An enemy rifle battalion and an antiaircraft battery defended the sector. The advance guard pressed into the northern portion of Njewinnomyskaja, overran a battery and moved on to the Kuma. A Russian force defended the railway station, but it was quickly ejected. The station house was soon assaulted and a fully loaded freight train captured. The advance guard had interdicted the Armawir–Grosny rail line. *Oberleutnant Graf* von Kageneck left behind two fighting vehicles to screen. The remaining four tanks moved through the locality, rattled across the 150-meter bridge and established a bridgehead on the far side of the raging river, along with the *2./Kradschützen-Bataillon 3. Feldwebel* Stever's platoon from the divisional engineers assumed the mission of safeguarding the bridge. His platoon destroyed three enemy bunkers, eliminated three mortars and one heavy machine

gun, took fifteen prisoners, and blew up two sections of track 1.5 kilometers from the locality. Five destroyed aircraft were discovered at the nearby landing strip, where three antiaircraft guns were also captured.

The *1. Panzer-Armee* sent the following radio message to the division: "Special praise for proving yourselves one more time!"

By reaching the Kuma, the division had booked another success, since it blocked the withdrawal route of the Soviets to the southeast. But as had always been the case previously, there were still large groups of scattered elements and stragglers to deal with, which were all attempting to break out to the east. For instance, one such element encountered the division logistics section, which was on its way to Woroschilowsk. Fighting ensued, in which the section suffered two dead (*Feldwebel* Komoss and *Soldat* Lessmann).

By and large, 6 August passed quietly. The division's forces took a break, wherever possible. The break was necessitated largely by the lack of fuel. Correspondingly, only reconnaissance was conducted to all sides. The patrols determined that large enemy forces were moving south on the roads leading towards Tscherkessk. Other Russians forces were temporarily blocking the road east of Pregradnoje. *Oberleutnant* Schewe's *8./Panzer-Regiment 201* of the *23. Panzer-Division* attacked those forces along with a few trains columns that happened to be nearby. The *23. Panzer-Division* conducted a reconnaissance-in-force to the east that day to secure the flanks.

Oberst Chales de Beaulieu was transferred out of the division about this time; his replacement was *Major* Pape. In his place, *Hauptmann* Cochenhausen assumed command of the motorcycle infantry battalion. *Oberstleutnant* Wellmann also left to take command of *Panzergrenadier-Regiment 126* of the *23. Panzer-Division*. The adjutant of the mechanized infantry brigade, *Hauptmann* Erdmann, assumed Wellmann's command. *Panzerjäger-Abteilung 670*, which had heretofore fought side by side with the comrades of the division, was reallocated to the *4. Panzer-Armee. Hauptmann* Mente assumed command of the *II./Panzergrenadier-Regiment 3.*

The weather was unbearably hot. New for the men of the division was the appearance of desert winds. In some places, the temperatures climbed to 35 degrees and more [95 Fahrenheit]. Enemy forces attacked the outposts of the *II./Panzer-Regiment 6* in the morning at Tatarskoje, to the south of Woroschilowsk. The combined fires scattered the Russians, who then took off to the southeast. An order from the corps arrived on 7 August, outlining new missions for the division: The objective for the division was Pjatigorsk. The objective for the *23. Panzer-Division* on the left was Mineralnyje-Wody.

The division established three battle groups to tackle the mission. *Oberst* Zimmermann (promoted 1 August) was supposed to guard the avenue of advance in the Njewinnomyskaja area with the *I./Panzergrenadier-Regiment 394*, the *II./Panzer-Artillerie-Regiment 75*, two companies of tanks, and some smaller elements. Zimmermann's elements would protect the open west flank of the advancing division. *Oberst* Westhoven led the second battle group, which consisted of *Kradschützen-Bataillon 3*, the *I./Panzer-Regiment 6*, the *II./Panzergrenadier-Regiment 394*, *Artillerie-Regiment 70*, the *III./Panzer-Artillerie-Regiment 75*, *Panzer-Pionier-Bataillon 39*, and other elements. *Oberst Freiherr* von Liebenstein assumed command of the third battle group of the *II./Panzer-Regiment 6*, *Pionier-Bataillon 52*, and other units. Based on the allocation of forces, Westhoven's battle group formed the main effort of the attack, while *Kampfgruppe von Liebenstein* was given the mission of advancing as far as Suworowskaja and assuming a flank guard mission in the direction of Tscherkessk.

As it turned first light the next day, the *3. Panzer-Division* started the advance that would take it into the Caucasus. *Kradschützen-Bataillon 3*, under its new and recently promoted commander, *Major* von Cochenhausen, left the out-

post positions around Njewinnomyskaja at 0300 hours and moved along the railway embankment to the southeast. The other elements of the division likewise moved out from their assembly areas. The entire division, including the command section, was on the move by 0330 hours. The motorcycles and fighting vehicles of the *I./Panzer-Regiment 6* got as far as Kursawskoje without stopping and without encountering the enemy. It was there that Soviet forces threw down the gauntlet for the first time that day, but they were thrown back by the companies of the advance guard. The movement continued along the Grosny–Rostow oil pipeline. Whenever the lead elements approached a pumping station, it would go up in flames.

The march continued through the heat and the dust. *Major* Pape's forces assumed the mission of guarding the western flank to cover the movement of the advance guard. The *5./Panzergrenadier-Regiment 394* remained behind to screen, along with antitank elements. The tanks and motorcycles rattling ahead were attacked several times by Russian aircraft, but that did not prevent the lead elements of *Oberst* Westhoven's battle group from advancing as far as Ssoluno-Dimitrikewskoje and establishing a bridgehead. There was a halt there as well, since all of the bridges had been blown up, and route and bridge reconnaissance needed to be conducted first. *Oberleutnant* Brandt's 1st Company of engineers was brought forward, along with Bridging Section 1. *Feldwebel* Knopke and his engineer reconnaissance element were the first to cross over the Kurasawka.

Hours passed before the lead elements could move out again. By then, *Kampfgruppe von Liebenstein* had closed up and pivoted to the southeast to take up flank guard. The *II./Panzer-Regiment 6* moved cross country over the fertile land with its rolling fields and green meadows. There were hardly any roads or trails off of the main road, with the result that movement had to be conducted by compass. The German soldiers could already see the snow-capped mountains of the Caucasus in the distance. The tankers of the *II./Panzer-Regiment 6* saw a single cloud above all of the other peaks, but it did not move. After moving for another couple of hours and then looking into the blue summer skies again, the cloud still had not moved. Then someone said a single word: "Elbrus." Yes, it was the 5,633-meter tall Mount Elbrus that was seen by the soldiers of the division for the first time on 8 August.

At 1715 hours, the advance guard moved out again on poor roads. It was slowly turning dark. *Kradschützen-Bataillon 3* reached the area north of Klangly. A tank ditch temporarily halted all forward movement. The division ordered the advance to stop around 2200 hours. *Kampfgruppe Westhoven* set up a perimeter defense about 10 kilometers northwest of Klangly for the night. The forces had covered nearly 180 kilometers in the tropical heat that day.

The night was hot and short. At 0245 hours, the engineers were already being called forward to the Kuma. The 3rd Company of the divisional engineers had reconnoitered crossing points. Bridging Section 1 started construction of a sixteen-ton bridge over the river and an additional sixteen-ton structure over a tributary. The first motorcycle infantry companies had also been summoned forward to the river, where they prepared to cross. Shortly after 0300 hours, the soldiers of the division started crossing the river. The crossing took a lot of time, since the bridging site was very narrow. Traffic piled up. But as soon as elements were across the river, the advance started again. This time, it led into the mountains. The routes sloped more and had more curves in them. While in the morning the only enemy forces seen were a seven-man mounted Cossack patrol, which was intercepted, there was increasing enemy resistance hour by hour later in the day. The Russians had dug in well in the mountain slopes and used the mountainous terrain for cover and concealment.

Major von Cochenhausen's *Kradschützen-Bataillon 3* was well in front of the division. At 0730 hours, it started attacking Smejka with the fighting vehicles of the *I./Panzer-Regiment 6*. Initially, the Soviets only put up slight resistance, but as the German soldiers advanced farther into the mountains—heights between 900 and 1,400 meters—the defense stiffened. The motorcycle infantry and tanks were unable to eject the enemy forces by themselves. They needed to wait for the arrival of the artillery and *Flak*. Once they arrived, the guns took the positions on the high ground under fire.

By 1300 hours, the advance guard had ejected the enemy forces along the eastern slopes of the mountains and was advancing in the direction of Karras. The battle group, which had been joined by the *I./Panzergrenadier-Regiment 394*, took the embankment between Smejka Mountain (994 meters) and the city of Mineralnyje Wody. *Oberst* Westhoven did not give his men much time to deploy into attack positions. The attack soon took place from the west and the north. The battle group overran the enemy and took the northern portion of Pjatigorsk, the "Five Mountain City," in the first assault.

The Soviets intended to defend the city with all of the means at their disposal. They had brought rifle and artillery brigades forward. The fighting along the northern edge of the city was tough and grim. It was not until the lead tanks of *Hauptmann* Rohrbeck's *I./Panzer-Regiment 6* had taken out a Russian 15-centimeter battery that the path was clear. *Kradschützen-Bataillon 3*, the *I./Panzergrenadier-Regiment 394*, and the *3./Panzer-Pionier-Bataillon 39* entered the city proper. There were individual skirmishes all over the city at street corners and within building complexes, which caused a number of casualties. They were soldiers from a NKVD division, an armor school, and a women's battalion that engaged the men of the *3. Panzer-Division*. Despite all difficulties, it was possible to get as far as Podhumok. A sharp engagement ensued for the sixty-meter bridge. The tanks of *Hauptmann* Rohrbeck, which had been able to get to the south bank in the first rush, had to pull back when they did not have any direct infantry support. Although the resistance on the south bank increased in the course of the day, the *2./Krad-schützen-Bataillon 3* was able to take the bridge and establish a narrow bridgehead in the afternoon with the support of the tanks and the guns of *Oberleutnant* Lange's *5./Panzer-Artillerie-Regiment 75*.

It was not only the fighting that took its toll on the soldiers, but the heat as well. The temperature climbed up to 52 degrees that day [125 Fahrenheit].

That afternoon, all of the forces of the *3. Panzer-Division* were headed in the direction of Pjatigorsk. *Oberst Freiherr* von Liebenstein was able to turn back an attack by a Soviet rifle battalion in the vicinity of Suworowskaja with his battle group. The tanks pressed across the 100-meter wooden bridge and reached the road to Pjatigorsk on the other side of the Kuma. The *II./Panzer-Regiment 6* turned southeast and reached the western approaches to the city around 1600 hours. The companies of *Kampfgruppe Pape* were in the city proper at the same time. The *5.* and *9./Panzergrenadier-Regiment 394* were the first to enter the city from that regiment, taking the area around the cemetery. The rest of the 2nd Battalion followed closely behind and was employed in the eastern part of the city.

Russian forces were still holding out in the southern part on the other side of the river and were preventing the German forces from crossing. *Oberst* Westhoven took command of all of the forces along the north bank in that sector and had them establish security for the night. The division headquarters had also arrived, setting up in the northern part of the city. *Kampfgruppe von Liebenstein* received orders to keep to the road open as far as Suworowskaja. The motorcycle infantry battalion remained in the western part of the city. It was adjoined by the *II./Panzergrenadier-Regiment 394*, which screened from Maschuk Mountain to the northern part of the city. In the evening hours, *Panzer-Regiment 201* of the *23. Panzer-Division* reached Pjatigorsk via Mineralnyje Wody. The regimental commander was *Oberst* Burmeister, who had led the *II./Panzer-Regiment 6* in the French campaign.

The very warm night was not a quiet one. The enemy probed the German lines with groups both large and small in an effort to identify the combat outposts and eliminate them. For instance, the *5./Panzergrenadier-Regiment 394* was attacked, taking casualties. *Feldwebel* Duwe, a terrific junior leader, was among the dead that night. Other Soviet elements pressed forward as far as the regimental command post and even to the quartering area for the division headquarters. Dangerous close combat ensued. The Russians, members of the NKVD division, knew how to fight in a determined and cunning fashion. The enemy artillery was not idle, either. An entire salvo of rockets from a Stalin organ landed in the firing positions of the 9th Battery of the divisional artillery in a fruit orchard and caused casualties.

The mission for the division on 9 August was to clear the northern portion of Pjatigorsk. The clearing operations proceeded in a deliberate manner. While that was being done, the armor regiment from the *23. Panzer-Division* protected the east flank of the division between Karras and Mineralnyje Wody. The latter locality fell to the neighboring division in the course of the day. The fighting for a crossing point over the Podhumok also tilted in favor of the division. The bridge position was finally in the division's hands.

The night was relatively calm, even though the enemy fired into the city on a regular basis with Stalin organs. The divisional headquarters was hit with them. The patrols launched by the Russians to probe the division lines were able be turned back. In the morning, the *I./Panzergrenadier-Regiment 394* arrived and was used to screen. *Kradschützen-Bataillon 3* crossed the Podhumok at noon and entered the southern part of Pjatigorsk. The enemy only offered sporadic resistance and was quickly pushed back. Just an hour after the start of the attack, all of the city was finally in German hands.

Oberst Zimmermann, who turned over sector command of Njewinnomyskaja to *Major* Richter, the commander of *Kradschützen-Bataillon 23* of the *23. Panzer-Division*, took charge of all of the forces of the *3. Panzer-Division* employed in the northern portion of the city. They reported to the headquarters of *Panzergrenadier-Regiment 3*. *Major* Pape and the headquarters of *Panzergrenadier-Regiment 394* assumed charge of the forces arrayed in the southern part of Pjatigorsk. The main focus was then to eliminate any remaining Soviet forces in the city, regroup the forces, take care of logistical requirements and initiate preparations for a continuation of the attack.

The corps ordered a temporary halt to all movements, since it first wanted the forested terrain in the mountains cleared. That was a necessary step, since the rear-area services of the corps were still along the Manytsch. So that those elements could move forward, the fuel that had been intended for the forward armor divisions was diverted. On that day, the *1. Gebirgs-Division* on the right reached Tscherkessk and secured the formerly open west flank of the division. The *1. Panzer-Armee* still held firm in its planning for taking the mountain passes south of Ordshonikidse and the oil region around Grosny.

Before all those movements commenced, there was some time for the soldiers of the division to take a look at Pjatigorsk and the beautiful surrounding countryside. The city was in the mountainous region of the Caucasus. The countryside, which the Greeks called the *Kauk-Asos*—"the land of the gods"—was magnificent. It was the realm of perpetual springtime. Despite the tropical heat, it was blooming everywhere. There were all sorts of trees: oaks, apricot, chestnut, nut, medlars, magnolias, cypress—to name but a few. The city proper was a first-class spa resort. From the times of the czars, the baths had drawn an international crowd. The hot springs were well suited for treating rheumatism and sciatica. The posters on the hotels and public buildings indicated that the spa activities had gone on until shortly before the city's capture by the *3. Panzer-Division*. There had been concerts and variety shows, as well as the presentation of operettas. Foodstuffs of all kinds were to be had for good prices; unfortunately, the prices climbed dramatically over the next few days. In addition, there were spoils-of-war to be had from an ice-house, as well as wine from a wine cellar near Karras. The troops were happy with their quarters, and the local populace generally appeared approachable and friendly. A few of the quarters even had European facilities, such as running water. Those were things that one no longer expected to see in Russia. In addition, there was opportunity to use the good sports facilities and tennis courts. Indeed, *Panzer-Regiment 6* immediately held a handball tournament to decide the "North Caucasus Championship."

Oberst Dr. Weissenbruch, the commander of the divisional artillery, was designated as the local area administrative commander so as to adjust civilian life with military requirements. A sense of trust quickly developed between the German commands and the Caucasian populace. The head of a mountain tribe appeared in full war paint and offered the military help of his tribe. Many Cossacks voluntarily reported to German headquarters, where they served as translators. During this period, *Generalmajor* Breith entertained the thought of volunteer formations.

The division received orders from the corps to occupy the neighboring resort town of Jessentuki on 12 August and to conduct reconnaissance into the mountainous region. But those orders were rescinded during the night, because it was directed that the enemy resistance at Karras be eliminated first. *Oberst Freiherr* von Liebenstein was given that mission. The *I./Panzergrenadier-Regiment 3* attacked, but it encountered superior enemy defenses by a rifle battalion at Shelsnowodsk, which had been reinforced with anti-tank guns. The 2nd Battalion of the regiment was pushed forward, which had heretofore been held back as the corps reserve. Supported by the additional battalion, von Liebenstein's forces ejected the enemy.

After that mission had been accomplished, von Liebenstein pivoted his forces to the southwest and in the direction of Jessentuki.

Hauptmann Rohrbeck's *I./Panzer-Regiment 6* took the picturesque town in short order, with the result that *Hauptmann* Erdmann's *I./Panzer-grenadier-Regiment 3*, which was following, hardly needed to be employed. The mechanized infantry occupied the town and conducted reconnaissance paralleling the mountain railway towards the south. *Oberleutnant* von Brauke's 3rd Company conducted the reconnaissance. The company moved its way forward along the mountain road as far as Kislowodsk, where the enemy put up a defense. When the company attempted to enter the thick woods outside of the village, it received such heavy fire that its advance came to a standstill. The battalion surgeon, *Assistenzarzt Graf* zu Solms, who was widely known not only for his height but also for his appetite and thirst, had his hands full, as did his medical personnel. The battle group started screening around Jessentuki.

Advance guards of the *XXXX. Panzer-Korps* started moving out again on the morning of 13 August. *Major* Pape, the commander of *Panzer-grenadier-Regiment 394*, led the division's advance guard, which consisted of the 2nd Battalion from his regiment, as well as the *2./Kradschützen-Bataillon 3*, the *III./Panzer-Artillerie-Regiment 75*, a 10-centimeter battery, a battery of *Flak*, and *Panzer-Pionier-Bataillon 39*. It quickly thrust thirty kilometers into the enemy's hinterland. To the south of Bage, the Soviets offered resistance, but it was broken. The motorcycle infantry company, riding to the front, reached the area five kilometers north of Malka at 0730 hours. Although no enemy infantry could be identified, the Russians fired artillery on the columns from well-camouflaged positions in the mountains. The motorcycle infantry held up and waited for the arrival of the mechanized infantry.

The German artillery went into position, and *Hauptmann* Kersten gave the guns permission to fire. The rounds slammed into the identified enemy positions, but the Soviets did not stir. No retrograde activities could be observed. The mechanized infantry battalion then received orders to advance against the western part of the village and block the road on the other side of the far bank.

Major Haspel moved his forces into attack positions in the depression-filled terrain. After a short artillery preparation, the infantry moved out at 1000 hours. *Oberleutnant* Pollmann's 7th Company took the lead, followed by the 6th Company, which was echeloned to the rear to protect the right flank. The mechanized infantry had dismounted, since it did not appear advisable to take along the vehicles given the enemy's fields of observation and the artillery fire. The men exploited the large sunflower and cornfields to advance. The 5th Company, brought forward on the left, arrived at the area one kilometer northwest of Malka in the blazing midday heat. Then there was no further advance, since the flood plains could be observed in their entirety by the enemy. Fires from heavy weapons forced the mechanized infantry to take cover and caused considerable casualties.

Major Haspel was badly wounded by shrapnel from an impacting round. *Oberleutnant* Schmidt assumed acting command of the battalion, until *Oberleutnant* Pollmann, the more senior officer, could arrive. In the afternoon, *Hauptmann* Stein assumed acting command of the battalion. He had been the battalion adjutant and had been placed on temporary duty, awaiting transfer to the homeland for a General Staff officer course.

The situation did not change. The Russian artillery stopped any attempt to advance. The afternoon saw counter-battery fire on both sides. The enemy had the advantage, since his batteries had been built into the mountains and could only be observed with difficulty. The 1st Company of motorcycle infantry and the 8th Company of the mechanized infantry took heavy losses.

It was not possible to cross Malka Creek that day. The mountain stream was in a raging flood stage, in contrast to what the military geographers had said. The creek had three tributaries of 4 to 8 meters in width and they were up to 1.5 meters deep. Since the night passed relatively quietly, the formations thought they might be able to cross the open bottomland quickly in the morning. Only *Feldwebel* Buchholz's platoon from the *6./Panzergrenadier-Regiment 394* had actually succeeded in making it as far as the village the previous day. On the morning of 14 August, the Soviets started the day with artillery fire from their dominant positions and continuous attacks from bombers. In the course of the day, it was determined that the Soviets had also reinforced the rifle formations and defensive positions along the entire riverbank.

Despite that, the corps ordered the establishment of a bridgehead at Malka. *Oberstleutnant i.G.* Pomtow, the division operations officer, personally went to the corps command post to stress the fact that there could be no success given the current situation. A friendly attack could only be successful, if the division were given sufficient additional forces or, as another possibility, the *23. Panzer-Division* be brought into sector and it also conducted an attack.

Most of the formations of the *3. Panzer-Division* were still in the area around Pjatigorsk, since only a small quantity of fuel had been brought forward. The corps sector itself had a depth of 400 kilometers, which made the supply situation very difficult. The *I./Panzergrenadier-Regiment 394*, the *II./Panzergrenadier-Regiment 3*, and *Pionier-Bataillon 52* were all employed in clearing the area around Shelesnowodosk, where scattered enemy forces were endangering the supply route.

The *1. Panzer-Armee* announced its intent to have the *III. Panzer-Korps* and the *XXXX. Panzer-Korps* pass around Malka and attack to the east. The *XXXX. Panzer-Korps* was given the mission of advancing on Naltschik via Bakssan. The corps thereupon ordered its two armor divisions to Ordshonikidse via Naltschik. They were to block the Grusinian Military Road to the north there, while holding it open to the south. The Romanian 2nd Mountain Division was temporarily attached to the corps for the execution of the operation. It was directed that the *3. Panzer-Division* conduct the main effort, while

the *23. Panzer-Division* block in the direction of the Terek, that is, to the east.

Generalmajor Mack's *23. Panzer-Division* moved out at 0800 hours on 15 August to launch that attack. The enemy resistance increased by the hour, and his employment of heavy bombers prevented a smooth move into the mountainous region of the Caucasus. There was no time that day to take in the spectacular scenery.

Hauptmann Stein's *II./Panzergrenadier-Regiment 394*, which was positioned up front at Malka, established that there were only weak Russian positions left along the river. A patrol from *Feldwebel* Buchholz's platoon was the first to cross the river, doing so at 0600 hours. An hour later, the entire platoon went across, then followed by the rest of the 6th Company. The 7th Company started crossing at 0900 hours. At first, the companies set up all-round defenses. They then conducted reconnaissance on both sides of the bridge, which the enemy had set alight. In the course of the day, Stein's battalion was able to cross the river, including its heavy vehicles. *Kradschützen-Bataillon 3* moved up to the east bridge. Reconnaissance patrols reported the area southwest of Malka as clear of the enemy.

Generalmajor Breith, whose command post was still in Pjatigorsk, issued *Major* Pape orders that afternoon to attack out of the bridgehead the next day. The *II./Panzer-Regiment 6* was to be prepared to follow, once fuel finally arrived and the engineer bridge was completed. Likewise, the batteries of the divisional artillery also prepared to move out. The division received new vehicles for *Panzergrenadier-Regiment 394* from Kharkov that day. In addition, the chief of one of the Tscherkessy tribes arrived and announced that he wanted to support the German forces. His tribe numbered 9,000 people and owned 1,300 horses and 9,000 head of cattle.

Major Groeneveld's *Panzer-Pionier-Bataillon 39* moved toward Malka. At 1700 hours, the 2nd Platoon of Bridging Section 1 started a sixteen-ton bridge of 19.2 meters, which was built on top of the destroyed road bridge. By necessity, the work was stopped when it turned dark, but the bridge was capable of supporting traffic starting at 0800 hours the following morning.

On Sunday, 16 August, the *XXXX. Panzer-Korps* attacked south. The *23. Panzer-Division* rapidly gained ground, and *Kampfgruppe Bachmann* took the locality of Bakssan. It was not possible to cross over to the south bank, however, since the enemy had established strong positions. The Soviets had destroyed all of the bridges and the water retaining wall. The waters of the raging Bakssan River prevented any crossing. Elements of the *23. Panzer-Division* turned west in an effort to find a crossing point at Kysburun.

At 0600 hours, *Oberst Freiherr* von Liebenstein assumed command of all of the combat elements of the division. The *II./Panzergrenadier-Regiment 394* was ordered to advance on Bakssan. By then, most of *Major* Frank's *II./Panzer-Regiment 6* and *Oberst* Weissenbruch divisional artillery had crossed the river. The *2./Kradschützen-Bataillon 3*, which was moving out front, was able to link up with *Kampfgruppe Bachmann* at Kysburun early in the afternoon, where they relieved elements of the *23. Panzer-Division*.

The headquarters of the *3. Panzer-Division* set up at the stud farm along the west side of Malka. The command staff followed the following morning.

The mission for 18 August: establish a bridgehead at Kysburun to the west of Bakssan, since it had been determined that there was no way to cross the eighty-meter-wide and raging river at the latter location. At 0800 hours, *Oberst* Dr. Weissenbruch, *Major* Pape, *Hauptmann* von der Heyden-Rynsch, and *Hauptmann* Stein went to the area two kilometers south of Kysburun 2[1] to reconnoiter and get a feel for the terrain. The ground dropped off steeply towards the river bottomland. Hardly anything could be seen of the enemy. It would be difficult to conduct a reconnaissance-in-force to the riverbanks, since the enemy could see everything from the high ground opposite. *Hauptmann* Erdmann's *I./ Panzergrenadier-Regiment 394* sent a reinforced raiding party in the direction of Kysburon 3. It was turned back by the Soviets and only returned when it started to turn dark, having suffered heavy casualties. The combat elements lost one tank and three *SPW's* that day, as well as suffering thirteen wounded.

The eighteenth of August was heavily overcast and marked by strong storms. The rivers swelled in the blink of an eye and became raging torrents. There was another monstrous storm in the evening. There was hail pelting down the size of small chicken eggs. But as quickly as the bad weather arrived in that region, it also disappeared equally rapidly. The commanding general, *General Freiherr* Geyr von Schweppenburg, arrived in the evening and visited the forces up front, along with the division commander. The corps recommended to the field army that it give up its attempt to break through to the south and, instead, swing east. The *1. Panzer-Armee* rejected the proposal.

At that point, renewed reconnaissance was conducted in the Bakssan area, since the *23. Panzer-Division* had been able to take a crossing point. *Oberleutnant* Brandt, the commander of the 3rd Company of the divisional engineers, reconnoitered a position for the *3. Panzer-Division*. He reported that a crossing was possible, if one man followed the other across the beams of the destroyed bridge. *Major* Pape brought the *II./Panzergrenadier-Regiment 394* forward to Bakssan to attempt the crossing. Additional reconnaissance was conducted in the course of the day. The division artillery dedicated five of its batteries and an attached *Nebelwerfer* battery in support. The mechanized infantry started filtering into Bakssan starting at 1900 hours. The operation was called off by the corps headquarters in the evening, however,

---

1. If a locality as split up into several distinct and separate areas but still retained the same name, it was frequently given a numerical designator or other modifier (size or cardinal direction, for instance) to distinguish it.

since an attack by the *23. Panzer-Division* in the direction of Naltschik promised more success.

The elements of the division still to the rear in the area around Pjatigorsk were assembled by *Oberst* Westhoven. At the same time, a battle group from the *23. Panzer-Division* under the command of *Oberst* Bodenhausen was attached to him. Both groups moved out during the course of 19 August from their quartering areas between Pjatigorsk and Mineralnyje Wody. After exerting a great deal of effort caused by congested traffic and the poor routes, both groups reached the area around Apollonskaja, far to the north of Bakssan. Depending on the development of the situation, the corps planned on employing those forces to either the south or the east.

By then, the enemy had been reinforced along the Bakssan. The floodwaters had made a rapid crossing impossible, since the bridge had been swept away. Since the enemy could observe the movement, a crossing across the blown up reservoir dam was not considered practical. Despite the unfavorable weather, the Soviets, for their part, were able to cross over to the north bank of the river. The outposts of the *I./Panzergrenadier-Regiment 3* were attacked along the high ground north of Kysburun 2, but they were able to hold their positions. In the evening, the *II./Panzer-grenadier-Regiment 394* took over the sector.

On 19 August, the *1. Panzer-Armee* agreed to allow the *XXXX. Panzer-Korps* to advance east. The *3. Panzer-Division* moved most of its elements towards Apollonskaja. The armor regiment left its positions along the river at night and moved back to Malka. Only *Haupt-mann* Stein's *II./Panzergrenadier-Regiment 394* remained in its positions, where it reported directly to the corps as a screening group. Late in the afternoon, Stein's battalion was relieved by elements of the Romanian 2nd Mountain Division, allowing it to move to rejoin the division.

The division prepared for operations in the area around Apollonskaja. *Artillerie-Regiment 70*, *Pionier-Bataillon 52*, and the *II./Lehr-Regiment "Brandenburg"* were attached to *Kampf-gruppe Westhoven*—consisting of *Kampfgruppe Zimmermann* and *Kradschützen-Bataillon 3*—in support. The division headquarters set up in Stanitza. The division commander, moving ahead, linked up with his brigade commander, *Oberst* Westhoven, around 0700 hours. While there, he informed him that he had been promoted to *Generalmajor*, effective 1 August.

Based on the reports he was receiving, *Generalmajor* Breith proposed the following to the corps: Advance from Apollonskaja to the east as far as Edissija and then turning south to take the bridges over the Terek. The corps approved Breith's recommendation.

The division moved up during the night. *Generalmajor* Westhoven's forces assembled in the area around Kurskaja–Kunowo. The armored regiment was around Sowjeyskaja, while *Oberst* von Bodenhausen and his battalions from the *23. Panzer-Division* was to the rear of Gornosawodjkaja. The division command post moved to Kurskaja. The advance east ordered by the corps was dependent, of course, on fuel being brought forward. For instance, the *III. Panzer-Korps* had been stalemated for days since no fuel had come forward.

During the morning of 21 August, it was very warm, even though the skies were cloudy. The Red Air Force was active starting at 0700 hours and disrupted German movements by rolling waves of attacks. It was not a rare occurrence to see thirty to forty aircraft loitering above the divisional sector at the same time. All different types of aircraft were represented. Since no German fighters were present, the *Ratas* and the twin-engine American bombers romped at will.[2]

While the division assembled around Kurskaja, increasing enemy pressure could be felt almost hourly. It was clear that a German attack

---

2. *Rata* is a German generic term for a Soviet fighter, although it does apply specifically to the Polikarpov I-16. The U.S. bombers were probably B-25 Mitchells.

on Mosdok would not come as a surprise. Combat and reconnaissance patrols established the presence of the recently introduced 8th Guards Rifle Division. Up to that point, the division had only encountered the 4th Rifle Division. Prisoner statements confirmed that the enemy was preparing Mosdok for the defense and was emplacing large minefields.

General der Panzertruppen Geyr von Schweppenburg discussed the situation with *Generalmajor* Breith. Since a *coup de main* directed against the bridges over the Terek promised no success, the division was to initially try to establish a bridgehead across the Lenin Canal and then advance from there with all of its forces. The division commander requested additional assets in the form of *Flak* and bridging sections, as well as sufficient fighter cover. Fortunately, for the division, all of its forces could be relieved from any out-of-sector commitments that day. The commanding general decided that evening to have the *3. Panzer-Division* wait another day so that sufficient fuel could be brought forward.

During the course of 22 August, the division regrouped for an attack on the Terek River line. *Oberst Freiherr* von Liebenstein formed a battle group consisting of the *I./Panzer-Regiment 6*, *Panzergrenadier-Regiment 3*, and *Panzer-Artillerie-Regiment 75*. His forces pulled forward in the course of the day east of Edissija. The elements of the *23. Panzer-Division* under *Oberst* von Bodenhausen followed and set up behind the positions of the armored regiment. Both of those groups received the mission to conduct small-scale reconnaissance-in-force efforts to the east that day to deceive the enemy concerning the division's actual attack plans.

Most of the division remained around Kurskaja under the command of *Generalmajor* Westhoven. It was organized into two groups. *Hauptmann* von der Heyden-Rynsch's *I./Panzergrenadier-Regiment 394* with attached artillery formed one of them. *Major* Pape commanded

the other battle group, consisting of the *II./Panzer-Regiment 6*, *Kradschützen-Bataillon 3*, the *II./Panzer-Artillerie-Regiment 75*, and the *II./Panzergrenadier-Regiment 394*. The enemy disrupted the formation movements from the air, especially in the afternoon. Once again there were vehicular losses and personnel casualties with the *4./Panzer-Regiment 6* losing *Oberfeldwebel* Krause, for instance. *Major* Gollob's fighter group[3] was directed to provide support to the division, and his pilots scrambled whenever a Russian showed himself in the skies. As a result, the enemy bomber attacks fell noticeably.

The twenty-third of August was a Sunday. The division was prepared to conduct its attack on Mosdok, with *Generalmajor* Westhoven on the right and *Oberst Freiherr* von Liebenstein on the left. As the sun rose over the horizon, Russian aircraft were already in the air. The advance guard of Westhoven's forces—led by *Oberleutnant* Pollmann and consisting of a tank company, a platoon from *Panzer-Pionier-Bataillon 39*, Pollmann's *6./Panzergrenadier-Regiment 394*, an infantry-gun platoon from the *9./Panzergrenadier-Regiment 394*, an artillery battery, a *Flak* platoon, and one heavy engineer platoon—moved out to launch the attack at 0400 hours. Suddenly, orders were received that the advance was to be halted until all of the columns could be completely refueled. The supply sections had not arrived in time because the weather had softened routes over the past few days. Finally, things were ready. At 0920 hours, the division issued orders for the attack.

Both battle groups headed south starting right at 1000 hours. Although enemy aircraft continuously attempted to disrupt the movements, they were unable to hold them up. By evening of that day, German fighters had shot down seventeen Soviet aircraft. *Oberleutnant* Pollmann's advance guard was able to move rapidly and reached the high ground south of Russkij by evening. It was there that the soldiers encountered stiff resistance for the first time. The mech-

---

3. *Jagdgeschwader 52*, one of the first *Luftwaffe* units to be equipped with the upgraded *Bf 109 G-2*.

anized infantry halted, and the artillery was brought forward, opening fire on Russian pockets of resistance.

Exactly one hour later, the mechanized infantry attacked. Pollmann rallied his mechanized infantry company forward, entered the enemy's first defensive positions and continued to advance. The enemy only put up token resistance at that point. At 1345 hours, the mechanized infantry reached Russkij. They immediately moved through the village, reaching the narrow Lenin Canal (two to four meters) and discovering a bridge that was damaged but still usable. The first men hastened across, with the rest of the company soon following. They then proceeded through the village to the main bridge to the east, which was completely undamaged. By then, most of the *II./Panzergrenadier-Regiment 394* and the *II./Panzer-Regiment 6* had closed up, reinforcing the bridgehead.

Kampfgruppe Liebenstein, advancing on the left, employed *Oberleutnant Graf* von Kageneck's *4./Panzer-Regiment 6* as its advanced guard. The fighting vehicles took the hills in front of the canal at the same time as the mechanized infantry of the *6./Panzergrenadier-Regiment 3*. They fired into the woods and vegetation, driving the Russians out. The vehicles then entered Grafskij, not giving the Soviets enough time to blow up the bridge.

Hauptmann Rohrbeck's *I./Panzer-Regiment 6* did not wait for the mechanized infantry to close up and continued to advance. The rail line at Wesselewskoje was reached at 1400 hours. The companies then turned in the direction of Mosdok. The enemy was no longer to be seen, with the exception of isolated riflemen making their way rearward. In short order, *Kampfgruppe Liebenstein* was outside of Mosdok. The accompanying artillery batteries took the city under fire. Many houses went up in flames. A church, which was identified as housing a Russian observation section, was set alight.

Kageneck's tank company had moved up to within 300 meters of the first houses of Mosdok. At that moment, a train appeared. *Feldwebel*

Thévoz, who was in the lead tank, thought for a moment that it was just a regular freight train. Then, he suddenly recognized armored turrets. There were already muzzle flashes. The Russian armored train rumbled towards the German fighting vehicles. An engagement developed that left a lasting impression. Firing entire broadsides, the Russian train approached the German company. The train raced close past a *Panzer IV*. Everything was shrouded in a thick cloud of gunpowder smoke. A direct hit from a tank main gun tore apart an oil tender and an ammunition wagon. The train exploded with a monstrous crash and remained in place, a burning wreck.

The tank company gathered at the church with the Oriental grave markers. Russian infantry was driven away with machine-gun fire. *Gefreiter* Jacobs was killed in the fighting.

Enemy antitank-gun positions had to be defeated by the battalion before *Hauptmann* Waldow's 2nd Company and *Oberleutnant Graf* von Kageneck's 4th Company could enter Mosdok proper. A few tanks ran over mines and remained behind, immobilized. With the forces available, the stiff resistance then encountered could not be overcome, and the attack stalemated for the time being.

Coming from the west, *Kampfgruppe Westhoven* had also reached the edge of Mosdok around 1600 hours. The 5th and 8th Companies of the armor regiment were in the lead and found themselves facing the first antitank-gun positions. The fight was no easier than the one conducted by the tankers' sister battalion. While the tanks were still engaging the enemy riflemen and antitank guns, an armored train appeared not too far from the rail station at Nowo Georgiewskij, opening fire on the command staff of the *3. Panzergrenadier-Brigade*. *Leutnant* Petri of the divisional signals battalion was killed. The tanks had to disengage from the one fight to go face the armored train. The main-gun rounds slammed into the steel body of the train from pointblank range. First one armored train that day, then this second one.

Another armored train appeared. Once again, a duel ensued between the German and Russian guns. Once again, the fighting vehicles had luck. An ammunition wagon on the train went up in the air. At the same time, the train slammed at full throttle into its predecessor, which was stopped on the track in front of it. A few of the cars flipped off and prevented the armored train from any further movement. *Major* Frank's *II./Panzer-Regiment 6* attacked one more time and overran everything that was in its way. The Russian armored trains, with their 7.62- and 12.7-centimeter cannons, were eliminated!

By then, the *II./Panzergrenadier-Regiment 394* had reached Mosdok. The 5th Company and the attached infantry-gun platoon from the 8th Company were the first to follow the fighting vehicles, reaching the area south of the railway line, about 300 meters for the edge of the locality. It had turned dark by then. It made no sense to try to advance into the city against a strong enemy. The bridges over the Terek could no longer be taken anyway, since the Soviets had sent them skyward in the afternoon during the tank attack. Both of the tank battalions were withdrawn from Mosdok in the darkness and set up an all-round defense in the open area outside of the city. Russian aircraft constantly tried to attack the German forces. The attached *Flak* had no opportunity to rest and had fired off all of its ammunition by morning.

The next day saw no change in the tactical situation for the division. Neither side took the upper hand. The enemy aircraft dominated the skies, however, and made life a "living hell" for the German soldiers. Friendly fighters put up a fight, but they were considerably outnumbered. Due to a shortage of ammunition, even the attached *Flak* batteries were powerless against that foe.

The enemy had reinforced his position in and around Mosdok. German patrols, which had been reconnoitering since first light, identified newly arrived Soviet formations. These were elements of the 6th, 8th, and 10th Airborne Brigades. The division recommended to the corps to wait a day for the attack and not move out again until 29 August. The corps turned down the recommendation.

Both of the battle groups, that of *Generalmajor* Westhoven and *Oberst Freiherr* von Liebenstein, started clearing the northern part of Mosdok in the morning. Patrols sent forward by the *II./Panzergrenadier-Regiment 394* reconnoitered until 0700 hours and went as far as the two churches on the city's outskirts. Enemy defensive fires forced the patrols to turn around. Elements dispatched along the rail line by the mechanized infantry and the engineers to reconnoiter also encountered defensive fires and had to turn back. An engineer section pressed east of the city to find a crossing point over the Terek, but the effort failed.

Hauptmann Rodenhauser's *1./Panzer-Regiment 6* was attached to the *II./Panzergrenadier-Regiment 394* and employed in support of the 6th Company to attack the enemy's flank at 1330 hours while advancing along the railway line. The tanks were stopped by a minefield, and the mechanized infantry could not cross the open terrain by themselves. The remaining tanks of *Hauptmann* Rohrbeck's battalion were able to join the fight in time, however, and the enemy positions could be cleared.

Three hours later, *Kradschützen-Bataillon 3*, the *II./Panzergrenadier-Regiment 394*, and the *I./Panzer-Regiment 6* attacked again to the south. The advance moved along the main road and towards the large, pretty church. As a result of friendly artillery fire, enemy resistance had weakened, and the companies were able to reach the church by the onset of darkness. The companies remained there and dug in for the night. Around 2100 hours, the sounds of fighting died down.

The night of 24–25 August passed without major disruption and gave way to a beautiful but humid summer day. In the division command post, which was located in Buguloff to the west of Graffskij, preparations for the crossing of the Terek were being discussed. The previous evening, the *XXXX. Panzer-Korps* had ordered the crossing for 26 August. Initial reconnaissance to that end had been ongoing since the early morning east of Mosdok. The hand-selected engineer patrols had returned without positive results, with the exception of a bend in the Terek at Galjugajewskaja, which was a possible crossing point. The difficulty with that, as elsewhere, was that the Soviets had taken up positions in the hills on the far side and could see everything in the river sector.

The situation in Mosdok finally started to turn more positive. *Kradschützen-Bataillon 3* and the *II./Panzergrenadier-Regiment 394* started their attacks at 0630 on the portions of the city occupied by the enemy. The batteries of the divisional artillery had supported the attack with a short but intense artillery preparation. *Kampfgruppe Pape* to one block after the other. The 5th Company of the mechanized infantry and the 2nd Company of the motorcycle infantry were the first ones to reach the banks of the river. A few minutes later, the 5th Company of the regiment arrived. It was joined shortly after that by the 6th Company of the regiment and the 3rd Company of the motorcycle infantry battalion. Mosdok was finally in German hands. *Hauptmann* Rodenhauser's *1./Panzer-Regiment 6* and elements of *Oberleutnant Graf* von Kageneck's *4./Panzer-Regiment 6* had helped clear the way for the dismounted forces. The enemy engaged the German forces fort he far bank of the river with artillery and mortar fire. *Leutnant Graf* Helldorf of the armor regiment was badly wounded by artillery fire while reconnoitering.

The companies positioned small outposts along the backs of the 150-meter-wide waterway, which allowed good observation to the far bank. Most of the mechanized infantry and motorcycle infantry forces were pulled back into the city, where there occupied widely dispersed positions. Once it turned dark, *Kradschützen-Bataillon 3* and the *II./Panzergrenadier-Regiment 394* were ordered out of Mosdok, since the division was in the process of regrouping. Only the *6./Panzergrenadier-Regiment 394* and the *1./*

Panzer-Regiment 6 remained behind. *Oberst* Zimmermann and the headquarters of *Panzergrenadier-Regiment 3* assumed command of those remaining forces in the city.

The division assembled north and east of Mosdok. The armor regiment was designated as the division reserve. The regrouping in the Graffskij and Medwedew areas took place in a moonlight night and were constantly disrupted by Russian bombing runs.

The field army was pressing for a forcing of the Terek. The order stated "that the fuel situation made the rapid taking of Ordsonikidse and Grosny impossible and that, as a result, the enemy had gained time to collect himself along the Terek and establish a line of resistance, in some cases with freshly introduced forces."

The breaking of that line of resistance was to fall to the *3.*, *13.*, and *23. Panzer-Divisionen*. The field army's plan looked beyond that and envisioned the *XXXX. Panzer-Korps* taking Grosny and the *LII. Armee-Korps* Ordshonikidse. The division received orders to establish a bridgehead at Galjugajenskaja and advance south. *Generalmajor* Westhoven, who was to lead the attack, went with *Oberst* Ullrich to reconnoiter the designated crossing point. He saw that there was commanding high ground on the south bank, from which the open approach routes could be dominated at great distance. He reported to the division commander that an attack and crossing at that point had no chance of success. *Generalmajor* Breith agreed with that assessment and presented it forcefully to the commanding general in the ensuing discussion. Schweppenburg indicated he understood and stated that he would await the results of other reconnaissance.

In an advance east, *Kradschützen-Bataillon 43* (*13. Panzer-Division*), which had been attached to the *3. Panzer-Division*, took Ischerskaja on the north bank of the Terek after a hard fight. A battle group from the *23. Panzer-Division* under *Oberst* Burmeister took Prochladny, west of Mosdok, and was thus able to link up with the *3. Panzer-Division*.

Additional reconnaissance for crossing points over the river was conducted during the night and at first light. *Major* Groeneveld, the division engineer, reported that a crossing at Ischerskaja was possible but very difficult.

The formations of the division had no enemy contact that day. The soldiers were able to finally get a good sleep for the first time after numerous days of combat under the hot sun. They were also able to take in the pretty countryside once more. Beyond the river were the majestic mountains of the Caucasus and their gigantic glaciers. The clear air allowed observation to the peaks that rose to more than 4,000 meters and were as far as 250 kilometers away. It was known that mountaineers of the *1. Gebirgs-Division* had already planted the Reich war flag on Mount Elbrus, the highest peak in the Caucasus, on 21 August. Contact between the soldiers and the local populace was cordial. The Caucasians, mostly shepherds and nomads, considered the German forces to be liberators from the yoke of Communism. On 19 August, the field army had issued a general order concerning "Treatment of the Caucasian Peoples" and well as distributing a pamphlet on the same subject.

The twenty-eighth of August was marked by preparations for the attack across the Terek, to which the *3. Panzergrenadier-Brigade* had been given the mission. New reconnaissance indicated that the crossing would most likely be difficult. Only one crossing point could be found, where it was possible to employ assault craft. The corps ordered the river to be crossed on 30 August and placed the corps engineer battalion in direct support of the *3. Panzer-Division*. The divisional formations used the day to rest, maintain weapons and vehicles and prepare for the fight. *Hauptmann* Mente's *II./Panzergrenadier-Regiment 3* returned to the division that day, after it had been in position for days on end at Prochladnaja. A replacement company of personnel arrived from the homeland in Kurskaja.

The weather was once again hot. Russian aircraft loitered constantly in the skies above. Some 160 aircraft were counted above the divi-

sion sector. *Generalmajor* Breith, whose health was not good, wrote in his diary: "Air oppressive. Affects health. Don't feel well; also under the effect of the upcoming very difficult attack. Although it has been prepared thoroughly and reconnoitered well, it still remains a risk."

The batteries of *Artillerie-Regiment 70* and *Panzer-Artillerie-Regiment 75* had scouted out their new firing positions and occupied them in the evening. Starting at 1800 hours, both battalions of *Panzergrenadier-Regiment 394* moved out widely dispersed in an effort to protect them form air attack. Only those most necessary command-and-control and communications vehicles were taken along. Field messes, ammunition vehicles and limbers remained to the rear. The night was completely quiet. The regiment had taken up positions in the completely destroyed Ischerskaja by 0400 hours. *Kampfgruppe Bodenhausen*, which was relieved there, reverted to corps control and was directed to attack north of the Terek to the southeast. That advance stalled out at Nikolajewskaja as the result of fuel shortages. The same held true for *Kampfgruppe Burmeister* to the west of Buguloff.

The division headquarters moved to Awaloff along the Lenin Canal. The houses were miserable huts that had been fashioned out of clay, grass, thatching and hard acacia wood. The divisional signals battalion collocated there. The first thing that *Generalmajor* Breith did when he got there was award the Knight's Cross to the commander of the *3./Panzer-Pionier-Bataillon 39*. *Oberleutnant* Brandt had been officially awarded the decoration on 20 August for his previous achievements. The German press characterized the award as follows: "*Oberleutnant* Friedrich Brandt . . . advanced ahead of the lead company in a reconnaissance vehicle and drove into the enemy aggressively, laying extraordinarily good groundwork for the continuation of the combat operations." Another officer of the division received a deserved high decoration that day as well. It was *Oberleutnant* Lange, the battery commander of the *5./Panzer-Artillerie-Regiment 75*, who received the German Cross in Gold.

FROM THE DON TO THE TEREK 91

The *3. Panzer-Division* received orders to pivot west as soon as the bridgehead at Ischerskaja was established, so as to facilitate the crossing at Mosdok for the *111.* and *370. Infanterie-Divisionen* of the *LII. Armee-Korps*. The *13. Panzer-Division* and elements of the *23. Panzer-Division* were employed against Grosny.

Generalmajor Westhoven held a conference with his commanders that afternoon. If the attack were to succeed, then the element of surprise had to be preserved under all circumstances. Correspondingly, the artillery could not register its guns. The commander of the observation detachment assured the commander that the firing plans would be with the batteries in a timely manner.

That evening, the two artillery regiments completed occupying their firing positions, as did the launchers of the attached *Nebelwerfer* elements. After 1800 hours, when it started turning dark, the mechanized infantry and the attached elements began their direct preparations for the crossing. The 1st Battalion of the mechanized infantry regiment was to form the first wave, along with the engineers, after the artillery had conducted a preparation on the enemy batteries and positions. The occupation of the final positions took place during the night. The enemy was in the air with the so-called "sewing machines"[4] in an effort to disrupt movements by the dropping of bombs. A few casualties were taken. Occasionally, some harassing rounds were fired from the far side of the river, but the enemy artillery was otherwise quiet. The *II./Panzergrenadier-Regiment 3* was positioned farther north and placed at the disposal of the brigade.

The clocks showed 0330 hours on Sunday, 30 August 1942, when twenty-six batteries of artillery with a total of seventy-five guns and ten rocket launchers opened their gullets at that second and spewed fire on the Russian positions on the southern banks of the Terek. The barrage rained down on the initial Soviet positions for ten minutes before shifting farther to the rear. At the same time, the mechanized infantry of *Hauptmann* von der Heyden-Rynsch's *I./Panzergrenadier-Regiment 394* hastened through the vegetation of the approaches to the riverbank, jumped into the assault craft held there for them by the engineers and then took off across the raging and rapid waters of the river to the south bank.

The enemy recovered quickly from his first shock. Russian artillery, especially mortars, fired ceaselessly into the crossing point. The enemy rounds hammered into the terrain along the riverbanks again and again. Hundreds of pieces of shrapnel shot through the air and tore the first gaps in the lines of the scrambling mechanized infantry. Rounds also impacted in the water, catching some of the death-defying engineers of *Pionier-Bataillon 52* and *Sturmboot-Kommando 906* (906th Assault Craft Detachment, a field-army asset). The German artillery was already firing on Mundar-Jurt, the first objective on the south bank of the Terek.

The brave commander of the mechanized infantry battalion, *Hauptmann* von der Heyden-Rynsch, was mortally wounded on the near bank. His adjutant, *Leutnant* Ziegler, fell with him, as did *Leutnant* Wurm. Despite the setback, the first German soldiers reached the far bank. Stout-hearted officers and noncommissioned officers rallied their men, jumping onto the sandy and marshy riverbank, taking cover, running a few meters, firing on the move and continuing the assault. *Oberleutnant* Eggert had assumed acting command of the battalion.

The empty assault craft raced back to pick up more soldiers. A few boats were torn apart by shells and sank forever onto the bottom of the raging mountain stream. But the second wave climbed into the watercraft and moved to the far

---

4. These were obsolete aircraft, including biplanes, that were employed at night, usually singly or in small groups, to fly harassing missions against German positions, where their low speed and lack of maneuverability did not matter. They were also referred to by a number of other names in soldier jargon, including "Staff Duty NCO."

bank. By 0530 hours, the 1st Battalion was across, along with elements of the *1.* and *2./Panzer-Pionier-Bataillon 39*, thus establishing a small bridgehead.

By then, the men of the regiment's 2nd Battalion had worked their way to the riverbank. Russian artillery continued to howl in. *Hauptmann* Stein, the battalion commander, was badly wounded in the upper thigh by mortar shrapnel as he attempted to board a boat and had to be taken to the rear. *Oberleutnant* Pollmann, the commander of the 6th Company, assumed acting command and led the second battalion of German soldiers to the far shore.

By then, the 1st Battalion had wrested the first 100 meters to the south from the enemy, run under the enemy artillery fire and reached the southern edge of the woods. The 5th and 7th Companies established contact with the 1st Battalion and held the front going back to the riverbank. Of the thirty-six assault craft employed that morning, there were only five intact by 0720 hours. No more soldiers could be taken across for the time being.

At the brigade command post, one could see clouds of dust along the south bank that were moving in the direction of the bridgehead and had to be coming from enemy columns racing in. At 0700 hours, *Generalmajor* Westhoven issued order: "Dig in and hold the bridgehead along the bend in the river!" Any continued attack by the weak forces against the strong enemy formations at Mundar Jurt would have been a senseless sacrifice. Since the assault craft were no longer available, the engineers started constructing ferries. They were torn apart by Russian artillery rounds while still being built. All of the artillery forward observers that had crossed were either dead or wounded, including *Oberleutnant* Liebke from the 5th Battery of the divisional artillery. Having reinforcements cross would have only led to additional casualties. *General der Panzertruppen* Geyr von Schweppenburg, who was at the brigade command post, agreed with the decision.

The *I./Panzergrenadier-Regiment 3* suffered 120 casualties that morning. The *2./Panzer-Pionier-Bataillon 39* was completely scattered. *Pionier-Bataillon 52* had suffered 30 percent casualties. Despite that, the men who had crossed over—whether from *Panzergrenadier-Regiment 394*, the *1.* and *2./Panzer-Pionier-Bataillon 39*, *Pionier-Bataillon 52*, *Sturmboot-Kommando 906*, or the *3.* and *7./Panzergrenadier-Regiment 3*—all held on to their small bridgehead.

The companies dug into the reeds along the bank as well as they could. After thirty centimeters, they were already running into water. The hours of the day seemed endlessly long. The heavens were filled with the rumbling of Russian aircraft engines and the howling of artillery rounds. German fighters also joined the fray against the enemy swarms, despite being outnumbered. Over the Terek, *Major* Gollob scored his 150th "kill" that day.

In the afternoon, Soviet riflemen attacked the bridgehead, but they were turned back. The enemy then withdrew. Other than the usual harassment bombing, the night remained relatively quiet, with only the occasional interruption of machine-gun fire. It was only possible to resupply the forces on the far bank by assault craft during the night.

As soon as it turned first light, the Russian bombers were back. The mechanized infantry were still in their positions in the woods and along the bend in the river. The German positions could be pushed forward somewhat, but it did not help much, since there was little in the way of observation or fields of fire. A broad, broken and vegetated terrain stretched in front of the battalions. It was only when the soldiers stood up that they could see over as far as the village. The forces remaining along the north bank regrouped. The *II./Panzergrenadier-Regiment 3* assumed responsibility for the outposts along the river. The enemy continued to hold the crossed-over forces in check. The Red Air Force forced the soldiers to remain pressed to the ground. On the other hand, the Russian riflemen did not attack until it turned dark. The *I./Panzer-*

grenadier-Regiment 394 was the objective of one such attack that day. German artillery fire was immediately called in, and it successfully scattered the attacking forces.

The situation in the bridgehead did not change. The companies located on the far bank conducted combat reconnaissance, feeling their way forward as far as the northern edge of Mundar Jurt. Many dead Russians were found in the reeds and vegetation. The crossed-over elements drew more and more enemy forces to the crossing site, some of which the Soviet leadership was drawing from the area around Mosdok. It was determined that there were four rifle battalions, four mortar battalions, one tank battalion and four artillery battalions in the area around Mundar Jurt. After an artillery preparation, the enemy attacked at 1800 hours, but his forces were again turned back.

The field army ordered that the bridgehead was to be held and that the division was to conduct a feint to deceive the enemy into believing that it was attacking in support of the *LII. Armee-Korps* of *General der Infanterie* Ott, which was intending to cross the Terek at Mosdok. Contrary to expectations, that operation succeeded quite rapidly on the morning of 2 September, since the Soviets had moved the bulk of their forces into the area south of Ischerskaja. The *LII. Armee-Korps* was able to send the first five battalions of *Generalmajor* Recknagel's *111. Infanterie-Division* across the Terek in the course of the morning and establish a fairly large bridgehead by the afternoon.

The area in front of the *3. Panzer-Division* continued to stagnate. The enemy at Mundar Jurt had transitioned to the defense. An assault detachment form *Panzer-Pionier-Bataillon 39* was able to advance across the eight-meter-wide and four-meter-deep tank ditch to the edge of the village, without encountering enemy resistance. In the afternoon, a Russian officer deserted, who brought along important signals documents with him. The division was able to get a firm grasp of the enemy situation. It was shown that *Panzergrenadier-Regiment 394* had tied down large numbers of Soviet forces.

Initially, there was no change to the situation on 3 September. The positions the enemy had evacuated during the day were reoccupied as soon as it turned dark, indicating an intent to attack. The night brought with it rain and even more softening of the marshy terrain. In addition, there was a plague of mosquitoes that was extremely unpleasant. As soon as it started to turn first light, the Russians attacked. This time, they attempted to reduce the positions directly along the riverbank, running into *Oberleutnant* Koblitz's *7./Panzergrenadier-Regiment 394*. Since the outpost lines were only thinly held and the requested friendly artillery fires did not have the desired effect, the company was pushed back 200 meters, and fierce close combat ensued. After that round of fighting, *Leutnant* Wedel's 1st Platoon consisted of only seven men.

The battalion sent help. The 2nd Company, augmented by elements of the 5th and 6th Companies, launched an immediate counterattack. When the *2./Panzer-Pionier-Bataillon 39* joined the fray, the enemy gave up. *Oberleutnant* Weigel's engineers went after the Russians with cold steel, took back the old position and drove the enemy back another 200 meters. The fighting ended at 1400 hours, with the Soviets leaving behind a lot of dead. But the German casualties were not light, either. The 7th Company suffered four dead and twenty-two wounded.

The order to evacuate the bridgehead, which *Generalmajor* Breith had requested continuously, arrived in the afternoon. Around 1800 hours, the first mechanized infantry elements disengaged from their positions. The 1st Battalion of mechanized infantry crossed the river in assault craft at 1830 hours. Company after company followed. The soldiers returned to Ischerskaja at two crossing points. Around 2230 hours, the 7rd Company, acting as rearguard, left the south bank of the Terek. Fortunately, the enemy did not disrupt the movements. After the last of the elements had crossed, Russian artillery fire continued to fall on the old positions.

The fighting to establish a bridgehead across the Terek at Ischerskaja was over. Sixty-two soldiers of *Panzergrenadier-Regiment 394* found their eternal resting place in Ischerskaja. Five soldiers, including *Leutnant* Dürrholz of the *2./Panzergrenadier-Regiment 394*, remained missing. The regiment standing its ground had enabled the *LII. Armee-Korps* to establish a bridgehead at Mosdok and allow operations to continue into the Caucasus. The performance of the *3. Panzer-Division* was praised by both the corps and the field army in general orders. *Generaloberst* Kleist, the commander in chief of the *1. Panzer-Armee*, sent the following telegram to the division:

> Despite all of the enemy's resistance and despite the weak forces, the corps attempted to create a crossing point over the Terek. . . . Considerably superior enemy forces stood in the way of that intent. Even if the effort to make the crossing did not succeed, the attack of the corps with the brave *3. Panzer-Division* had worked decisively in favor of the field army's intent. In its stubborn defense in a markedly difficult situation in the bridgehead, the division had tied down so many forces on the ground and in the air that the *LII. Armee-Korps* succeeded in crossing at Mosdok with strong elements. . . . I extend my thanks and great appreciation to the battalions in the bridgehead at Ischerskaja!

The commanding general of the *XXXX. Panzer-Korps, General der Panzertruppen Freiherr* Geyr von Schweppenburg, also praised the actions of the division in a telegram: "That illustrious feat of arms had drawn so many enemy forces of the enemy towards it and fixed them that a surprise crossing of the Terek could be achieved at another location. Honor the fallen and the warriors of Ischerskaja!"

Church in Mosdok.

Oberstleutnant Pape. His *Panzergrenadier-Regiment 394*
held the point farthest southeast along the Eastern Front.

Oberst Westhoven and
Oberstleutnant Pape discuss
the situation in Mosdok.

Destroyed Soviet armored
train at Mosdok.

The commanding general, *General der Panzertruppen* Geyr von Schweppenburg, arrives in Mosdok. In the middle is the division commander, *Generalmajor* Breith, and to his left is *Oberstleutnant* Pape.

The view along the Terek.

Field service in Awaloff.

A Cossack troop that was attached to the *3. Panzer-Division*.

The bridge over the Terek at Mosdok.

Oberleutnant Friedrich Brandt, commander of the *3./Panzer-Pionier-Bataillon 39*.

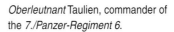

Oberleutnant Taulien, commander of the *7./Panzer-Regiment 6*.

Hauptmann Erdmann, commander of the *I./Panzergrenadier-Regiment 3*. He was posthumously awarded the Knight's Cross.

Hauptmann Volckens, commander of the *7./Panzer-Regiment 6*.

CHAPTER 4

From the Terek to the Don: The Battle for the Caucasus

The month of September saw the German summer offensive of 1942 in the outer edges of the Caucasus finally come to a standstill. The Soviets had constructed strong defensive positions along the south bank of the Terek, as well as along the roads leading over the passes, and had been able to move strong forces into them over the course of the previous few weeks. The Soviet 44th Army had the advantage of the rising ground from which its observers could see far into the lower terrain along the north bank.

The Terek itself was a major natural obstacle. The river originated in the glacier region of the 5,000-meter-high Kasbek. It flowed through Ordshonikidse and emptied into the Caspian Sea. The waterway was up to 500 meters wide in places and five meters deep. It flowed at a rate of 3.5 meters a second. The river is interlaced with sandbanks and islands, features shallows, is marked by stony or marshy banks, and has hardly any fords. The path of the Terek from out of the mountain region leads it through marshy, vegetated terrain. The southern bank, that is, the enemy side at the time, is mountainous and forested.

The *3. Panzer-Division* was given the mission of establishing defensive positions along the Terek in front of Ischerskaja. On 4 September, the division issued its first orders in that regard. The defensive sector of the division ran from Mosdok to the bend in the Terek east of Ischerskaja. *Kradschützen-Bataillon 3* screened on the right with a reinforced company, while the *I./Panzergrenadier-Regiment 3* was in the middle and *Kampf-*

gruppe Westhoven on the left. The *II./Panzer-grenadier-Regiment 3* was responsible for defending Ischerskaja. The badly battered *Panzergrenadier-Regiment 394* and *Panzer-Pionier-Bataillon 39* were pulled back. *Oberst Freiherr von Liebenstein* received orders to be prepared for operations south of Mosdok with the main body of the armored regiment. The security of the rear area, especially around the division command post in Awaloff, was assumed by a troop of volunteers of Uzbeks, Cherkessians and Cossacks, all led by *Oberleutnant* Brandes of *Kradschützen-Bataillon 3*.

The nights had already turned cooler, which made the days that much nicer. It was a magnificent late summer. The rear-area services, which had set up along the banks of the Lenin Canal, experienced the last blossoming of the cotton fields. The plantations were fed by the fresh water of the canal and were thus able to grow well in the salty steppes. From their quarters, the soldiers had a magnificent view of the powerful mountain world of the Caucasus.

The Red Air Force and the frequent mortar barrages disturbed the "idyll" on more than one occasion. The Russian aircraft concentrated on the bridge site at Mosdok and the attack of the *LII. Armee-Korps* south of the river. For some days there had been a cloud of smoke and fire above Mosdok proper. The forces paid a considerable price in blood. The corps surgeon, *Generalarzt* Dr. School, was among the dead from that period.

The *XXXX. Panzer-Korps* transitioned to the defense along a line running Ischerskaja–Staro Lednew. The corps' mission: "secure the eastern flank of the field army by conducting aggressive operations."

After initial success, the attack of the *LII. Armee-Korps* south of Mosdok came to a halt. The Soviets employed tanks in counterattacks, which pushed the infantry divisions back as close as five kilometers from the Terek. It was directed that *Kampfgruppe Liebenstein*, consisting of *Panzer-Regiment 6*, *Panzergrenadier-Regiment 3*, the *3./Panzer-Pionier-Bataillon 39*,

and a mixed battery, screen the left flank of the *LII. Armee-Korps*.

The *3. Panzer-Division* remained with its remaining formations and the attached *Kampfgruppe Brückner* of the *23. Panzer-Division* on the north bank of the river and reconnoitered to the east. A field replacement battalion arrived in Pjatigorsk that day, and the artillery also received replacements. The vehicle situation caused concern, however. *Panzer-Regiment 6* had 118 fighting vehicles on its books, but only a portion was operational. The lack of replacement and spare parts made itself felt.

Panzergrenadier-Regiment 394 relieved its sister regiment by evening. The regimental command post and the two battalions set up in Ischerskaja, which would later become a bulwark of the division's defense in the wake of many large-scale attacks. On 10 September, *Hauptmann* Rode assumed command of the 1st Battalion. In September 1941, he had received the Knight's Cross as an *Oberleutnant* in a motorcycle infantry battalion.

The regiment's positions were improved to become strongpoints over time. An interconnected and deeply echeloned defensive system developed along the eastern, southern and western edges of Ischerskaja over the next three months. After almost all the houses in the city had been destroyed by airpower or artillery, the headquarters elements, heavy weapons and reserve forces established themselves in livable bunkers. An underground city developed. For instance, there was a connection passage between the commander of the *I./Panzergrenadier-Regiment 394* and his adjutant, *Oberleutnant* Oberhuber, and from there to the senior noncommissioned officer and then to the individual platoons. An underground bathing facility with three large changing rooms was even established.

The forward positions of the regiment were outside of Ischerskaja. *Oberfeldwebel* Albrecht and his few mechanized infantry, augmented by a heavy mortar and a 5-centimeter antitank gun, held "Albrecht Hill" along the Grosny–Machatsch–Kala rail line. *Leutnant* Wallraff's

6th Company occupied the brickworks, while *Leutnant* Wedel's 7th Company, covered the center portion of the battalion sector. The 2nd Battalion gradually came to hold an outpost line that extended from the Nowo-Galjujewskaja rail station to the Alpatowo Collective Farm

Oberst Freiherr von Liebenstein and his battle group moved to Mosdok during the night of 8–9 September. It did not start crossing the Terek until 0600 hours on the morning of 9 September, since it was impossible to conduct ferry operations in the darkness. The battle group reported to the *LII. Armee-Korps*. After the tanks and the mechanized infantry had crossed the river, they had to also get across a tank ditch, which had been bridged over by engineers. Enemy aircraft had identified the movements and attempted to disrupt the assembly areas by means of rolling attacks.

The battle group then moved out with the *2./Panzer-Regiment 6* on the right and *1./Panzer-Regiment 6* on the left. Following closely behind in the second wave were the *I./Panzergrenadier-Regiment 3* and the *4./Panzer-Regiment 6*. Those elements were followed by the 2nd Battalion of the divisional artillery. After moving two kilometers—the enemy unexpectedly pulled back—the elements turned left. At that point, the tanks encountered strong antitank defenses. While the *4./Panzer-Regiment 6* covered the flank, *Hauptmann* Rodenhauser's *1./Panzer-Regiment 6* attacked the enemy, knocking eight guns out of commission and eliminating or damaging seven Soviet fighting vehicles. A second line of resistance, which was well camouflaged by a tall field of sunflowers, was likewise broken through. *Oberstleutnant* Reinicke, the commander of the attached artillery, moved with the lead tanks and directed the fires of his batteries. The enemy's artillery positions finally had to be assaulted before the battle group reached the village of Terek around 1800 hours. By doing so, the bridgehead around Mosdok was expanded by some ten kilometers.

The Armed Forces Daily Report of 10 September announced the achievement as follows:

"A German battle group from an armor division pushed back an attacking massed enemy force along the Terek, broke into the enemy's artillery positions and destroyed batteries."

That night, *Kampfgruppe Liebenstein* set up an all-round defense around Terek. Patrols sent out in the morning identified an enemy armor staging area southeast of the village. *Oberleutnant Graf* von Kageneck's *4./Panzer-Regiment 6* was ordered to conduct an attack with limited objectives against the enemy position. The company eliminated the initial enemy outposts. But the enemy then put up such a stubborn defense, especially around the waterworks, with his heavy antitank guns and antitank rifles that the German fighting vehicles had to be ordered back. The armored regiment then continued to hold its positions around Terek, even though enemy low-level air attacks and artillery salvoes made life difficult for the soldiers. The tankers breathed a sigh of relief when the companies of *Panzergrenadier-Regiment 3* arrived in the afternoon to relieve them.

On 11 September, the Soviets took the initiative on the southeastern corner of the German front. Supported by tanks, strong Russian forces attacked north of the Terek to the west along the railway line. *Kampfgruppe Brückner* of the *23. Panzer-Division*, which was pushed forward to the east, got in a tight spot. *Generalmajor* Westhoven was placed in charge of defending the eastern flank. He hurried to Mekenskaja to the command post of *Oberst* Brückner, who was subordinated to him. Westhoven had one tank company, the motorcycle infantry battalion and four batteries of the divisional artillery brought forward. *Kradschützen-Bataillon 3* was relieved by *Panzergrenadier-Regiment 394* in order to report to *Generalmajor* Westhoven. At the last moment, it was possible to bring the vehemently attacking enemy forces to a halt. Nonetheless, heavy enemy artillery fire continued throughout the night, especially along the road, as did air attacks.

The situation turned more threatening the next day. Supported by heavy artillery, the Russians attacked the battle group from the east. It was only by employing the remaining reserves that an envelopment for avoided for the time being. New enemy forces were identified in the course of the day that were in the process of attempting to outflank the arduously established line of defense. *Generalmajor* Westhoven breathed a sigh of relief when *Hauptmann* Fechner, who had once been assigned to *Panzer-Regiment 6*, reported in with the *II./Panzer-Regiment 201* of the *23. Panzer-Division*. While on the move, the battalion was employed against the northern flank of the enemy forces, by conducting an enveloping maneuver via Kalenkoff. Together with the *I./Panzergrenadier-Regiment 123* of the *23. Panzer-Division*, the tanks pushed strong enemy forces back south. When they did that, they ran into the fires of *Major* Cochenhausen's *Kradschützen-Bataillon 3*. While defending against those enemy forces and later taking part in their elimination, *Leutnant* Hess, the acting commander of the *4./Kradschützen-Bataillon 3*, particularly distinguished himself and was later inducted into the Army Honor Roll.

In the evening, it was found out that the enemy had reached Kapustin with forces that had advanced further to the north and that elements had crossed the Terek to the rear of the battle group. Since there were no more forces available to prevent an envelopment, a retrograde movement was ordered for 2100 hours to a passage point organized east of Ischerskaja by *Oberstleutnant* Pape.

The retrograde movement of the forces occurred during the night without significant interference from the enemy. German patrols and reconnaissance aircraft identified ongoing movements to the north. The Soviets started an attack against the exposed flank to the west at Naidjenowskoje. *Hauptmann* Fechner's tanks, supported by *Major* Kersten's 3rd Battalion of artillery, was employed against those movements several times. In aggressive movements, his forces scattered two battalions and forced the enemy to halt. In Awaloff, enemy cavalry pressed to within 500 meters of the division command post. It was *Oberleutnant* Brandes with a *SPW* and his troop of Cossacks who created some breathing space there. Later on, *Major* Groeneveld's *Panzer-Pionier-Bataillon 39* was brought to the area to provide security.

The division had no more reserves. The threat to the open east flank grew ever larger. Relief came in the form of the return of *Panzer-Regiment 6* to the division, as well as the attachment of *Panzer-Regiment 201* from the *23. Panzer-Division*. *Oberst Freiherr* von Liebenstein returned from across the Terek with his battalions and occupied a staging area around Graffskij. In the course of the day, additional reinforcements arrived in the form of elements from *Oberst* Burmeister's *Panzer-Regiment 201*.

The fifteenth of September saw clear and cooler weather. The first signs of fall appeared. Two big attacks against *Kampfgruppe Westhoven* were turned back. *Kampfgruppe Liebenstein*, with its fifty tanks, and *Kampfgruppe Burmeister*, with its thirty-five tanks, were ordered to envelop the enemy north of *Kampfgruppe Westhoven* and attack him. Burmeister's battle group was attached to von Liebenstein for command and control purposes. Because of the poor road network, the battle groups only made slow progress and did not reach Naidjenowskoje until the afternoon. The Soviets pulled back to Mekenskaja and to the northeast. The enemy force, consisting of elements of three brigades, could not be pursued. The superior numbers of Russian artillery forced the German formations to halt. The enemy fires hit the sector of *Kradschützen-Bataillon 3* especially hard.

Once again, the medical personnel of *Oberstarzt* Dr. Zinsser had their hands full. *Stabsarzt* Dr. Lehmann-Braun and his 1st Medical Company set up a main clearing station in Russki. *Oberfeldwebel* Winzker, the platoon leader of the 2nd Ambulance Platoon, set up a forward clearing station in Ischerskaja. The number of casualties was large and could barely be managed. The ambulances available to the division were soon no longer adequate for the demand. The forces in the field were constantly asking for medical personnel, but there was a lack of ambulances and replacement parts for the vehicles.

Along the Terek, *Major* Steinbrecher's *Pionier-Bataillon 52* relieved elements of *Panzergrenadier-Regiment 394*, which were sent off to be incorporated into the eastern-facing sector. Ischerskaja was also fortified towards the west as well, since Russians forces succeeded again and again in crossing a bend in the Terek unnoticed and causing confusion in the rear of the front lines.

During the night of 15–16 September, *Oberst Freiherr* von Liebenstein prepared his battle group, consisting of *Panzer-Regiment 6*, the *II./Panzer-Regiment 201*, and the *II./Panzer-Artillerie-Regiment 75*, to attack. He had received the mission of eliminating the enemy forces north of the Lenin Canal and in front of the northern wing of *Kampfgruppe Westhoven* and, in the process, of linking up with *Kampfgruppe Burmeister*. The attack with fifty-seven fighting vehicles started at 0700 hours. The attack initially headed east. Then, moving through Staro Ledneff, it turned south to Hill 113, where it pivoted to the west and in the direction of *Kampfgruppe Burmeister*, which was attacking to the east. The fighting was tough. The Russian riflemen, who had dug in well, defended bravely from their foxholes. The Russian forces were equipped with numerous antitank rifles, which the snipers used against vision ports and oil pans. After the tanks had moved back and forth and the accompanying riflemen had dismounted, the enemy was gradually wiped out. When the lead attack elements approached the northern wing of *Kradschützen-Bataillon 3*, the pincers closed. Four hundred prisoners were taken and twenty artillery pieces, twenty-one antitank guns, and thirteen mortars captured or destroyed. Despite that, the friendly losses weighed heavily. Among others, *Leutnant* Löffler of *Panzer-Regiment 6* was killed and *Oberleutnant* Schewe of the *8./Panzer-Regiment 201* was badly wounded.

After a short rest during a night that was quite cool, the two armored regiments moved out again on 17 September around 0700 hours. This time, they headed in the direction of Alpatowo on the canal. The tank battalions swung out far to the east and south. The Russians defended stubbornly. The numerous antitank rifles were a special danger for the German fighting vehicles. *Panzer-Regiment 201* alone took thirteen losses. *Leutnant* Kipp, the well-proven adjutant of the *II./Panzer-Regiment 6*, was killed during an attack on a position on Hill 113. The tank attack proved successful in the end, however. The Soviet X Guards Corps gave up in its efforts to advance west and transitioned to the defense.

On the other hand, the Soviets outside the bridgehead at Mosdok to the south of the Terek had considerably reinforced their forces. After they had already achieved air superiority for several days in that area, they started a counteroffensive on 19 September. *Oberst* Zimmermann's *Panzergrenadier-Regiment 3* could only turn back those attacks by employing all of his forces. The *13. Panzer-Division* on the right had a worse time of it and had to give up its forward positions that day.

There was no slackening of the tension along the northern wing of the *3. Panzer-Division*, either. The division formed a ready reserve on 18 September, consisting of *Panzer-Regiment 6*, the *III./Panzer-Artillerie-Regiment 75*, the *1./Panzer-Pionier-Bataillon 39*, and the *1./Kradschützen-Bataillon 3*. That force moved into the area around Spornij. For the next several days, it was the mission of that group of forces to send patrols deep into the Russian lines and behind the front and immediately report any concentrations of the enemy.

At that point, the senior command levels realized that any further advance in the Caucasus with the forces available was impossible. Since the main effort was on Stalingrad by then, Hitler ordered the German forces in the Caucasus to go on the defensive on 18 September. It was directed that the *1. Panzer-Armee* conduct mobile defensive operations with its armor forces. *Generalmajor* Breith stated he could not conduct those operations on 18

September, since his tanks were in need of maintenance and repair.

The respite granted him did not last long. Whenever the situation in the north was cleared up, trouble started in the south. The Soviets were increasing their pressure along the Terek in the direction of Ischerskaja. The aircraft with the Red Star were constantly in the air. Within a ninety-minute period on 19 September alone, more than twenty-two air attacks of Ischerskaja were counted.

After preparations like that, the Soviets were able to cross the Terek with four rifle battalions at Beno Jurt. The *3. Panzer-Division* launched an immediate counterattack. The first effort fell flat. The enemy facing the forces of *Pionier-Bataillon 52* and the *8./Panzer-Regiment 6* was too strong. It was possible to seal off the penetration, however. *Oberleutnant* Schmidt, the adjutant of the *I./Panzer-Artillerie-Regiment 75*, was killed during that fighting.

That night, additional enemy formations, including artillery pieces, were brought across the Terek. Once again, the clever improvising of the enemy was a cause for amazement. The Russians had built gigantic ferries that could transport 120 men at a time across the raging river. Starting at 0400 hours, the enemy was already firing artillery and rocket launchers on the German positions at Ischerskaja. The command post of the *II./Panzergrenadier-Regiment 394* received a direct hit from a bomb, but there were only minor casualties, fortunately. A short while later, a Russian rifle regiment moved out to attack from the west.

The *7./Panzergrenadier-Regiment 394* was in position there; *Oberleutnant* Schulze had only assumed command two days previously. The mechanized infantry allowed the Russians to approach close to the positions before opening rapid fire all at once. The company exploited the Russians' surprise and launched an immediate counterattack. *Unteroffizier* Königstein was the first to rise up with his squad and charge the Soviets. The example the brave junior noncommissioned officer set was electrifying. The 7th Company took the enemy position in a powerful charge and drove the Soviets to the river. The enemy left behind seventy dead, twenty-seven prisoners, five mortars, eight antitank rifles, and much more.

Oberst Freiherr von Liebenstein was directed to command the forces in the central portion of the southern sector. He was told to form a ready reserve that was to be prepared for commitment at any time. Forming the battle group were *Major* Frank's *II./Panzer-Regiment 6*, elements of *Panzer-Pionier-Bataillon 39*, and *Hauptmann* Erdmann's *I./Panzergrenadier-Regiment 3*, which had been relieved on 20 September at Mosdok.

The situation around Ischerskaja was finally cleared up on 21 September. The Soviets no longer succeeded in establishing a firm foothold on the north bank of the Terek. The *II./Panzergrenadier-Regiment 3* was pulled out of its positions along the Mosdok bridgehead and returned to division control. With the return of the battalion, the division had all of its organic assets again. In addition to elements of the *23. Panzer-Division*, also reporting to the division were *Bau-Bataillon 538* (538th Construction Battalion), *Pionier-Bataillon 52*, the *II./Nebelwerfer-Regiment 62*,[1] and the *3./Lehr-Regiment 800 "Brandenburg."*

During those days, *Oberstleutnant Freiherr* von Türckheim, the commander of *Panzerjäger-Abteilung 543*, left the division in order to assume a duty position at a senior administrative office. He was replaced by *Hauptmann* Hoffmann. *Hauptmann* Michels, the senior company-grade officer of the battalion, had been badly wounded.

On 22 September, the Soviets started continuous attacks against the eastern flank of the division. The first assault was between Terek and the Lenin Canal. Division formations, led by the *I./Panzergrenadier-Regiment 394*, were able to

---

1. Possibly *Nebelwerfer-Regiment 52*, which was employed in this sector at the time. There was no *Nebelwerfer-Regiment 62*.

turn back four Russian battalions. At that point, the enemy focused his efforts north. *Krad-schützen-Bataillon 3* was alert and did not allow any Russians through. But since friendly aerial reconnaissance had reported that the Soviets were being reinforced further to the north, the entire armor regiment was moved there. The fighting vehicles knocked out six Russian tanks, including one KV-I.

Pionier-Bataillon 52, positioned to the south, was the target of a strong Soviet attack at 0430 hours on 23 September. The engineers and the attached batteries turned back the enemy at Hill 116, inflicting heavy casualties. In all, 220 dead were counted in front of the engineer battalion positions. At that point, the Russians pulled back and transitioned to the defense. *Panzer-grenadier-Regiment 394* was able to take back the ground that had been lost along the rail line.

During the day, there was heavy enemy artillery fire, including salvoes of rockets from Stalin Organs, on the positions of *Kradschützen-Bataillon 3*. In addition, bombers attacked and gave the motorcycle infantry hardly an hour of respite. To the northeast, the Russians approached Kapustin with strong forces, including tanks and cavalry. A reconnaissance-in-force conducted by *Oberleutnant* Fiehl's *2./Panzer-Regiment 6* was able to get as far as Staro Ledneff, but any further advance had to be broken off because of a strong enemy armored presence.

The armored regiment was reinforced during the night by the *II./Panzer-Regiment 201*, two batteries of the divisional artillery, and the *1./Panzergrenadier-Regiment 126*.[2] The *I./Panzergrenadier-Regiment 3* prepared during the cold and moonlight night to follow the tanks in the attack. Moving via Naidjenowskoje, the *I./Panzer-Regiment 6* attacked in the direction of Staro Ledneff around 0700 hours. In hour later, it was in German hands. The companies then turned to the west to force the enemy into the guns of *Kradschützen-Bataillon 3*. But the enemy

proved stronger that time around. He had brought up heavy antitank guns, which stopped the *I./Panzer-Regiment 6* from well-camouflaged positions. The battalion was able to cross the open terrain in a bold maneuver and set up in a vegetated area. The casualties were considerable. The 2nd Company of the armor regiment suffered four dead (*Feldwebel* Kirschke and *Gefreiter* Hentschel, *Gefreiter* Sudnek, and *Gefreiter* Träger).

The *II./Panzer-Regiment 6* and the *II./Panzer-Regiment 201* were unable to support the stalled advance of their sister battalion, since they were themselves under heavy fire. Russian tanks suddenly appeared in front of that battle group, but three of them were knocked out. *Oberst Freiherr* von Liebenstein called off the operation and pulled back with his two battalions behind the lines of the motorcycle infantry battalion between Spornij and Staro Ledneff. In all, six tanks were total losses, while eleven were damaged. The Soviet 4th Guards Rifle brigade also took its hits as well. It suffered eighty dead and lost seven fighting vehicles and seven heavy antitank guns.

Things went better in the south that day, with the engineers of *Pionier-Bataillon 52* scoring a success. The well-placed fires of *Major* Kersten's 3rd Battalion of artillery had softened up the Russians to the point where they fell back to the Terek and crossed it when the engineers moved out to attack. A great deal of materiel was captured, and the formation was able to move up to the riverbank.

The constant back and forth of the grueling fighting, in which neither side was able to score a resounding success despite all of the dogged determination and tenacity, caused both sides to scale back their efforts. The Soviets temporarily called off their efforts to force the *3. Panzer-Division* back from the Terek. But the German forces were also much too weak to bring about any type of decision. Both friend and foe used

---

2. The *SPW* company of the regiment. The regiment was commanded by *Oberstleutnant* Wellmann at the time, who formerly was a company commander in *Schützen-Regiment 3*.

the next three days to collect their forces, reorganize, and improve their positions. The Soviets pulled back from the eastern side of the defensive positions. Many Red Army soldiers used the opportunity to desert. Most of the deserters were Georgians, Armenians, and Caucasians. The following deserters were counted in the division sector on 23 September: 6 officers and 156 enlisted personnel. On 25 September, it was 2 officers and 210 enlisted personnel. Two days later, on 27 September, the number within the corps sector was 14 officers and 523 enlisted personnel.

In the fall of 1942, the German Army in the East underwent a number of changes in its senior commands. The personnel changes were tied to the general situation along the front. After it was determined that the two offensives directed against Stalingrad and the Caucasus would not lead to success, there were disagreements between the field commands and the Army High Command. *Generalfeldmarschall* List, the commander in chief of *Heeresgruppe A*, was the first one to lose his post. Hitler had already replaced him as early as 10 September, and the Armed Forces High Command assumed direct leadership of the field-army group. Two weeks later, there was a break between Hitler and his chief of staff, *Generaloberst* Halder. The effects were felt even at the *3. Panzer-Division*. The commanding general of the *XXXX. Panzer-Korps*, the former distinguished commander of the *3. Panzer-Division*, *General der Panzertruppen Freiherr* Geyr von Schweppenburg, went home on 26 September, since his health had deteriorated rapidly over the previous few weeks. He took leave of his forces with the following words:

> At the hour of my departure from the *XXXX. Panzer-Korps*, I look back with gratitude and pride in all of the accomplishments that this battle-tested corps brought to fruition in its march to victory across the Oskol, through the eastern Ukraine, over the Don and the Manytsch, and as far as the mountains of the Caucasus.

> I commemorate our dead comrades.

> I extend my wishes for continued military good fortune and additional success to the corps and all of you.

Generalmajor Breith became the acting commanding general, until *Generalleutnant* Fehn, the former commander of the *5. Panzer-Division*, arrived on 28 September to assume formal command.

The division continued to conduct combat patrols to the east and the south. One patrol reached an area three kilometers outside of Naurskaja, while others got to the area around Kapustin. All of the patrols reported that the enemy was being reinforced. Moreover, additional armored trains had been seen. During the night, the Soviets, for their part, pressed westward and occupied Alpatowo without being discovered.

On the next day, the division established a battle group under *Hauptmann* Erdmann, consisting of the *I./Panzergrenadier-Regiment 3*, the *1./Kradschützen-Bataillon 3*, and a mixed company from the *II./Panzer-Regiment 6*, which received the mission of advancing to the southeast. The battle group moved out from Staro Ledneff. The Soviets put up a stiff defense, but they were unable to contain the momentum of the attack. Under the command of *Major* Frank and *Hauptmann* Erdmann, the battle group was already on hotly contested Hill 113 by noon. The attack continued south. The enemy in front of the eastern portion of the division sector was ejected after *Hauptmann* Rode's *I./Panzergrenadier-Regiment 394* joined the fight and assaulted Hill 103 west of Alpatowo. The Russians left behind 400 prisoners. On that day, the *II./Panzergrenadier-Regiment 3* and the *II./Panzer-Regiment 6* suffered seven dead and twenty-five wounded. The last day of September turned out to be a successful one for the *3. Panzer-Division*.

The beginning of October was marked by magnificent weather and highlighted once more the beauty of the countryside. The mountain range of the Caucasus stretched to the south, while the huge steppe was to the north and east, sometimes taking on the appearance of a desert. The forces of the division worked industriously on improving their positions, since it appeared certain that the German Army would spend the winter in that region. The vehicles were integrated into the localities. The units of the division support command, which had its command post in Kurskaja, established issue points for rations and materiel. On 2 October, the division received the reequipped *I./Panzer-Artillerie-Regiment 75*, which had been in Kharkov up to then undergoing a reconstitution. The following elements remained attached to the division: *Pionier-Bataillon 52*, *Feldzeug-Bataillon 8* (8th Ordnance Battalion), *Artillerie-Abteilung 777* (*Mörser*), *Beobachtungs-Abteilung 23*, the *III./Nebelwerfer-Regiment 62*, and *Bau-Bataillon 538*. Later on, the division also received the *Nordkaukasisches Bataillon 802* (802nd North Caucasus Battalion), the *II./Artillerie-Regiment 60*, the *2./Artillerie-Regiment 800*,[3] and the *5./Artillerie-Regiment 46*.[4]

Generalmajor Breith received a telegram on 3 October informing him that he was to report immediately to the Army High Command. Effective 1 October, he had been transferred to the unassigned officer manpower pool. With that, a commander left the division who had commanded it magnificently. His successor was designated as the commander of the *3. Panzergrenadier-Brigade*. Since *Generalmajor* Westhoven was on home leave at the time, *Oberst Freiherr* von Liebenstein assumed acting command in his stead. The commander of the 2nd Battalion of the divisional artillery, *Oberstleutnant* Reinicke, assumed command of the artillery regiment. For the time being, the armored regiment was under the acting command of *Major* Frank. *Major* Stockmann assumed command of the armor regiment's 2nd Battalion. *Generalmajor* Breith left the division on 6 October. He was accompanied by *Hauptmann* von dem Knesebeck, who turned over his position as the division intelligence officer to *Oberleutnant* Twardowski. The two traveled to Winniza, where Breith took his leave of Hitler, and then on to the homeland. *Hauptmann* Böttge, the commander of the signals battalion, was transferred to the Army High Command; *Major* Helfritz took his place.

The front lines had not stagnated to positional warfare, however. On 2 October, the motorcycle infantry battalion launched an attack on Hill 113 to improve its positions. The advance encountered a prepared enemy and cost one company one dead, one wounded and seven *SPW's*. The three days that followed were filled with increased patrol activity in order to obtain a clear picture of the enemy situation. The Russians were constantly moving their formations, bringing groups of forces and weapons across the Terek and then taking them back again. It was assumed they were preparing for a new attack.

The assumptions were correct. At 1345 hours on 5 October, enemy artillery fired a barrage on the German positions along the eastern sector. The 5th, 6th, and 7th Guards Rifle Brigades attacked north of Ischerskaja and along the Lenin Canal. The division's formations had been warned by deserters and were prepared for the Soviet operation. The divisional artillery fired with everything it had and stifled the Soviet attacks in front of the lines until the onset of darkness. The location of the firing positions of a mortar battalion, which had been betrayed by a deserter, were taken under concentrated fire and destroyed.

The Soviets used the next few days to regroup their forces. On 8 October, they attempted to break through at Ischerskaja again. The first blow hit the *6./Panzergrenadier-Regiment 394*,

---

3. This unit cannot be found in the records.

4. A separate artillery regiment, with separately deployable artillery battalions, of which the 2nd Battalion was allocated to the *LII. Armee-Korps* during this time period.

which was able to turn back the attack with the assistance of rocket launchers. During the fighting, the heavy machine-gun squad of *Unteroffizier* Becker particularly distinguished itself. A short while later, the Russians succeeded in crossing the Terek again and attacking the outposts of the *7./Panzergrenadier-Regiment 394*. Once again, the enemy was turned back once heavy weapons, tanks, and several *SPW's* were employed.

Those enemy efforts were repeated again two days later. That time, the Russians also employed ten tanks. The sector of *Hauptmann* Mente's *II./Panzergrenadier-Regiment 3* was the focus of the enemy attack. In the end, the Russians gave up in their effort. Six enemy fighting vehicles were left alight in and in front of the German positions. Only one tank succeeded in getting across the railway line, but it was also knocked out.

The combat squadrons of the *VIII. Flieger-Korps* were finally back in the air that day. They flew sorties to the south above the heads of the soldiers. A few hours later, dark clouds rose from behind the mountains. The black clouds even obscured the sun for a while. It was not discovered until the next day that it had been the smoke from the burning oil tanks at Grosny.

On 10 October, the Soviets launched an attack with the IV Cossack Guards Cavalry Corps from the steppes against the thinly held outpost lines of *Korps z.b.V. Felmy*,[5] which was employed to the north of the *XXXX. Panzer-Korps*. The Soviet offensive in that sector failed as well, and the enemy suffered heavy casualties. It was demonstrated there, as it had also been in the sector around the *3. Panzer-Division*, that the Azerbaijani and Caucasian forces employed by the Soviets had little combat value. It was only the native Russians who did well. Many of the non-Russian forces deserted when given the chance, as was demonstrated in the sector of the *II./Panzer-grenadier-Regiment 394*, where thirty-five Caucasian soldiers found their way to the German lines to desert on that 10 October.

The situation turned somewhat quieter, although both sides continued to conduct reconnaissance and combat patrols. The German forces increasingly concentrated their efforts in constructing more permanent-like positions, with bunkers being built, barbed wire set up and minefields emplaced. The rear-area services formed two alert companies, which were referred to as "Awaloff" and "Mosdok." *Major* Peschke, the commander of the division's field-replacement battalion, personally oversaw the infantry training of those companies.

The daily logs of the *II./Panzergrenadier-Regiment 394* for 14 October reflect what it was like on a typical day in the middle of that October 1942: "No changes in the enemy situation. The enemy continues to remain passive and has not changed his dispositions. The forces manning Ischerskaja are gradually growing stronger and the number of bunkers grows from day to day. Larger-sized bunkers needed to be built for the field kitchens and the headquarters administrative areas. Since the former could not be removed from the vehicles, there was a considerable movement of earth involved."

At the end of October, the 2nd Battalion listed the construction efforts it had initiated in and around Ischerskaja: 86 dugouts, 4,710 meters of trench line, 89 sleeping bunkers, 33 ammunition bunkers, and 23 field-kitchen and administrative dugouts. In addition, 2,070 meters of barbed wire had been emplaced. The Red Air Force, which dominated the air space, continuously attacked those dugouts. The low-level attacks, during which the division command post was also not spared, were the most dangerous ones.

As a result of the critical fuel situation, vehicular movement between the battalions of *Panzer-grenadier-Regiment 394* in Ischerskaja and the

---

5. Special-Purpose Corps Felmy. The corps headquarters was formed in late September from *Sonderstab F* (Special Headquarters Felmy), which had been part of the military mission to Iraq and also tasked with handling Arab issues for the Armed Forces High Command. By April 1943, it became the nucleus of the *LXVIII. Armee-Korps*.

trains elements dug in along the Lenin Canal west of the town were restricted. Contact was maintained by means of a truck route, which was nicknamed the "Pape Courier," which had a regular schedule.

Generalmajor Westhoven assumed command of the division on 15 October. The situation at the time: The division, reinforced by many different formations, covered the eastern flank of *Heeresgruppe Kaukasus* from its overextended positions, jutting far out to the east. Between Mosdok and Ischerskaja, the defense of the southern portion of the division's frontage was made easier by the presence of the Terek. There was still a threat, however, from the banks, which were broken up and vegetated, and the fact that the Russians had terrific observation into the areas behind the German front from the elevated terrain on the south bank. An especially dangerous spot was the bend in the river to the west of Ischerskaja.

To the east and the north, where the positions turned north, the terrain offered good fields of observation to the Germans. It was trafficable practically everywhere for armored vehicles. As a result, it was possible for the armored elements of the division to conduct attacks or counterattacks, as the situation demanded. Of course, the suitability for armor was also of benefit to the enemy as well, who was also able to commit his tanks to an attack virtually everywhere.

A new threat to the flank of the division arose in the north. The steppes, which had previously been difficult to negotiate due to the deep sand and lack of water, started to become trafficable for formations of all types as a result of the fall rains and the ensuing frost.

In the south, along the Terek, the forces were arrayed as follows (right to left): *Bau-Bataillon 538*, the *Nordkaukasisches Bataillon 802*, *Pionier-Bataillon 52*, and *Panzer-Pionier-Bataillon 39*. *Panzergrenadier-Regiment 394* continued to man the bulwark of Ischerskaja, with its 2nd Battalion oriented south and its 1st Battalion ori-

ented east. Adjoining to the north were the Cossack Troop, *Kradschützen-Bataillon 3*, and *Feldzeug-Bataillon 8*. In a salient jutting far to the east was the armor regiment with its combat outposts; its main body was held farther to the rear, ready to move, as needed. Most of the artillery, mortars and rocket launchers were positioned between Ischerskaja and Kriwonosoff. The rear-area services were between Schefatoff and Buguloff on the Lenin Canal. A Cossack formation adjoined them to the north.

Kampfgruppe Zimmermann and the 3rd, 4th and 9th Batteries of the divisional artillery, the latter under *Hauptmann* Wykopal, were still south of the Terek.

A few changes of duty positions that took place in November are worthy of note. Based on a *Führer* directive of 6 November, the headquarters of the mechanized infantry brigade was inactivated. The command post in Kriwonosoff was torn down. The commander of the armored regiment, *Oberst Freiherr* von Liebenstein, was transferred to the unassigned officer manpower pool on 8 November. Later on, he would go to Africa as a *Generalmajor* and commander of the *164. leichte Afrika-Division*, where he led the division through the hard fighting to the very end in Tunis. For the second time, *Oberst* Munzel returned to the regiment after convalescing from wounds. Exactly one week later, the news arrived that the division operations officer, *Oberstleutnant i.G.* Pomtow, was to be transferred to Africa as well. He would be named as the chief of staff of the *XC. Armee-Korps*[6] in Tunisia. The division had much to owe to this General Staff officer, who was universally respected. His successor was the former logistics officer of the *XXXX. Panzer-Korps*, *Oberstleutnant i.G.* Voss. Protestant Pastor Heidland, who was wounded in September, was temporarily replaced by Chaplain Sieburg.

In September, three officers received the German Cross in Gold: *Oberstleutnant i.G.* Pomtow, the division operations officer; *Major* Kersten,

---

6. Also listed as the *LXXXX. Armee-Korps* by various sources.

the commander of the *III./Panzer-Artillerie-Regiment 75*; and *Hauptmann* Lingk, the commander of the *3./Panzerjäger-Abteilung 521*. That was followed in October by four others: *Major* Streger, the commander of *Panzerjäger-Abteilung 521*; *Hauptmann* Rodenhauser, the commander of the *1./Panzer-Regiment 6*; *Leutnant* Harbeck, an acting commander in *Krad-schützen-Bataillon 3*; and *Oberfeldwebel* Kantah, a platoon leader in the *1./Panzergrenadier-Regiment 394*.

When the movements of enemy forces, most likely the newly identified 63rd Cavalry Division, were observed heading to the northwest, *Oberst* Munzel was given the mission of eliminating them by advancing to Nyrkoff and then pivoting north in the direction of Staro Bucharoff.

On 30 October, *Kampfgruppe Munzel* started to move out, news was received that the enemy had penetrated the lines at the "Western Village," and that the status of the Cossack Troop was unknown. *Kampfgruppe Munzel*, consisting of the *I./Panzer-Regiment 6*, elements of the *I./Panzergrenadier-Regiment 3*, and elements of the divisional artillery, left behind weak outposts and continued its original attack. A company of antitank riflemen was eliminated at Nowo Ledneff. Staro Bucharoff and the high ground around it were full of enemy forces. Since the enemy had also reinforced his forces at Kapustin by then and was advancing west, the fighting at Staro Bucharoff was broken off. The battle group was directed south and attacked Kapustin from the east. Two battalions were eliminated there after offering stiff resistance. In all, 14 officers and 450 enlisted personnel were taken prisoner. The enemy's casualties were very high. Unfortunately, the division also suffered casualties. The *2./Panzergrenadier-Regiment 3* suffered seven dead, including all of the company messengers. The battle group then returned with most of its forces to its original line of departure.

By then, another battle group had been formed under *Major* Frank. It was employed in retaking the "West Village," and it captured fifty Russians in the process.

It was confirmed that Russian cavalry was threatening the open north flank of the division. To combat those forces, a battle group was formed under *Oberleutnant* Hagenguth, the acting commander of *Panzerjäger-Abteilung 543*, at Konsowatt. Its mission was to increase patrolling activity to the north and northeast.

The first snow fell on Sunday, 11 November, exactly one month later than the previous year. The snow flurries, which were mixed with hail, delayed the planned operations of *Kampfgruppe Munzel* for a day. The reinforced *I./Panzer-Regiment 6* of *Hauptmann* Rohrbeck remained halfway to its objective on the steppes. It was not identified by the enemy, however, and it moved out the following morning at first light. The fighting vehicles moved on a widely dispersed line, entered Artaschikoff by surprise and then advanced on Staro Bucharoff. Tank main guns and machine guns eliminated a Russian cavalry regiment in bivouac. The enemy was in no position to offer a deliberate defense. Three hundred sixty-five prisoners remained in German hands, and ten infantry guns, eight antitank guns, and numerous antitank rifles were captured or destroyed. For his bold actions, *Hauptmann* Rohrbeck was later inducted into the Army Honor Roll.

Despite its success, that operation brought with it the sobering realization that the mechanical condition of the fighting vehicles was not sufficient for any large-scale operations. The wear and tear on materiel was considerable, and there were hardly any replacement parts available. It was only the inventiveness of the maintenance officers and the industriousness of the maintenance companies that kept the tanks and *SPW's* combat operational. In addition, there were insufficient supplies of fuel, which severely limited freedom of operation.

There were no serious incidents in the other sectors of the division. The formations worked tirelessly on improving their positions and conducted combat reconnaissance to the east. They also launched combat raids across the Terek. In general, the Soviets remained on the defensive.

An attack against *Kradschützen-Bataillon 3* on 10 November was turned back. The onset of bad weather made all movements difficult. The forces, which saw large numbers of soldiers suffering from infectious diseases like jaundice, stomach catarrh and kidney catarrh over the previous weeks, attempted to conduct training. Noncommissioned officer courses were held, firing practice conducted and alert companies established.

Since the *1. Panzer-Armee* was assuming that the enemy was pulling forces out of the sector, the division received orders to try to tie up enemy forces by means of limited-objective attacks.

Oberst Munzel thereupon received orders from the division to advance on the "Sugar Loaf" and the "Seven Hills" with the armored regiment, reinforced by two companies from *Hauptmann* Rode's *I./Panzergrenadier-Regiment 394*, along with the regimental engineer platoons. The battle group was to move south from Hill 113. While *Major* Stockmann's 2nd Battalion of the armor regiment, along with the mechanized infantry, attacked the enemy from the front, it was directed for the 1st Battalion to envelop the enemy and roll up from the west. The attack had to be postponed several times because of the morass created by rainfall. On 17 November, however, the attack could be launched.

While Stockmann's forces moved out against the enemy positions, the *I./Panzer-Regiment 6* succeeded in reaching the Lenin Canal northwest of Alpatowo within three-quarters of an hour, thanks to an aggressively led attack. The 1st Battalion took seventy-eight prisoners and knocked out two T-34's. Since the Russians fled to the southeast, *Hauptmann* Rohrbeck made the decision on his own to pursue.

The battalion initially moved in a column of twos, echeloned out towards the open side. The tanks initially made good progress through the difficult terrain, when all hell broke out over it. The battalion had moved into a trap: Antitank guns protected by mines. Russian antitank gun fire suddenly slammed against the tanks from three sides. In addition, there was the crack of antitank-gun rifles from hidden bunkers and the dull thud of mortars from the far side of a reverse-slope position.

Hauptmann Rodenhauser's 1st Company, bringing up the rear, raced forward to help. His company also ran into heavy fire. Two vehicles were set alight. On top of everything else, three T-34's appeared and advanced on the German fighting vehicles. At pointblank range, the *Panzer IV's* were able to knock out two Russian tanks. The third one escaped in the general chaos.

There was no choice but to break off the fight. The battalion pulled back along the same way it had come. The tanks assembled at a solitary building on a collective farm. Russian artillery suddenly started raining down. *Hauptmann* Rohrbeck fell victim to the first round, and the life of a daring and successful armor commander was gone.

The failure of the one group had effects on the other one as well. The mechanized infantry and the *1./Panzer-Regiment 6* had moved from their assembly areas by echelons, where they advanced frontally on the enemy positions. Initially, the mechanized infantry made good progress under the covering fire provided by the *I./Panzer-Regiment 6*. Once in the enemy positions, the mechanized infantry was exposed to massive mortar fire and suffered heavy casualties. The tank battalion, which was closing in, encountered a minefield. The first two fighting vehicles were lost. The battalion was no longer able to support the mechanized infantry; instead, it had to go around the dangerous spot. The mechanized infantry companies, left up to their own devices, continued their assault. The succeeded in running under the mortar fire and entering the enemy positions. Position after position was taken in close combat in the broken terrain. *Leutnant* Hinsch of the *3./Panzer-grenadier-Regiment 394* was shot through the chest at pointblank range. The battalion suffered 6 dead and 20 wounded. While clearing the deeply echeloned enemy defensive positions, more than 100 prisoners were taken. The tankers were able to capture another 200 Soviets and 10 antitank guns. On that day, the armor regiment suffered 21 wounded and dead and 4 missing. In addition, it had lost nine tanks. The bloody losses of the enemy were even worse.

Volckens's company, which was employed south of the canal at the same time to deceive the enemy and protect the other efforts, succeeded in rolling up the enemy positions to the north and inflicting heavy casualties. The company was able to disengage from the enemy without him following.

For their part, the Russians attacked on 18 November at several spots. In each case, it was with several companies. All of the attacks were turned back. In the days that followed, the Russians placed artillery fire on the front-line positions and the rear areas. An enemy armored train appeared several times at Alpatowo.

On 22 November, the division commander, who was the acting commanding general as well, held a commander's conference. It was occasioned by the announcement from the field army that no more fuel would be brought forward for the foreseeable future. Those were effects of the impending catastrophe at Stalingrad, which hung like a Sword of Damocles above all of the formations employed in the Caucasus, especially the *3. Panzer-Division*, which was the farthest to the southeast.

Some of the enemy formations were apparently unreliable; they were usually composed of members of Caucasian clans. There were deserters almost every day. On 21 November, five officers and sixty-nine enlisted personnel deserted in the sector of the *I./Panzergrenadier-Regiment 394* alone. The positional warfare was used to conduct a propaganda war as well. For instance, the Russians set up a large poster at Ischerskaja with the following text: "Your death is in the Caucasus! Save yourselves! Desert!" A German patrol tore down the poster the next evening and put a different one in its place: "We're coming, but with our weapons! Stalin's going *kaputt*!"

At the announcement of the code word "Ant," the division had to order the immediate transition of all supply activities to *panje* carts. Since

the overextended front was only thinly occupied and many sections were only monitored by patrols, there were unique episodes that frequently occurred. For instance, the headquarters of the 2nd Battalion of the divisional artillery was in a house in Awaloff. Once, there was a knock on the door. The battalion adjutant, *Leutnant* Gerlach, opened. Was he ever surprised when he found himself facing a Russian patrol. Making a spur-of-the-moment decision, he yelled at the Ivans and, with help from *Leutnant* Sporns, who was hastily summoned, convinced the confused Russians, who were gazing in, to disarm.

In the rear areas, the division had set up military cemeteries to provide the fallen with a worthy final resting place. The units were required to provide graves officers, who were charged with maintaining designated cemeteries. They facilities were found at the following locations: Ischerskaja (*Panzergrenadier-Regiment 394*), Schefatoff (*Kradschützen-Bataillon 3*), Stoderewskaja Main Clearing Station (2nd Medical Company), Stoderewskaja rail station (*Pionier-Bataillon 52*), Besorukin (*Panzer-Artillerie-Regiment 75*, Mosdok (division support command), Graffskij (*Panzer-Regiment 6*), and Russki (1st Medical Company). By the end of November, there were already 148 soldiers from *Panzergrenadier-Regiment 394* buried at Ischerskaja. Field services were held on *Heldengedenktag* at all of the cemeteries. The division's chaplains and commanders delivered eulogies. Since 26 July, the divisional artillery had suffered 8 officers and 98 enlisted personnel dead, 25 officers and 385 enlisted personnel as wounded, and 7 cannoneers as missing.

On 24 November, *Generalleutnant* Henrici assumed command of the *XXXX. Panzer-Korps*. He had been the commander of the *16. Infanterie-Division (mot.)*, which had been the sole German division watching the gigantic Kalmuck Steppe between the *3. Panzer-Division* and the front at Stalingrad. The new commanding general released a general order (excerpt): "I extend my greetings to the proven troop elements of this armored corps, especially the *3. Panzer-Division*, which is familiar to me from peacetime and which stood by my side this past winter in the best spirit of military comradeship with its tanks. In these serious times, we want to quickly gain one another's trust and together take down every enemy who grapples with us, especially at this especially exposed portion of the front."

The new commanding general arrived in Ischerskaja on 27 November and visited the outermost German strongpoint on the southeast corner of the Eastern Front. All of the signs were there that the Soviets would start a new offensive shortly. *Panzergrenadier-Regiment 3* was back across the Terek, after its battalions had spent almost two weeks in position along the Grusinian Military Road. The regiment was designated the corps reserve for a short period.

From left to right, the battle groups at the time were commanded as follows: *Major* Steinbrecher (*Pionier-Bataillon 52*), *Major* Groeneveld (who also commanded elements of *Lehr-Regiment "Brandenburg"* and the *Nordkaukasisches Bataillon 802* in addition to his own battalion), *Oberstleutnant* Pape, and *Oberst* Munzel. The divisional artillery, augmented by the *II./Artillerie-Regiment 60* and a rocket-launcher battalion, was concentrated around Ischerskaja. The artillery commander was *Oberstleutnant* Reinecke.

As the result of ground and air reconnaissance, as well as patrol activity, it was determined the enemy was being reinforced and conducting movements in a northwesterly direction. For instance, a patrol from the motorcycle infantry battalion encountered elements of the recently introduced 416th Rifle Division in the area around Kapustin. According to the senior commands, the enemy was concentrating about two divisions, along with cavalry and tanks, in the area of Terekli Mekleb. Within the *3. Panzer-Division*, *Major* Cornelius, the commander of the *IV. (Flak)/Panzer-Artillerie-Regiment 75*, was directed to form a blocking position, if the enemy attack actually took place. *Hauptmann* Hoffmann, the commander of *Panzerjäger-*

Abteilung 543, was given command of a mobile reserve force. The desert had become trafficable after the onset of frost, with the result that there was an increased threat along the open northern flank of the division.

The enemy's winter offensive in the southern portion of the Eastern Front started on 30 November. Several field armies between Stalingrad and the Caucasus charged against the German positions. The Soviet 44th Army, positioned north of the Terek, had the mission of defeating the *XXXX. Panzer-Korps* with its X Guards Rifle Corps and V Don Cossack Guards Cavalry Corps. Its objective was to reach the Atschikulak–Mosdok road. The main effort of the offensive was directed against the cavalry group of the corps. Those were mostly volunteer troops of Eastern peoples under the over-all command of Oberst von Jungschulz. The Soviet main effort also hit the northern wing of the *3. Panzer-Division*, where *Kampfgruppe Munzel* screened across a broad frontage with groups of forces.

On the morning of 30 November, Soviet artillery placed barrage fire on the dugouts of the armor regiment and the motorcycle infantry battalion. Russian infantry, about one and one-half divisions strong, as well as cavalry, attacked across a broad front about TEN kilometers north of Ischerskaja. The entire division was alerted! The men of the motorcycle infantry battalion jumped out of their log cabins and bunkers, moved up behind their mortars and machine guns and received the attacking Russians with defensive fires that caused the first wave to stop in its tracks.

Kampfgruppe Hoffmann, along with the *2./ Panzer-Regiment 6*, was attacked by Russian tanks at Kretschetoff. The Russian forces attempted again and again to bypass the German positions by swinging far to the north. *Oberleutnant* Fiehl and his tank company launched an immediate counterattack and, together with *Panzerjäger-Abteilung 543*, was able to knock out twelve Russian tanks. In addition, 300 prisoners were brought in. After that, the fighting died down.

A counterattack conducted by *Kampfgruppe Stockmann* in the direction of Naidjenowskoje brought temporary relief. Some 140 prisoners were taken and six antitank guns captured.

The first of December was marked by a surprising success. It was a unique incident, the likes of which were only possible in the strongpoint defense being conducted in the Kalmuck Steppe. *Hauptmann* Volckens's *7./Panzer-Regiment 6* had been sent north to reinforce *Kampfgruppe Hoffmann* and the threatened northern flank of the division. The fighting vehicles churned through the terrain. An hour passed, then a second one. It seemed as though the company had gotten somewhat off course. The fuel gauges slowly started to move towards empty. *Hauptmann* Vol-

ckens had his company close up and halt. He wanted to wait until his supply section caught up. A portion of the company was located in a depression not far from Mitrofanoff.

All of a sudden, the tanks sent out as outposts identified movements in the steppe. Binoculars! Something was moving! There was one column, then another and then a third. Volckens sounded the alert! He knew that his company had not yet been seen, and fate was offering him a prize. As the great king of Prussia said: "A soldier needs to have his luck!"

The company formed up to attack. The tanks buttoned up and the main guns loaded. Volckens issued his order by radio: *"Panzer marsch!"* The *Panzer III's* and *IV's* advanced into a completely

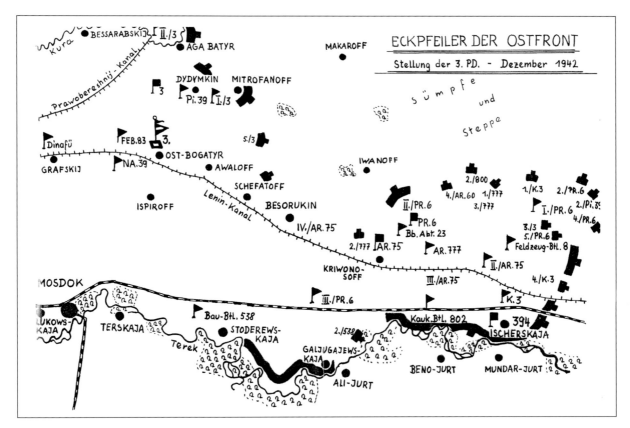

Bulwark of the Eastern Front
Position of the *3. Panzer-Division* (December 1942)
Kanal= canal; *Dinafü* = Division Support Command; *FEB.83* = *Feld-Ersatz-Bataillon 83*; *Bau-Btl.538* = *Bau-Bataillon 538*;
Kauk.Btl.802 = *Kaukasisches Infanterie-Bataillon 802*

surprised brigade that was moving up in its entirety. The enemy fled head over heels across the steppe and left behind large quantities of infantry guns, machine guns, small arms and pieces of equipment. Two 12-centimeter field pieces and ten 7.62-centimeter antitank guns were overrun. When three T-34's started to defend, they were soon put out of commission. Hundreds of dead and wounded and pieces of equipment were left on the battlefield. The tank company did not suffer a single loss. Later on, Volckens received the Knight's Cross for his bold actions in preventing a deep thrust into the deep flank of the corps.

Since there was the danger that the field-replacement battalion and the *III./Panzer-Regiment 6* of Prince Christian zu Schaumburg-Lippe could be subordinated to non-divisional entities in the crush of events during that critical time, both elements were brought forward into the divisional area.

Although the initial enemy attacks had collapsed, the enemy was still pressing forward everywhere. The division commander ordered *Kampfgruppe Munzel* to evacuate Hill 113 during the night. The position that had jutted out far to the east had been held for weeks and hotly contested, but it was time to shorten the line and bring the forces back to Spornij.

In the northern screening sector, located further to the rear, the enemy had apparently been able to score a penetration against the Cossack troops and eastern people's volunteer battalions of *Oberst* von Jungschulz. According to aerial reconnaissance and patrol activity, two divisions had broken through in the area around Aga Batyr. *Kampfgruppe Hoffmann* was constantly being attacked by large enemy forces. The enemy was also attacking along the entire eastern sector of the division. In some cases, the attacks were supported by tanks. The *1./Kradschützen-Bataillon 3* was encircled for a while, and the command post of the *I./Panzer-Regiment 6* was also threatened.

Ischerskaja was being attacked from both the south and the east. That afternoon, the enemy's penetrations were sealed off and eliminated as a result of concentrated fires, especially those from the artillery, which showed tremendous effect. All of the enemy's attacks had been turned back with heavy losses to the enemy.

Kampfgruppe Zimmermann, the corps reserve, was committed against the Russian forces that had broken through at Aga Batyr. Zimmermann's forces succeeded in ejecting the enemy, who defended stubbornly. The infantry guns of the regiment proved to be especially effective in that engagement. *Oberfeldwebel* Kruse of the *7./Panzergrenadier-Regiment 3* once again distinguished himself through his bravery. By evening—it was already turning dark at 1500 hours—Zimmermann's forces had entered Aga Batyr and relieved the Cossacks and their German officers holding out there. Among the spoils of war were ten armored cars, twenty antitank guns, five artillery pieces, eight heavy mortars, and two regimental flags. In addition, 200 prisoners were taken. The 12th Guards Cavalry Division had been defeated. Among the captured papers was a letter from Kaganovitch[7] to the commander of the division.

In order to close the gap, *Hauptmann* Erdmann's *I./Panzergrenadier-Regiment 3* was given the mission of moving via Scherstobitoff and Kretschetoff to establish contact with the left wing of *Kampfgruppe Munzel*. Munzel's forces supported the attack by advancing north with elements, resulting in the taking of more than 1,000 prisoners.

By the evening of 4 December, all of the attacking enemy forces along the eastern sector of the division's front had been turned back. The enemy, supported by tanks and artillery, was also contained in the north as well.

The wear and tear on the tanks forced the armor regiment to consolidate vehicles into one battalion under *Major* Stockmann.

---

7. A Communist functionary and friend of Stalin's. During this period of the war, he was a member of the Military Council for the North Caucasian and Transcaucasian Fronts. He played a major role in bringing about the great food famines of 1932–33.

A major cause of concern during the fighting during that period was the fuel and ammunition situation, just as it had been in the past. The artillery, which was vital in helping maintain the thinly-held positions, had to economize. At the beginning of December, there were only 1,500 rounds of light howitzer ammunition, 500 rounds of heavy howitzer ammunition, 500 rounds of 10-centimeter ammunition and 300 mortar rounds available for three days. The logistics lines of communication ran along the same railway line as that needed for establishing the new defensive frontage at Rostow and to its north—necessitated by the collapse of the Southeast Front as a result of the encirclement of Stalingrad—and for the relief effort for Stalingrad, as represented by *Panzerarmee Hoth*.

It comes as no wonder that there were only completely insufficient amounts of supplies earmarked for the Caucasus in that catastrophic situation. The commands of the various divisions only heard vague indications of a severe setback in the north at the end of November. Nevertheless, the prospect was held that the enemy would be brought to a standstill.

On 5 and 6 December, the Russians continued their attacks with strong forces along the entire front north of the Terek. Effectively supported by *Oberstleutnant* Reinicke's agilely led artillery, *Panzergrenadier-Regiment 394*, *Kradschützen-Bataillon 3*, and *Feldzeug-Bataillon 8* drove off the enemy and inflicted heavy casualties, even though two armored trains had been employed in the Alpatowo. The situation turned dramatic in the northeast. The battle groups of Munzel, Erdmann, and Hoffmann had to move out against numerically superior enemy forces again and again. Sometimes defending, sometimes attacking, the men defeated individual or massed elements of the enemy, taking hundreds of prisoners and preventing the foe from advancing. *Hauptmann* Erdmann and his men successfully attacked in all directions in the area around Kretschetoff.

For six days, the division was in constant heavy combat against five rifle and three cavalry divisions, three rifle brigades, five separate regiments, one tank brigade, and one fighting-vehicle battalion.

The division commander pointed out to the chain of command that the division's successes in hitting all of the enemy formations at the right moment—created by skillful regrouping and the initiative of the battle groups—were only granting temporary relief. The division's current positions could not be held over the long haul with the addition of new forces, since the areas between the positions were too large, the mobile forces too weak and the excessive demands continuously placed on both bodies and materiel too great. In addition, the fuel available was insufficient for mobile operations. The commanding general responded that the deficiencies had been reported in a most pressing manner to the field army, but neither reinforcements nor fuel was to be counted on.

In order to clear up the situation around Kretschetoff once and for all, *Kampfgruppe Erdmann* moved out again on 7 December. On the previous day, it had taken 1,400 prisoners and captured four artillery pieces and many weapons there. The battle group encountered hard-fighting, well-entrenched enemy forces, and it had to swing out several times in an effort to envelop them. While doing so, Erdmann's *SPW* was hit by a mortar round. He was killed immediately, as were *Unteroffizier* Mirre and *Unteroffizier* Apostel. At that moment and in the most important sectors, the division lost one of its most capable officers, a man who had a great future ahead of him. In addition, the battalion administrative noncommissioned officer, *Feldwebel* Tegeler, was also killed that day. Two company commanders, *Oberleutnant* Busch of the 1st and *Oberleutnant* Seifert of the 2nd, were lost to wounds. *Hauptmann* Volckens of the armored regiment immediately assumed command of Erdmann's forces until *Hauptmann* Biegon could arrive. Volckens's forces were able to take another 600 prisoners. A senior supply sergeant from the 1st Battalion took another 100 prisoners along the supply route to Kretschetoff.

On 8 December, the alarming news filtered in that the enemy was at Besomkin, that is, to the rear of the position and was advancing not far from the road. The only available reserves, the field replacement battalion of *Major* Peschke, was alerted. The corps was also requested to release its reserves and to place them under the command of *Oberst* Zimmermann. The request was granted and Zimmermann, attacking from the north with the *II./Panzergrenadier-Regiment 3* and tank support, succeeded in pushing back the enemy after tough fighting and taking 300 prisoners.

As a precautionary measure on 7 December, the division had ordered preparations for an evacuation of Ischerskaja and a movement of the main line of resistance back to Stoderewskaja–Besorukin–Dydymkin–Stoderewskij. It was directed that all efforts must be made to evacuate all of the materiel in Ischerskaja, especially the ammunition, as well as the equipment, without any casualties. In addition, a new main line of resistance was to be established immediately. Up to then, it had only been planned to use it as a interdiction line and, as a result, it did not have any reinforced bunkers. Within the *II./Panzergrenadier-Regiment 3*, *Leutnant* Steinacker was given the mission of preparing the new position for his formation around Stoderewskaja.

Of course, the Soviets observed those preparations with their aircraft. For days on end, the enemy machines had scampered in the air space above interruption. The *Flak* was unable to do much against them, since the 8.8-centimeter guns were primarily employed in ground-combat roles. The Red Air Force was also active during the night, constantly dropping parachute flares, which lit up the terrain.

On 9 December, the division sent out the code word "Schlieffen." That meant that the positions jutting out far to the east, including the village of Ischerskaja itself, were cleared for withdrawal. The withdrawal movement started early in the morning. *Panzergrenadier-Regiment 394* and its attached elements and *Mörser-Abteilung 777* pulled back in such a manner that the companies most exposed were withdrawn first, pulling back

through the other positions to the rear. The deliberate withdrawal in a leapfrog manner worked without a hitch.

The *7./Panzergrenadier-Regiment 394* was the first to pull back, starting from the ferry house. It screened south of Ischerskaja. It was followed by the *3./Panzer-Pionier-Bataillon 39*, which then passed the mechanized infantry of the 5th Company. The 5th Company then took up a passage line at the Terek rail station. After those movements were completed, the main body of *Hauptmann* Müller-Röhlich's *II./Panzergrenadier-Regiment 394* disengaged. The 6th Company was sent off in the direction of Kriwonossoff, where it screened the village as part of *Kradschützen-Bataillon 3*. The *I./Panzergrenadier-Regiment 394* of *Hauptmann* Rode formed the rearguard, along with the *2./Kradschützen-Bataillon 3* and the *3./Panzer-Pionier-Bataillon 39*.

The lead elements of *Hauptmann* Müller-Röhlich's forces reached the Stoderewskaja rail station around 2200 hours, occupying the main line of resistance. *Hauptmann* Kunkel's *Bau-Bataillon 538*, which had been screening the bend in the river there, then moved to occupy the trenches in the village proper. The Russians did not pursue, with the result that the positions in the new main line of resistance could be improved the following day. The *II./Panzergrenadier-Regiment 394* occupied its positions as follows: The 7th Company remained on the rail line. It was adjoined on the left by the *2./Nordkaukasisches Infanterie-Bataillon 802*, with its Cherkessians under the command of *Oberleutnant* Litschmann. To the right of the 7th Company was the 3rd Company of the Cherkessians, under the command of *Oberleutnant* Zaag. The *3./Bau-Bataillon* screened up to the Terek. A battle group reporting to *Oberleutnant* Rövekamp was in an intermediate position at the Terek rail station. It consisted of the battalion's 2nd and 5th Companies, as well as some artillery. Contact between Stoderewskaja and Galjugajewskaja was maintained by a platoon from the 7th Company.

An *ad hoc* formation from the armor regiment under the command of *Hauptmann* Dewitz set up in the area around Kriwonossoff to cover the other retrograde operations. The tanks mastered the difficult mission by conducting an active defense and launching some immediate counterattacks to all sides. Unfortunately, all those were pinpricks that could not prevent the Soviets from gaining ground to the west. The enemy had identified the weak points of the German defenses. Kriwonossoff was soon enveloped on three sides. *Hauptmann* Dewitz pulled his tanks and antitank elements back to the edge of the village and set up an all-round defense. The antitank platoon of *Panzergrenadier-Regiment 394* was sent to Dewitz's location to lend support. But it was not needed in joining the fray, since the Russian fighting vehicles stopped outside of the village for unknown reasons.

The Soviets were more active to the north. They repeatedly attacked the outposts of *Panzergrenadier-Regiment 3* and *Major* Peschke's *Feld-Ersatz-Bataillon 83*. In the course of 9 and 10 December, the field-replacement battalion suffered twelve dead and twenty-four wounded. The mechanized infantry forces suffered eight dead and nineteen wounded during the same period. The weather was miserable. It rained until it started to snow during the night of 10–11 December. *Major* Groeneveld's battle group was also attacked. The attacks could not be stopped until they were about 200 meters from the main line of resistance. *Major* Cochenhausen's motorcycle infantry battalion did not allow the enemy to make it through Dowlatkin.

Munzel's and Hoffmann's battle groups disengaged from the enemy, only to be hard pressed again in all sectors over the next few days by strong forces.

As recorded in the division daily logs, there were numerous differences between the division and higher levels of command over the next few days concerning the conduct of operations. *Generalmajor* Westhoven was of the opinion that the formations should be pulled back to the new main line of resistance in a single bound, so that enough forces would be there to establish the new position and, above all, allow the forces to catch their breath and maintain their armored vehicles. According to orders from the field-army group, attacks by strong groupings of combat forces were to delay the advance of the enemy until the arrival of new forces. Despite objections from the division that renewed mobile employment of *Kampfgruppe Munzel* would more than likely result in serious loss of materiel and success was questionable, the higher level of command ordered his forces to attack from the Tomasoff area in the direction of Kretschetoff–Scherstobitoff to eliminate enemy forces reported in the steppe there.

On 11 December, the regimental headquarters, *Panzer-Abteilung Stockmann*, the *I./Panzergrenadier-Regiment 3* (minus its 1st Company), *Kradschützen-Bataillon 3*, the *I./Panzer-Artillerie-Regiment 75* (minus one battery), and an armored reconnaissance section moved out. By the onset of darkness, the battle group succeeded in scattering enemy rifle columns and taking 400 prisoners. During the night, the forces set up an all-round defense and continued their reconnaissance-in-force the next morning. The battle group advanced across the steppe, widely dispersed. All of a sudden, ten T-34's and ten tanks of American manufacture appeared off to the left. They had not been identified by the battle group's armored reconnaissance section or by a friendly scout aircraft that happened to be flying overhead. Before the companies could react to the newly appeared enemy force, several tanks had been set alight. The Soviets exploited their surprise and fired with everything they had. In short order, eight German tanks and eight *SPW's* were burning or immobilized on the battlefield. The *7./Panzer-Regiment 6* lost all of its tanks. *Hauptmann* Volckens, the youngest Knight's Cross recipient of the regiment, had an arm shot off and died two days later. It was only the artillery that prevented worse from happening to the battle group.

Oberst Munzel immediately issued orders to return to the line of departure. The artillery covered the retrograde movement of the battle group, even though the forward observer was chased two kilometers away by the Russians. Despite that, he was still able to reach his battery. With some difficulty, the battle group reached its sector.

On 12 December, *Panzergrenadier-Regiment 394* gave up its intermediate position after the Soviets had conducted several thrusts toward the new main line of resistance in the course of the day. To do so, the enemy had to forfeit 226 prisoners, twelve machine guns, five antitank rifles, and a number of small arms. The disengagement from the intermediate position took place during the night. The 6th Company had no problems, although the 2nd Company that followed had a more difficult time of it, since the darkness made it difficult to find the way along the muddy routes. By morning light, however, the mechanized infantry had found their way back to the Stoderewskaja rail station. *Panzerkampfgruppe von Dewitz* finally also showed up, after having had to make a difficult move via the Terek rail station to Stoderewskaja.

In its new sector, the division established four battle groups. In the south, *Oberstleutnant* Pape held command over *Panzergrenadier-Regiment* 394 and the attached *Bau-Bataillon 538* and the *Nordkaukasisches Infanterie-Bataillon 802*. His command post was in Wesselowskoje, west of Mosdok. *Oberst* Zimmermann screened the area east of Schefatoff–Awaloff with the *II./Panzergrenadier-Regiment 3*, the field-replacement battalion, and attached engineers. *Major* Cochenhausen's motorcycle infantry was positioned east of Dowlatkin. *Oberst* Munzel held the area around Tomasoff with *Panzer-Regiment 6* and the *I./Panzergrenadier-Regiment 3*. All the way in the north was *Kampfgruppe Hoffmann*. *Oberstleutnant* Reinicke's divisional artillery and the attached mortar elements were distributed throughout the divisional sector to form points of main effort and ensure effective fire concentrations. The division command post was in East Bogatyr. The *III./Panzer-Regiment 6* of *Hauptmann* Prince zu Schaumburg-Lippe was in

Schefatoff. Since the battalion could not be equipped with armored vehicles because of the catastrophic vehicle situation, its men were employed as infantry. The companies, which had only just arrived from Kharkov, where they had been established, performed their unfamiliar mission well and were able to turn back the first Russian attacks against Schefatoff.

The enemy conducted major air attacks against the artillery positions. Around Tomasoff, the Red Air Force hit *Mörser-Abteilung 777* and also struck against the command post of the *I./Panzergrenadier-Regiment 3* in the village. The Soviet aircraft attacked in groups of ten to fifteen machines, which were always escorted by the same number of fighters. On a few occasions, German fighters suddenly showed up and gave chase.

In the days that followed, there were again large-scale attacks by Russian infantry and many tanks against the weak and widely separated strong-points of the division. There were new crises by the hour, intensified by the fact that the terrain was broken up by numerous depressions and the constant excessive wear and tear on the armored elements made only a portion of them operational at any given time. *Panzer-Pionier-Bataillon 39* gave a heroic account of itself. Two companies were overrun by tanks. Despite that, the men remained unflappable in their positions, completely cut off. The infantry that followed the tanks was driven off. It was not until next day that the overrun men were relieved by an immediate counterattack launched by *Hauptmann* Biegon's

When the positions of *Feldzeug-Bataillon 8* on the right wing were penetrated and individual Soviet tanks started making their way towards the artillery positions at high speed, *Hauptmann* Biegon led two *SPW's*, two *Panzer III's*, and two 7.5-centimeter self-propelled antitank guns on a trust into the right flank of the enemy forces that had broken through. While the lead Soviet tanks attacked a battery of the divisional artillery and were literally stopped between the guns, Biegon's forces took some commanding high ground from which it was able to engage a large number of high-value targets anywhere from 400 to 1,000 meters. In short order, six enemy tanks with mounted infantry were destroyed by the antitank guns. Unlimbering artillery pieces were shot to pieces with high-explosive rounds and the Soviets, some of whom were marching in company columns, were forced to the ground by on-board machine guns.

In the sector of *Kradschützen-Bataillon 3*, the enemy tanks were shot to pieces by light field howitzers and antitank guns in and behind the main line of resistance. The enemy infantry that had broken through between the strongpoints was driven back by means of immediate counterattacks. There were also intense attacks conducted in the sector of the *II./Panzergrenadier-Regiment 3*.

Bad news began arriving from the sector of the friendly forces to the north at Dydymkin, where Russian tank forces and infantry had broken through. In the sectors of *Kampfgruppe Hoffmann* and the *II./Flak-Regiment 24*,[8] where little infantry protection could be spared, the enemy tanks were stopped between the guns. In a short amount of time, *Leutnant* Noack's *1./Panzer-Regiment 6* knocked out six enemy tanks and numerous trucks. The Russians were well armed and were able to resupply their overwhelming amounts of artillery with lots of ammunition, since the supplies from the United States that were transported through Persia made it into the theater quickly. Of the tank regiments that were identified, the 221st and 225th were outfitted with T-34's and T-70's, while the 123rd had exclusively American tanks.[9]

By nimbly changing the attachment relationships, employing an extraordinary flexibility in the fire direction of the artillery, constantly forming new assault detachments and employing the weak armored elements for immediate counterattacks, it was always possible to prevent a catastrophe at the last moment. Whenever the situation was not clear, *Generalmajor* Westhoven would hurry to a hot spot, personally issue orders and remain in contact with the division operations officer, *Oberstleutnant i.G.* Voss, through wire or radio.

In the course of that constant and generally heavy combat, considerable casualties were taken. It was especially among the infantry that their numbers kept growing smaller. The organization of the division was a colorful, mixed bag; the organic elements only formed the framework. In the thirty-five kilometers of frontage, there were construction battalions, ordnance battalions, Russian volunteers, *Flak* battalions impressed into infantry and armor support in dire emergencies, alert companies, and separate engineer detachments. On top of all that, there was the worrisome scarcity of ammunition and fuel. The nagging thought never disappeared that there might not be enough to fend off the next attack. A lack of batteries also made it necessary to curtail radio usage. The radio operators and switchboard operators performed magnificently. Despite the constant high message traffic, the heavy artillery fire that continuously tore up the landlines and the many enemy penetrations, the signalers always provided the leadership with the vital communications connections.

In the southern sector, where *Oberstleutnant* Pape was in command, the enemy had pushed forward. On 16 and 17 December, he attacked several times from Galjugajewskij with armored support. On 19 December, there was an even more intense attack, this time supported by twenty tanks, heavy artillery, and mortars. The enemy's effort collapsed right in front of the main line of resistance in the massed fires of the artillery. A lost strongpoint was retaken by the bravely fighting Caucasians in an immediate counterattack. In the sector of *Kampfgruppe*

---

8. A *Flak* regiment whose two battalions and headquarters were habitually employed separately from one another. The 2nd Battalion reported to the *15. Flak-Division* during this period.

9. These were probably M3A3/A5 diesel-engine Lee/Grant's, which the Russians did not like since they were far inferior to the T-34, except for crew comfort.

Zimmermann, an enemy attack conducted by two regiments and twenty tanks against the left wing of *Kradschützen-Bataillon 3* at Besokurin ground to a halt in the face of well-placed artillery fire. The enemy pressure continued to be strong in the sector of *Pionier-Bataillon 52*. *Panzer-Regiment 4* (13. Panzer-Division), commanded by *Major* Morell, was placed at the disposal of the division for a few days. The regiment conducted several attacks and took 400 prisoners. Thanks to an active defense, the battle groups of Stockmann and Biegon were also able to contain the enemy and even push him back. It was a miracle that their vehicles were still operational in light of the continuous operations and the insufficient supply of spare parts. The maintenance companies and sections performed superhuman efforts.

Although the defense prevailed on the evening of 19 December against the enemy forces that were attacking along the entire front, the enemy moved up during the night and dug in. Although the friendly counterattacks created some breathing room, there were not enough infantry forces to comb through the terrain and occupy it.

Over the next few days, the constant movement of columns among the enemy was observed. There were also infantry and tank attacks all across the front. One bright spot was the report that an armored train was blazing like a torch after being hit several times.

A large-scale attack was launched across the entire front on 24, 25, and 26 December, the Russian infantry attacked over and over again. Packs of Russian armor supported them by fire. The tanks frequently tried to break through with mounted infantry. There was heavy fire on all of the positions from artillery, mortars and rocket launchers. In that situation, the few remaining operational tanks and *SPW's* had to be employed in support at the hot spots or to seal off and clear up penetrations. Thick fog frequently made observation difficult. It did carry the sounds of armor movement a long distance, however, and enabled the timely identification of enemy attacks.

A focal point of the operations was the area around Tomasoff, where *Hauptmann* Rode's *I./Panzergrenadier-Regiment 394*, as part of *Kampfgruppe Munzel*, was constantly being attacked. It was there that one forward observer particularly distinguished himself. He was overrun by tanks but remained in his observation post, where he forced the following infantry to seek cover due to the well-placed artillery fires he called in. The tanks that had broken through were taken care of in the rear area. The ones that had halted in front of the main line of resistance took the German positions under fire. But the battalion held. One company alone brought in 400 prisoners.

Then it was Christmas. There were no signs anywhere that the Soviets would let up over the holidays. The artillery fire continued unabated. *Oberfeldwebel* Lesch of the *6./Panzergrenadier-Regiment 3* conducted a patrol on Christmas Eve. He advanced as far as six kilometers behind the enemy front with two other soldiers and three Cossacks. He observed the approach march of a Russian regiment and brought two captured officers back.

Despite the continued combat activity, the division logistics officer and the division support command had been preparing for the celebration for some days. Personal demand items had been obtained and there were sufficient amounts of Christmas mail and packages, even though many of the packages still had not arrived from the homeland. A few of the companies even put up Christmas trees. Who knew how they had obtained the trees in an area where there were no growing trees for some distance? Whoever had a commercial radio and could set the dial to the German shortwave radio directed to the southeast could hear the sounds of bells from the homeland. The division's chaplains and commanders held simple celebrations, with *Panzer-Regiment 6* holding its in a sheep stall. In the sector of the *I./Panzergrenadier-Regiment 394*, Cossacks sang their Christmas songs in the commander's bunker.

The division commander visited several companies in position along the front lines. When he returned and distributed Christmas gifts to the various sections of the division headquarters, the news burst in that ten enemy tanks had moved forward to Hill 139.4 at Dowlatkin shortly before darkness. That hill was occupied by a platoon from *Kradschützen-Bataillon 3* and dominated the terrain to the west. As a result of the concentrated fires from the tanks, the motorcycle infantry were held down in their holes and could not engage the Russian infantry. They were driven back. With the support of a few tanks and a platoon from the *I./Panzergrenadier-Regiment 3*, the strongpoint was later retaken.

The *XXXX. Panzer-Korps* announced its successes for the month of December in a general order. According to the corps, the forces of the corps, primarily the *3. Panzer-Division*, accomplished the following in captured or destroyed: "8,037 prisoners, 1,037 deserters, 68 tanks, 27 armored cars, 34 artillery pieces, 74 antitank guns, 223 mortars, 286 antitank rifles, numerous small arms and materiel, including two regimental standards captured by the *I./Panzergrenadier-Regiment 3*."

On Christmas Day, the tried and tested acting commander of the *8./Panzer-Regiment 6*, *Leutnant* Becker, received the German Cross in Gold.

That Christmas Eve, the entire division was involved in heavy fighting across its sectors. The enemy's heavy artillery fire continued without pause. Since the enemy attack on the positions of *Kradschützen-Bataillon 3* had resulted in the loss of almost an entire platoon and the battalion had no more reserves, two platoons from *Panzer-Pionier-Bataillon 39* were sent forward during the night to reinforce the motorcycle infantry manning Hill 139.4. *Hauptmann* Hoffmann received the mission of reconnoitering a position for emplacing antitank guns that could place flanking fires on the hill. The tank company positioned in Awaloff received orders to be prepared to defend at first light from a position behind the high ground.

The measures proved themselves when the Russians attacked there again the next morning.

Three tanks were knocked out and prisoners brought back after an immediate counterattack was conducted. Christmas Eve was barely over when the Russian guns opened fire in front of the sector of the *I./Panzergrenadier-Regiment 394*. *Hauptmann* Rode's mechanized infantry sprang out of their bunkers, and the forward observers manned their scissors scopes. The Soviets were coming. At least thirty tanks were moving ahead of the riflemen. The commands went to the firing batteries, the antitank-gun positions and the machine-gun nests: "Fire!" Christmas morning was filled with the sounds of bursting and crashing rounds, the whine of rifle bullets, the detonation of hand grenades, the rattling of tanks and the moaning of those hit. After the sounds of battled ebbed a few hours later, twenty enemy tanks were alight: T-34's and American vehicles. The Soviets had to pull back.

On 25 December the following entry was made into the daily logs at 1300 hours:

Oberst Munzel relayed his impressions to the division commander, after he had inspected his entire sector this morning. According to him, the enemy artillery fire continued to be very heavy and well placed today. The enemy attacks were stopped early by friendly artillery fire, and the enemy infantry has suffered great losses. As a result of placing tanks behind the main line of resistance, the friendly tanks were ready for operations quickly and were able to turn back every effort to roll up the main line of resistance.

In that round of fighting, the brave acting commander of the *1./Panzer-Regiment 6*, *Leutnant* Noack, was killed. The next few days passed relatively quietly. It was only in the headquarters and the rear-area services that the work tempo was high. The *1. Panzer-Armee* had ordered measures taken to be prepared to withdraw from the Caucasus; they were to be kept secret. As a result of the threatening developments around Stalingrad and the headlong advance of the Russian field armies to the Dona and the Donez, *Heeresgruppe A* was suddenly threatened with being cut off in a major way. Pressed by the field-army group, which was led by *Generaloberst* Kleist at the time, Hitler was just then coming to the decision to pull the most exposed portion, the eastern wing with the *1. Panzer-Armee* of *General der Kavallerie* Mackensen, back to a line running Pjatigorsk–Praskoweja. At the time, the *1. Panzer-Armee* consisted of the *III. Panzer-Korps* (*General der Waffen-SS* Steiner) with the *13. Panzer-Division*, the *370. Infanterie-Division*, the Romanian 2nd Mountain Division, and *Kampfgruppe Steinbauer*; the *LII. Armee-Korps* (*General der Infanterie* Ott) with the *50.* and *111. Infanterie-Divisionen*; and the *XXXX. Panzer-Korps* (*Generalleutnant* Henrici) with the *3. Panzer-Division*, *Gruppe Felmy*, and *Kampfgruppe Jungschulz*.

It was a relief to all concerned when the division operations officer returned from the corps headquarters on 30 December with the news that a withdrawal to a line running Budenowsk–Woronzowo–Aleksandrowskoje was planned (Movement Directive: *Winterwetter*—"Winter Weather").

At 1700 hours on 31 December, the corps order for *Winterwetter* was received. It was to be executed starting at 1700 hours on 2 January 1943 and proceed in stages. Preliminary movements for non-combat elements were to be started during the night of 31 December–1 January.

The unit and formation leaders received the necessary orders and directives. According to them, all non-operational vehicles were to be taken to the rear or rail-loaded at Mosdok. At the same time, all elements were to get rid of superfluous equipment.

As it dawned on New Year's, thick fog obscured the steppes, with the result that observation was very limited. During the night, the guards had heard the rattling of vehicles for hours on end. The hours slowly passed, and the fog only lifted slowly. All of a sudden, the earth started trembling. A firestorm rained down on the neighbors of the division to the north from hundreds of artillery pieces. The fires soon started shifting south, reaching the left wing of the division, where the light *Flak* were positioned. Russian rounds then started falling on the positions of *Panzergrenadier-Regiment 3* and *Panzer-Regiment 6*. Fortunately, in the sector of the *I./Panzergrenadier-Regiment 3*, the barrage fires were too short. The thick fog did not allow anything at all to be identified. Instead, one heard the thunder of the engines of many tanks in between the detonations of the impacting rounds. Were they ours or were they theirs? At the command post of *Kampfgruppe Munzel*, that fact could not be ascertained with certainty. Contact had been lost with the elements to the front.

Enemy tanks and rifle formations were attacking at the boundary between the division and *Kampfgruppe Jungschulz*. They overran the light *Flak* within the division sector and continued to advance west. *Major* Stockmann's tank battalion established a blocking position. The companies and platoons were widely dispersed, since no one knew where the enemy would turn. At the location of the *2./Panzer-Regiment 6* of *Oberleutnant* Fiehl, one heard the sound of fighting. *Oberfeldwebel* Blaich, a Knight's Cross recipient, and his platoon were suddenly facing sixty-two Russian tanks when the fog lifted for a moment. The situation was completely confused. *Major* Cochenhausen moved his companies forward.

Panzergrenadier-Regiment 3 was also attacked by the enemy. Some of the outposts had already been overrun. Soviet tanks were feeling their way along the Kura far to the west. It was there that *Oberfeldwebel* Kruse, a Knight's Cross recipient of the 7th Company, demonstrated his cold-bloodedness. Not losing his composure, he gathered his men and rallied them to resist. Without any type of artillery support, the mechanized infantry went after the Soviets, taking out the enemy riflemen and destroying several tanks. Later on, Kruse received the Oak Leaves to the Knight's Cross for his bold actions.

Based on the dangerous development, *Generalmajor* Westhoven ordered the initiation of the retrograde movements that day, deciding not to wait until the following day. During the afternoon of 1 January, the rear-area services, supply elements, logistics sections and trains elements moved out of their quarters. The batteries moved out of their positions somewhat later and were positioned and ready to fire behind the Prawobereshny Canal at Chotajew that night.

The southern sector of the division was not ordered to move out until the morning of 2 January. Although the enemy pressed against the positions of *Panzergrenadier-Regiment 394* since the early-morning hours, he was turned back at all locations, despite the heavy fog. Around 1400 hours, the *1./Nordkaukasisches Infanterie-Bataillon 802* was the first unit to leave its dugouts and move to the rear. The *II./Panzergrenadier-Regiment 394* and *Pionier-Bataillon 52* evacuated their positions by the onset of darkness, without being bothered by the Russians. In contrast, Russian tank elements had latched themselves to the heels of the *I./Panzergrenadier-Regiment 394*. During the cold winter's night that followed, contact was lost with the enemy. In the darkness, the 1st Battalion used the map to occupy its designated positions in the main line of resistance. Early the next morning, it discovered it had already been partially bypassed. The battalion headquarters was almost caught, and it was only with difficulty that the battalion was able to fend off the superior numbers of the enemy and his tanks. Given covering fire by its attached antitank platoon and an alerted rocket-launcher battery, it was able to disengage from the enemy and occupy a better position along the edge of a village.

Panzergrenadier-Regiment 3 disengaged from the enemy, although it was still threatened by eighty tanks on its left flank. *Major* Stockmann's armored group was committed to the southwest of Pijew against approaching T-34's. A bitter engagement ensued, which the German companies could only conduct as a delaying action. *Leutnant* Huhn and the tankers of his company particularly distinguished themselves. Nonetheless, the German forces had to pull back to the

west in the end. The employment of the tanks had made the retrograde movements of the mechanized infantry easier, however. By 1800 hours, all of them had reached the new main line of resistance. *Panzergrenadier-Regiment 394* remained east of Durtujew, while *Panzergrenadier-Regiment 3* was positioned around Russkij.

At Russkij, the approach of large Soviet armor elements was observed. *Generalmajor* Westhoven employed the divisional antitank battalion. When it reached the front lines, it immediately opened fire. *Panzerabteilung Stockmann*, which was covering the retrograde movements, was ordered to turn north by radio by the division operations officer to attack the enemy in the rear. That measure resulted in success. The Russians took considerable casualties and pulled back.

Because of the fog and the hoarfrost that developed as a result of the thaw, the armor regiment encountered many difficulties. The timely issue of fuel for the columns to keep them moving was a problem. For instance, the dismounted *III./Panzer-Regiment 6* of *Hauptmann* Prince zu Schaumburg-Lippe had to be relayed to the rear by trucks.

The newly designated armored regiment commander, *Oberstleutnant* Schmidt-Ott, assumed his duties in that most difficult situation. On 3 January, *Oberst* Munzel was transferred out of the division, along with the regimental surgeon, *Stabsarzt* Dr. Zülch. *Oberst* Oskar Munzel, who received the German Cross in Gold after his departure, became the commander of the tactics department at the armor school in Wünsdorf. *Oberst* Reinicke was also replaced in command of the divisional artillery around this time by *Oberst* Lattmann.

The Soviet Transcaucasus Front started its offensive on 3 January. The forces of Generals Chomenko and Melnik were able to cross the Terek the same day and take back Mosdok. The Russian field armies then pressed hard to the west and kept on the heels of the withdrawing German divisions. The *II./Panzergrenadier-Regiment 394* and *Pionier-Bataillon 52*, moving on the right wing of the division, were put in a tough spot on more than one occasion by enemy tanks and cavalry. The 5th Company of the mechanized infantry was scattered and was only able to cross the bridge over the Kura at Kurskaja at the last minute, before it was blown up.

The division moved to the northwest toward the Kuma in several march serials. The left wing, moving over bad and softened routes across the steppe, reached the river line at Woronzowo. As a precautionary measure, passage lines had been established there, where the forces had a chance to catch their breath and rearm and refuel to a relatively good extent. The scattered companies were assembled and reorganized. The formations fighting on the right wing disengaged from the enemy—sometimes only with the greatest of difficulty—and moved through the Gorkaja *balka* to the Kuma. The river line was reached by all elements of the division on 7 January, signaling the end to the first phase of the withdrawal. In order to remain relatively mobile, the division ordered all vehicles that were in tow and no longer able to be repaired with available means to be destroyed.

Strong enemy formations then managed to cross the Kuma in the sector of the right-hand neighbor, the *111. Infanterie-Division*, and enter Soldatsko-Aleksandrowskoje. The division immediately dispatched *Hauptmann* Müller-Röhlich's *II./Panzergrenadier-Regiment 394* there in order to protect its own flank and throw the enemy back. But when the battalion was attached to *Infanterie-Regiment 50* at some point between the rail station along the Kuma and Soldatsko-Aleksandrowskoje, it was already too late. The Soviets had taken both bridges and were leading additional forces across the river. The battalion went into position at the rail station and turned back all attacks, even after the infantry battalions pulled back. It was not until the danger arose that the battalion could be bypassed during the night that it pulled back to the division sector. The next day, it was attached to the armor regiment to screen in Ssolkolowskij. The Soviets crossed the river with additional forces during the night of 9–10 January, with the result that the

division had to disengage from the river line and pull back to the northwest along two roads (leading through Aleksandrowskoje and Tschernolesskoje). The armored regiment and *Hauptmann* Müller-Röhlich's battalion attacked the enemy forces, which were supported by tanks, on 11 January. There were some tough tank-on-tank engagements, before the enemy finally pulled back to the southeast. The badly shrunken *Infanterie-Regiment 50* of *Oberst* Friemel had linked up with the division's forces and participated in the immediate counterattacks.

The Russians then turned toward the northwest in an effort to envelop the *3. Panzer-Division* from there and to cut it off from the road. *Hauptmann* Rode's *I./Panzergrenadier-Regiment 394* engaged the enemy at Sablja and turned back all of his attacks.

Soviet divisions under Generals Korotejew and Koslow broke through north of Mineralnije Wody and threatened the *13. Panzer-Division*, which was holding there. *Generalmajor* Westhoven ordered the *II./Panzergrenadier-Regiment 394* to pull back at midnight in order to form a battle group with the *3./Panzer-Artillerie-Regiment 75* and a group from *Panzerjäger-Abteilung 543* to assist the sister armored division. Just as the men got ready to move out, the report came in that the *13. Panzer-Division* had disengaged from the enemy and the mission was no longer needed.

The continued withdrawal of the *3. Panzer-Division* in the direction of Aleksandrowskoje proved to be increasingly difficult. A few vehicles slid off the icy roads and others got stuck in roadside ditches and could only be recovered by means of tanks or artillery prime movers. Despite the black ice and the darkness of night, the division finally reached the area around Kruglolesskoje and Blagodarnoje.

There were several instances during the time of fuel not being brought forward by rail. The division would be immobilized for a while, while the Russians continued to move and then block the logistics lines of communication. Thanks to the admirable inventiveness and toughness of the fuel-truck drivers, the vehicles always eventually succeeded in getting through and reaching their units.

The division fought its way farther back to the northwest and encountered rear-area service entities along the railway line northeast of Woroschilowsk, while the few tanks of the division conducted an attack south of Aleksandrowskoje against cavalry and rifle formations in an effort to get the neighboring *50. Infanterie-Division* out of a dangerous situation. The movements, which were always conducted after the onset of twilight and along iced-over and pitch-black roads, were a dangerous undertaking.

Up to the start of evening twilight, the enemy would push himself forward to within penetrating distance of the "positions." The formations had to disengage in those critical situations and reach their vehicles. It was not the time for a vehicle to break down or get hit. Those types of critical moments occurred almost daily during the first phase of retrograde operations. The forces were then on the move during the night, moves which were usually difficult and not without a lot of delays. The rearguards then had to close back up with their formations. As it turned first light, the new "position" was reached. In reality, it was simply open terrain. The forces had to dig in as best they could and once again wait for the pursuing enemy. No one would think much about sleep.

The movement to the west and the northwest developed into a race between the Russians and the *1. Panzer-Armee*. It was frequently the case that Russian formations were much farther west than the German divisions, which had to defend to the east while suffering through the misery of a withdrawal. A mixed enemy formation succeeded in getting to Srgiejewskoje, along the road between Aleksandrowskoje and Nadesha, and blocking the withdrawal route. The division command post was also there. The *I./Panzergrenadier-Regiment 394* was cut off. There were no longer any communications with the division or the regiment. *Major* Cochenhausen, who was with the battalion, since one of his companies

was attached to it, decided to reestablish communications. Against the advice of *Hauptmann* Rode, Cochenhausen and his driver took off into the darkness. A motorcycle messenger, who had been sent along, reported a short while later that the staff car had rammed into a T-34 on the road and was burning. Despite that, the commander of the motorcycle infantry battalion found his way back to the mechanized infantry battalion command post a short while later.

Hauptmann Rode then decided to clear the road in the moonlit night and attempt to link up with the division. Without suffering any losses, an attached assault gun platoon, along with a dismounted company, was able to set alight at pointblank range four out of eight enemy tanks that were waiting in an ambush position along behind a reverse slope. The remaining enemy tanks were able to save themselves by fleeing at high speed.

The reinforced *I./Panzergrenadier-Regiment 394* passed through the area that had been cleared out with four columns next to one another. It was trailed by a powerful rearguard. In the process of moving past the burning tanks, there was even time to recover the officer's trunk of *Major* Cochenhausen, which had been placed on the rear deck of one of the vehicles as a spoil of war.

On 15 January, the *3. Panzer-Division* ended the second phase of its withdrawal. There was a short break, whereby the maintenance sections continued to work feverishly in an effort to get all vehicles more or less capable of movement back into operational status. Many of the units only had half of their authorized strengths of trucks, staff cars, motorcycles and prime movers. A makeshift solution that proved beneficial was the presence of the *panje* sections, which had been established as a precautionary measure.

The third phase of the withdrawal started on 18 January. The *3.* and *11. Panzer-Divisionen* used the same road to move back across the railway line at and around Woroschilowsk to Michailowskoje. From there, they moved via

Isobilnaja to Nowo-Aleksandrowsk, north of Armawir. With that, the division again crossed the road it had used five months previously, when it had advanced into the Caucasus with verve and confidence.

At this point, it would be appropriate to remember the assistance in arms provided by the Caucasians.

The continued movement back to the northwest went somewhat more smoothly than previously, despite the bad road network. The Soviets were no longer pressing so hard. Hitler, who initially wanted to leave the entire field-army group in the Kuban bridgehead, issued orders on 22 January that portions of the *1. Panzer-Armee* were to reach the Don via Rostow. On 24 January, the order was amended to include the entire field army. It was to be allocated to *Heeresgruppe Don*, which found itself in extremely heavy fighting with torn-open fronts.

Crossing the Kuban, the *3. Panzer-Division* reached the area around Tichorezk on the rail line to Rostow on 23 January. That same day, a battle group composed of the *II./Panzergrenadier-Regiment 394*, the *IV. Panzer-Artillerie-Regiment 75*, one platoon of *Panzerjäger-Abteilung 543*, and one *Flak* platoon from the *10./Panzergrenadier-Regiment 394*, was ordered by the corps, which was located in Fastowezkaja, to screen the northern flank of the *1. Panzer-Armee*. The battle group moved out along a difficult route to Nesamajewskaja, where it arrived on the morning of 24 January. *Hauptmann* Müller-Röhlich organized his forces. *Oberleutnant* Schulze, the commander of the 7th Company, received the mission of reconnoitering to all sides with his attached *Flak*, antitank gun, and infantry gun assets and to establish contact with the Cossack squadrons operating across the sector and *SS-Panzer-Grenadier-Division "Wiking,"* adjoining on the left.

The main body of the battle group then continued moving in the direction of Plosskaja. The weather had turned around; a frost had returned and the softened roads once again turned completely solid. The situation was uncertain. The mechanized infantry elements were surprised by two Russian tanks in Plosskaja on 25 January. The Russian tanks shot two self-propelled *Flak* and one infantry gun to bits. The mechanized infantry defended as best they could. The two howitzers that were brought forward could not fire as a result of the terrific cold, which froze up their mechanisms. But an unknown cannoneer succeeded in knocking out a Russian tank with an antitank rifle, thus putting an end to the nightmare.

Oberleutnant Schulze ordered his forces to pull back to Nowo-Iwanowskaja. Soviet formations were moving about in the sector in front of him, but there was no enemy contact. *Panzergrenadier-Regiment 394* established a second battle group under *Oberleutnant* Arnoldt. It consisted of the 9th and 10th companies of the regiment and one platoon from *Panzerjäger-Abteilung 543*. It was sent to Besorowskij in order to block along the Jeja. Both of the groups blew up all of the bridges outside of the villages, in addition to their screening and reconnaissance assignments.

Oberleutnant Dietrich's *5./Panzergrenadier-Regiment 3* underwent an odyssey of sorts. When the company's communications were lost, the unit lost contact with its parent battalion. After two days spent snaking its way at night between enemy columns and occasionally marching ahead of them and fighting its way through, the company reached the regiment—albeit without vehicles—where it was enthusiastically greeted, since it had already been written off.

It was not until 26 January that there was fighting again. This time it was in the form of skirmishes with cavalry, which were quickly driven away after a few rounds from the howitzers of the 4th Battery of the divisional artillery. *Kaukasisches Infanterie-Bataillon 802* was also integrated into the lines of the division. That day, the battle groups identified elements of the Soviet I Cavalry Corps, consisting of the 9th, 10th and 30th Cavalry Divisions. The XII Guards Cavalry Corps adjoined to the south. All of those forces were oriented to the northwest in the direction of Rostow.

Oberst Zimmermann was given command of the sector along the Jeja on 26 January. His 9th and 10th Companies, under the combined command of *Oberleutnant* Comberg, relieved *Gruppe Arnoldt*. The enemy's 151st Infantry Division attacked the Caucasian infantry battalion in Kalnibolotskaja on 28 January, forcing the Caucasians back. *Kampfgruppe Schulze* pulled back as well in order not to be cut off. The mechanized infantry then started screening in Nesamajewskaja. The battle group of the *II./Panzergrenadier-Regiment 394*, which was being led at that point by the commander of *Panzerjäger-Abteilung 543*, *Hauptmann* Hoffmann, since *Hauptmann* Müller-Röhlich had turned ill, was relieved by the Caucasian battalion during the night of 29–30 January, whereupon the mechanized infantry returned to the division.

The *3. Panzer-Division* was east of Irinowka, where the forces of the 9th, 10th, and 30th Cavalry Divisions were assaulting its positions, especially those of *Kradschützen-Bataillon 3*. The tanks that were still operational conducted an advance to the east as far as Rossoschinskij, where they established contact with the *11. Panzer-Division*. The latter division and SS-*Panzer-Grenadier-Division "Wiking"* were part of the *III. Panzer-Korps*. *Generalleutnant* Breith assumed command of the corps from *General der Waffen-SS* Steiner during this period.

By the end of January, the division had a frontage extending some 120 kilometers. That allowed most of the remaining formations of the *1. Panzer-Armee of General der Kavallerie* Mackensen to pull back through Rostow. On 30 January, the only forces of the field army forward of the Don were the headquarters of the *XXXX. Panzer-Korps*, the *General-Kommando z.b.V.* (Felmy's corps), and the troop units of the *3.* and *11. Panzer-Divisionen* and the *444. Sicherungs-Division*.[10]

The *3. Panzer-Division* moved ever closer to Rostow each day. On 31 January, its rear-area services reached the road to Rostow, after moving from Kuschtschewskaja through Bataisk. The division had set up a collection point at Bataisk, which directed the forces to Ssambeck, north of Rostow. *Hauptmann* Prince zu Schaumburg-Lippe ran the reception point, which collected all of the division elements and organized them, as they appeared.

The retrograde movements of the troop formations did not always go according to plan on the icy roads. It was imperative to not only deal with the hard-pressing formations of the Soviet 44th Army and the cavalry formations, but also with the rigors of the weather. The march routes were in indescribable condition and demanded the utmost from man, horse and engine. The columns moved next to one another back towards Rostow on the roads. There were disruptions that led to stoppages that lasted for hours. It was possible at the last moment to redirect the trains and horse-drawn columns that had been ordered into the Kuban bridgehead across the ice bridge over the Don Delta towards Rostow.

A tank driver from the *2./Panzer-Regiment 6* has provided a firsthand account of the demands placed on the forces at the time. At the time of the narrative, the company had only two operational *Panzer IV's*, one of which had the crew of *Feldwebel* Kraatz, *Gefreiter* Sternberg, *Gefreiter* Sasse, and *Gefreiter* Kullrich:[11]

> As a result of damage to the fuel pump, we had to move to the rear. Half lying on the turret floor, the loader had to operate the emergency hand pump. The snow was

---

10. 444th Security Division, originally formed in March 1941 using a large number of personnel from the *221. Infanterie-Division* as cadre. As implied by its designation, the division was really intended not for frontline operations, but for protecting rear-area installations. As much as can be ascertained, the division probably had a reinforced infantry regiment at the time (coming from the *221. Infanterie-Division*), as well as battalion equivalents of Turkestani and Cossack volunteers, an artillery battalion, and a tank company.

11. For unknown reasons, the fifth member of the crew is not mentioned.

crunchingly hard; it was -20 [-4 Fahrenheit]. Our tracks looked like polished chrome; the winter extensions had long since been worn round.[12] A slightly precipitous, mirror-smooth icy road. The tank started sliding. The crew jumped off. The tank landed in a frozen-over road ditch. The immediate efforts to turn and back up caused the blanket of ice to break. The *Panzer IV* sank deeper and deeper; water was already seeping through the ground vents, which were no longer tight. Only the turret jutted out. The motor gave up! Then it turned night. It was pitch black. Long columns plodded past, but the ranks grew thinner each time. An order came by radio: Hold on! We're coming! There was hardly any movement on the road any more. We were freezing and filled with uncertainty. All of sudden, engine noises. The Russians? No, it was the maintenance officer, Bärwinkel, with two eighteen-ton prime movers. You could always rely on him. Each of the prime movers was towing a *Panzer III*. Bärwinkel came to us and looked everything over. No way we were going to blow it up! The prime movers were blocked; a *Panzer III* served as a brace. Using the winch, the tank was pulled out, turning over twice. Water, ice and leaking oil transformed the interior of the fighting vehicle in a crazy manner. We moved on. We reached our regiment . . .

Similar events transpired a thousand times that winter. In the end, it was the toughness and proficiency, not to mention the bravery, of the individual soldiers of all ranks that allowed them to deal with the vicissitudes of the terrain and the constant threats from partisans, stragglers and scattered enemy units.

The final rearguards of the division, elements of both mechanized infantry regiments and the 1st Battalion of the divisional artillery, crossed the bridge over the Don in Rostow during the night of 1–2 February. In a period of exactly four weeks, the *3. Panzer-Division* had been the last division of the *1. Panzer-Armee* to engage an ever-pressing enemy force over a stretch of 700 kilometers. The losses in tanks, trucks and other vehicles were higher than those that had been sustained during the withdrawal from Tula in the first winter catastrophe of 1941–42.

The commander in chief of the *1. Panzer-Armee*, *General der Kavallerie* Mackensen, wrote:

> That the retreat could be concluded successfully . . . is primarily thanks to the magnificent leadership and attitude of the *3. Panzer-Division* on the open flank and the left flank of the field army! I would like to openly express that here as the former commander in chief, who was responsible, to honor the wonderful division. *Generaloberst* Kleist characterized the retreat of the field army as a "masterpiece" when I reported to him by telephone. That renown is due to no small extent to the division mentioned.

The division, which temporarily quartered in the Taganrog area, was attached to the *LVII. Panzer-Korps* of *General der Panzertruppen* Kirchner. *General der Panzertruppen* Henrici, the commanding general of the *XXXX. Panzer-Division*, took his leave of the division in a general order dated 6 February 1943, in which he said, in part:

> The *3. Panzer-Division*, fighting as part of the corps ever since 29 May 1942, has finally departed the *XXXX. Panzer-Korps*

---

12. The so-called *Ostketten* ("Eastern tracks") were extension that fit onto the ends of the normal track in an effort to decrease ground pressure and thus increase mobility in snow, ice, and soft ground. Low ground pressure was a well-known deficiency of German tanks until the introduction of the *Panther* and *Tiger*, which had significantly wider tracks.

effective 29 January 1943. It particularly distinguished itself in decisive attacks during the summer offensive of 1942 through verve and offensive spirit, living up to its reputation. In the even more difficult defensive fighting along the Terek, it had proven its magnificent, unshakeable defensive strength in holding firm against superior numbers . . . 10,000 prisoners taken, 150 tanks destroyed, 36 artillery pieces, and 76 antitank guns destroyed or captured . . . has proven what a brave and cohesive force can accomplish. It can always be proud of that.

Nebelwerfer support the efforts to establish a bridgehead over the Terek at Ischerskaja.

Attack on the far side of the Terek into the steppe. This image was taken during an attack through a vision port of an *SPW*. The *SPW* seen ahead was that of the commander of the *I./Panzergrenadier-Regiment 3, Hauptmann* Erdmann.

Men of *Panzergrenadier-Regiment 394* cross the Terek in pneumatic rafts.

The next squads to cross make their way to the riverbank.

Military cemetery at Ischerskaja. The graves were established in four rows. A large cross was placed at the rear of the cemetery overlooking everything.

Soldiers and officers take their leave of fallen comrades at Ischerskaja.

Dedication of the division headquarters in Awaloff on 12 October 1942.

The command pennant and the "bear" in the division headquarters.

Building housing the division commander and the operations staff. The structure was built by the division itself.

A Cossack reconnaissance section along the Terek.

Oberstleutnant i.G. Voss, the division operations officer during difficult times.

Generalmajor Westhoven assumed command of the division on 1 October 1942.

Withdrawal from the Terek. *Hauptmann* Biegon, the acting commander of the *I./Panzergrenadier-Regiment 3*, with his adjutant, *Leutnant* Arnim, and the radio noncommissioned officer, *Unteroffizier* Korwandtke.

CHAPTER 5

From the Don to the Donez: The Battle for Kharkov in 1943

The major Russian offensive of the winter of 1943 tore apart the entire German southern front in the space of a few weeks. *Generalfeldmarschall* Manstein assumed command of all of the German forces between the Don and the Donez. It was intended for the newly formed *Heeresgruppe Don* to prevent the Soviets from entering the Donez industrial area. By then, the *6. Armee* of *Generalfeldmarschall* Paul had capitulated in Stalingrad. With its inadequate forces, the *4. Panzer-Armee* of *Generaloberst* Hoth, which had been sent in to relieve the beleaguered force, had been unable to break through to the *6. Armee*. In the process, it was also badly battered; it was busy trying to reestablish a cohesive front. The formations of the *1. Panzer-Armee* of *Generaloberst* Mackensen were conducting retrograde operations at the end of January and beginning of February in the area northwest of Rostow. The divisions were attempting to reorganize their forces. The enemy field armies succeeded in reaching the Donez and crossing the iced-over river. Just as they had the previous year, they entered the industrial area between Slawjansk and Isjum.

Italian and Romanian forces were streaming westward, uncontrolled.

The *3. Panzer-Division* was moving north along the Taganrog–Gorlowka rail line. Snowdrifts and exhaustion on the part of the drivers led to stoppages, delays and accidents. The columns became widely separated and could only be held together by liaison officers on sleds. About 100 vehicles were stranded on the road to Nikitino in a snowstorm. The division had established a collection point there. The men had to dismount their vehicles again and again to shovel the snowed-over routes clear or give stranded vehicles a push.

On 3 and 4 February, the division gradually assembled its battalions and other troop elements in that village. At noon on 4 February, *Panzergrenadier-Regiment 3* and *Kradschützen-Bataillon 3* headed in the direction of Gorlowka along newly reconnoitered and snow-cleared routes. Since no better routes were to be found north of Nikitino, *Generalmajor* Westhoven decided to reroute the division through Stalino in an effort to get to the next march objective, Artemowsk. It was difficult to command and control, since radio silence was ordered for all of the forces.

The order for radio silence was lifted somewhat starting on 6 February, since Soviet formations were already pressing on Kramatorskaja north of Artemowsk. The field army directed that the *3. Panzer-Division* was to be employed immediately, and it was to occupy a defensive position to the north. *Oberst* Zimmermann's *Panzergrenadier-Regiment 3* and *Major* Cochenhausen's *Kradschützen-Bataillon 3* were given all available fuel. Those forces reached the area north of Nowo-Aleksandrowka that same day, and both elements had immediate contact with the enemy.

The main body of the still operational portions of *Panzergrenadier-Regiment 394* arrived in Artemowsk on 7 February. Many of the overworked vehicles and prime movers of the divisional artillery were no longer capable of being driven and disappeared in the snow. Weeks of tireless work on the part of the maintenance sections and companies would pass before they would be operational again.

In Artemowsk, *Generalmajor* Westhoven reported in to his predecessor, *Generalleutnant* Breith, to whose *III. Panzer-Korps* the division was attached. Since the enemy was already advancing west to the north of Artemowsk and the *7. Panzer-Division*, which was positioned there, had to extend its wings too far, the divi-

sion was ordered to relieve portions of the neighboring division. *Panzergrenadier-Regiment 3* and the fighting elements of *Panzer-Regiment 6* had already swung to the northwest to block the Soviets at Rai-Aleksandrowka. *Kradschützen-Bataillon 3* had already moved through Woroschilowka, and *Panzergrenadier-Regiment 394* was directed to establish contact with the motorcycle infantry. The 2nd Battalion of the latter regiment, which *Hauptmann* Müller-Röhlich again commanded, launched an attack against Woroschilowka with *Oberleutnant* Schulze's 7th Company. The Soviets had reestablished themselves there. Despite strong resistance, the mechanized infantry were able to enter the village and throw the Russians back to the high ground at Petrowskoje. With that, contact was also reestablished with *Kradschützen-Bataillon 3*.

The 6th Company was directed to relieve non-divisional elements at Bondarnoje at the same time. The forces to be relieved could not be located, with the result that the company was left to its own devices in the pitch-black night. Preparations for the defense had not yet been completed, when an enemy ski patrol suddenly showed up in the middle of the company area. The enemy entered the positions that had just been established. They overran *Oberfeldwebel* Bremer's platoon, and he was killed in the fighting. The enemy exploited his surprise and moved into the center of the village, where he pushed back the machine-gun squads and was also able to scatter *Feldwebel* Skerka's platoon.

Hauptmann Müller-Röhlich, who was making the rounds with *Leutnant* Schöninger, ran into the advancing Russians. The officers alerted the headquarters section of the company. Leading the drivers, messengers and radio operators, the officers launched an immediate counterattack against the Soviet ski troops. Artillery from the *7. Panzer-Division*, which was still in position in the area, joined the fray, and it was possible to hold up the Soviets for the time being. Since the enemy was constantly being reinforced, however, Bondarnoje had to be evacuated eventually. In the process, *Leutnant* Möller, the acting company commander, and *Leutnant* Schöninger were badly wounded.

By then, the regiment was readying forces for an immediate counterattack. *Hauptmann* Müller-Röhlich moved out around 0800 hours with his 5th and 7th Companies, reinforced by a *Panzer IV*, two self-propelled antitank guns and four self-propelled *Flak*. Both of the reinforced companies advanced step by step against the stubbornly defending enemy. After two hours of fighting, they were able to advance all the way to the east side of the village. The 1st Battalion was then employed against those remaining Soviet forces, reinforced by the heavy weapons of the 2nd Battalion that were on hand. Shortly after the onset of darkness, that portion of the village had also been retaken. The spoils of war included the taking of forty prisoners and the capture of four antitank guns, six machine guns, and eight antitank rifles. Since the 2nd Battalion had been considerably battered—the 6th Company, for instance, had only one *Feldwebel* and one machine-gun crew left—it was relieved by the 1st Battalion.

While *Panzergrenadier-Regiment 394* was finding itself facing a dangerous situation in Bondarnoje on the night of 8–9 February, its sister regiment, *Panzergrenadier-Regiment 3*, scored a major success on the other wing of the division. *Oberst* Zimmermann's battalions had advanced far to the north. The 1st Battalion, which *Hauptmann* Dittmer had assumed command of only recently, was approaching the important transportation hub of Slawjansk along the road east of Kramatorskaja. The city had played an important role the previous year, when it became a pivot point for the fronts. It appeared that the same thing was going to happen again in 1943.

Enemy motorized and horseback forces had succeeded in crossing the Donez northeast of Slawjansk and breaking through the German defensive positions. It became the mission of the *I./Panzergrenadier-Regiment 3* to establish contact with the forces that were pulling back and to prevent the continued advance of the Russians.

Patrols sent forward determined that the city was full of enemy forces. Up to that point, however, the mechanized infantry had not run into any enemy combat outposts.

Hauptmann Dittmer wanted to exploit the opportune situation and decided to conduct a surprise attack from the march. The companies of the 1st Battalion mounted their vehicles, got their weapons ready, turned over the engines of the *SPW's* and rattled at high speed into Slawjansk, just as they had done at Rossosch half a year earlier. The enemy was so surprised by the "bum rush" that he barely had any time to put up a defense. By the afternoon, the men of the 1st Battalion were in charge of the important city not far from the Donez. *Hauptmann* Dittmer later received the Knight's Cross for the bold deed.

At the beginning of February, the Russians started another offensive, and it led to a deep penetration of the German front. After Kharkov fell, the enemy advanced with armor forces to the southwest, reaching a point just before the crossings over the Dnjepr at Dnjepropetrowsk, which also interdicted the logistical lines of communication and the lines of retreat. Once again, the enemy was to the rear of the German front. After hard fighting, it was possible to bring the Russians to a standstill and then transition to a counterattack.

To that end, the division received orders from the *1. Panzer-Armee*—it reported directly to the field army at this point—to take the banks of the Donez. *Stukas* were allocated as part of the preparation, and the attack was conducted on 28 February by the armored battle group of the division under the command of *Major* Stockmann (adjutant: *Oberleutnant* Adamek). The tanks were supported by *Hauptmann* Müller-Röhlich's *II./Panzergrenadier-Regiment 394*. In Nikolajewka, the Soviets defended stubbornly with tanks and Stalin organs. Despite that, the village was taken. In the process, an intact Stalin organ fell into German hands. On 1 March, the village was combed again, followed by the taking of Raigorodok. Moving from Kalenki on 2

March, three villages along the Donez were taken. The route to the river was clear.

Panzergrenadier-Regiment 394 established itself along the river between Dranowka and Sakotnoje and prepared to defend. *Panzergrenadier-Regiment 3* screened in the bend of the Donez northeast of Slawjansk. The divisional artillery set up firing positions throughout the divisional sector. *Panzergrenadier-Lehr-Regiment 901* was temporarily attached to the division and expanded the screening area as far as west of Lissitschansk. The division headquarters with the command staff was in Artemowsk. The 2nd Medical Company set up a clearing station there as well, and the local populace was also treated. Russian female military surgeons assisted the German doctors.

The non-combat or non-combat-capable elements of the division—trains, division support command elements, and remaining elements of regiments and battalions no longer capable of combat operations—was placed under an *ad hoc* headquarters led by *Oberst* Schmidt-Ott and moved to Stalino. After the Soviets broke through to the area around Stalino and to its west in mid-February, Schmidt-Ott was given orders to move his detachment to the area west of Dnjepropetrowsk. His columns started moving out on 18 February. They moved through Pokrowskoje and then across the large Dnjepr reservoir at Saporoshje and then on to the Kamenskoje area, about 35 kilometers west of Dnjepropetrowsk.

For the rear-area elements, the month of March saw a period of intense training, reconstitution with new personnel and materiel and the reorganization of formations. Both officers and enlisted personnel went about improving their quarters and taking up neglected maintenance on the vehicles. This all alternated with drills, firing practice and classroom instruction. During their free time, the soldiers could frequent the bathing facility or take in a movie at the Armed Forces Theater.

The armored regiment disbanded the 3rd Battalion. The remaining companies were consolidated to form the 3rd and 6th Companies, which

were given to the respective battalions. In his rear area, *Oberst* Schmidt-Ott thus had two tank headquarters companies at his disposal (*Leutnant* Lippoldt and *Oberleutnant* Zobel), as well as three tank companies: the 5th (*Hauptmann* Büschen), the 6th (*Hauptmann* Heuer), and the 7th (*Oberleutnant* Steindamm). Serving as Schmidt-Ott's adjutant was *Hauptmann* Oelrich. *Major* Peschke's *Feld-Ersatz-Bataillon 83* raised a defensive company for screening along the Dnjepr. *Major* Groeneveld's *Panzer-Pionier-Bataillon 39* provided an alert platoon of six noncommissioned officers and forty-two enlisted personnel for the same purpose. *Major* Helfritz's *Panzer-Nachrichten-Abteilung 39* established a fixed communications center that was able to cover the 500 kilometers of distance to the division command post in Artemowsk without any problems.

The front lines along the Donez quieted down that month. The enemy in front of the *III. Panzer-Korps*, the *XXXX. Panzer-Korps*, and the *LVII. Panzer-Korps* transitioned to the defense. The German forces were also able to set up defensive positions along the river line that had been captured and dig established trenches and dugouts. At the beginning of the new month, the *4. Panzer-Armee* started preparations to take back Kharkov. To finish those preparations, the division's armored group was employed by an infantry division to clear out the Russian bridgehead at Isjum.

That attack was not successful. Instead, it collapsed in the face of enemy fires, since the promised *Luftwaffe* support did not materialize. From their positions on the high ground, the Soviets were able to fire into the approaching tanks and *SPW*'s with their antitank guns and artillery. After ten minutes, all of the vehicles were either hopelessly stuck or shot up. The division then ordered the battle group to move back to its line of departure. In the month of March, in that fighting and in other engagements, the armored regiment lost the brave acting commander of the 8th Company, *Oberleutnant* Huhn, and the dashing battalion surgeon, Dr. Rieseneder. Within the 2nd

Company, *Feldwebel* Hessler and *Feldwebel* Hochstein were killed, as was *Gefreiter* Kleist. The medical platoon of *Assistenzarzt* Dr. Fritzsche moved to Radionowka, north of Artemowsk, where it set up a forward clearing station. By 4 April, 347 soldiers had been treated, including those with spotted fever.

The Donez area, which was important for the war economy, was once more completely in German hands. To the north of the *1. Panzer-Armee*, it was possible to close out the winter fighting with the recapture of Kharkov. Then, as a result of the melting snows, the muck and mud no longer allowed major movements.

A general order from the Supreme Command stated:

> Finally, the period of just holding out was over, and the hour of the counterattack had arrived. In addition to the battle-tested soldiers of the Army and the *Waffen-SS*, newly introduced divisions entered the fight. The Russian has been taken down on the essential portion of the front by the combined violent assault and the constant heroic operations of the *Luftwaffe*. Kharkov is once more in our hands. . . . As a result of your bravery and the change in the fortunes of war that it ushered in, you have created the prerequisites for yourselves so that I can, effective today, lift the ban on leaves so that it will be possible for you, my comrades, to increasingly be able to visit your homeland and your loved ones, whose thoughts, hopes and prayers have been with you during this winter more than ever before.

On 26 March, the division received orders to transfer its positions and screening sectors to the *38. Infanterie-Division*. It was to be withdrawn from the front for a reconstitution. The *XXX. Armee-Korps* of *General der Artillerie* Fretter-Pico, to which the division reported, directed that the reconstitution area be located in the area between Konstantinowka and Kramatorskaja.

The combat forces moved into the rear area of the field army. The command staff followed on 4 April. The rear-area services that had been in Kamenskoje were ordered to Konstantinowka in the first half of April. At that point, the division had all of its formations and elements again. The reconstitution effort then took off at full speed. Replacements in men and materiel arrived; weapons and vehicles were issued; training was conducted; and field exercises took place. The formations had the opportunity to grow into powerful combat units again.

The *Panzertruppe* underwent general organizational changes in March and April. With Directive 16840/43, The High Command of the Army redesignated the "Fast Forces" (*schnelle Truppen*) as the "Armored Forces" (*Panzertruppen*). Oversight was provided by the Inspector General of the Armored Forces, with the newly titled duty position having come into effect on 28 February. *Generaloberst* Guderian assumed the weighty responsibility as the first Inspector General. His headquarters immediately issued guidance for the reorganization of the armor divisions. The motorcycle infantry battalions were reorganized and redesignated as *Panzer-Aufklärungs-Abteilungen* (Army High Command Directive 3047/43, dated 23 March 1943).

The division reorganized as follows over the next few weeks:

- Command and Control: Division headquarters, with map section and military police section
- Armor: *Panzer-Regiment 6*, with two battalions, each with a battalion headquarters and headquarters company and three line companies.
- Mechanized Infantry: *Panzergrenadier-Regiment 3* and *Panzergrenadier-Regiment 394*, each with a regimental headquarters and headquarters company and two battalions each. Each battalion was comprised of one headquarters and headquarters company with four line companies. The regiment's 9th Company was an infantry-gun unit and the 10th Company was a *Flak* unit. The *I./Panzergrenadier-Regiment 3* remained the division's only fully mechanized battalion (*SPW*-equipped).

- Armored Reconnaissance: *Panzer-Aufk-lärungs-Abteilung 3* had a headquarters and headquarters company, four line companies and a supply company. The four line companies: The 1st Company was an armored car unit; the 2nd Motorcycle Infantry Company (Tracked) was equipped with halftracks; the 3rd Motorcycle Infantry Company (Wheeled) retained motorcycles and trucks; and the 4th Light Company (mechanized) had half-tracks.
- Antitank: *Panzerjäger-Abteilung 543* had a headquarters and headquarters company and two line companies, one motorized (1st), and one self-propelled (2nd).
- Artillery: *Panzer-Artillerie-Regiment 75* with a headquarters and headquarters battery and two line battalions. *Schwere Artillerie-Abteilung 714 (mot.)* was integrated into the divisional artillery as the 1st Battalion. *Beobachtungs-Batterie (Panzer) 75* was the flash ranging battery for the divisional artillery.
- Air Defense: *Heeres-Flak-Artillerie-Abteilung 714* consisted of a headquarters and headquarters battery, two heavy batteries, and one light battery.
- Engineers: *Panzer-Pionier-Bataillon 39* with a headquarters and headquarters company and three line companies, with the 1st and 2nd being motorized and the 3rd being armored (*SPW*).
- Replacements: *Feld-Ersatz-Bataillon 83* with five companies.
- Signals: *Panzer-Nachrichten-Abteilung 39* with a landline company (1st) and a radio company (2nd).
- Division Support Command: A headquarters element with one truck company (120-ton lift capacity), three truck companies (90-ton lift capacity), a supply company, and a fuel section (50 cubic meters of fuel). In addition, there were two medical companies, two maintenance companies, one administrative company, one bakery company, one meat-processing company, three ambulance platoons, and one motorized field post office.

The formations also reorganized internally. For instance, the tank companies were standardized. The company headquarters had two *Panzer III's*; the 1st Platoon, five *Panzer III's* with the long 5-centimeter main gun; the 2nd Platoon, five *Panzer III's* with the short 7.5-centimeter main gun; and the 3rd Platoon, five *Panzer IV's* with the long 7.5-centimeter main gun.

The mechanized infantry battalion had only four line companies, with two additional companies at regimental level (infantry gun and *Flak*). The headquarters company had twelve *R75* motorcycles, two three-ton prime movers, and two 7.5-centimeter antitank guns.

The divisional artillery started to receive the *lFH 18/40*, which was an updated version of the old workhorse with a muzzle brake. Its development had been pursued while the former commander of the 2nd Battalion, *Oberstleutnant* Wöhlermann, had been the head of the development and testing directorate of the army's weapons agency.

The *Flak* battalion had two batteries of 8.8-centimeter *Flak* and one battery of 3.7-centimeter *Flak*. Adding in its light section, the battalion had an end strength of 22 officers, 142 noncommissioned officers, and 600 men.

The division proper had authorized levels of major equipment at the time as follows:

45 *Panzer IV's*
63 2-centimeter *Flak*
12 10.5-centimeter light field howitzers (towed)

52 *Panzer III's*
6 2-centimeter quad *Flak*
12 10.5-centimeter light field howitzers (self-propelled)

483 Motorcycles
8 3.7-centimeter *Flak*
12 15-centimeter heavy field howitzers (towed)

2,703 Vehicles (other types)[*]
8 8.8-centimeter *Flak*
6 15-centimeter heavy field howitzers (self-propelled)

---

*This includes 292 armored vehicles as well.

There were also personnel changes within the organization. The division commander, *General-major* Westhoven, was promoted to *Generalleutnant*, effective 1 April. The former division logistics officer, *Major i.G.* Dankworth, was transferred. He was replaced by *Hauptmann i.G.* von dem Borne, a nephew of the former division operations officer. *Oberleutnant* Wrede from the armored regiment became the new assistant division intelligence officer. *Oberst* Zimmermann, the highly competent commander of *Schützen-Regiment 3/Panzergrenadier-Regiment 3* in both peace and war, became the commander of a replacement regiment. He was awarded the German Cross in Gold after his transfer for his achievements. *Oberstleutnant* Wellmann assumed command of that regiment. *Major* Peschke, the former commander of the field replacement battalion, became the new commander of the *II./Panzergrenadier-Regiment 394*, with *Hauptmann* Biegon taking Peschke's place.

During those days of rest, deserving officers and noncommissioned officers of the division received their well-earned awards. The Knight's Cross was presented to *Hauptmann* Dittmer (*I./Panzergrenadier-Regiment 3*) and *Oberfeldwebel* Steinführer (platoon leader in the *II./Panzergrenadier-Regiment 394*). The following personnel received the German Cross in Gold from February to the end of April (presented in the order given): *Feldwebel* Wiedenhöft (*2./Panzer-Regiment 6*), *Oberleutnant* Berg (*7./Panzergrenadier-Regiment 3*), *Unteroffizier* Lindemann (*4./Kradschützen-Bataillon 3*), *Oberfeldwebel* Reiss (*1./Panzergrenadier-Regiment 394*), *Oberfeldwebel* Lesch (*6./Panzergrenadier-Regiment 3*), *Hauptmann* Müller-Röhlich (*II./Panzergrenadier-Regiment 394*) *Hauptmann* Hagenguth (*1./Panzerjäger-Abteilung 543*), *Oberleutnant* Schulze (*7./Panzergrenadier-Regiment 394*), and *Feldwebel* Dentler (*7./Panzergrenadier-Regiment 394*).

The month of April brought nice weather with it and soon allowed the rigors and hardships of the fighting during the withdrawals of the last few months to be forgotten. Summer arrived early in the Ukraine. The division conducted training feverishly. The issuance of the weapons and vehicles made rapid progress. Noncommissioned officer courses were conducted. The bridging section of the divisional engineers had the following equipment on 20 April: eight pontoons, four supports, eight stringers, and eight surface sections. The new equipment was loaded on trucks in a manner that allowed two complete sections to be installed. An exercise was conducted by the *3./Panzer-Pionier-Bataillon 39* with a battalion from *Panzergrenadier-Regiment 3* under the watchful eyes of the division commander. In it, a 19.2-meter-long section of sixteen-ton bridge was built across the Torez.

The twentieth of April was a "holiday" for the division.[1] Many officers and noncommissioned officers were promoted and awards presented. The division band played at village and town squares. The divisional engineers hosted a multifaceted athletic competition. The soldiers competed in 100-, 200-, and 400-meter runs, in bicycle riding and in a mixed relay race involving motorcycles, floats, wheeled vehicles, runners, and *panje* carts. A soccer match between the divisional artillery and the engineers brought the sunny day to a close.

A terrific variety show that had its origins in the armor regiment in the winter of 1941–42 continued to entertain the soldiers. It was augmented by Russian artists and was always greeted by thunderous applause whenever it performed. The cabaret was called the *Panzersprenggrenate* ("Armor High-Explosive Round").

It was possible to celebrate Easter appropriately. The division's supply elements brought forward extra personal-demand items. There were chocolates, bonbons, eggs, cakes, and, it goes without saying, alcohol as well. In the middle of that training period, new orders arrived on 29 April. The division had to leave its quarters

---

1. Not mentioned here, and obvious to any German of the period, is that this was Hitler's birthday, which was always the occasion for a "training holiday" in peacetime and, when permissible, in wartime as well.

within twenty-four hours. As it turned dark, it marched in the direction of Barwenkowo and Podolje. For unknown reasons, however, the movement was stopped the next day. Starting on 1 May, the division basically remained in the area it had reached. The formations of the division, which had been strung out in the long march serials, assembled in Podolje. The regiments, battalions and detachments resumed training, until the spring rains in the first days of May turned the fertile Ukrainian soil into a sea of mud.

On 9 May, an order to move back to the previous location was unexpectedly received. For the most part, the elements of the division reached their former quarters around Konstantinowka by evening and settled back in. Intermittent training and reconstitution efforts were continued for the next ten days. Only *Oberst* Pape's *Panzergrenadier-Regiment 394* did not return to the division fold. Effective 10 April, the regiment had been designated as the ready reserve of the *XXX. Armee-Korps*. Initially, the two battalions of the regiment were positioned in the area south of Lissitschansk. The 2nd Battalion of *Major* Peschke then moved to Solotarewka. A few days later, *Major* Rode's 1st Battalion moved to the area around Messarosch.

The Soviets were attempting to establish a bridgehead in the bend of the Donez and were continuously attacking the infantry divisions in position there. The Red Air Force supported those efforts, but they were never crowned with success. *Panzergrenadier-Regiment 394* was never committed as the reserve and was thus able to continue its training program on a limited scale. Two weeks later, the regiment's 9th and 10th Companies, as well as the 2nd Battalion, moved into the area around Nowo-Aleksandrowka–Brjanzewka. That was followed for a couple of peaceful weeks. After the 1st Battalion was also relieved of its mission and returned to Konstantinowka, the available time allowed the regiment to grow into a combat-capable cohesive whole.

At the beginning of June, *Generalleutnant* Westhoven was able to present additional German Crosses in Gold. The following recipients were honored: *Hauptmann* Deich (company commander in *Panzer-Aufklärungs-Abteilung 3*), *Oberleutnant* Voutta (company commander in *Panzer-Aufklärungs-Abteilung 3*), *Oberleutnant* Möllhoff (company commander of the *3./Panzer-Pionier-Bataillon 3*), *Oberfeldwebel* Rüdenberg (*Panzer-Aufklärungs-Abteilung 3*), and *Unteroffizier* Blass (*Panzer-Aufklärungs-Abteilung 3*). *Oberleutnant* Huhn, the fallen commander of the *8./Panzer-Regiment 6*, received the award posthumously.

Woroschilowsk burns in January 1943.

Ischerskaja, 1942. *Oberst* Pape, the commander of *Panzergrenadier-Regiment 394*, at the forward command post and in discussion with *Leutnant* Oberhuber, the adjutant of the 1st Battalion.

Proper signage is the be-all and end-all of rapid troop movement for a mobile force. At first glance, the signpost is confusing, but for those in the know it was a lifesaver, especially for supply personnel.

Members of the headquarters of the *I./Panzergrenadier-Regiment 394* in Dranowka in the spring of 1943 (from left to right): *Gefreiter* Oerter, *Unteroffizier* Witte, *Gefreiter* Titje, *Unteroffizier* Hünecke, *Gefreiter* Elch, Wolga-Meier, and *Obergefreiter* Praske.

The columns of the division make their way tortuously through the snow and ice along the banks of the Asovian Sea.

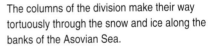

Hauptmann Dittmer, the commander of the *I./Panzergrenadier-Regiment 394*, received the Knight's Cross for his role in the assault on Slawansk with his battalion in February 1943.

Oberstleutnant Friedrich Feldhuß, the commander of *Feld-Ersatz-Bataillon 75* and the division support command.

Position along the Dnjepr in March 1943.

Panzer-Nachrichten-Abteilung 39 in Konstantinowka in May 1943. The men are preforming maintenance on signal equipment.

Signaleers, the indispensible helpmates of the fighting forces. Here: a landline section of the *I./Panzergrenadier-Regiment 394*.

View inside the work space of a radio truck, the *Funk-Kraftfahrzeug 17*. Here: *Obergefreiter* Rudi Thom.

The cabaret of the division, the *Panzersprenggrenate* ("The Armor-Piercing Round") performs in Kharkov.

Field services in Konstantinowka in May 1943. Here: Pastor Drews, the Protestant chaplain.

A motorcycle messenger assigned to the 4./*Panzergrenadier-Regiment*, Günter Apelt.

Oberfeldwebel Gerhard Steinführer, a platoon leader in the 2./*Panzergrenadier-Regiment 394*.

Major Deichen, the commander of *Panzer-Aufklärungs-Abteilung 3*.

Oberleutnant Karl-Heinz Sorge, the commander of the 5./*Panzer-Regiment 6*.

Oberst Wellmann, the commander of *Panzergrenadier-Regiment 3*.

CHAPTER 6

From the Donez to the Pena: Operation Citadel

The Soviet winter offensive of 1942–43 had not only brought with it extreme danger for the southern field-army group, it had also torn open the central portion of the Eastern Front. The Red Army succeeded in reducing the positions of *Heeresgruppe Mitte*. North of Bjelgorod, the Soviet forces had driven a deep wedge into the German front. The salient was nearly 500 kilometers long. It jutted like an arrow along the boundaries between the southern and central field-army groups, serving as a point of departure for any new offensive.

The "boil" needed to be removed. On 15 April, the Operations Directorate of the Army General Staff released Operations Plan No. 6 (Log entry: 430226/43, SECRET). The order, signed by Hitler, directed, in part:

I have decided to conduct the "Citadel" attack as the first offensive this year, as soon as the weather allows it. Correspondingly, this attack is of decisive importance. It needs to give the initiative into our hands for the spring and the summer. Correspondingly, all preparations must be conducted with the greatest circumspection and energy. The best formations, the best weapons, the best leaders and large amounts of ammunition are to be committed to the points of main effort. Every leader, every man must been inculcated with the importance of this attack. The victory at Kursk needs to be a signal to the world.

To that end, I order:

1. Objective of the attack is to encircle the enemy forces found in the Kursk area by means of a concentrated, aggressively conducted and rapidly executed advance by one field army each from the area around Bjelgorod and south of Orel and to destroy them by means of concentric attack . . .

2. . . .

3. Moving from the line running Bjelgorod–Tomarowka, *Heeresgruppe Süd* breaks though a line running Peilepy–Obojan with massed forces and establishes contact with the attacking field army of *Heeresgruppe Mitte* at Kursk and to its east . . .

4. . . .

5. The staging of the forces of both field army groups is to be done exploiting all possible camouflage, diversionary and deception measures and in such a manner that it is far enough from the lines of departure that the forces can attack on the sixth day following issuance of the order by the Army High Command, effective 28 April. Accordingly, the earliest attach date is 3 May . . .

Generalfeldmarschall Kluge's *Heeresgruppe Mitte* and *Generalfeldmarschall* Manstein's *Heeresgruppe Süd* started their preparations for Operation Citadel in the middle of April.

Both of the field army groups firmed up their own front lines after the heavy fighting of the winter, sent armored divisions back for reconstitution, conducted operations to straighten out sections of the front and slowly sent the designated attacking forces into their assembly areas. *Heeresgruppe Mitte* designated the *9. Armee* of *Generaloberst* Model, the former commander of the *3. Panzer-Division*, as its attack force. It was intended for that field army to advance southeast on Kursk from areas south of Orel with its three armor corps. The *2. Armee* of *General der Infanterie* Weiß on the right was to remain in the area between Ssewsk and Sumy with its infantry divisions and hold its ground, oriented to the east. The *4. Panzer-Armee* of *Generaloberst* Hoth was the attack force of *Heeresgruppe Süd*. It was to attack northeast from the area north of Kharkov. *Armee-Abteilung Kempf*[1] of *General der Panzertruppen* Kempf was to the right and was charged with a flank guard mission to the east. The German forces—a total of 433,000 men, 3,155 armored vehicles, 6,763 field artillery pieces, and 1,850 aircraft—were organized as follows at the start of the attack:

Northern Pincer: 9. Armee (from left to right)
- *XXIII. Armee-Korps* with the *78. Sturm-Division* and the *216.* and *383. Infanterie-Divisionen*
- *XXXXI. Panzer-Korps* with the *18. Panzer-Division* and the *86.* and *292. Infanterie-Divisionen*
- *XXXXVII. Panzer-Korps* with the *6. Infanterie-Division* and the *2., 9.,* and *20. Panzer-Divisionen*
- *XXXXVI. Panzer-Korps* with the *7., 31., 102.,* and *258. Infanterie-Divisionen*
- *XX. Armee-Korps* with the *45., 72., 137.,* and *251. Infanterie-Divisionen*
- Reserves: *4.* and *12. Panzer-Divisionen* and the *10. Panzergrenadier-Division*

Southern Pincer: 4. Panzer-Armee (from left to right):
- *LII. Armee-Korps* with the *57., 255.,* and *332. Infanterie-Divisionen*
- *XXXXVIII. Panzer-Korps* with the *3.* and *11. Panzer-Divisionen, Panzergrenadier-Division "Großdeutschland,"* and the *167. Infanterie-Division*

---

1. The equivalent of a field army, with three corps, one of which was armored (*III. Panzer-Korps*).

- *II. SS-Panzer-Korps* with the *SS-Panzer-Grenadier-Divisionen "Leibstandarte SS Adolf Hitler," "Das Reich,"* and *"Totenkopf"*

Flank Guard: *Armee-Abteilung Kempf* **(from left to right):**
- *III. Panzer-Korps* with the *6., 7.,* and *19. Panzer-Divisionen* and the *168.* and *198. Infanterie-Divisionen*
- *XI. Armee-Korps (Korps Raus)* with the *106.* and *320. Infanterie-Divisionen*
- *XXXXII. Armee-Korps* with the *39., 161.,* and *282. Infanterie-Divisionen*
- Reserves: *XXIV. Panzer-Korps* with the *17. Panzer-Division* and *SS-Panzer-Grenadier-Division "Wiking"*

The Red Army was aware of the German offensive planning and had started preparing for the upcoming battle in the middle of April. The measures taken and movements made by the Russians did not remain hidden to the various levels of command, but the extent of them was not known until the actual start of the operation.

Just like their German opponents, the Soviets had their best and most powerful formations moved into the Kursk salient. Marshall Zhukov assumed command of all the forces in that sector. Marshall Wassilewski and Political Commissar Malenkov, the future successor to Stalin, were at his side to give advice. The Red Army had the following field army groups in the Kursk area at the beginning of July:
- Central Front (Commander in chief: General Rokossowski): 13th, 48th, 60th, 65th, and 70th Armies and the 2nd Tank Army
- Woronesch Front (Commander in chief: General Watutin, with Political Commissar Khrushchev): 38th, 40th, and 69th Armies, the 6th and 7th Guards Armies and the 1st Tank Army
- Southwest Front (Commander in chief: General Konjew): 5th Guards Army and 5th Guards Tank Army

The enemy had transformed the terrain all around Kursk into a strong system of fortifications. The terrain was studded with wire obstacles and minefields, dug-in tanks (including KV-I's) as semipermanent gun bunkers and stationary batteries of flamethrowers. Marshy depressions and steep valleys were cleverly incorporated into the defensive network as tank obstacles. The infantry was in well-prepared bunker positions. In addition, there was the fact that the enemy had been in his positions for weeks and was well acquainted with the terrain.

During the afternoon of 15 June, the code word arrived at the division to move to its tactical assembly area. The forces moved to the west. The division headquarters followed at 2015 hours. The march objective was initially held secret. It was only the fact that that columns were marching on the same roads they had six weeks previously that provided a clue.

The movement, which was conducted at night, led through Wesseloje to Losowaja over the next few days. The trains, which had remained in the former billeting areas, were brought up to the frontline forces, following the combat formations. *Generalleutnant* Westhoven, who had taken up quarters in Losowaja South, along with the command staff, was directed to a tactical assembly area south of Merefa (near Kharkov) on 17 June. The division scheduled its movement to start at 1930 hours.

The division rolled on during the night through the Ukrainian countryside. The next few days were marked by magnificent summer weather, but the first drops fell from the skies on 26 June. Then there was a downpour. In the blink of an eye, the ground was softened up, with the result that many vehicles got stuck. Fortunately, most of the formations of the division had already reached the quartering areas around Paraskoweja. A few battalions were able to use the remaining six days to get themselves into "shape." Other elements, especially the signalers, had to move tortuously through the muck, since they had been short on fuel to begin with.

On 29 June, the movement continued west. The nighttime movement to Walki proved to be a test of endurance for both men and machines, since the rain did not let up. The columns of the division moved in a wide arc to the west of Kharkov and to the north. Bogoduchow was transited; Pisarewka reached. Columns from a number of divisions got jammed up. That was a sure sign that "something" was in the works. Elements of the division moved at the same time on the same march route to Gaiworon as battalions from *Panzergrenadier-Division "Großdeutschland."* The routes had become quagmires. The movement got delayed, so much so that a portion of the forces did not reach their quarters until after it had turned light. After the rain stopped, the ground dried up quickly due to the heat.

From Gaiworon onward, the formations of the division were able to use the road all by themselves; it led due east to Bjelgorod. The lead elements reached Chotmyshsk on 1 July, where the division command post was established.

There was not much time left to get set up, maintain equipment and vehicles and get familiar with the terrain. The operations order for Citadel had arrived. On the morning of 3 July, the division's elements received the documents necessary for what would prove to be the last and greatest German offensive on the Eastern Front. The offensive was scheduled to begin on 5 July, with the direction of attack for the division to the northwest.

General der Panzertruppen Knobelsdorff's *XXXXVIII. Panzer-Korps* (Chief of staff: *Oberst i.G.* Mellenthin) had been directed to attack due north. The division was to be employed on the left wing of the corps. *Panzergrenadier-Division "Großdeutschland"* was to adjoin to the right. It, together with the *11. Panzer-Division*, was to form the main effort of the corps. The *332. Infanterie-Division* was employed to the left of the *3. Panzer-Division* in a flank-guard role. The attack itself was to be launched through the infantry division's positions.

Facing the division was the 6th Guards Army of Lieutenant General Tschistjakow. The enemy forces the division would first encounter were the 67th and 71st Guards Rifle Divisions, which had occupied well-built field fortifications between Dragunskoje and Gerzowka. Behind them and south of the Pena was the 90th Guards Rifle Division. Intelligence traffic indicated that the enemy field army was holding two more corps in reserve. They were expected to be committed when the attack started. The forces in question were the III Corps (Mechanized) with the 1st, 3rd, and 10th Mechanized Brigades, the 1st Guards Tank Brigade, and the 49th Tank Brigade and the VI Tank Corps with the 22nd, 122nd, and 200th Tank Brigades and the 6th Motorized brigade.

The division was in terrific spirits. The officers and noncommissioned officers had been tested in combat and worked well with their units. The troop elements had been well trained during the period of rest and prepared for their mission; they were in shape physically and mentally. The materiel had been overhauled, replaced and supplemented. It was a rare occurrence when a attack was so carefully prepared. Nonetheless, no one harbored any doubts that the upcoming fighting would be difficult, based on the German knowledge of the enemy situation and the difficulties of the terrain.

It was imperative initially to take the forward Russian positions. It was not possible to employ tanks at the outset in the hilly terrain, which had been heavily mined and was crisscrossed by marshy, creek-filled depressions.

Panzergrenadier-Regiment 3, minus its 1st Battalion, and *Panzergrenadier-Regiment 394* were to make the initial attack, supported by combat engineers. The armored group of *Oberst* Schmidt-Ott, consisting of the armored regiment, the *SPW* battalion and the mechanized company of the divisional engineers, was held back. At first light on 4 July, the division command post was moved to Sybino.

The Soviets remained relatively quiet. Their batteries placed harassment fires on the marshy terrain and the villages at irregular intervals. It slowly became the afternoon. The rainy weather of the previous few days had yielded to sunshine. When it showed 1500 hours on the watches, there were suddenly the sounds of *Stuka* engines in the air. At the same time, the battery officers of the divisional artillery gave their units orders to fire. Guns of all calibers started firing on the enemy positions, which were hit from the air by the German machines at the same time. Operation Citadel had started.

The mechanized infantry got ready to move out from their bunkers and trenches. At 1530 hours, the soldiers in field gray jumped up, exited their positions and raced towards the Russian lines . . . hand grenades detonated, mines exploded, and shots rang through the air. The artillery started shifting its fires farther to the rear.

Right after the start of the attack, a downpour started.

The main effort of the attack for the division was in the sector of *Oberst* Pape's *Panzergrenadier-Regiment 394*. The regiment's mission was to advance north, get to the Bjelgorod–Gotnja rail line and take the village of Gerzowka. *Generalleutnant* Westhoven accompanied the regiment in its attack, maintaining contact with the command staff by means of a wire that was strung along the advance route.

The Soviet 71st Guards Rifle Division put up a brave defense in spite of the extremely heavy casualties it had taken as a result of the artillery and the bombing. The Russians fought stubbornly for every meter of ground. The mechanized infantry had to "chew their way through," foxhole-to-foxhole and dugout-to-dugout. The engineers got no rest. One mine obstacle after the other had to be cleared.

Progress was slow. The *I./Panzergrenadier-Regiment 394* had to bear the main burden of the fight. The battalion commander, *Major* Rode, was wounded, and *Hauptmann* Eggert stepped in to assume acting command. Later on, he was also wounded and was replaced by *Hauptmann* Voutta of the armored reconnaissance battalion. The 3rd Company of the battalion was especially hard hit.

The battalion finally reached the rail line and crossed it. The resistance on the part of the Soviet riflemen outside of Gerzowka subsided.

The mechanized infantry, engineers and antitank elements pushed the enemy back. Gerzowka was reached as the sun set across the land. The fighting for the last remaining ruins of buildings took place. The thirty-year-old Knight's Cross recipient *Fahnenjunker-Oberfeldwebel* Steinführer rallied the men of his platoon in the 2nd Company through his personal courage and his circumspect leadership and got them to give another effort. The men of the company assaulted the Russian pockets of resistance and took the day's objective before the onset of night. Steinführer was later inducted into the Army Honor Roll for this action.

The division chaplain, Father Ruzak from Vienna, evacuated wounded from minefields in heavy artillery fire without waiting for the arrival of the requested mine clearing section. The men had been wounded by mines that had exploded in the dense minefields.

The division, which had achieved its day's objective and ejected the enemy forces, pushed *Major* Stockmann's *II./Panzer-Regiment 6* forward during the night as far as the positions that had been reached by the mechanized infantry regiments. Even as they were approaching, some of the fighting vehicles were lost to mines. The enemy placed heavy artillery fire on the assembly areas and approach routes. The fire forced the formations to constantly disperse and made it difficult to organize for the continuation of the attack.

The divisional artillery of *Oberst* Lattmann moved forward during the night. At precisely 0500 hours on 5 July, it opened the next day's attack with an artillery preparation. *Luftwaffe* flying formations also supported the advance directed against the localities on the high ground. The mechanized infantry had already started advancing. The armor battalion was behind the mechanized infantry in position in order to give covering fire, eliminate pockets of resistance and turn back immediate counterattacks. Numerous minefields and marshy bottomland made a rapid advance difficult. The engineers were busily engaged in putting down corduroy roads and constructing provisional crossing points for the heavy vehicles. The enemy defended energetically everywhere and, in the afternoon, launched immediate counterattacks supported by tanks. They were forces of the 1st Tank Army of Lieutenant General Katukow, which had been brought forward rapidly. Those forces advanced primarily against the *11. Panzer-Division* and *Panzergrenadier-Division "Großdeutschland,"* but the two divisions were able to turn back their attackers.

The division's attack to the northwest proceeded slowly and deliberately. The companies of *Oberstleutnant* Wellmann's *Panzergrenadier-Regiment 3* cleared one Russian position after the other. The advance was constantly being delayed because of the Russian tanks that had been dug-in an antitank pillboxes. They could only be identified and eliminated at very close range. The enemy riflemen fought bravely but, in the end, they had to yield to the pressure of the grenadiers. The regiment was able to take another piece of high ground, but then it had to stop due to a lack of ammunition. While there, the mechanized infantry were able to free a group of captured Germans. Among the freed captives, *Obergefreiter* Mogel of the *2./Panzergrenadier-Regiment 3* was able to find his uncle. The enemy collected himself and started to conduct immediate counterattacks.

By noon, the engineers were able to construct provisional crossings over the streambeds, with the result that the fighting vehicles could finally pull forward to support the mechanized infantry. After much effort, the bridging section was finally brought forward. It had been hopelessly stuck around the railway embankment with its heavy vehicles due to the softened-up road network. It wasn't until the warming rays of the sun started drying the clay that the doubtful efforts to free up the section met with success. *Generalleutnant* Westhoven ordered a bridge across Beresowy Creek at 1530 hours. Fifteen minutes later, the bridging vehicles of *Unteroffizier* Lohrengel started arriving. The *2./Panzer-Pionier-Bataillon 39* of *Oberleutnant* Weigel

and the Bridging Section of *Oberleutnant* Mertens immediately got to work erecting a 19.2-meter-long sixteen-ton bridge, which was completed at 1650 hours.

From Gerzowka, *Oberst* Pape's *Panzergrenadier-Regiment 394* launched a frontal assault against the enemy's main line of resistance. The 1st Battalion led the assault, while the 2nd Battalion followed, echeloned to the left rear.

At that point, the *II./Panzer-Regiment 6* could be brought forward. Shortly after the bridge had been completed, *Major* Stockmann sent the platoon of *Leutnant* Aschermann of the 2nd Company to help *Panzergrenadier-Regiment 3*. The tanks advanced across the high ground to the forward positions of the mechanized infantry and, advancing together, ejected the Russians from the grain fields. By doing so, they also prevented a Soviet immediate counterattack, which had just been getting underway. The mechanized infantry were able to continue their advance.

By then, most of the rest of the armored battalion had closed up. The companies advanced on a wide front and, together with the mechanized infantry, slowly pushed the Soviets back. The companies had a difficult time of it due to the artillery, rocket launchers, antitank guns, antitank rifles and antiaircraft weaponry. It was possible to turn around the Russian tanks that attacked the advancing *Panzergrenadier-Regiment 394*. It was impossible to continue advancing, however, due to a belt of mines.

Oberst Pape, who was always leading from the front, was wounded one more time while he was reconnoitering outside of Korowino. *Major* Peschke assumed acting command of the regiment, while the commander was evacuated. Pape's personal example and terrific leadership qualities had made the impending success possible. With one final effort, the mechanized infantry and the tanks of the *II./Panzer-Regiment 6* took Korowino, a village on a dominant piece of high ground, as it turned twilight.

At the same time, *Panzergrenadier-Division "Großdeutschland"* succeeded in taking Tscherkasskoje, which meant that both of those key

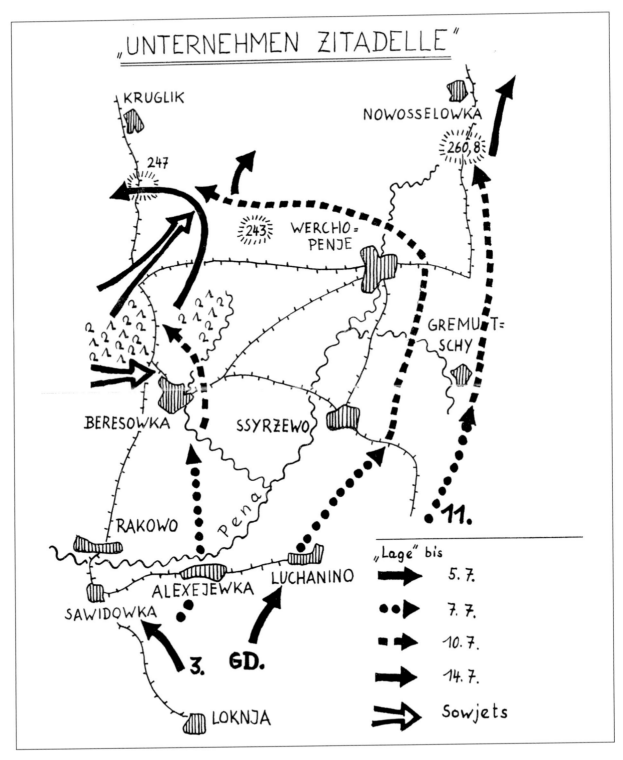

Operation Citadel

Lage = Situation

positions of the enemy's defenses were in German hands at the end of that blazingly hot day.

The last objective to be taken was the bottleneck at Krassnyj-Potschinok. *Oberleutnant* von Veltheim and the light platoon of the tank battalion took off in an effort to capture it by a *coup de main*. The young officer used a burning windmill as an orientation point. The enemy resistance was weak, with his forces pulling back rapidly to the positions along the Pena. The officer remained close on the heels of the Russians and was the first one of his platoon to enter Krassnyj-Potschinok. He was later inducted into the Army Honor Roll for this action.

Up to that point, the attack had proceeded as expected and discussed among the commanders, even though there was the friction of war.

The night was by no means quiet. Outposts were established, resupply conducted. Patrols were out the entire night. The 3rd Company of the division engineers and the bridging section of *Feldwebel* Valentin built a 9.6-meter-long sixteen-ton bridge at the northern outskirts of Krassnyj-Potschinok between 0515 and 0600 hours.

The 67th and 71st Guards Rifle Division had pulled back to their Pena Position to the northwest. Starting during the day and continuing into the night, the sounds of tanks being moved forward from the rear into the Pena Position could be heard, in the Soviet effort to prevent a thrust on Obojan.

The Pena flowed from north to south and turned west around Alexejewka. The river coursed through marshy bottomland. The only place to cross it was at Rakowo, where there was a bridge. The division attempted to take that bridge in a *coup de main*.

Oberleutnant Steindamm's *7./Panzer-Regiment 6* was sent to conduct the reconnaissance-in-force along the river. The company moved the many kilometers to the river in battle formation down the slope. Initially, the tanks moved without interference, as if at a training area. In the distance, some 3,500 to 4,000 meters away, the strongly fortified Rokowo could be seen. When

the tanks had covered approximately half of the stretch, the enemy initiated his defensive fires. The Russian artillery had registered on that bit of terrain and forced the company to disperse even further.

By then, the rest of the battalion had moved forward under *Major* Stockmann's command and formed up to attack. The 5th Company attacked on the left, the 7th in the middle, and the 6th on the right. The 8th Company, echeloned to the rear, provided covering fire. The batteries of the divisional artillery that had been pushed forward started firing on Rakowo. A frightening shortage of ammunition forced the guns to scale back their firing.

The Russian artillery was concentrating exclusively on the forty tanks that were attacking. The German fighting vehicles made only slow progress. Soviet antitank guns were firing without a let up from Rakowo. Even more dangers was the fires received from the dug-in T-34's and the American-built tanks. Despite that, the tanks closed to within 600 meters of the village. *Hauptmann* Büschen's 5th Company then ran into concentrated fires and had to pull back. The platoon leader of the 1st Platoon, *Oberleutnant* Biesoldt, received a direct hit, and only his driver survived. By then, the 6th Company on the right had reached a depression, where it was safe from Russian artillery but was constantly attacked by Russian fighter-bombers. The battalion's advance came to a standstill.

At that point, *Leutnant* Aschermann and his platoon seized the initiative, even though the tanks were almost out of ammunition. He issued orders to the 2nd Platoon to attack. The other two platoon leaders of the 7th Company, *Hauptfeldwebel* Rust and *Oberfeldwebel* Hoppe, immediately followed. They were joined by *Oberfeldwebel* Krotke and his platoon from the 5th Company. The bridge over the Pena was in sight of the approaching tanks. All of the drivers stepped on it. The bridge was palpably close to Rust and Hoppe as they raced towards it. But, in the next instant, there was a loud cracking noise. The bridge flew into the air. The tanks stopped and had no other choice but to pull back. Despite taking a round to the front slope of his vehicle, *Leutnant* Aschermann's crew was able to take out one more Russian antitank gun. At that point, the fighting vehicles ran out of ammunition. The 8th Company provided covering fire from the high ground and laid down a wall of smoke, under the cover of which the forward tanks were able to pull back. Despite the heavy fires it had received for several hours, the battalion had only three tanks it needed to write off, although there were dozen of others that sustained battle damage and had to be pulled out of the fighting temporarily.

Alexejewka was occupied by the armored reconnaissance battalion and placed heavy fires on the enemy forces on the far side of the Pena. The Soviets constantly employed their fighter-bombers and regular bombers, which attacked the assembly areas, approach routes and bridges in waves. The engineer sections that had been brought forward to Krassnyj-Potschinok for possibly erecting a bridge over the Pena had to be pulled back to Korowino on account of the constant bombing.

Generalleutnant Westhoven, whose command staff was still on Gerzowka, reported back after personally reconnoitering that it was no longer possible to break through the Pena Position. By then, the Soviets had brought their VI Tank Corps forward. *Panzergrenadier-Division "Großdeutschland"* on the right was also unable to make any forward progress by means of frontal assault. It had shifted its efforts to the east. The corps then ordered the *3. Panzer-Division* to also shift east so as to use a bridgehead established by *Füsilier-Regiment "Großdeutschland"* at Luchanino in order to then attack to the north and northwest.

The Red Air Force was very active during the night. But its attacks were unable to prevent the division from disengaging in its sector and moving east in the direction of Luchanino. *Hauptmann* Deichen's *Panzer-Aufklärungs-Abteilung 3* remained the sole combat formation in the old sector, where it also screened the movements in the areas around Alexejewka and Sawidowka. To the left, the reconnaissance battalion had established contact with *Aufklärungs-Abteilung 332 (332. Infanterie-Division)*.

The combat elements of the *3. Panzer-Division* moved out at first light on 7 July. The march route led through Krassnyj-Potschinok. The armor regiment and the *I./Panzergrenadier-Regiment 3* formed the lead element this time, reaching the area around Luchanino by noon. The engineers took up their bridge in Krassnyj-Potschinok and then followed the columns. Likewise, the supply elements were quickly brought forward along the march route.

The closer the division got to Luchanino, the more obvious it became that the village was in the hands of the Soviets—despite the earlier reports. In the distance, one could see a fairly large number of German tanks burning. While attacking east of Syrzewo, the armored regiment of *Panzergrenadier-Division "Großdeutschland"* had been caught in a trap. The recently introduced *Panzer V Panther*, in which high hopes had been placed, caught fire easily.[2] Not an encouraging sight.

The division commander raced forward to get a better feel for the situation. It turned out that the attack of *Füsilier-Regiment "Großdeutschland"* had stalled at Luchanino and to its east. The village stretched along both sides of the creek and had been transformed into a small fortress with bunkers and trench lines. A barren ridgeline rose behind the creek, from which every German movement could be observed. An attack could only be successful, if it were care-

---

2. Actually, all of the *Panthers* employed at Kursk were issued to two separate tank battalions, *Panzer-Abteilungen 51* and *52*, and attached for command-and-control purposes to *Panzer-Brigade 10*, which was attached to *"Großdeutschland"* tactically during the initial stages of the fighting—hence the confusion concerning the units of assignment. Part of the problem with the *Panther* is that it was rushed into frontline service before all normal trials could be completed. The *Panther* went on to become one of the most famous medium tanks of the war and considered to be one of the best. The *3. Panzer-Division* was eventually equipped with a battalion of them as well.

fully planned. The job of taking Luchanino then fell to the *3. Panzer-Division*, to which the *"Großdeutschland"* fusiliers were attached, as well as a heavy artillery regiment.

Panzergrenadier-Regiment 394 and *Füsilier-Regiment "Großdeutschland"* formed up east of Luchanino to conduct the attack. *Panzergrenadier-Regiment 3*, minus its 1st Battalion, was given the mission of attacking the village from the southeast. *Generaloberst* Hoth, the commander in chief of the *4. Panzer-Armee*, appeared twice at the division command post, located in a defile, in the course of the day. It was not until the two artillery regiments—both under the unified command of *Oberst* Lattmann—reported that they were ready to fire that *Generalleutnant* Westhoven issued the order to move out to the infantry elements. Thanks to the magnificently directed artillery fires and the support of tanks, it was possible to take the high ground north and northwest of Luchanino with few casualties by the evening of 7 July.

Panzergrenadier-Regiment 3 had a much tougher time of it. *Oberstleutnant* Wellmann's regiment, supported by *Hauptmann* Büschen's *5./Panzer-Regiment 6* and *Oberleutnant* Möllhoff's *3./Panzer-Pionier-Bataillon 39*, attacked Luchanino directly. The enemy, who had transformed each structure into a small fortress, defended stubbornly. The mechanized infantry and fighting vehicles pressed forward methodically. Turning out one pocket of resistance after the other. Moving through the village, they finally reached the creek. The tanks provided covering fire from the high ground. It was not possible to build a bridge, however, since the Soviets were placing massed artillery and mortar fire on the positions of the companies.

The Russians fires increased in intensity by the hour. Later on, fighter-bombers joined the fray and illuminated the countryside as bright as day with parachute flares. The crashing of bombs, the howling of the rounds and the bursting asunder of buildings all combined to provide a nighttime concert from hell. The situation of the forces in the village became untenable. The mechanized infantry sought cover under the steel bodies of the fighting vehicles from the devilish fire. In order to avoid casualties, the division ordered the forward positions to be vacated temporarily during the shelling. Despite the heavy fire, the movement back was successful. Fortunately, the casualties and equipment losses were not too great. The *5./Panzer-Regiment 6* lost only one fighting vehicle, which crashed into a defile during the night. The engineers did need to leave behind some vehicles. Unfortunately, the mechanized infantry also suffered some injuries when some tanks pulled back and ran over some men on the ground.

The divisions of the *XXXXVIII. Panzer-Korps* advancing to the right of the *3. Panzer-Division* had also forced the Russian positions by the morning of 8 July and were facing less strongly defended terrain. *Panzergrenadier-Division "Großdeutschland"* attacked that morning west of the road in the direction of Obojan. Its first objective was Syrzewo on the Pena. *Panzer-Regiment 6* was attached to *"Großdeutschland"* in support.

The attack by *"Großdeutschland"* picked up steam. The 5th and 6th Companies of *Panzer-Regiment 6* formed the spearhead of the left wing. They were closely followed by the 7th and 8th Companies of the regiment. To the right, *Panzer-Regiment "Großdeutschland"* attacked as well. The *7./Panzer-Regiment 6*, whose commander, *Oberleutnant* Steindamm, was wounded by a round to the lungs, was then employed on the left as a flank guard. The attack by the two regiments met with considerable success; the enemy was ejected. By 1350 hours, the men of the *I./Panzergrenadier-Regiment "Großdeutschland"* were entering Syrzewo.

Early in the afternoon, *Generalleutnant* Westhoven went to the location of the *7./Panzer-Regiment 6*, which was temporarily being commanded by *Leutnant* Aschermann, in order to reconnoiter the terrain. The tank company was thereupon attached to *Panzergrenadier-Regiment 3*, which was moving out on Luchanino. The fighting vehicles headed west. But after a few meters, the first three vehicles ran over mines and were disabled. By the time the company reached the command post of the *II./Panzergrenadier-Regiment 3*, which was to be the main effort of the divisional attack, it only had four operational vehicles left.

By then, *Hauptmann* Mente's *II./Panzergrenadier-Regiment 3* had already positioned itself for the attack. The Soviets placed the positions that had been won under constant artillery fire, which was being directed from the high stone church steeple in Beresowka. Although the German batteries continuously tried to take out the steeple, their efforts were not crowned with success.

After a short preparation by mortars, Mente's men moved out. They encountered the first enemy line of resistance after advancing only 150 meters. The remaining three fighting vehicles of the 7th Company—those of *Leutnant* Aschermann, *Feldwebel* Appich, and *Unteroffizier* Urban, with the fourth tank of *Feldwebel* Rust having already fired off its ammunition—fired into the Russian position in the defile, which was finally taken by the mechanized infantry. The men continued their advance, only to run into a second line of defense. It was also taken, after storming the bunkers and trench line. Then a third line was assaulted. By then, there were only two fighting vehicles left to provide coverage. By evening, the east bank of the Pena had been reached.

To help support the attack, the division had ordered *Panzer-Aufklärungs-Abteilung 3* to cross the creek west of Luchanino from its positions around Alexejewka. The effort failed due to the heavy enemy fire. At that point, the armored reconnaissance battalion was sent over to the right wing of the division. It appeared that the enemy was slowly wavering there and pulling back. The lead elements of the *11. Panzer-Division* and *Panzergrenadier-Division "Großdeutschland"* were only eleven kilometers from Obojan, the first major objective of the *4. Panzer-Armee*, on the evening of 8 July.

The Soviets realized that the situation was a threatening one for them and committed more and more forces into the battle. The enemy formations that heretofore had been facing the *3. Panzer-Division* moved back to the north and west and established themselves between Werchopenje and Beresowka, orienting to the west. The enemy was attempting to hold open the road to Obojan with all the forces at his disposal. The Soviets regrouped the forces of the III Corps (Mechanized) on 8 July in such a manner that the enemy forces arrayed in front of the *3. Panzer-Division* were positioned as follows (from left to right): 67th Guards Rifle Division, 2001st Tank Brigade, 22nd Tank Brigade, 112th Tank Brigade, 6th Motorized Brigade, and the 90th Guards Rifle Division.

For the time being, the division was still not affected by the massing of the armor forces of the Russians, some of which employed the latest version of the T-34 with the long 8.5-centimeter main gun.[3] The division's mission for 9 July was to screen along the Pena and clear the marshy east bank, where there were still a lot of Russians hiding. Combing through the area was not simple, because many of the Russians still had antitank rifles and they were familiar with the densely mined terrain.

The division, which moved its command staff that day to Syrzew, southeast of Syrzewo, directed the armored reconnaissance battalion into the area around Werchopenje to protect the right flank. The losses in equipment within the division and the casualties taken were not insignificant. The light platoon of the 1st Medical Company established a forward clearing station in the clay huts of Syrzewo on 9 July. Over the next three days, the handful of medics had to care for more than 200 wounded.

The battle, which had its share of high points, continued without letup. The forces of both sides were defending and attacking, day and night. *Panzergrenadier-Division "Großdeutschland"* also started to turn west, and the attack on Wercho-

---

3. The T-34/85 was not introduced until early 1944.

penje commenced. Both the division's armor regiment and armored reconnaissance battalion participated in that thrust. Intense engagements developed between the *Panthers* and *Panzer IV's* and the T-34's. Both antagonists fought doggedly and made sacrifices. The tank of *Oberleutnant* Taulien, the new commander of the *7./Panzer-Regiment 6*, was knocked out. In the end, the Germans gained the upper hand and Werchopenje could be taken. In addition, *"Großdeutschland"* took Hill 258.5 near Werchopenje and Hill 244.8 on the road to Obojan. That hill turned out to be the deepest point of penetration into the Russian front.

The weather turned again. The skies became overcast, and it rained. There was a storm during the night. The change in the weather prevented the enemy from employing his numerous bombers and fighter-bombers, and the German attack on Werchopenje brought with it an unexpected success. It was possible to capture a permanent bridge that was capable of carrying tracked vehicles. The bridge was reinforced by the engineers and supplemented. That same night, the engineer battalion sent its 2nd Company and a bridging section forward, which succeeded in building a 9.6-meter-long sixteen-ton bridge by morning.

The penetration north of Werchopenje was exploited by the *3. Panzer-Division*. *Oberst* Schmidt-Ott's *Panzer-Regiment 6* advanced from Hill 258.5 west of the Pena to the south while, at the same time, *Oberstleutnant* Wellmann's *Panzergrenadier-Regiment 3* and *Major* Peschke's *Panzergrenadier-Regiment 394* thrust across the Pena to the west between Luchanino and Syrzewo. All of the combat forces of the *3. Panzer-Division* were attacking, and the thrust landed square in the middle of the enemy's retrograde operations. The mechanized infantry moved aggressively and took the attack objective of Beresowka, an elevated village that dominated the crossings at Luchanino. The liaison officer of the *II./Panzergrenadier-Regiment 394*, *Leutnant* König, distinguished himself through extraordinary bravery. He was killed, never

knowing that he would be inducted into the Army Honor Roll. In all, 1,700 prisoners were taken, with the *1./Panzergrenadier-Regiment 394* bringing in 70 of that number all by itself.

In the evening, the division received orders to call off the continuation of the attack planned for the next day. It was to immediately swing to the north in order to attack Obojan to the left of *Panzergrenadier-Division "Großdeutschland"* after completing preparations.

As it turned night, the division regrouped its forces towards the north. *Panzergrenadier-Regiment 3* prepared for the attack north of Werchopenje. Behind it were *Panzergrenadier-Regiment 394* and the *II./Panzer-Regiment 6*. The movements through Werchopenje were going faster at that point, since the engineers had set up a sixty-ton bridge in the meantime with the help of construction companies. But before those operations could get underway, the enemy would deliver his own decisive blow.

The division headquarters sent the command staff to Werchopenje. *Hauptmann* Deichens's armored reconnaissance battalion, reinforced by a company from *Panzerjäger-Abteilung 543 (Sfl)*, received orders during the night to relieve a mechanized infantry battalion from *"Großdeutschland"* on the high ground north of Kruglick and, by doing so, screening the open left flank of the *3. Panzer-Division*, which was to attack north. That high-ground position became a bulwark of the front. During the relief, enemy riflemen, supported by fighting vehicles, attacked by surprise from the Kubasosskskij Defile against the outposts of the extended ridgeline. As a result of the critical situation that ensued, *Major* Franz's *Sturmgeschütz-Abteilung "Großdeutschland"* remained in its former positions and helped to turn back the enemy's attack. Soon after that occurred, *Major* Franz received new orders from his division and disengaged his assault guns.

The reconnaissance battalion had no contact with other forces in its two kilometers of sector. After the enemy attack had been turned back, the troops set about improving their positions only to soon report the approach of tanks and trucks about two to three kilometers away. They were headed south along a ridgeline farther west. More tanks and other vehicles were constantly seen along the ridgeline road to the west of the Kubasosskskij Defile. They appeared to be concentrating for an operation northwest of Beresowka.

With the very first reports, the division started to fear that the enemy was preparing an attack against the open deep flank of the division and the *4. Panzer-Armee*. There was no contact with the *167. Infanterie-Division*, which was following to the left rear. The operations officer, *Oberstleutnant* Voß, was sent to the corps headquarters to gain permission for most of the division to hold up until the situation was clarified and to be able to be employed immediately, if a flank attack materialized. Even though the higher command did not share the same opinion and insisted on execution of the original orders, *Generalleutnant* Westhoven left the *II./Panzergrenadier-Regiment 394*, the antitank battalion and the divisional engineers behind.

When more reports came in from the reconnaissance battalion that enemy armor forces were continuing to advance, the *II./Panzergrenadier-Regiment 394* and the antitank battalion received orders to immediately occupy Hill 258.5 west of Werchopenje. The division commander raced to the location to discuss the matter with the two battalion commanders. As they were conferring, Russian tanks appeared directly in front of the small group. The men jumped into a shell hole as fast they could and were overrun by the tanks. At that critical moment, the crack of antitank guns could be heard. Two Russian tanks were hit. The lead platoon of the antitank elements had unlimbered and fired at practically pointblank range. The confusion that erupted among the enemy forces was utilized by *Generalleutnant* Westhoven to run back, give instructions to the mechanized infantry battalion and issue orders from a communications center, that had been sent for-

ward as a precautionary measure, to the artillery for concentrated fires on the new enemy grouping. The division's armored group received orders to turn around and launch an immediate counterattack.

Even those measures might not have come in the nick of time, had not *Hauptmann* Deichen saved the situation by means of a bold decision. Using his light *SPW* company and the brave self-propelled antitank-gun company, he attacked the surprised enemy in the flank. Several T-34's were knocked out and the enemy riflemen suffered heavy casualties from the machine guns firing from the *SPW's*. For his courageous decision, Deichen later received the Knight's Cross.

While *Hauptmann* Deichen continuously struck at the enemy in the very essence of maneuver warfare, there was desperate fighting against the Soviet X Tank Corps between Hill 258.5 and Beresowka. In time, a line of resistance could be established there. *Oberstleutnant* Wellmann led his mechanized infantry in immediate counterattacks. On that day, he needed his universally famous *1000 WW—1000 Worte Wellmann*[4]—more than a few times. *Hauptmann* Dittmer, the commander of the *I./Panzergrenadier-Regiment 394*, who had sworn not to shave once during all of Operation Citadel, provided the laconic remark: "And another beautiful day comes to a close!" The commander of the 5th Company, *Oberleutnant* Rövekamp, was later inducted the Army Honor Roll for his brave and circumspect leadership that day.

In the afternoon, *Generalleutnant* Westhoven was able to reassemble and regroup his beleaguered forces. The *3. Panzer-Division* was west of Werchopenje at that point, oriented to the west. It had transitioned to the defense, turning back all of the thrusts of the massed Soviet X Tank Corps through the evening. For the time being, the enemy's attack into the deep left flank of the *4. Panzer-Armee* had failed. The lines of communication to the rear remained open.

---

4. The 1,000 Words of Wellmann.

The next day, the fighting between Werchopenje and Beresowka continued with undiminished intensity. The Russians attacked constantly with tanks and infantry. Despite the exhaustion of the German forces, the scales seemed to shift in their favor at the course of the day. Thanks to the forcefulness of the leaders, it was possible to form assault detachments and smoke out pockets of resistance. Only a few tanks were still operational, however. The vehicles in need of repair were with the maintenance sections, but they had not been able to get any more replacement parts.

Nothing was heard from *Panzergrenadier-Division "Großdeutschland"* that day.

The night of 13–14 July finally some quiet on the battlefield. The officers and enlisted personnel breathed a sigh of relief. Whoever was not absolutely needed for guard duty fell into a death-like sleep. When the new day dawned, the skies were clear and it was sunny again. There was a howling in the air, but it was not the sound of Russian shells this time. Instead, it was squadrons of *Stukas*. Starting at 0600 hours, the aircraft attacked the Soviet forces to the west of the division in waves. That helped perk up the soldiers.

The Soviets then started their efforts to clear a path for their tanks and riflemen with their bombers. Despite their continuous efforts, the *3. Panzer-Division* held. In the afternoon, the two mechanized infantry regiments, accompanied by tanks, even attacked to the west. They enveloped the large tract of the Tolstoje Woods concentrically on three sides and ejected the newly introduced forces, the 184th and 219th Rifle Divisions. Assault guns from *Panzergrenadier-Division "Großdeutschland"* reestablished contact with the *3. Panzer-Division* in the evening and closed the gap between the two formations.

The hard but successful fighting for the forces died down towards night, when there was

another cloudburst that softened up the road network. Because of it, the divisional artillery was unable to participate in the final phase of fighting, since all of its prime movers had gotten stuck. The mechanized infantry had to hold wherever they found themselves at the time. It was not until next morning that the storms let up. Both of the regiments attacked again and advanced as far as the western edge of the Tolstoje Woods. But most of the enemy rifle divisions had succeeded in escaping to the west by then. Despite that, the division claimed seventy enemy tanks as spoils of war; they had gotten stuck in the marshlands of the woods.

That was the last success for the *XXXXVIII. Panzer-Korps* during the battle, indeed for the entire *4. Panzer-Armee*. The German forces had reached the culminating point. It was clear that the Kursk salient could no longer be reduced with the forces on hand.[5] The enemy proved stronger and, what weighed even more heavily: The *Panzertruppe* had suffered losses from which it would never be able to recover. The German Army started the offensive with sixteen fully equipped armored divisions; by the middle of July, they had all forfeited a large portion of their combat power.

In the end, Hitler realized that he had to break off the battle. On 14 July, he called the offensive off. The German forces had given their all, but the Soviets were superior. *Generaloberst* Model's *9. Armee* had penetrated the Russian front to a depth of anywhere from 14 to 18 kilometers, but then his formations had come to a standstill in front of the Soviet positions. *Generaloberst* Hoth's *4. Panzer-Armee* had penetrated up to thirty-five kilometers. The lead elements of the two field armies were only 100 kilometers apart. In addition, *Armee-Abteilung Kempf* had also penetrated up to 18 kilometers, before his divisions came to a halt. The enemy left 32,000 prisoners in German hands. The Red Army

---

5. This was the general thinking at the time this book was written. More current research indicates that the Germans may have met with success, at least in the south, had they pressed on for several more days. Strategically, this proved impossible, as Hitler basically called off the offensive due to the Allied landings on Sicily and the requirement to send forces to that theater in response.

suffered 17,000 dead. The German forces suffered 3,300 dead and 17,000 missing and wounded. Even if the Russian losses were higher, the German Armed Forces were no longer in a position to cover its losses. The greatest German loss, however, was the bleeding white of the *Panzertruppe*. For that reason, the Battle of Kursk was of even more significance than the Battle of Stalingrad as the turning point of the campaign in the East. The initiative had passed forever into the hands of the Red Army.

The next few days saw the German forces defending. The Soviets started attacking everywhere. The German forces then started moving back to their lines of departure. The neighboring division, *Panzergrenadier-Division "Großdeutschland,"* was pulled out of the line expeditiously to be employed elsewhere. It relieved over the course of two days by elements of the *3. Panzer-Division*.

The fighting around Werchopenje, the Tolstoje Woods and Gremutschij continued with unfinished harshness. The 2nd Medical Company of *Oberstabsarzt* Dr. Koch established a clearing station in the stone school building at Werchopenje, which was visible from a great distance. The medics and the surgeons knew how tough the fighting was. The doctors worked for thirty-six hours straight at the operating tables. In the space of three days, the company took care of 350 badly wounded men.

The division remained in its positions until 18 July. It was adjoined on the right by the *11. Panzer-Division* and by the *332. Infanterie-Division* on the left. The mechanized infantry, engineers, radio operators, antitank gunners, tankers and cannoneers remained in their fox holes, camouflaged their vehicles, pulled guard and defended whenever the Russians attacked with fighting vehicles or infantry. Everyone was asking himself the question: "How much longer?"

Then, at 1600 hours on 18 July, the division command post received orders: "Get ready to move immediately! We are pulling out!" No one had time to think about what the order meant. All of a sudden it was pack up and move out! As the lead elements formed up to move out that evening, there was a downpour. The weather matched the mood the officers and men found themselves in.

In the midst of pouring rain, softened-up roads and the dark of night, the men moved along the same road to the south that they had taken in days of fighting. The road, which several columns were using at the same time, was soon backed up, since the heavier vehicles got stuck in the mud. The difficult movement took the formations of the division through Tscherkaskoje-Butowo and then on to Luchanino. The sun did not start shining again until noon on 19 July, drying the road so that movements again became more fluid.

The Soviets identified the fact that the German forces were pulling back; they pursued immediately. The few operational fighting vehicles of the *II./Panzer-Regiment 6* and *Panzergrenadier-Regiment 394* formed the rearguard. They had to fend off the pursuing enemy forces on more than one occasion. Since the *Luftwaffe* was no longer seen in the skies, the Russians possessed air superiority and exploited it accordingly. The enemy forces were able to press ahead by surprise to Luchanino on 19 July. It was solely thanks to the brave actions of the *7./Panzer-Regiment 6* and its new commander, the always dependable *Leutnant* Sorge, that the enemy attack did not tear apart the German columns.

The enemy continued to press harder by the hour and covered the rearguards with well-placed artillery fire. As early as the next day, Russian tanks pressed into the gap between the *3.* and *11. Panzer-Divisionen*. *Panzergrenadier-Regiment 394* immediately turned around and threw itself at the Soviet forces between Gremutschij and Syrzewo. *Major* Peschke's battalion launched an immediate counterattack. Despite considerable losses, the regiment was able to hold back the enemy. *Hauptmann* Bieler, the new commander of the 2nd Battalion, and his men particularly distinguished themselves. The division was able to hold a line running Syrzewo–Beresowka–Rakowo.

The fact that the disengagements from the enemy always succeeded, was due in large part to the divisional artillery and its unflappable observers. *Major* Weymann's 2nd Battalion was frequently in the thick of things. During the afternoon of 21 July, the *XXXXVIII. Panzer-Korps* ordered that the division was to pull back across the Pena to the south during the night, leaving behind strong rearguards.

It turned out to be a difficult day for *Hauptmann* Dietrich's *5./Panzergrenadier-Regiment 3*, which was a part of the rearguard and had to hold its positions until the evening. Despite repeated enemy attacks, the company held. In accordance with its orders, it did not disengage from the enemy until around 2130 hours.

That same evening, the division started its retrograde movements across the Pena, which were executed without a hitch. The last few companies of *Panzergrenadier-Regiment 394* followed the next morning. With the completion of that movement on 22 July, the division had found itself back at the point it had started on 4 July. Occupying the trenches this time were the formations of the *332.* and *255. Infanterie-Divisionen.* The columns of the division were passed through the lines and collected in the area around Chotymsk and to its south in the course of the day.

The division headquarters, which established itself in Sseretino, received orders from the field-army group at noon that it was allocated to the *1. Panzer-Armee*, effective immediately, and was to start moving to the area north of Kharkov. That signaled the end to another chapter of the division's history.

General der Panzertruppen Knobelsdorff, the commanding general of the *XXXXVIII. Panzer-Korps*, took his leave of the division on 22 July with the following general order:

As of today, the *3. Panzer-Division* leaves the *XXXXVIII. Panzer-Korps* in order to be sent elsewhere for new utilization. I am filled with pride to be able to express my thanks and appreciation to the division for its terrific achievements. The division accomplished the missions assigned to it in an exemplary manner: It broke through the heavily built-up fortifications of the enemy, along with the neighboring divisions, and played a major role in the decisive envelopment and encirclement movements of the corps along its western flank.

Let my best wishes accompany the division on its way to new assignments.

The commander in chief of the *4. Panzer-Armee*, *Generaloberst* Hoth, directed personal correspondence to the division, in which it stated, among other things:

Coming from another sector, the division had an especially hard time of it in conducting an attack along the left wing in unfamiliar terrain. Boldly attacking, the division broke deeply through the enemy's main battle area on the first day of attack and executed its thankless mission of covering the left flank of the entire attack in an exemplary manner. It played a major role in weakening the offensive combat power of the enemy. It can be proud of its success.

I wish to express my utmost recognition to the division.

After the fighting at Kursk, the following members of the division were awarded the German Cross in Gold for their noteworthy contributions to the operations: *Major* Weymann, the commander of the *II./Panzer-Artillerie-Regiment 75*; *Major* Stockmann, the commander of the *II./Panzer-Regiment 6*; *Oberfeldwebel* Krotke of the *5./Panzer-Regiment 6*; and *Oberfeldwebel* Sydow of the *8./Panzer-Regiment 6*.

Elements of *Panzer-Regiment 6* assembling for Operation Citadel in the Bjelgorod area at the beginning of July 1943.

Major Peschke, Knight's Cross recipient and commander of the *II./Panzergrenadier-Regiment 394*.

Generalleutnant Westhoven in his command *SPW*. Standing behind him is *Oberleutnant* Kleffel. Note the relatively unusual addition of the 3.7-centimeter antitank gun to a radio version of the *Sd.Kfz. 251*.

Female Red Army soldiers captured in the Bjelgorod area, along with their commissar.

CHAPTER 7

From the Mius to the Dnjepr: Fighting for the Ukraine

The Russian leadership used the commitment of practically all of the reserves and armor divisions of the Eastern Front as a result of Operation Citadel to launch a major offensive along the Mius. Factoring into the decision was the fact that a penetration into the Ukraine would make the harvesting of the grain, which was so important for Germany, impossible.

The initiative had passed on over to the enemy. He would retain that initiative through the end of the war. On 17 July, the enemy moved across the Mius with the 5th Shock Army, the 2nd Guards Army, and the 28th Army in the area around Demitrijewka Jassinowskij, penetrating deeply.

The *6. Armee* gave *General der Waffen-SS* Hausser's *II. SS-Panzer-Korps* the mission of throwing the enemy back across the river. Since Operation Citadel had been given up by then, other formations became available, including the *3. Panzer-Division*.

By 26 July, the division reached the area around Losowaja, moving along roads that were sometimes dusty and sometimes softened up from rain. The road conditions negatively affected the road movements considerably. The tracked elements of the division were loaded on trains at Kharkov. The men of the division were familiar with the route, since they had used it, after all, just a short time ago. The command staff moved through Losowaja to Grischino. On 27 July, it went on to Krassnogorowka and, on the next day, through Stalino to Leski.

The constant demands placed on the vehicles and the poor road network combined to make the number of mechanical losses for the division climb significantly. Since the corresponding replacement parts had not arrived, it was almost impossible to effect repairs in the short term. Other losses were sustained from Russian bombers, as well as the explosion of an ammunition train in Charzyssk on 28 July.

The division commander was ordered to a conference at the headquarters of the *II. SS-Panzer-Korps*, where he was informed that the attack would take place from north to south as follows (arrayed from west to east): *23. Panzer-Division, SS-Panzer-Grenadier-Division "Das Reich," SS-Panzer-Grenadier-Division "Totenkopf," and SS-Panzer-Grenadier-Division "Leibstandarte SS Adolf Hitler."* The *3. Panzer-Division* would follow behind the *"Leibstandarte."* In the middle of the conference, a telephone call came in from the *6. Armee*, stating that the entire operation might be doubtful. Later on, the decision was made to continue the operation, but without the *"Leibstandarte,"* which was to be immediately rail loaded to Italy. The *3. Panzer-Division* was to take the place of the *"Leibstandarte."*

On 28 and 29 July, the division reached the area around Gurschewyj, right behind the front. The regiments and battalions moved into their tactical assembly areas during the night of 29–30 July, from which the *"Leibstandarte"* was departing. Personal-demand items were distributed, and the supply sections brought ammunition forward. The rest of the *II. SS-Panzer-Korps* had closed in. The *3. Panzer-Division* formed the left wing and had established contact with the *306. Infanterie-Division*, which was to hold out in its positions.

The enemy's offensive had already reached its culminating point by this point; the Russians had transitioned to the defense. The division's intelligence section published an intelligence estimate on 29 July. It could be gleaned from the document that the following enemy divisions were arrayed in front of the *3. Panzer-Division* alone (left to right): the 126th Infantry Division, the 4th and 10th Guards Rifle Divisions, and the 32nd Tank Brigade. The focal point of the efforts of the XXXI Corps was on the left, where its tank brigade adjoined both the II and the IV Corps (Mechanized).

The right half of the attack terrain consisted of completely barren terrain, practically without cover. In the lefthand sector, there were small groups of vegetation and folds in the ground, which helped the mechanized infantry but also the enemy. The division employed its armored group on the right—which, it should be mentioned, had very few tanks—under *Hauptmann* Dittmer. On the left, *Panzergrenadier-Regiment 394* was given the attack mission. *Panzergrenadier-Regiment 3*, minus its 1st Battalion, was held in reserve.

The attack by the *II. SS-Panzer-Korps* started at 0810 hours on 30 July across the entire front. The Soviets quickly recovered from the initial shock of the *Stuka* attack and stubbornly went about defending.

Enemy bombers and fighter-bombers flew in extended formations above the bursts of fire from the 2-centimeter *Flak* over the battlefield and bombed and strafed almost continuously. Among the enemy positions, there were many dug-in tanks.

Initially, the attack by the armored group made good progress, but then it ran into a dense minefield. It turned out to extend across all of the terrain that was trafficable for tanks. The brave *3./Panzer-Pionier-Bataillon 39* attempted to clear lanes through the minefield while receiving covering fires from the tanks and the artillery.

Panzergrenadier-Regiment 394 had been directed to take the villages of Peresej and Srubna to open up the enemy's front and clear the way to the Mius north of Demitrijewak. *Oberstleutnant* Beuermann had just taken command of the regiment on 24 July. *Hauptmann* Eggert's 1st Battalion attacked Srubna, but it stalled outside of the village. Likewise, the 2nd Battalion was unable to take Peresej. The Russian fighter-bombers covered the mechanized infantry so thoroughly, that they were barely able to lift their heads. Hours passed, without the situation changing. Gigantic mushrooms of smoke from the artillery impacts and bomb detonations obscured the sun for periods of time. Considerable losses were taken.

The night that followed remained relatively calm. It seemed as though the enemy wanted to catch his breath. When the first pale light of morning arrived in the east on 31 July, the battle flared up again. The division ordered its artillery batteries forward, and they placed a short preparation on the enemy positions. The mechanized infantry and the attached tanks attacked one more time. The enemy's resistance in that bulwark of the Soviet positions appeared to have increased, however.

The engineers accomplished incredible things in the sector of the armored group, and they were finally able to create lanes in the minefield. But when the *I./Panzergrenadier-Regiment 3* advanced through, it quickly encountered a second minefield.

It was breached, as well as a third, before the armored group of *Hauptmann* Dittmer finally entered the enemy positions. But there were not enough forces to capitalize on that success. The division commander ordered the attack to be stopped, but the enemy was to be deceived into thinking it was continuing by means of fire.

The friendly forces to the right, *SS-Panzer-Grenadier-Division "Totenkopf,"* had not been blessed with success up to that point, either. On the other hand, the *23. Panzer-Division* was able to score a decisive breakthrough along its open wing, which also had positive effects for *SS-Panzer-Grenadier-Division "Das Reich."*

Panzer-Artillerie-Regiment 75 was immediately sent into the sector of the *23. Panzer-Division* and helped it in its farther advance. At the same time, the *3. Panzer-Division* received orders to disengage from the enemy during the night so as to be attached to the *XXIV. Panzer-Korps,* which was attacking from the south. Things did not turn out that way, however.

At the end of the fighting, the Mius Position was taken back and the Russians suffered heavy losses. Although the division did not achieve a success that was immediately apparent, it did tie up enemy forces through its tough

attacks, thus effectively contributing to victory at another location.

The very next day, the divisions received orders to immediately move north. Soviet forces had overrun the German front at Bjelgorod, north of Kharkov. They had already achieved deep penetrations into the sector of *Armee-Abteilung Kempf*. The enemy's thrust was directed to the south and to the west of Kharkov. It apparently had the objective of cutting off the formations that were arrayed in a semicircle around the major city. The field-army group expedited the movement of the division there, as well as the two SS divisions, *"Das Reich"* and *"Totenkopf."*

The columns rolled out of the Charzyssk–Makejewka area through Jassinowataja, Konstantinowka, Podolje, and Nowaja Wodolaga toward Kharkov. The approach march indicated the severity of the fighting that was to come, since enemy fighters and fighter-bombers loitered over the march columns and attacked them constantly.

The closer the forces got to Kharkov, the worse it got. Columns of trains vehicles and supply elements blocked the roads. There were disabled vehicles to the left and right of the road.

On 6 August, the lead elements of the division reached Kharkov and were immediately directed north. The division headquarters, which followed from Nowaja Wodolaga to Nowo Bawaria, a suburb of Kharkov, was briefed on the latest situation. Ever since 4 August, the *III. Panzer-Korps* had been involved in extremely heavy defensive fighting. Soviet armor forces had broken through at Tomarowka that day and had advanced as far as Bogoduchoff. The enemy had attacked the corps command post, whereby the commanding general, *General der Panzertruppen* Breith, had been wounded. It was only the employment of the corps signals battalion, which attacked ten T-34's in close combat, that the corps headquarters was saved.

Speed was of the essence. Without waiting for the tracked vehicles or the divisional artillery, which had to be transported by rail, the mechanized infantry were committed in the area around Dergatschi. Advance parties established contact with the *168. Infanterie-Division* and elements of the *6.* and *19. Panzer-Divisionen.* It was possible to establish a more-or-less cohesive front. Greatly anticipated, the divisional artillery and the *II./Panzer-Regiment 6* arrived on 7 August.

The enemy kept attacking with tanks and infantry and had enormous numerical superiority. The divisional armored reconnaissance battalion succeeded in entering Solotschew and establishing an all-round defense with the village as its pivot point. To the northwest of the village, it was possible to establish a defensive position with the light *SPW* company along Ridgeline 208.5. While the Soviets attempted to enter the village west of the rail line—mostly with infantry—from the north, they attacked from the east over and over again with tanks. They advanced past Solotschew to the south and separated the battalion for a while from its rearward lines of communication. Despite all that, it was possible to hold the village and also destroy two of the three enemy tanks that had entered it.

Major Deichen's men were able to hold the positions that had been hastily occupied and went after the tanks that had broken through with mines and shaped charges. *Oberleutnant* Kunze and *Pionier* Möhring of the *2./Panzer-Pionier-Bataillon 39* eliminated two T-34's in close combat.

Panzergrenadier-Regiment 394 was also able to stand firm against all attacks. Wherever the enemy would break through or infiltrate, a few courageous men would seal them off or launch an immediate counterattack, despite their exhaustion. The 10th Company of the regiment, the self-propelled *Flak* company, particularly distinguished itself under *Hauptmann* Arnoldt and the future *Leutnant* Dr. Bayer. Without any cover at all, they moved against the enemy and shot him to pieces with their 2-centimeter guns. The commander of the 2nd Battalion, *Hauptmann* Bieler, was captured after putting up the bravest of defenses. The commander of the 1st Battalion, *Hauptmann* Müller-Röhlich, and his

adjutant, *Leutnant* Henk, were wounded. The brave commander of the 5th Company, *Oberleutnant* Röverkamp, and the forward observer from the 1st Battery of the divisional artillery, *Leutnant* Schweigler, were among the dead.

Fortunately, the *Stukas* were active that day and joined the fray on the ground again and again. The fighting vehicles of the *II./Panzer-Regiment 6* were also successful. The *Panzer IV's* were able to give the mechanized infantry powerful support. Tank engagements that lasted for hours ensued, but the German tanks remained the victors in the end. *Oberleutnant* Taulien's 7th Company did the best, with both *Oberleutnant* Taulien and *Unteroffizier* Eggers racking up the score. More than twenty T-34's were knocked out by the two of them, with both later receiving the Knight's Cross.

The fighting for Kharkov continued. During the second night, the division established contact with its neighbors, the *168. Infanterie-Division* and *SS-Panzer-Grenadier-Division "Das Reich."* Despite that, the situation remained serious. A downpour around noon interrupted the hard fighting for a while. But the Russians started attacking again along the entire division frontage soon afterwards. On 10 August, the divisional artillery fired more than 2,800 shells, establishing a record. Both the *II./Panzer-Regiment 6* and *Panzerjäger-Abteilung 543* were successful that day, knocking out a total of forty-six enemy fighting vehicles.

The armored reconnaissance battalion continued to have to fend off large attacks from its strongpoint at Solotschew on the left wing. In the process, the battalion became encircled. *Stukas* and an armored train brought some relief.

Late in the afternoon of 10 August, orders were received directing that the battalion pull back from the strongpoint. By then, however, the situation had evolved to the point where it was no longer possible to pull back on the road east of the Uda. Enemy tanks were to the rear of the battalion and were covering the road. At the last minute, the only remaining usable bridge over the river to the south of the village was reconnoitered. Even though the load capacity was barely enough for the armored vehicles, the companies started withdrawing unnoticed from the enemy at the onset of darkness. The battalion succeeded in bringing all of its vehicles to the west bank.

The front was pulled back to a line running Dergatschi–Fesski during the night of 10–11 August. As a result of a cloudburst, the withdrawal went unnoticed by the enemy. In the morning, friendly reconnaissance determined that the Russians had pulled their tanks off to the north. On 11 August, the division received reinforcements in the form of thirteen *Tigers* and an *SPW* company from *SS-Panzer-Grenadier-Division "Das Reich."* The division was attached to *General der Panzertruppen* Raus's *XI.*

Armee-Korps, since the *III. Panzer-Korps* was moved farther west.

In Kharkov proper, there were already signs of dissolution. Rear-area services were fleeing in a panic. The rations depots were rapidly emptied, if they hadn't already been plundered. All of a sudden, the local populace turned aggressive and harassed the departing soldiers. Shortly after midnight on 12 August, Russian artillery started to take the northern portion of the city under direct fire.

While enemy shells were setting the houses of Kharkov on fire, four Soviet rifle divisions attacked the positions of the *3. Panzer-Division* in the morning. *Oberstleutnant* Beuermann's *Panzergrenadier-Regiment 394* was once more in the thick of things. *Hauptmann* von Kleist's

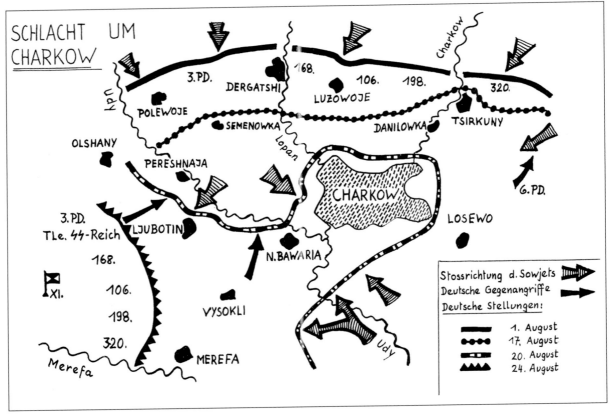

Battle of Kharkov
Stossrichtung d. Sowjets = Direction of advance of the Soviets; *Deutsche Gegenangriffe* = German counterattacks; *Deutsche Stellungen* = German positions

1st Battalion and *Hauptmann* Arnoldt's 2nd Battalion could only hold their sectors with difficulty. When the Russians entered Dergatschi, *Major* Stockmann's tanks were able to eject them. Likewise, *Oberstleutnant* Wellmann's *Panzergrenadier-Regiment 3* was able to contain a Soviet attack.

The reconnaissance battalion had been assigned another sector, and it suffered additional losses in the wake of strong Soviet attacks. *Oberleutnant* Wittmack, who had just assumed command of the 2nd Company, was badly wounded and died a short while later.

A few *Panzer IV's* were sent to the reconnaissance battalion in the course of the day. With their help, it was possible to knock out five T-34's. The battalion was then sent to another threatened position. Once there, the platoon leader of a *Tiger* platoon reported in to the battalion command post. His employment required the permission of the division, but the mere fact that the tanks were on hand gave the reconnaissance soldiers in their positions a boost and a feeling of unconditional security. Those feelings were short lived, since the tanks rolled off a short while later to be committed elsewhere.

It was obvious that the front could not be held much longer there. In the afternoon, the command staff moved to Peresetschnaja, outside of Olschany. The vehicles and the non-essential equipment were moved back to the Olschany area. The forward clearing station, which had handled 420 wounded in the space of four days, was moved from Kurortskaja to Jemeljanoff. The establishment of rearward positions was started everywhere.

On Friday, 13 August, the Soviets attacked at first light. The German positions were placed under a hail of artillery fire. By conducting immediate counterattacks, both of the mechanized infantry regiments gained some breathing room. Russian tanks broke through the positions of the reconnaissance battalion, which had been reduced to eighty men. Friendly fighting vehicles helped maintain contact between the battalions and prevented the left wing from being

ripped completely open. The division received *Grenadier-Regiment 351* from the *167. Infanterie-Division* as a reserve force, although the regiment only mustered 200 men and could only occupy a thin screening line.

The division commander was forced to watch his forces, which had been overextended for weeks, shrink in numbers in the defensive positions. At every opportunity possible, he recommended the evacuation of Kharkov, which would considerably shorten the extended frontage. The immediate chain-of-command was of the same opinion. The highly competent commander in chief of the field army, *General* Kempf, was relieved because he insisted upon the evacuation of Kharkov.

When the Soviets achieved a breakthrough in the sector of *Generalmajor* Chales de Beaulieu's *168. Infanterie-Division*, the corps issued orders to pull back. A short while later, the forces were ordered to halt their movements. A *Führer* order had arrived that stated that Kharkov was to be held at all costs.

The Russians started a barrage fire on 14 August that was reminiscent of the battles of attrition of World War I. Friendly losses climbed by the hour. Russian artillery observers had infiltrated through gaps in the front and were directed fires from the rear on artillery positions, troop concentrations etc. We were able to eavesdrop on their radio traffic, but it proved impossible to find them. There was absolutely no support from the *Luftwaffe*. The division pulled back in the direction of Polewaja in the face of overwhelming numbers. The Soviets pursued immediately. Their tanks sometimes reached the German fallback positions before the Germans did. The men of *Panzergrenadier-Regiment 3* were not just a little surprised when they found themselves being attacked from the rear by T-34's.

It was blazingly hot in the Ukraine on 15 August. The soldiers of the division were still involved in heavy fighting. *Panzergrenadier-Regiment 394* was being continuously attacked at Polewaja. What was left of the regiment held out in front of the village and, later on, in the ruins of the houses. The Russians attacked on three sides. The bled-white companies continued to defend and push the enemy back innumerable times. The remaining operations guns of the divisional artillery fired with everything they had. Twelve enemy tanks were counted burning in front of the regimental lines.

Since the division no longer had any reserves, the infantry of a destroyed division were sent in as reinforcements.

The fighting continued under the blast furnace of the August sun. The division command post in Peresetschnaja was under constant fire. There were no more rear-area services; the front was everywhere. Soviet aircraft dropped leaflets with the following text: "Comrades of the *3. Panzer-Division*! We know that you are brave soldiers. Every second one of you wears the Iron Cross. But every second one of us carries a mortar." Those words did not seem to be exaggerated when the division underwent yet another monstrous firestorm on 16 August.

Panzergrenadier-Regiment 3 carried on a dogged fight with the enemy. The Russians were able to repeatedly infiltrate through the high sunflower fields though the German lines. They had to smoke them out gradually in close combat, frequently with the aid of flamethrowers. The 1st Battalion lost two of its company commanders, *Oberleutnant* Ulbrich and *Oberleutnant* Lohse. The last remaining *SPW's* were consolidated into a battle group under the command of *Leutnant* Gruschwitz. *Panzergrenadier-Regiment 394* had an even worse time of it. The men, who had not slept for days, continued to hold out in Polewaja. The ammunition for the heavy weapons had long since been used up. The enemy fire created more and more gaps in the lines. *Hauptmann* von Kleist and the highly competent commander of the 9th Company, *Oberleutnant* Dr. Lobedanz, died a soldier's death, along with many other officers, noncommissioned officers and enlisted personnel. *Oberleutnant* Goppel assumed acting command of the 1st Battalion. When the Soviets attacked the village from the southeast on 16 August, the regiment was cut off

from the division. The regimental adjutant, *Hauptmann* Steinmüller, became a rallying point for the formation. When the Russians attacked the regimental command post, he created some breathing room by means of an immediate counterattack conducted by a hastily assembled group of men. His bravery later resulted in induction into the Army Honor Roll. *Hauptmann* Deichen was finally able to reestablish contact with the last six *SPW's* of his reconnaissance battalion. The security platoon of the division headquarters under *Oberfeldwebel* Heinz was also employed in that effort. Only four men from that platoon returned from the operation, Heinz was not one of them.

Panzer-Regiment 6, the backbone of the division, was decimated. The fighting elements had inflicted heavy casualties on the Russians, but they were at the end of their rope. *Leutnant* Zeislinger and *Oberfeldwebel* Kamin had been killed; *Oberst* Schmidt-Ott and *Oberleutnant* Adamek (8th Company) wounded. *Oberleutnant* von Veltheim led the remaining operational tanks, which the new commander of the 2nd Battalion, *Major* Lühl, had consolidated into one company.

The devotion to duty and the mental toughness of the men was deserving of admiration. For weeks on end, they had been embroiled in a grueling and bloody defensive battle against a gruesome enemy, who vastly outnumbered them, both in men and materiel. Fighting individually or in small groups, with no contact with friendly forces to either side, frequently attacked from the rear, they held out, since they knew that giving up their positions would endanger their neighbors. It was a quiet heroism that usually remained hidden. The emotional and physical stress of such situations was far greater than any successful attack.

Rockets from Stalin organs howled through the air shortly before 0500 hours on 17 August, introducing a new Soviet large-scale attack. The Russians rolled against the positions of *Panzergrenadier-Regiment 394* with twenty-four T-34's. The men toughly defended the ruins and foxholes. But the enemy had entered Polewaja and was also on Hills 201 and 204. *Oberstleutnant* Wellmann charged forward with a colorful battle group that had been hastily assembled. For a short while, the soldiers were successful, but then the enemy started attacking from the east and into the flank. Additional immediate counterattacks on the part of the regiment to dislodge the enemy failed; the employment of *Stukas* was also unable to change anything. The situation appeared doubtful, but *Oberstleutnant* Wellmann was still able to hold back the enemy that evening with elements received from *Panzergrenadier-Regiment 3*, *Grenadier-Regiment 331 (167. Infanterie-Division)*, and *Panzer-Aufklärungs-Abteilung 3*. The T-34's turned back to the southeast; the situation was saved for the division. The enemy tanks soon hit the neighboring *168. Infanterie-Division* in the flank, however.

The new field army commander in chief, *General der Infanterie* Wöhler, gave the division commander to understand while visiting the division command post that "what will happen is what has to happen." That statement was a relief, inasmuch as it meant that the senseless fighting would be broken off.

The *3. Panzer-Division* finally gave up its positions around Polewaja, receiving the corps' permission to occupy the "Friedrich II" Line to the rear. The command staff moved back from Peresetschnaja to Samorodskij.

Panzergrenadier-Regiment 394 occupied new positions around Peresetschnaja, which had been evacuated of civilians. The regiment consisted of a sole battle group, which was commanded by *Hauptmann* Arnoldt. The remaining elements of the *I./Panzergrenadier-Regiment 3* under *Major* Dittmer disengaged from the enemy. As the rearguard, they had to race through Russian columns at full throttle to get back to the German lines, as the Soviets were nipping at the German heels. The T-34's that rolled forward at first light posed a new danger to the decimated *Panzergrenadier-Regiment 394*.

When the Russian tanks attacked, the division alerted its armored battle group. *Oberleutnant*

von Veltheim moved immediately to Peresetschnaja and had his vehicles deploy for the attack at the edge of the village. *Leutnant* Aschermann led the remaining tanks of the 5th and 7th Companies, while *Feldwebel* Holstein directed the efforts of the 6th Company and *Oberfeldwebel* Bartels the 8th. Despite the heavy fire, the fighting vehicles rattled up the slowly climbing terrain and engaged the T-34's in the positions of the mechanized infantry. A hard-fought engagement ensued between the sixteen Russian tanks and the German ones. The Soviets appeared to have taken the upper hand—*Feldwebel* Holstein had already been killed—when *Leutnant* Aschermann attacked by surprise from a defile with the remaining seven *Panzer IV's* and engaged the Soviets at pointblank range. Eleven Soviet tanks went up in flames. *Oberfeldwebel* Müller and *Unteroffizier* Banecki pursued the fleeing Russians and each knocked out an additional T-34. The situation had been cleared up once again.

A few hours later—it was the anniversary date of the Red Air Force—Soviet bombers and fighter-bombers attacked Peresetschnaja and the road to Ljubotin. One of the attacks was flown by sixty fighter-bombers; the German defensive weaponry was unable to do anything against them. The Soviets initiated a large-scale attack to the west of Kharkov, in an effort to cut off the city. The 5th Tank Army attacked at the same time from the east. The front lines of the *320. Infanterie-Division* of the *XXXXII. Armee-Korps* collapsed. Tanks poured through the gap and were able to get as far as the tractor works east of Kharkov.

Based on the heavy casualties of the previous few days, the division was forced to take the headquarters of *Panzergrenadier-Regiment 394* out of the line. All combat-capable units of the regiment—no more than the equivalent of two companies—were attached to *Panzergrenadier-Regiment 3*. *Oberstleutnant* Beuermann was entrusted with reorganizing the regiment in the rear, since the area around Welki was also seeing increasing partisan activity.

Russian barrage fires on the morning of 19 August woke the men from a short, restless sleep. Enemy riflemen and tanks advanced against *Panzergrenadier-Regiment 3*, which was able to turn back the enemy forces in tough close combat. A few hours later, the Russians placed a barrage fire on Peresetschnaja. The remnants of *Panzergrenadier-Regiment 394*, which were still holding there, were too weak to hold back the enemy. Even the four tanks that were attached in support were not enough to stop the enemy. It was not until an immediate counterattack launched by *Oberfeldwebel* Bartels with eight *Panzer IV's* of the 8th Company that some breathing room was obtained. The mechanized infantry dug in anew in the vicinity of the fighting vehicles.

The field army approached the evacuation of Peresetschnaja in the evening. A company from the reconnaissance battalion, reinforced with a few tanks and engineers, served as rearguard for the movement across the Uda. The engineers blew the last bridge into the air. The division pulled back behind the Uda to a line running Ljubotin–Kharkov. The division command post was established in Mischtschenkoff.

The division was widely dispersed. The infantry forces could only be directed to positions in general terms. The main brunt of the defense was borne by the nimbly led artillery of *Oberst* Lattmann, the tanks and antitank elements, the *SPW's* of the *I./Panzergrenadier-Regiment 3*, and *Panzeraufklärungs-Abteilung 3*. The prerequisites for success were the maintenance of good communications and a decisive but agile leadership.

On the following day, 20 August, reports from artillery observers and forces in the field indicated that the enemy was bringing forward strong forces in front of the division sector. There were thick clouds of dust over all of the depressions and folds in the ground. Reconnaissance aircraft identified large concentrations of armor, with fifty tanks in Peresetschnaja alone. There was not enough artillery ammunition to engage those concentrations effectively. *Stukas*

were requested. Their bombs caused great mushroom clouds of smoke to rise from the earth. It proved fortuitous that new tanks arrived about that time, so that the combat power of the armor battalion could be increased somewhat.

At 0500 hours on the morning of 21 August, the enemy started placing barrage fires on the division's positions again. When enemy tanks started rolling against the left-hand portion of the division sector, they were effectively engaged by the *5.* and *6./Panzer-Regiment 6* under *Hauptmann* Heuer. The lead T-34's were knocked out, and the remaining twenty turned away. The Russian infantry were forced to take cover by the divisional artillery. The tanks were tied up by the Soviet tank concentrations, however.

In the righthand sector of the division, to the east of Kasarowka, there was a new danger brewing to face the *II./Panzergrenadier-Regiment 3*. For hours, it could be seen with the naked eye that enemy tanks were concentrating. They could attack at any moment, and there was no defensive weaponry of note against them.

The division was promised the *Panther* battalion from *SS-Panzer-Grenadier-Division "Das Reich."* The battalion was rolling in from the homeland after it had been issued the new tanks there. The question: Would it arrive in time? The detraining was delayed by an enemy air attack, which disabled six of the *Panthers*. The enemy tank masses then started approaching the positions of the *II./Panzergrenadier-Regiment 3*. They overran the main line of resistance, but then the *Panthers* arrived. Fifty enemy tanks were knocked out, and the rest turned back, where they were passed through their lines by other armor formations. The enemy infantry disappeared as well. For the time being, the enemy stopped his attacks. A great defensive success had been scored, especially since *SS-Panzer-Grenadier-Regiment "Deutschland,"* which was sent to the division during the night, was able to seal off and eliminate an enemy penetration by means of an immediate counterattack. There were not enough forces to continue the attacks past the main line of resistance, however.

Despite that, the division had thwarted the intent of the enemy to break through the German front at that location in an effort to encircle the German divisions still fighting in Kharkov. *Hauptmann* Brandt, the regimental adjutant of *Panzergrenadier-Regiment 3*, was later inducted into the Army Honor Roll for his part in those operations.

The next day, the enemy started feeling his way forward again, but there were no large-scale attacks. The Red Air Force attacked day and night.

Finally, on 22 August, Kharkov was evacuated. *General der Infanterie* Wöhler made the decision on his own. Hitler was able to come to terms with it.

The movement of the infantry divisions to the west necessitated some shifting of forces within the *XI. Armee-Korps*. The *3. Panzer-Division* remained on the left wing. The front needed to be straightened out a bit in the area around Olschany next to the neighboring *SS-Panzer-Grenadier-Division "Das Reich."* The division's armored reconnaissance battalion was entrusted with that task. *Oberleutnant* Kleffel's 4th Company, reinforced with a platoon of tanks under *Leutnant* Aschermann and a platoon of mechanized infantry, rolled forward. The enemy identified the German intent and placed protective fires on the terrain. The fighting vehicles were able to make it through the artillery fire, but the mechanized infantry had no such luck. At that point, the operation was called off. *Oberleutnant* Kunze's *2./Panzer-Pionier-Bataillon 39* was sent forward at first light. The battle-tested engineer company occupied the position and was able to hold it against every enemy attack.

An attack planned for *SS-Panzer-Grenadier-Regiment "Deutschland"* on 28 August had to be cancelled, since the artillery was not in a position to adequately support the advance. The regiment was taken out of the front in the course of the day and sent back to its parent division.

Panzergrenadier-Regiment 3 continued to hold its sector around Ljubotin. The Russians continuously reinforced their elements there and exerted pressure against the railway embankment. The mechanized infantry were positioned within the fruit orchards, in the fields and in the *balkas*. The Soviets infiltrated with substantial forces. *Major* Dittmer committed his 3rd Company to an immediate counterattack, and his mechanized infantry were able to eject the enemy force. As they continued their advance, they ran into heavy fire, which was supported in part by T-34's. The company was effectively wiped out. By noon, the following had found their way back: *Oberleutnant* Litzmann, *Gefreiter* Tenning (radio operator), a medic, and two soldiers. A few hours later, a few more scattered soldiers reappeared. The enemy attacked the returned elements. In the process, one T-34 got stuck in marshland. An unknown mechanized infantryman, who had just arrived with the last trainload of replacements from the homeland, jumped on the steely monster and tossed a hand grenade into the open hatch. The T-34 flew into the air. The brave nineteen-year-old soldier received the Iron Cross, Second Class, directly from the hands of *Major* Dittmer on the battlefield. It was the last joyful act he experienced; a short while later, he was killed.

As a result of the shortening of the corps frontage on 24 August, the *3. Panzer-Division* also received a narrower sector. Contact with the friendly forces to both sides was established. The command staff of the division moved to Jemeljanoff at noon. Even though the enemy did not attack, his artillery continued firing on all movements and caused considerable losses, even at the division command post.

The weather continued to be summery and warm. During the afternoon of 25 August, the division was radioed movement orders for a withdrawal. Since the landlines had been destroyed, the movement order could only be transmitted by radio. The neighbors to both sides had already departed by the time the division started its own movements. The reconnaissance battalion and *Grenadier-Regiment 331* moved slowly back to the south. *Panzergrenadier-Regiment 3* moved back to Spartessy, while the remaining elements of *Panzergrenadier-Regiment 394*, *Grenadier-Regiment 339*, *Panzerjäger-Abteilung 543*, and *Panzer-Pionier-Bataillon 39* did not move out until the following day.

The Soviets followed the withdrawal movements. Temporary penetrations in the sectors of the reconnaissance battalion and *Grenadier-Regiment 331* were dealt with by means of immediate counterattacks. The *I./Panzergrenadier-Regiment 3* got caught in artillery, and the *SPW* of the commander, *Major* Dittmer, was hit just after he had dismounted. The crew of *Unteroffizier* Wodtke, *Unteroffizier* Böttrich, and *Gefreiter* Hilpert was killed. The commander of the 3rd Company, *Oberleutnant* Litzmann, was killed by a round to the head. He could not be evacuated by his men, since the Soviets were pressing too hard.

Preparatory measures on the part of the corps had led to the establishment of rearward positions in the area around Bortschany. Elements of the divisional engineers, including the bridging sections, had started digging foxholes and heavy weapons positions and emplacing minefields since 22 August. Starting at 1600 hours on 28 August, the division began occupying that line. The division command post was located in Kawalenkoff.

The combat elements of the division left their positions on 29 August. Elements from the neighboring *Waffen-SS* formations relieved the mechanized infantry. The battle group consisting of *Major* Lühl's *Panzer-Regiment 6* and the engineers of *Panzer-Pionier-Bataillon 39*, who helped delay the advance of the enemy by the emplacing of numerous mines, formed the rearguard. The rearguard started pulling back during the night of 29–30 August. The command staff moved to Nowo-Iwanowka. Effective 0000 hours on 30 August, the division was attached to the *III. Panzer-Korps*. The commanding general, *General der Panzertruppen* Breith, visited his old division the next day. The *3. Panzer-Division* had been designated as the corps reserve and remained west of Walki.

General der Panzertruppen Raus took his leave of the division the next day, 1 September, in a general order that stated: "The *3. Panzer-Division* held up to the overwhelming superiority of the enemy forces in a heroic manner and pushed them back . . . again and again . . . in bold counterblows. The division garnered unforgettable laurels at Polewaja and Ssinolizowka. . . . It is both an honor and a duty for me to highlight the exemplary devotion to duty and bravery of the division and the successes it achieved in the bloody struggle. . . . May success in combat remain constant to this brave division!"

The Battle for Kharkov was over. As the wing division of the *XI. Armee-Korps*, the *3. Panzer-Division* had contributed significantly to the defensive effort. The success of the division was mirrored in part by the award of the Oak Leaves to the Knight's Cross to *Oberst* Wellmann (promoted effective 1 September). For their parts in the fighting, the following soldiers were awarded the German Cross in Gold:

- *Panzergrenadier-Regiment 394*: *Hauptmann* Arnoldt, *Hauptmann* Eggert, *Oberleutnant* Motz, *Leutnant* Ossenbünn, *Oberfeldwebel* von Krenzki, *Oberfeldwebel* Schroeder, and *Feldwebel* Strucken
- *Panzergrenadier-Regiment 3*: *Hauptmann* Comberg and *Hauptmann* Dietrich
- *Panzer-Regiment 6*: *Oberleutnant* Adamek and *Oberleutnant* Kölle
- *Panzer-Artillerie-Regiment 75*: *Hauptmann* Wykopal (commander of the 1st Battalion)
- *Panzer-Aufklärungs-Abteilung 3*: *Feldwebel* Haase (2nd Company)

The successes the division achieved at Kharkov were great, but the losses were also large. The division was in dire need of rest and reconstitution. *Panzergrenadier-Regiment 394* had suffered the most. Based on its head count, the regiment was only able to muster a ready battalion that consisted of elements of the headquarters of the 2nd Battalion, the 2nd, 3rd, 5th, and 6th Companies and regimental assets. The artillery was hoping for reinforcement in the form of a fourth battery for each battalion, as well as a self-propelled battalion. One thing was certain, however, was the fact that the *I./Panzer-*

Regiment 6, which had been detached from the division before Operation Citadel, was not coming back. It was sent to France for new equipment training on the *Panther* and eventually was incorporated into the *Panzer-Lehr-Division*, where it fought in the West.

The Soviets followed the withdrawal movements and penetrated through a gap in the main line of resistance on 31 August. A hastily assembled battle group under the command of *Oberst* Schmidt-Ott eliminated the first penetration in the morning. A few hours later, the mechanized infantry reporting to *Oberst* Wellmann pushed the Soviets back across the main line of resistance in another area. Five Soviet divisions were facing the *3. Panzer-Division*. Despite that, the enemy's rifle regiments were unable to penetrate at any location. The front held.

During the first two weeks of September, fighting flared up for individual farmsteads with grim harshness. In the sector of the neighboring forces, there was only occasional combat patrols. Elements of the *3. Panzer-Division* pushed back the constantly attacking Russians by means of immediate counterattacks. For a while, the following formations were attached to the division: *Grenadier-Regiment 385*, the *II./Artillerie-Regiment 223*, and *Aufklärungs-Abteilung 223* (all from the *223. Infanterie-Division*).

During the night, *Major* Dittmer assembled a response force out of his companies, the *4./ Panzer-Aufklärungs-Abteilung 3*, and the *7./ Panzer-Regiment 7*. At daybreak, it took the collective farm at Kirassirski. *Oberleutnant* Veltheim attacked the Soviet positions in the left flank with his tanks. The fighting vehicles overran fifteen antitank guns and could not be stopped until they reached a deep defile. *Oberfeldwebel* Hoppe then found a way around it. The tanks entered the collective farm by surprise and smoked it out. The mission was accomplished.

The armored battle group of *Oberst* Schmidt-Ott was constantly on the go as the "fire brigade" in an effort to contain penetrations. When *Aufklärungs-Abteilung 223* was encircled by the Russians, the word went out once more: *"Panzer*

marsch!" The *Panzer IV's* rolled through the tall corn and sunflower fields, and the fighting vehicles broke through the lines of the enemy. *Oberfeldwebel* Hoppe advanced into the village, overran the first antitank gun, shot a battery to pieces and cleared the way for the following tanks. The tankers relieved the encircled battalion.

Since the tank crews were employed day and night—sometimes on the lefthand side of the division's sector, sometimes on the right—the regiment started swapping out crews so that individual crews could go to the trains for a few days in "rest quarters." The battle group's leaders—*Hauptmann* Heuer, *Oberleutnant* de Voss, *Oberleutnant* Veltheim, and *Oberleutnant* Taulien—took turns, as did the other officers, noncommissioned officers and enlisted personnel. One time, the combat elements participated in an attack conducted by *Panzergrenadier-Division "Großdeutschland."* *Oberleutnant* Taulien was wounded during that operation, and *Leutnant* Aschermann stepped in to replace him.

On 8 September, Soviet riflemen assaulted the village of Konstantinowka on the left wing of the division. The two motorcycle companies of *Panzer-Aufklärungs-Abteilung 3* had to pull back in the face of the heavy enemy pressure. It was possible for *Hauptmann* Deichen to retake the lost terrain with the help of *Oberleutnant* Kleffel's light *SPW* company and *Leutnant* Aschermann's tanks. The force also succeeded in driving the Soviets back to the creek bottomland and taking 100 prisoners. In addition, *Leutnant* Kossel of the *7./Panzer-Regiment 6* was able to establish contact with the neighboring division. When the Soviets felt their way forward the next day in the vicinity of Kowaltschuki, *Hauptmann* Hoffmann's *Panzerjäger-Abteilung 543* knocked out all five of the T-34's conducting the probe. The enemy did not succeed in entering the village with a concentration of tanks until 10 September. Once again, it was the armored reconnaissance battalion and the armor battle group that drove out the Soviets by means of an immediate counterattack. *Leutnant* Kossel and

Feldwebel Reske each knocked out a T-70. With those "kills," the *II./Panzer-Regiment 6* had been able to knock out a total of 200 enemy tanks since 5 July (two months).

On 12 September, the Soviets directed an assault against Kolomak, where the trains of the armored regiment were located. *Hauptmann* Heuer's tankers were "on top of things," and were able to turn back the Russian tanks. The engagements continued throughout the period. They did not bring any change to the situation, but they also did not allow the German soldiers to get any rest. The main clearing station of the division at Tarapunka was overcrowded. In just the first few weeks of September alone, the surgeons and medics treated 315 wounded.

The division started a systematic training program for its replacements in its rear area. Non-commissioned officer preparatory courses were conducted and maintenance work completed. Positions were improved and support services for the troops were initiated. Correspondents, still photographers and filmmakers from the Army High Command arrived and started a modest campaign of psychological warfare. The military police took inventory of the grain, the number of agricultural machines and related matters. The days were cloudless and warm, but the nights were already very cool.

On 9 September, the division command post moved to Stepanowka and, four days later, to Nagalnij. The commanding general of the *III. Panzer-Korps* visited in order to take his leave. The corps headquarters was being withdrawn from the sector for another mission. *General der Panzertruppen* Breith concluded his general order with the following words: "With my best wishes for continued successful feats of arms, I couple my desire to be able to have the division under my command once again."

Effective 16 September, the division was attached to the *XXXXVII. Panzer-Korps*. That same day, orders arrived directing the initiation of retrograde movements for the *8. Armee*.

According to the orders, the formations would move to lines of resistance that had been established to the rear and remain at each one for twenty-four hours.

During the night of 16–17 September, the German formations started pulling back. The tankers and the engineers were once again the forces that veiled the movements until first light, emplaced mines and then pulled back themselves. *Unteroffizier* Eggers of the *7./Panzer-Regiment 6* distinguished himself in the process by dint of his considerable pluck. He moved into enemy columns with his *Panzer IV* and stirred them up. The engagements were no longer as intense as the previous ones, but they also caused casualties. *Leutnant* Ruth from the tank force and *Leutnant* Kurz from *Einsatz-Bataillon 394*[1] were killed during that period.

The retrograde movement of the division proceeded nearly without a hitch. The division, whose command post moved from Nowo-Kutschebewka to Terentjewka on 19 September, reached Poltava with some of its elements that day. The rearguard was formed by the armored reconnaissance battalion and the two tank sections of *Oberleutnant* Taulien (7th and 8th Companies) and *Leutnant* Sorge (5th and 6th Companies).

The area around Poltava on 20 September was already showing all the signs of an evacuation. The streets were filled with columns, with fleeing or displaced civilians moving among them, as well as herds of cattle. Russian aircraft were constantly dropping bombs among those concentrations. The division's main clearing station had been located in the former 770th Field Hospital in the city ever since 7 September.

The men of the division were allowed no rest. The command staff had just moved through Poltava to Demidowka, when counter-orders were received. The division was to get to the area northeast of Tscherkassy as soon as possible. An enemy attack there had torn a gap between the *III. Panzer-Korps* and the *XXIV.*

---

1. The unofficial designation given to the remnants of *Panzergrenadier-Regiment 394*, which effectively could field only an *ad hoc* battalion.

Panzer-Korps, and Russian tanks were rolling through it toward the Dnjepr.

The division turned around during the morning of 21 September. The division logistics officer, *Hauptmann* von dem Borne, together with support from the division support command commander, *Oberstleutnant* Feldhuß, had established a rearward support point at Kirowograd, where all nonessential vehicles and equipment were sent. By then, the combat elements were moving via Globino to Omelnik. It was difficult to make forward progress, since there were many columns on the road, which were all attempting to get over the Dnjepr at Krementschug. At Omelnik, the division turned to the northwest and made it as far as Schownin.

Oberst Wellmann received orders to take charge of the screening of the approaching division. Partisans were becoming noticeable and executed an ambush against an advance party of the divisional artillery at Perwomaisk on 22 September. *Panzergrenadier-Regiment 3*, minus its 1st Battalion, and *Hauptmann* Eggers's *Einsatz-Bataillon 394* and *Hauptmann* Wykopal's *I./Panzer-Artillerie-Regiment 75* established an all-round defensive position between Perwomaisk and Zagorodischtsche.

A light but continuous rainfall on 23 September soon made all the roads muddy. Reconnaissance conducted as far as the rail line in the morning did not result in any enemy contact. *Hauptmann* Deichen's reconnaissance forces and *Oberleutnant* Veltheim's tanks conducted wide-ranging operations as far as the creek bottomland at Bul-Borowka. Elements of the division occupied defensive positions in the afternoon. The reconnaissance battalion screened south of Wlikije-Kanewzy, where it adjoined *Panzergrenadier-Regiment 3* and *Einsatz-Bataillon 394*, which was positioned around Riminz. The division command post was in Irklejew, where the commanding general also established his headquarters.

The next day, the division was directed to hold open the Dnjepr crossings for *SS-Panzer-Grenadier-Division "Wiking."* To that end, the reconnaissance battalion, the tank section and the *I./Panzergrenadier-Regiment 3* attacked The village was taken without sustaining heavy casualties. That meant the mission was complete and the designated screening line had been reached. The SS division was able to pull back via Tscherkassy. The *3. Panzer-Division* started its own crossing after midnight, after rear-area elements had reached the west bank of the Dnjepr the previous day. The reconnaissance battalion, the *SPW* battalion and a platoon from the *7./Panzer-Regiment 6* were attached to the *11. Panzer-Division*, which was the last major formation to cross the river. The combat elements moved during the night through Wlikije, Kanewzy and Dubinka to the bridgehead. The division command staff had set up in Dubijewka.

The rearguards of the *3. Panzer-Division* disengaged from the enemy during the night. As the men moved through the villages along the east bank in their *SPW's*, they were greeted at various times with flowers by the locals. They thought they were greeting the Russians. The crossing with the last elements took place during the night of 25–26 September without any difficulties. With the crossing, the division left the Eastern Ukraine.

The new defensive lines of the division that had to be occupied ran along the banks of the Dnjepr northwest of Tscherkassy. The right-hand boundary was the Tscherkassy–Tchapajewka rail line; the lefthand boundary the villages of Oswidcwok–Kedinagora. The division headquarters was in Russkaja-Poljana. The assembly area for the division trains was in the area between Smela and Goroditschte. The forces in the field were hoping that they would be able to recover a bit in improved positions after the intense fighting of the last few months. Those hopes were dashed. The building of the field fortification had yet to begin, since Hitler had forbidden the construction of defensive positions behind the Dnjepr by reasoning that the presence of such rearward positions was detrimental to the resolve to fight. There were no bunkers at all along the river.

The exhausted mechanized infantry, cannoneers and engineer then had to fend for themselves. Since the new sector was fairly wide, it was only occupied in strongpoint fashion. To construct dugouts for living and for improving the road network, construction parties from the *Organization Todt* and the 1st Company of the divisional engineers were used. *Hauptmann* peters was placed in charge of supervising the construction efforts. During the first several days in position, there was no enemy contact.

Optimists believed they were going to spend the coming winter in those positions. Just after midnight on 28 September, the division received new orders. It was to turn over its positions the next day and immediately move northwest. The Soviets had established bridgeheads at the bend in the Dnjepr, as well as to the south at Kanew. The *3. Panzer-Division* was directed to reduce the Russian bridgehead at Sseliischtsche in the sector of the *57. Infanterie-Division*. The division had already had to move the 6th and 7th Companies of the armor regiment (*Oberleutnant* de Voss and *Oberleutnant* Veltheim) to that area on 26 September when the Soviets first started crossing the river. Without any preparations, the two companies attacked the enemy forces and succeeded in getting near the river. But the infantry forces did not arrive. The fighting vehicles had to return to their lines of departure.

The advance parties of the division found themselves starting the 100-kilometer march on the morning of 29 September. The movement proceeded along the west bank of the Dnjepr in partisan-infested territory. The main body of the division followed on 30 September, after the *11. Panzer-Division* and *SS-Panzer-Grenadier-Division "Wiking"* had assumed responsibility for the division's sector. The *SPW* battalion screened towards the wooded areas, where three Russian airborne brigades had been identified. The extremely sandy, broken up and wooded terrain between Schelepuki and Michailowka posed a special challenge. Around 1800 hours on that day, the front-line forces had occupied their quartering areas. The command staff of the

division set up in Kurilowka. The commanders were already going forward into the area of operations that evening in order to prepare for the attack. Since the artillery was unable to close into its areas on time, the operation was postponed for twenty-four hours. That provided more time for reconnaissance.

The terrain in front of the bridgehead was not good for an attack. Just before the Dnjepr, there was a barren ridgeline, which offered the enemy terrific fields of observation into the German rear area and prevented the Germans from seeing the bridge. Leading to the ridgeline were deep *balkas*, which the German forces could not see into. The employment of tanks was only possible along an 800-meter-wide section of terrain that led directly towards the barren high ground.

The operation was to be initiated on 2 October with a thirteen-minute artillery preparation, which had a heavy artillery regiment in general support. The attack force was lead by the regimental headquarters of *Panzergrenadier-Regiment 394* (*Oberstleutnant* Beuermann). It consisted of *Hauptmann* Eggers's *Einsatz-Bataillon 394*, reinforced with seven assault guns, an eighty-man group from *SS-Panzer-Grenadier-Division "Wiking,"* which was led by *SS-Hauptsturmführer* Dorr, and the weak *I./Panzergrenadier-Regiment 3*, which was led by *Hauptmann* Brandt, who was replacing *Major* Dittmer, who had been transferred to be a regimental commander and who was killed shortly thereafter. The latter force was reinforced by tanks, and it was given the mission of attacking along the narrow strip of terrain up the hill, while the other two infantry groups initially took the *balka* to the south.

The battalions took up their tactical assembly areas. The tanks and the assault guns got bogged down in rain-softened ground during the movement during the night and were not in place on time. Despite that, the attack was launched at the designated time.

When the first tanks arrived an hour later and churned their way through the deep ground with difficulty, they received heavy artillery and anti-tank-gun fire and took losses.

Einsatz-Bataillon 394 was unable to achieve success. The enemy's pockets of resistance in the deep defiles could not be engaged by the artillery. Heavy casualties were taken. The SS element had more success. It advanced through the *balka* and took Hill 2.1. The division commander, who was at the command post of *Einsatz-Bataillon 394*, ordered that battalion to stop its attack and follow the SS elements at their point of penetration. The new attack, which started at 1100 hours after an artillery preparation, started out with more success. It broke through an enemy position, but then it got bogged down in a minefield, where the assault guns took losses. The enemy started launching immediate counterattacks, and resistance flared up again in the defile. The enemy had already ferried too strong of a force across the river, and the strong enemy artillery presence on the east bank could not be effectively engaged. A continuation of the attack promised no success and would only lead to considerable casualties. The division ordered it called off.

The division's armored reconnaissance battalion was attached to an infantry division at the time to help seal off and eliminate a Russian bridgehead southeast of Pekari. In the completely broken up and occasionally marshy terrain along the banks of the river, it was only possible to establish contact with the infantry, who were in strong-points along the west bank of the river, with the greatest of difficulties. During a counterattack, which led to numerous casualties, the village of Pekari was taken by the battalion's armored cars, working in conjunction with the motorcycle infantry. *Leutnant* Romeike of the 3rd Company was later inducted into the Army Honor Roll for his bravery.

The forces occupied new positions between Otudenez and Butschak. Because there was a lot of woods and a number of defiles, the terrain was not good for the defense. On top of that, there were the Russian airborne forces to the rear who, together with the partisans, made the rear areas unsecure. The assigned sectors were wide and contact could only be maintained by means of radio. The *57. Infanterie-Division* was to the right in front of the division, while the *112. Infanterie-Division* adjoined the infantry to the left.

The next two days were focused on regrouping the force and improving positions. The artillery was reorganized. A reserve force consisting of *Panzerjäger-Abteilung 543*, the *II./Panzer-Regiment 6*, and the divisional artillery, was positioned behind the forward battle groups. The divisional engineers, supported by *Bau-Bataillon 440*, mined all of the terrain in the division's sector. In one day alone in the western sector, the 3rd Company of the divisional engineers emplaced 480 mines.

The enemy remained quiet during this period. It was not until the night of 6–7 October that he started launching combat raids that led to temporary penetrations. When the Soviets ripped open the positions of the *3./Panzergrenadier-Regiment 394* in the early morning hours of 8 October, it was a boldly conducted immediate counterattack by the regiment's 10th Company (2-centimeter *Flak*) that restored the situation. The tank element also registered a success the next day in the same area. Since the enemy was continuing to reinforce his elements all along the front, the improvement of the German trenches was pursued with all means possible. On 8 and 9 October, *Major* Schwing's division engineers emplaced more than 3,400 mines. The villages behind the front were set up for all-round defense. All of the various units stepped up their efforts to protect bridges in the wake of partisan activity. *Oberst* Wellmann established a battle group, which he used to locate and engage Soviet airborne forces and partisans that were attempting to conduct ambushes. During one of those operations, the divisional signals battalion suffered two men as missing-in-action and the bridging section had three wounded.

Around 0500 hours on 12 October, the enemy started an attack after a heavy artillery preparation. Four rifle regiments assaulted the German positions at Otudenez and Glitschino. The Russian battalions started to move out while the Russian artillery was still placing fires on the German positions. The divisional artillery replied in kind, but it was limited to firing 400 light howitzer rounds a day. There was heavy street fighting in Otudenez. *Einsatz-Bataillon 394* finally evacuated the village, along with the *1./Panzer-Pionier-Bataillon 39* and the *1./Bau-Bataillon 410*, and moved back to Hill 225. The battalion suffered considerable losses. The commander, *Hauptmann* Eggert, was wounded. His successor, *Hauptmann* Peters, was badly wounded shortly thereafter, so that *Hauptmann* Gappel became the third battalion commander that day.

Hauptmann Busch's *II./Panzergrenadier-Regiment 3* had to give up Sselischtsche, but it was finally able to stop the enemy's attack. The enemy came to a standstill in front of Lühl's section.

In the afternoon, the fighting ebbed. The German forces set up for the defense in their new lines, while additional concentrations of the enemy were identified. Initially, the nighttime hours passed quietly, but Russian tanks and riflemen attacked the positions of the *6./Panzergrenadier-Regiment 394* at 0230 hours. *Oberleutnant* von Veltheim's tanks were alerted immediately. The tanks advanced against the enemy forces that had penetrated and drove them back through the open area, which was covered with large stands of corn and sunflower crops. As a result of that immediate counterattack, the positions along the main line of resistance that had been lost the previous day around Bobriza were retaken around 0500 hours. *Leutnant* Breith of the *4./Panzergrenadier-Regiment 394* was killed during that round of fighting. *Oberleutnant* Taulien, the commander of the *7./Panzer-Regiment 6*, was once again wounded. In the afternoon, the corps provided the division with the *4.* and *5./Artillerie-Regiment 71*[2] and *Werfer-Regiment 52* as additional artillery support.

The next three days passed without major combat. The divisional engineers were busy with improving the positions and emplacing mines along the division sector. The operations of the engineers received high praise and both *Oberleutnant* Kunze, the commander of the 2nd Company, and *Leutnant* Gäbel, a platoon leader in the 3rd Company, were later inducted into the Army Honor Roll.

The situation remained unchanged until the end of the month. The Soviets did not undergo any efforts to expand their bridgehead in the sector of the *3. Panzer-Division*. Indeed, they withdrew forces there. Occasionally, there were still artillery fires. The occasional combat patrol was turned back.

The troops were constantly exerting themselves to improve their positions, despite the poor fall weather, and establish a deeply echeloned trench system. All of the elements not employed directly at the front were employed in the construction of positions to the rear. Through 29 October, the bridging section reported it had constructed 39.6 kilometers of shallow trenches, 6.1 kilometers of standard trenches, 198 machine-gun positions, 5 antitank gun positions, 13 infantry gun firing points, 55 bunkers, 15 observation points, and 491 dugouts.

At the end of the moth, the division was attached to the *XXIV. Panzer-Korps* of the *4. Panzer-Armee*. The award of the German Cross in Gold was a symbol of the achievements of the division in October: *Oberfeldwebel* Paschek (*1./Panzergrenadier-Regiment 3*), *Oberfeldwebel* Klingbeil (*4./Panzergrenadier-Regiment 3*), and *Hauptmann* Gaebler (*4./Panzer-Artillerie-Regiment 75*).

A few personnel changes took effect at the end of October. *Generalleutnant* Westhoven, who intended to take a home leave, received notice on the day before that he had been reassigned to the officer manpower pool of the Army. The general officer had led the division thirteen months—during a period that was

---

2. The *II./Artillerie-Regiment 71* was a field-army and corps asset.

among the most difficult the division had faced—after he had already led the rifle brigade of the division. Until the end of the war, Westhoven remained true to the *Panzerwaffe*, first in a position at *Panzergruppe West* in France and then as an Assistant Inspector General and Commander of the Armor Schools.

Acting command of the division was temporarily entrusted to *Generalmajor* Chales de Beaulieu, who had been the commander of *Panzergrenadier-Regiment 394* for some time. Unfortunately, that appointment did not sit well with Hitler, since de Beaulieu had been the chief of staff of *Generaloberst* Hoepner, who had earned the disfavor of the *Führer* after he had withdrawn a corps that was threatened with encirclement.

The new official commander of the division became *Generalleutnant* Bayerlein, who had been the operations officer of *Generaloberst* Guderian and, later on, the chief of staff of *Generalfeldmarschall* Rommel.

There were additional changes within the divisional staff. *Oberstabsarzt* Dr. Stribny replaced *Oberstarzt* Dr. Zinnser as the division surgeon, after the latter was in an incapacitating accident. The division intelligence officer, *Hauptmann* Twardowski, was transferred out of the division to attend a General Staff officer course, and the former assistant division operations officer, *Leutnant* Dr. Pauck, assumed his duties. *Oberleutnant* Schauseil became the new assistant division operations officer and *Hauptmann* Funcke the headquarters commandant.

Generaloberst Guderian at the division command post in August 1943. *Oberstleutnant i.G.* Voss, the division operations officer, explains the situation using a map.

Tanks and motorcycle infantry on the move. By this stage of the war, the *Panzer II's* were used primarily as reconnaissance assets.

Communications center for the *I./Panzergrenadier-Regiment 3* during the fighting for Kharkov in August 1943.

A *Tiger* during a break in operations along the edge of Kharkov. The heavy tanks were a welcome attachment to support the division.

CHAPTER 8

From the Dnjepr to the Bug: The Fighting between Tscherkassy and Kirowograd

On 28 October, vastly superior enemy forces attacked the *6. Armee* between the Dnjepr and the coast of the Asovian Sea and obtained a breakthrough.

On 2 November, the enemy command launched a new large-scale offensive against the *4. Panzer-Armee*. On 5 November, the enemy took Kiev and, advancing farther to the west, also took the important railway transportation hubs Fastow, Shitomir, and Korosten, which were so vital for the field-army group.

On 11 November, the division operations officer, *Oberstleutnant i.G.* Voss, held a conference with the division's adjutants at the command post in Litwinez. He explained the situation thusly:

As for upcoming employment, all options are on the table from being pulled out of the line to staying here forever. It has been raining since yesterday, and that is proving restrictive on troop movements. The *General* will not allow his division to be fragmented. The Soviets have withdrawn two armored divisions unnoticed from the bridgehead to the north and three rifle divisions in front of us; they have gone to Kiev, taken the city, advanced to the southwest and occupied Fastow and Wassilkow. The potential for us being employed there is less than being withdrawn from the line and held as corps reserve.

On 10 November, it started to snow. Early in the afternoon, orders arrived at the division for it to be pulled out of the line and move to Kagarlyk. For the time being, both of the mechanized infantry regiments remained in position. On 11 November, the division was ready to move out. The command staff departed two hours later and, moving through Masslowka, reached the area around Kagarlykskaja–Ssloboda on muddy routes and passing through miserable villages. The combat elements followed the next day and quartered in Kagarlyk.

The division found sufficient time with the forces available to prepare for the designated counterattack. Not all of the battle groups made it in time to the new location. The armor regiment, for instance, only had the fighting vehicles of the 5th and 6th Companies, which were consolidated into a single company. The reconnaissance battalion and *Panzergrenadier-Regiment 3* would bear the brunt of the upcoming fight.

The attack started at 0700 hours on 13 November. The batteries that had closed up initiated the proceedings. The mechanized infantry and the motorcycle infantry were able to cover the first hundred meters rapidly. The advance then literally bogged down in the mud. In addition, the Soviets had dug in well along the high ground and also brought heavy antitank weaponry into position. As a result of the deep *balka*, the armored vehicles were scarcely able to advance to either the north or to the east. In the afternoon, the division called off the operation. The forces pulled back to the former main line of resistance.

During the night, the division transitioned to the defense. The sectors had to be extended to the southeast, with the final frontage being twenty-five kilometers across. The enemy disrupted the occupation of the positions and the relief of the neighboring formations several times by means of artillery. Over the next few days, the division was able to improve its sector, which was relatively quiet but which eventually went al the way to the Dnjepr. The work of the positions was stopped during the evening of 18

November, since it was expected that the division could be called out of the line again at any minute. Up to that point, the bridging section alone had constructed 9.9 kilometers of continuous trenches, 1.1 kilometers of communications trenches, thirteen machine-gun positions, and twenty-one rifle dugouts.

The orders to depart arrived on 19 November. The division was directed back to the so-called "B" Line, which was a main line of resistance that had been established north of Strilowka. It was to be passed through the lines there by elements of the *10. Panzergrenadier-Division* and the *34. Infanterie-Division*. The retrograde operation took place on the night of 20–21 November, completely unnoticed by the enemy.

The catastrophic vehicle situation posed a special problem. At the time, some 30 to 40 percent of all vehicles were either with the maintenance platoons or companies. Major Riessberger, the Division Maintenance Officer, had already started a weeding-out process for the vehicles a few days previously in order to try to obtain a "pure fleet" status. Those vehicles selected were to be cannibalized as a result of the poor spare-parts situation. The individual formations reorganized their vehicles. Within *Panzergrenadier-Regiment 394*, it was decided that a company would have two complete platoons and half of a heavy platoon that had the following vehicles: the command section—three staff cars; the company messenger(s)—one heavy motorcycle; each complete platoon—three trucks; the half platoon (heavy)—one staff car and one truck; the company trains—six trucks. Captured vehicles were not affected by the decision.

When the division pulled back, it had enough fuel but not enough oil. Once that was received, the retrograde actions proceeded without a hitch.

The movement of the division back through Shitnegory and Paripssy to Solowjewka, which was reached on 24 November, turned out to be no easy march. The rainy weather had so softened the routes that the vehicles were only able to crawl along them. The columns became separated by kilometers and lost all cohesion. The mud period had started. Since there was radio silence along the route, many a commander did not know where his units were. The division command post was established in Solowjewka on 24 November, even though the locality was already overcrowded with elements of *SS-Panzer-Grenadier-Division "Leibstandarte SS Adolf Hitler"* and the *19. Panzer-Division.* Effective that day, the division was attached to the *XXXXVIII. Panzer-Korps* of *General der Panzertruppen* Balck. It was intended for the corps to attack in the direction of Kiev with its attached divisions—the *3., 8., 19.,* and *25. Panzer-Divisionen* and *SS-Panzer-Grenadier-Divisionen "Leibstandarte SS Adolf Hitler"* and *"Das Reich"*—and then swing to the southeast in order to form a pocket. The orders for the attack arrived in the evening, but a few minutes later the orders were rescinded. The division was turned around and sent to Belaja Zerkow for a new assignment.

Most of the division made it to Belaja Zerkow along the same bad routes by 26 November. The division was attached back to the *III. Panzer-Korps,* which was a part of *General der Infanterie* Wöhler's *8. Armee.* The division was assembled in that area in order to be transported from there to the Tscherkassy sector. The enemy had broken through there and was threatening the city. Since a total of forty trains was necessary to transport the division, it movement was broken down into two serials. The combat elements and the command staff rode in the initial transport so that they could be employed immediately.

The first train of the division arrived at its detraining station of Bobrinskaja at 1000 hours on 27 November. *Einsatz-Bataillon 394,* which had been led by *Major* Peschke since 18 November, moved out as the lead element to Smela and took up screening positions that night in the Bjelooserje area. The division commander and operations officer went to Konstantinowka (vicinity of Smela) to establish contact with *General der Panzertruppen* Breith. The situation: Russian airborne forces and partisans had attacked the German positions at Tscherkassy from the rear, while regular forces moved across the Dnjepr directly towards Tscherkassy at the same time. The Russian objective was the encirclement of Tscherkassy. The *III. Panzer-Korps* was holding its own along a thinly held security line on both sides of the city with *SS-Panzer-Grenadier-Division "Wiking,"* the *72. Infanterie-Division,* formations of *Organization Todt,* and native forces.

SS-Panzer-Grenadier-Regiment "Germania," which was in position at Dubijewka, was attached to the division. The SS men had to pull back in the face of overwhelming numbers. Since the possession of the village was of importance to the corps for its flank security during the planned attack, the locality was ordered to be retaken. *Generalmajor* Bayerlein directed that to be done on 29 November. After a short artillery preparation, the SS mechanized infantry regiment and the *3./Panzergrenadier-Regiment 394* moved out to attack at 1100 hours. Against all expectations, the enemy was surprised and pulled back from the northern portion of Dubijewka. By retaking the village, the original main line of resistance was back in German hands. In addition to twenty-six prisoners being taken, seven antitank guns, five mortars, and eight machine guns were captured.

At 1800 hours on 29 November, the *III. Panzer-Korps* ordered the division to attack Tscherkassy to relieve the *72. Infanterie-Division,* which had been encircled by the Russians. Since most of the division arrived in the Smela area during the day, the preparations could only be made expeditiously. Two battle groups were formed. The righthand one under *Hauptmann* Brandt consisted of the *I./Panzergrenadier-Regiment 3* and a tank combat element of eight *Panzer IV's.* Brandt's forces assembled in the railway junction north of Chozki. The lefthand group, consisting of *Einsatz-Bataillon 394* and the *II./Panzergrenadier-Regiment 3,* was led by *Major* Peschke and assembled around Bjeloserje. The divisional artillery placed one battalion each in direct support of the battle groups.

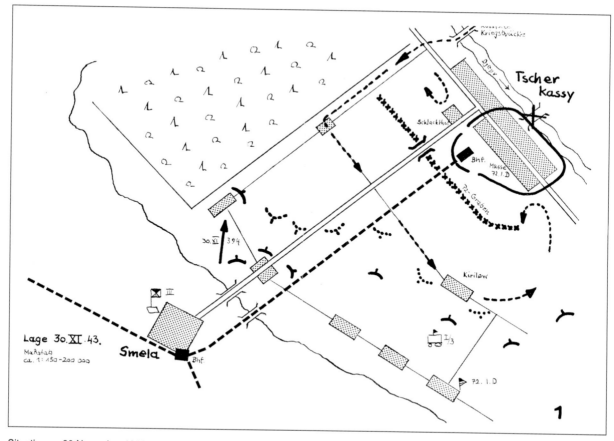

Situation on 30 November 1943

Scale: approximately 1:150,000–200,000

Russische Kriegsbrücke = Russian engineer bridge; *Schlachthof* = Slaughterhouse; *Bhf. = Bahnhof* = Rail station; *Masse 71.ID* = Main body of *71. Infanterie-Division*; *PzGraben* = Tank ditch

The attack started at 0500 hours on 30 November, with Brandt's forces in the spearhead. The thrust was directed against the enemy field fortifications on the Smela–Tscherkassy road. The fighting vehicles of *Oberleutnant* de Voss, *Leutnant* Sorge, and *Leutnant* Theimer broke the resistance of the enemy's well-camouflaged 7.62-centimeter antitank guns, which had been hidden in haystacks. By doing so, they cleared a path for the mechanized infantry, who were able to take Jankiwka around 0800 hours. *Hauptmann* Brandt then focused on his next objective, the Kirolowka–Russkaja Poljana road. That road was reached without appreciable resistance.

The enemy then started to put up a fight. He allowed the tanks to rumble past, then turning his attention to the following mechanized infantry. The close-in fighting along the road became tougher and tougher. The tanks were engaging T-34's at long range.

The Soviets had established themselves within the Nowyj Pachar collective farm. *Hauptmann* Busch's *II./Panzergrenadier-Regiment 3* struggled for that strongpoint for hours before it finally fell into his hands. At the same time, *Einsatz-Bataillon 394* attacked the enemy forces west of Lake Rakita, while *Major* Deichen's reconnaissance battalion cleared the terrain northwest of the collective farm and screened in

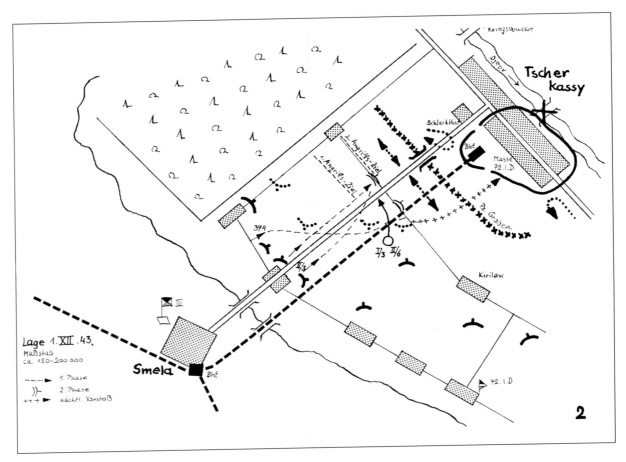

Situation on 1 December 1943

Scale: approximately 1:150,000-200,000

nächtl. Vorstoß = Night advance

the direction of Russkaja Poljana. The individual battle groups took their objectives by 1500 hours and occupied the rail line to Kirolowka.

The corps pressed hard for establishing contact that day with the forces encircled in Tscherkassy. Correspondingly, *Generalmajor* Bayerlein ordered a continuation of the operation prior to the onset of darkness. *Kampfgruppe Brandt*, with only three operational SPW's and three *Panzer IV's*, moved out right at 1500 hours. Since an attack in the previous direction promised little success because of the unfavorable terrain and the increasingly stiff resistance of the enemy, *Hauptmann* Brandt

opted to attack down a field path east of the railway line.

Brandt's forces crossed the railway line before the onset of darkness and turned north. A tank ditch was reached, but it was not being watched. After a short while, a detour was found. The battle group rolled out again. It was 1800 hours when the designated recognition signals—parachute flares—hissed skyward.

The corps ordered a continuation of the attack during the night and a rolling up of the enemy's positions. It directed the attack was to start again at 0500 hours (1 December). But the Russians beat the Germans to the punch. Starting at 0430 hours and coming from Dubijewka, the enemy attacked the positions of the recently introduced *Füsilier-Bataillon 157*,[1] as well as the Nowyj Pachar collective farm and Hill 111.5. By concentrating the few remaining operational *Panzer IV's* and some *Flak*, the wind was finally knocked out of the sails of the enemy's thrust. The postponed German attack was launched at 1100 hours.

The *II./Panzergrenadier-Regiment 3, Einsatz-Bataillon 394*, and *Panzer-Aufklärungs-Abteilung 3* all advanced fluidly. There was no significant resistance encountered until the tank ditch south of Tscherkassy was reached. The companies of *Einsatz-Bataillon 394* took the obstacle, and assault guns, *SPW's* from the reconnaissance battalion and *Panzer IV's* immediately started to cross. The military facilities along the southern edge of the city were soon reached. A short while later, at 1345 hours, the area around the slaughterhouse was taken. *Hauptmann* Brandt approached with his forces. A wide corridor had been created leading into Tscherkassy. The battle groups of the *72. Infanterie-Division*, which had been encircled for days, were relieved.

The division continued its attack without stopping in an effort to take the northern portion of the city. There was stubborn fighting at numerous strong-points, especially around the labor office. The attack was halted when it turned dark. The continuation of the attack planned for the morning had to be postponed, since the tanks were not operationally ready in time.

The third of December proved to be the day of *Panzer-Pionier-Bataillon 39*. The Soviets attacked around 0600 hours, but they were turned back. When the Russians prepared to attack Nowyj Pachar for the second time, *Major* Schwing and his engineers attacked the enemy by surprise, inflicting heavy losses. After the engineers had reorganized, they advanced on Kirolowka, which had been fortified. Heavy fighting developed around noon on the main road and to the north. The engineers were not shaken, and they pushed the enemy back, taking the village around 1530 hours. By doing so, they eliminated a threat to the flanks for the division. Later on, *Major* Schwing received the Knight's cross for his actions that day.

The Russians continued their attacks around Tscherkassy. That morning, they succeeded in infiltrating the thin German screening lines in the vicinity of the tank ditch and going around the left wing of the division. The *3./Panzergrenadier-Regiment 394*, whose acting commander, *Leutnant* Wendt, had replaced the previous acting commander, the badly wounded *Leutnant* Ossenbühn, launched an immediate counterattack. Wendt was badly wounded in the process and replaced by *Leutnant* Zimmermann. The Russians soon established a ring around the company, which was fighting in isolation. A relief effort was launched, with *Major* Peschke and his engineer platoon and a few self-propelled guns attacking frontally, while *Hauptmann* Brandt came up from the south with a few *SPW's* and some *Flak*. A path was cleared to the encircled company, and the Russian forces sealed off.

On 4 December, the Russians attacked the field-expedient fortifications of the engineer battalion. The engineers were able to stand firm and, supported by a few tanks, were able to occupy the cemetery at Kirolowka at 0930 hours after an immediate counterattack. A battalion from *SS-Panzer-Grenadier-Division "Wiking"* and the *II./Grenadier-Regiment 331*[2] advanced along the rail line, with their efforts slowly winning ground. The grenadiers and the SS mechanized infantry attacked the railway embankment

---

1. The reconnaissance battalion of the *57. Infanterie-Division*. The reconnaissance battalions of infantry divisions were changed from *Aufklärungs-Abteilungen* to *Füsilier-Bataillone* around this time, when reconnaissance assets of the infantry divisions received additional manpower and motorization (occasionally mechanization) to allow them to better perform economy-of-force missions, which was increasingly being required as Germany almost universally went over to the defensive.

2. The badly battered regiment from the *167. Infanterie-Division*. By February 1944, the regiment would be further bled white and referred to as *Regimentsgruppe 331*.

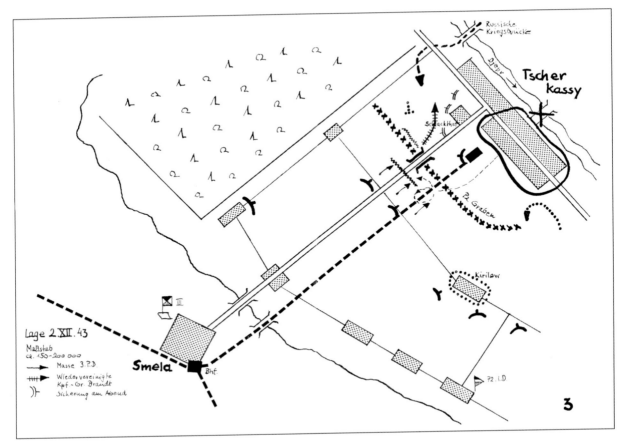

Situation on 2 December 1943

Scale: approximately 1:150,000–200,000

Masse 3PD = Main body of the *3. Panzer-Division*; *Wiedervereinigte Kpf-Gr Brandt* = Reunited *Kampfgruppe Brandt*; *Sicherung am Abend* = Evening outposts

together and pushed out the enemy forces east of the line. The last remaining Russian forces in the brickworks outside the southern portion of Tscherkassy evacuated their positions during the night. They were able to escape unnoticed through the thin German outpost lines. When the German attack started up again at 0500 hours, it hit nothing but thin air. The Soviets had pulled back as far as the heavily vegetated terrain west of Kirolowka.

Later on, the Soviets attempted to thrust into the division's flank, coming from the area around Dubijewka. The Soviet attack collapsed in the face of the defensive fires. The tank ditch was taken by the time it turned dark, and Hill

117.9 was assaulted. The signaled the end of the initial fighting for Tscherkassy. The Daily Report of the Armed Forces High Command commented on the successful conclusion to the fighting. The *3. Panzer-Division* was not mentioned. *Generalmajor* Bayerlein composed a sharp message to the corps in that regard and wrote:

The fact that five 8.8-centimeter *Flak* and six guns of 2-centimeter caliber from the *Flak-Division* employed in sector were captured, that likewise the same fate befell elements of the armored artillery [battalion] of the *Division "Wiking,"* that the previously named division's attack on Kirolowka was turned back despite the support of twenty-four assault guns and the village was later taken under the leadership of the *3. Panzer-Division* with the support of ten assault guns, the fact that all of the successes that were mentioned in the Armed Forces Daily Report in the area of combat operations around Tscherkassy were successes of the *3. Panzer-Division*, especially the relief of the encircled elements of the *72. Infanterie-Division* in Tscherkassy and the elimination of enemy groups of forces that had broken through. . . . The casualties that the *3. Panzer-Division* sustained during the attack and the hard defensive fighting approached nearly 800 men. . . . Despite that, the division always attacked with success and defeated the Russian divisions. Those were achievements that cannot be attributed to the troop elements mentioned in the Armed Forces Daily Report.

During the period from 3 to 5 December, the three most difficult days, the division had successfully fought against three rifle divisions, one airborne division, one guards rifle division, and one tank brigade. During the same period, the division took 216 prisoners and captured or destroyed ten tanks, thirty-one artillery pieces, forty antitank guns, thirty-one mortars, seventy-six machine guns, ninety-two antitank rifles, and a large quantity of small arms.

The division transitioned to the defense on 6 December. The main line of resistance ran along a narrow sector west of the Tscherkassy–Bjeloserje road. The formations reorganized and ready reserves were created. Despite the black ice and the rain, the positions had to be improved. An engineer detail under the supervision of *Feldwebel* Hedrich repaired three bridges around Stepanki, since the assembly area for the division reserve was located there.

The next three days were filled with the routine of positional warfare. While the division was busy trying to reorganize its forces—the

headquarters of *Panzergrenadier-Regiment 3* assumed command over *Einsatz-Bataillon 394* once more, for instance—the enemy prepared for a counterattack. In a surprise move, he placed a half-hour artillery preparation on the German front between Tscherkassy and Russkaja Poljana starting at 0600 hours on 9 December. Groups of Soviet tanks attacked to the southwest in the area around the slaughterhouse and Nowyj Pachar. T-34's overran the outpost lines and moved from the south against the slaughterhouse one time and then across the railway embankment another time. The lack of mobile antitank forces made itself felt. The German forces had to slowly pull back from the road. The enemy fighting vehicles advanced with great verve and reached the woods around Hill 110.5. They were thus able to drive a wedge between *Einsatz-Bataillon 394* and the *72. Infanterie-Division*. The fighting raged back and forth. In the end, the division's formations were able to win the upper hand.

Generalmajor Bayerlein committed the remaining elements of the *II./Panzer-Regiment 6* to an immediate counterattack. The tanks advanced along the railway embankment and reached the tank ditch at 1015 hours, where they were supposed to link up with *Einsatz-Bataillon 394*, attacking to the east. The battalion took back Hill 110.5, which was filled with enemy forces. After that, however, its attack bogged down. A battalion from *SS-Panzer-Grenadier-Division "Wiking"* was inserted into the line to the left, while the artillery took up new firing positions. Arrayed that way, the attack was to continue the following morning.

During the night, the corps ordered the division to eliminate the enemy forces at the slaughterhouse and to restore the old main line of resistance. It was to place its Schwerpunkt on the right wing. At 0530 hours, *Hauptmann* Wykopal's *I./Panzer-Artillerie-Regiment 75* placed a short artillery preparation on the Russian positions. An SS tank company attacked, while *Einsatz-Bataillon 394* followed. The *II./Grenadier-Regiment 331* screened the flank northeast of the collective farm. The mechanized infantry reached the railway embankment in a series of bounds and then assaulted the railway crossing guard's house. All of the railway facilities of Tscherkassy could be seen. The Russian artillery had registered its guns in a very exacting fashion on this sector, however. A salvo of Stalin organ rockets hit the command post of *Einsatz-Bataillon 394*. The radio vehicle received a direct hit, which killed the crew. Another salvo of rockets followed. *Major* Peschke was badly wounded. Before *Oberarzt* Dr. Schubert could attend to his commander, Peschke died. The commander, who had proven himself so well in many a critical situation, would later be posthumously awarded the Knight's Cross.

The division continued its attack. The SS fighting vehicles advanced to the slaughterhouse, while the *II./Panzer-Regiment 6* of *Major* Lühl moved against Hill 108.3 and to the northeast. The area between the railway station and the road was taken after a tough fight, although not all of the former main line of resistance could be retaken. The *72. Infanterie-Division*, tied up by enemy forces, was unable to follow the *3. Panzer-Division*. The positions the division was occupying were not in a good location, and they could only be hastily improved. The formations in the rear worked ceaselessly on improving the rearward trenches. On 11 and 12 December alone, the division's bridging section dug 820 meters of continuous trenches, seven machine-gun stands, two antitank-gun firing positions, twenty-two infantry dugouts, and seven bunkers at Kirolowka.

During the night of 10–11 December, the enemy remained relatively quiet, but he attacked with tanks around 0900 hours in the sector of the friendly forces to the right, where *Pionier-Bataillon 72* and the *II./Grenadier-Regiment 331* were pushed back. *Einsatz-Bataillon 394*, under the command of *Hauptmann* Schulze, remained in its old positions during the day, but it pulled back at night. The Soviets were constantly reinforcing their elements and, on 12 December,

advanced as far as the railway embankment. This time, the immediate counterattack launched by the division did not work. Since the mechanized infantry elements were also in no position to defend themselves without assistance, the divisional artillery's time had come. The batteries placed one salvo after the other on the Russian positions, thus preventing a penetration. The Russians advances on the morning of 12 December hit the *2./Panzergrenadier-Regiment 394* and the neighboring grenadier companies especially hard. During the fighting there, three T-34's were knocked out.

The field army then ordered a general withdrawal to the Tjassmin Line. The situation in the area of operations farther to the south made it necessary to evacuate the Tscherkassy area. It was directed for the *3. Panzer-Division* to assemble in the Smela area, with *Panzergrenadier-Regiment 3* being designated as a corps reserve and sent to Bjeloserge. Early in the afternoon, the division command staff moved to Popowka. The battalions moved out of their positions around 1600 hours. The *2./Panzergrenadier-Regiment 394* and the tank elements remained as a rearguard. Starting at 1800 hours, they started moving back through Kirolowka. The Russians attempted to disrupt the movements using the concealment provided by the darkness, but they were pushed away in an immediate counterattack launched by tanks and self-propelled guns. By first light of 14 December, the division had reached its new staging area. That signaled the end of the fighting around Tscherkassy for the division. Later on, three officers received the Knight's Cross for the exemplary leadership of their formations and units: *Major* Schwing, the commander of *Panzer-Pionier-Bataillon 39*; *Major* Peschke, the commander of the *II./Panzergrenadier-Regiment 394*; and *Oberleutnant* Sorge, the commander of the *5./Panzer-Regiment 6*.

On 13 December, the *III. Panzer-Korps* sent a telegram to the headquarters of the *8. Armee*, which stated, in part:

At the conclusion of the heavy fighting for Tscherkassy, the corps recommends the 3. Panzer-Division of Berlin, under the command of *Generalmajor* Bayerlein, receive a by-name mention in the Armed Forces Daily Report. In the period from 29 November to 13 December 1943, the division bore the main brunt of the fighting. . . . During that period, the division successfully conducted twenty-eight attacks and nine counterattacks and turned back fifteen enemy attacks that were supported by tanks. In the process, 511 prisoners were taken and 1,182 enemy dead were counted, with another 3,000 estimated. Fifty-two tanks and one assault gun were destroyed; 36 artillery pieces, 115 antitank guns, 45 mortars, 163 machine guns, 298 submachine guns, and 96 antitank rifles were captured. Together with the friendly forces to the right, the division badly battered the following enemy forces during the fighting: The 7th Guards Airborne Division, the 254th Rifle Division, the 62nd Guards Infantry Division (one regiment), and the 113th Tank Brigade.

The division had not assembled all of its formations in the new quartering area, when it already received an alert and orders. The 8. *Armee* radioed at 0800 hours on 14 December: "Enemy withdrawing to the southwest. *XXXXVII. Panzer-Korps* is attacking Kamenka from the south. Request your support!" The division formed a battle group under *Hauptmann* Brandt that consisted of elements of the *SPW* battalion, the armored regiment, the antitank battalion, and the 2nd Battalion of the divisional artillery. It was immediately sent moving. Early in the afternoon, the force reached the area around Kamenka. By evening, the enemy had been ejected from the village, which was then occupied. But that did not mean that the mission of Brandt's forces, which were reinforced during the night by the reconnaissance battalion, was over. *Major* Deichen's reconnaissance battalion

and the remainder of the battle group attacked Tomaschewka on 15 December. The motorcycle infantry and the mechanized infantry took the village, but they did not have the combat power to clear the woods to its west and south.

On 16 December, the division formed two battle groups to better conduct its screening mission. The *II./Panzergrenadier-Regiment 3*, commanded by *Oberstleutnant* Fleischauer, received the reconnaissance battalion and the remaining tanks of the *II./Panzer-Regiment 6* in support. Fleischauer's forces moved to Bondyrewo and screened towards the east. The *SPW* battalion screened south from Tomaschewka. *Oberstleutnant* Beuermann's *Panzergrenadier-Regiment 394* was held in the Smela area as a ready reserve.

As early as the next day, the *Einsatz-Bataillon* of the regiment, under the command of *Hauptmann* Müller-Röhlich, was ordered to the sector of the *57. Infanterie-Division*, where the enemy had broken through. Beuermann's forces, reinforced by the 3rd Battalion of the divisional artillery, had to conduct an immediate counterattack on 18 December without any preparations or knowledge of the terrain. The first effort to penetrate the enemy's lines succeeded. The mechanized infantry then bogged down in the jungle-like thickets against a stubbornly defending enemy force. *Oberleutnant* Gaedtke was killed. The 2nd, 3rd, and 6th Companies were temporarily encircled by the enemy. It was only with some difficulty that they were able to slog their way through the marshland as far as the west bank of the river.

The next day saw no change in the situation. The Russians had firmly established themselves in the thickets and did not allow the Germans to approach a single step. *Oberleutnant* Rosemeyer assumed command of the *Einsatz-Bataillon*. *Generalmajor* Bayerlein arrived there during the day and was briefed on the situation. He was able to get the battalion released from attachment to the *57. Infanterie-Division* and instead be employed in guarding the bridgehead at Bjeloserje.

Starting on 21 December, the corps issued its intent to improve and reinforce the main line of resistance. The *3. Panzer-Division* and the *57. Infanterie-Division* were directed to take the necessary preparatory measures, which meant that both divisions were to be employed in taking Hill 115.3. But the Russians beat the Germans to the punch and moved out to attack at first light. It seemed that the German attack plan had been revealed to the Russians due to the carelessness of some personnel on telephone lines. The Russians selected a construction battalion as the object of their attack, and the battalion was unable to stand fast in the wake of the assault. It was only the immediate commitment of *Einsatz-Bataillon 394* and a battalion from the *57. Infanterie-Division* that the situation could be cleared up. The fighting to seal off the point of penetration prevented the German attack on the hill to start on time.

Oberstleutnant Fleischauer's battle group made good progress. The 2nd Battalion was able to assault the high ground to the southeast. The division commander accompanied the battalion, that he then instructed to turn toward Drody. The elements of the *57. Infanterie-Division* under *Oberst* Zunke remained on the hill. The enemy did not give up, however. He launched an immediate counterattack against the hill and ejected Zunke's infantry. The infantry division there-

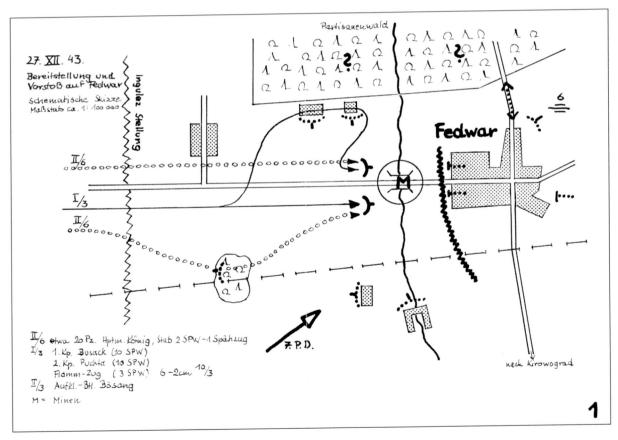

Preparations for an Attack on Fedwar (27 December 1943)

Schematic scale: approximately 1:100,000

M = Mines

Partisanenwald = Partisan Woods

upon finally decided to give up the densely wooded terrain and take up positions on the west side of the marshland.

A conference concerning the intended movement of the *3. Panzer-Division* was conducted at the division command post at Popowka late in the evening of 21 December. *Einsatz-Bataillon 394*, which had suffered four dead, seventy-two wounded, and twenty-four missing over the course of the recent fighting, was released from attachment to the *57. Infanterie-Division* on 22 December and returned to the division fold. In the night that followed, the *3. Panzer-Division* pulled its combat forces out of the main line of resistance and assembled them south of Smela.

Since it was certain that the division would have to evacuate its quarters on 24 December, it was decided to celebrate Christmas Eve on 23 December. It had snowed and had been freezing for days on end, with the result that the countryside presented a "Christmasy" picture. The division support command had secured sufficient personal demand items and the division post office had managed to get large amounts of mail forward. The individual troop elements started celebrating as early as the afternoon. The divisional engineers celebrated at the village square with a large bonfire. The adjutant of the *SPW* battalion, *Leutnant* Blasig, visited the dugouts of the battalion dressed up like Santa Claus. For his Christmas present, *Oberfeldwebel* Koczula of the *6./Panzergrenadier-Regiment 3* received the German Cross in Gold. That award had also been presented in the past month to *Oberst* Lattmann (*Panzer-Artillerie-Regiment 75*), *Hauptmann* Biegon (*Feld-Ersatz-Bataillon 83*), *Hauptmann* Schmidt (*5./Panzer-Artillerie-Regiment 75*), *Hauptmann* Oelrich (adjutant of *Panzer-Regiment 6*), *Oberleutnant* Kleffel (*4./Panzer-Aufklärungs-Abteilung 3*), *Oberleutnant* Harzer (*1./Panzer-Pionier-Bataillon 39*), *Oberfeldwebel* Tiemann (*6./Panzergrenadier-Regiment 394*), and *Oberwachtmeister* Ostwald (*5./Panzer-Artillerie-Regiment 75*).

The order for the movement of the division to the Nowo Migorod–Kanish area was issued during the evening of 23 December. The columns started marching around 0500 hours on the morning of Christmas Eve. Since the roads were iced over, the movement had its share of difficulties. Most of the division reached the designated staging area around Kanish and to its west around noon. *Panzer-Regiment 6* and *Panzergrenadier-Regiment 394* formed the rearguard and followed on Christmas day. By then, new attack orders had arrived: "Attack by the *10. Panzergrenadier-Division* and the *3., 6.,* and *11. Panzer-Divisionen*, along with elements of the *14. Panzer-Division* and *Artillerie-Division 310 z.b.V.,*[3] on 27 December against the enemy forces at Fedwar to close the gap between the *III.* and *XXXXVII. Panzer-Korps.*

The intent was for the three armored divisions to close a considerable gap in the front at Fedwar. The *3. Panzer-Division* was to protect the left wing of the *III. Panzer-Korps* during its attack east. The objective was to establish contact with the *XXXXVII. Panzer-Korps* south of Omelgorod in order to encircle the enemy forces that had broken through. In an effort to conceal the intent of the operation, the tactical assembly areas could not be occupied until the night of 26–27 December. All of the formations participating reached their assembly areas in time, with the result that the attack started at 0600 hours. The batteries that had been brought forward placed a short artillery preparation on the identified Russian positions. The *II./Panzer-Regiment 6*, commanded by *Hauptmann* König, rolled forward. His battalion was closely followed by the two mechanized infantry regiments, the antitank battalion, the 2nd Battalion of the divisional artillery, and the divisional engineers.

The formations, led by the tank companies of *Leutnant* Schlüter (5th) and *Leutnant* Theimer (6th), rapidly pressed into the enemy strongpoints

---

3. A short-lived artillery headquarters formed for command-and-control purposes by the *8. Armee* in late 1943. It was probably employed here to control all of the various artillery assets of the various divisions involved in the attack.

and ejected the forces there. The Russians were surprised by the vehemence of the German attack and pulled back the first few hours. Female soldiers[4] were among the prisoners; they had put up a particularly stubborn defense. Ljubomirka was taken in an assault. The bridge west of Fedwar fell into the division's hands intact. Hill 215.1, west of the city, was occupied. The *II./Panzergrenadier-Regiment 3* played a large role in those successes. A penetration into the enemy's front lines had been achieved.

Long-range Russian artillery started to make its presence felt and caused considerable losses. Enemy rifle formations, supported by tanks, launched an immediate counterattack. The medics, who had established a main clearing station in Kanish, set up forward clearing stations in Ssen-towo and Ljubomirka. *Generalmajor* Bayerlein lent new impetus to the attack in the afternoon, and the men of *Panzergrenadier-Regiment 3* and the *II./Panzer-Regiment 6* moved out once more. The armored group went around Fedwar to the north and rolled up the Russian positions. The *II./Panzergrenadier-Regiment 3* penetrated into the western portion of the city shortly after 1400 hours. *Einsatz-Bataillon 394* followed. The early onset of darkness unfortunately prevented the taking of the entire city. It was not until the next morning, around 1000 hours, that all of Fedwar was firmly under German control.

---

4. The original German uses *Flintenweib*, for which there is no really good English equivalent. It is pejorative in nature and roughly equivalent to "soldiers in skirts."

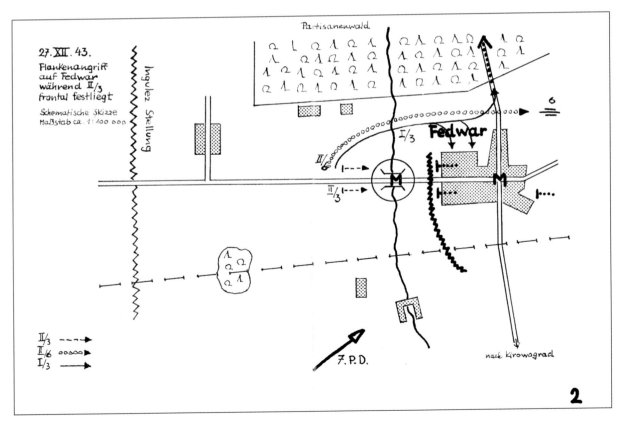

Flanking Attack on Fedwar
(*II./Panzergrenadier-Regiment 3* bogged down)
Schematic scale: approximately 1:100,000

On 28 December, the division moved out to attack northeast in the direction of Grigorjewka. The woods were full of the enemy and heavily mined. Despite that, the division was able to take good points of departure for the continued attack. The mechanized infantry penetrated into the sophisticated woodland positions the enemy had established and cleared them, one after the other. Around noon, the enemy's resistance intensified. T-34's launched an immediate counterattack. Intense tank-versus-tank engagements ensued, with seven T-34's being knocked out. Once that was done, the path was clear for the mechanized infantry. Grigorjewka, which had been heavily fortified and manned, and the high ground to the west were taken in a nighttime attack.

The fighting on 30 December focused on firming up the newly established main line of resistance and fending off enemy immediate counterattacks. The armor battalion and the reconnaissance battalion attacked once more during the afternoon. The intent was to establish contact with the *XXXXVII. Panzer-Korps*. Contrary to expectations, the operation went well. After a short while, the battle groups established contact with the lead elements of the *302. Infanterie-Division* coming from the north. The enemy had pulled back out of the gap he had entered. The attack by the *III. Panzer-Korps* had been a complete success.

The *3. Panzer-Division* remained in the new positions, and the division command post was

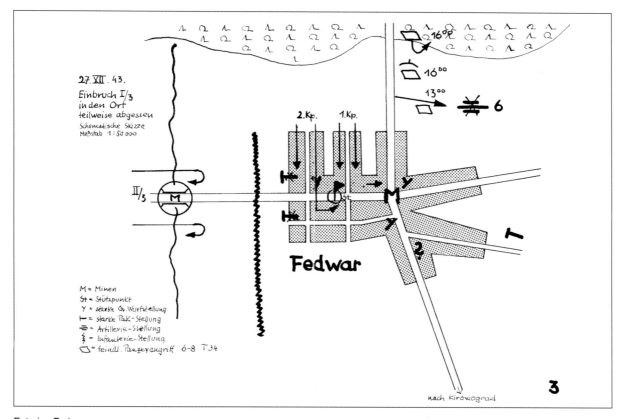

Entering Fedwar
(some elements dismounted)
Schematic scale: approximately 1:100,000
M = Mines; *St* = *Stützpunkt* = Strongpoint
2.Kp = *2. Kompanie*

moved forward to Tarassowka. Fortunately, the casualties sustained over the course of the operations were minimal. New Year's passed quietly. At midnight, the men let colorful parachute flares hiss into the dark skies. *Generalmajor* Bayerlein experienced the New Year as a guest of the *II./Panzer-Regiment 6* and *Panzer-grenadier-Regiment 394*.

In its daily report of 30 December, the *III. Panzer-Korps* highlighted the achievements of the *3. Panzer-Division* as follows:

[The division] performed magnificently during those days of attack under the exemplary leadership of its commander. The division, on the northern wing of the corps . . . carried the main burden of battle. Even though it was constantly attacked and threatened along the northern flank by the V Guards Mechanized Corps, the division succeeded in taking the locality of Fedwar—of decisive importance for the entire operation—on the first day of the attack. It blocked the main road to the south that led through the city and thus . . . made . . . the attack by the enemy . . . impossible. . . . Of the prisoners and spoils-of-war already reported, the following are attributable solely to the *3. Panzer-Division*: 656 prisoners; 7 tanks; 8 assault guns; 3 self-propelled antitank guns; 94 machine guns; and 100 horses. . . . Once again, a request is made for a by-name mention of the division in the Armed Forces Daily Report.

At the start of 1944, the Red Army was attacking across the entire Eastern Front. The focal points of the enemy's offensive efforts were in the north at Leningrad and at Narwa. In the south, the spearheads were between Korosten and Fastow, to the west of Kiev, and in the area between Tscherkassy and Kriwoi Rog. *General der Infanterie* Wöhler's *8. Armee* defended in the latter sector with *General der Artillerie* Stemmermann's *XI. Armee-Korps*, *Generalleutnant* Lieb's *XXXXII. Armee-Korps*,

and *General der Infanterie* Buschhagen's *LII. Armee-Korps*, which was brought in later.

During its movement to the west of Kirowograd, the division was halted. It was attached to the *XXXXVII. Panzer-Korps* on 2 January and ordered to be ready to move at a moment's notice. The tracked vehicles prepared for rail transport. In the midst of all that, the surprising news arrived at the division headquarters that *Generalmajor* Bayerlein was being reassigned to assume command of the *Panzer-Lehr-Division*, which had just been activated. Because of what was happening at the time, Bayerlein retained command of the *3. Panzer-Division* for another few weeks, however.

The loading of the armored elements was called off. All of the division was to road march to the area around Kirowograd by 5 January. Since it was freezing during the night and the day was filled with sunshine, the movement proceeded without interference. The air was already filled with the thunder of the new fighting. The large-scale Russian offensive in the area around Kirowograd against the *8. Armee* had started that morning at 0600 hours. In just a few hours, 177,000 artillery shells plowed up the earth around Kirowograd. Marshal Zhukov's Southern Front was attacking the positions of the *4. Panzer-Armee* and the *8. Armee* with the 1st and 2nd Ukrainian Fronts. Three enemy field armies were storming the sector of the *XXXXVII. Panzer-Korps* and the *LII. Armee-Korps* alone. The 53rd Army, the 5th Guards Army, and the 7th Guards Army were pushing the German divisions back. The enemy ripped open the front on both sides of Adshamka and then pressed on Kirowograd with eleven major formations.

On the morning of 5 January, the *3. Panzer-Division* entered the city. *Generalmajor* Bayerlein received a briefing at the corps command post: The *10. Panzergrenadier-Division* had been badly battered north of the city and was pulling back in its direction. The *3. Panzer-Division* was directed to advance as quickly as possible to the north from the Lelekowka area so as to stop the retrograde movements and close the gap.

To carry out that mission, the reinforced divisional armored reconnaissance battalion was committed at 1500 hours to attack Terbowka. By then, the Soviets were already rolling past Kirowograd with more than 600 fighting vehicles to attack into the deep rear of the German forces.

The command post of the *XXXXVII. Panzer-Korps* in Mal. Wiski was threatened. Oberst von Bernuth defended that area with an assortment of differing forces. That meant that the *3. Panzer-Division* had already been bypassed before it had even commenced operations.

The division's counterattack started at 0600 hours on 6 January. *Hauptmann* König's *II./Panzer-Regiment 6* and *Hauptmann* Brandt's *I./Panzergrenadier-Regiment 3* formed the spearhead. The objective was to block the enemy's logistical lines of communications and link up with the *11. Panzer-Division*, which was coming from the north. The attack was powerfully executed and the Soviets recoiled. The village of Lelekowka, located on a hill north of Kirowograd, was taken. The tanks and the *SPW's* continued forward. Fifteen 7.62-centimeter antitank guns were destroyed, and a few T-34's went up in flames. By the onset of darkness, the division had occupied the high ground at Roshnatowka. By then, the divisional artillery had used up almost all of its ammunition, since the supply columns had been unable to follow. In contrast, the enemy was reinforcing his elements by the hour. As a result, the attack had to be stopped. There were only five kilometers left to the spearhead of the *11. Panzer-Division*.

The Soviet VII Mechanized Corps crossed the Ingul River at Ssewerinka and blocked the road west of Kirowograd. The *XVIII. Panzer-Korps* entered the southern part of the city, where stubborn house-to-house fighting ensued. All hell broke out in Kirowograd, with panic practically breaking out. Dark clouds of smoke billowed over the streets. Columns, trains elements, administrative services and female auxiliaries moved rearward as quickly as possible. *Oberarzt* Dr. Mohr was directed to evacuate the burning

main clearing station at midnight and make his way to the division. But there were hardly any operational medical vehicles, with the exception of a heavy prime mover, onto which the worst of the wounded were loaded. The less seriously wounded were placed into a truck. The column slowly snaked its way out of the city.

With the seventh of January came the certain realization that Kirowograd had been encircled by the enemy. Patrols determined the following by noon: Russians tanks were in Obosnowka, along the Ingul, in Gruskoje and at the passing point in Lelekowka. The road, the only logistics lines of communication to the west, had been blocked by the Russians. A ring had been formed around the *3. Panzer-Division*. *General-major* Bayerlein came to a bold decision. After consulting with the commanders of the *10. Panzergrenadier-Division*, the *14. Panzer-Division*, and the *376. Infanterie-Division*, which were also encircled in Kirowograd area, he would have his division break out to the northwest at Kanish and then, operating from outside the ring, advance against Kirowograd to relieve the other divisions. There had not been any contact with the corps command post in Mal. Wiski for several hours, since a battle group of the 67th Tank Brigade that had broken through had scattered the headquarters element there. Correspondingly, Bayerlein's decision was his and his alone.

The division assembled in the northeastern portion of Kirowograd and in the area around Lelekowka starting at 1400 hours. The enemy disrupted the concentrations with sporadic artillery fire. It was intended for the reinforced *II./Panzer-Regiment 6* to form the spearhead. The wheeled vehicles of the remaining division elements formed up into four groups. The flanks were directed to be screened by the *SPW's* of *Panzergrenadier-Regiment 3* and the self-propelled vehicles of the *Flak* battalion. The reconnaissance battalion would form the rearguard and screen to the division's rear.

When it started to turn dark and the clocks showed 1600 hours, *Generalmajor* Bayerlein,

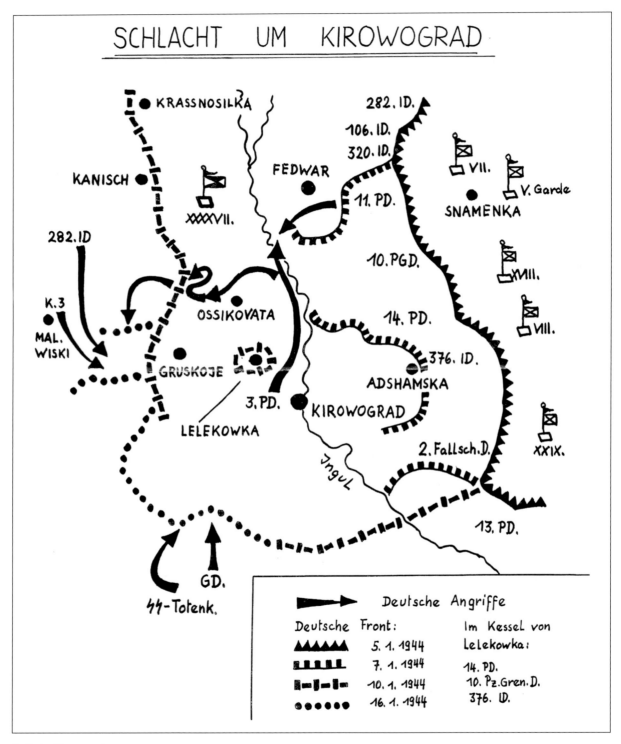

Battle for Kirowograd

Deutsche Angriffe = German attacks; *Deutsche Front* = German Front; *Im Kessel von Lelekowka* = In the Lelekowka Pocket

who was in the lead element, gave his orders to start the operation: *"Panzer marsch!"* That initiated a division movement that could be called truly unique. With the tanks spread out ahead of it in an inverted wedge, the division advanced against the Russian defensive positions. All of a sudden, the lead tank went up in flames and illuminated the snow-covered battlefield. Hit by an antitank gun! That was followed by numerous impacts. The formations did not hesitate and continued moving. The Russians were apparently surprised by the "gigantic" force approaching them, since everything appeared larger and more numerous at night. In some cases, they abandoned their recently constructed positions in a panic, which were taken practically without a fight. Only the one tank and a few trucks fell victim to the Soviet guns during the first attack.

Towards midnight, the division encountered strong resistance along the road, but *Hauptmann* König and his tanks were able to eliminate it. The road was soon cleared, and the remaining groups soon followed. The lead tank elements reached Iwanowka and Wladimirowka towards morning. It was there that they encountered the lead elements of the *11. Panzer-Division*. The division had gotten out.

On 8 January, the division was still essentially between the encircled battle groups in Kirowograd and the *11. Panzer-Division*, which was positioned south of Fedwar. Finally, contact was reestablished with the corps. After consulting with the commanding general, Bayerlein was instructed to take the so-called "Sparrowhawk" Line along the Ingul, attack in the direction of Lelekowka (where the division had broken out the previous day) and relieve the three cut-off divisions. The division regrouped for the mission. The armored group, consisting of the *II./Panzer-Regiment 6* and elements of *Panzergrenadier-Regiment 3*, attacked east. Since the armored group did not make any progress, *Generalmajor* Bayerlein, changed his plan: He had the group pull back in view of the enemy, making it look like it was retreating. Once it was out of view of the enemy, he had the

forces turn around and regroup in a large depression. In the meantime, the divisional artillery was placing everything it had on Ossikowata. The tanks and *SPW's* rolled forward towards the village. They entered the village as the last artillery shell was impacting. "Close your eyes and get in there!" The division commander was in the lead elements of the armored group.

The Russians never even had a chance to fire. The attack was a complete success. The mechanized infantry cleared the village, while the tanks moved on towards Kirowograd. The Soviet 48th Mechanized Brigade suffered approximately 400 dead and 500 prisoners, as well as the loss of forty antitank guns. The division initially set up an all-round defense at Ossikowata.

The commanding general of the *XXXXVII. Panzer-Korps, General der Panzertruppen* Vormann, wrote about those bold and therefore successful operations a decade later in his memoir entitled *Tscherkassy*:

By then, the VII and VIII Mechanized Corps had encircled the *3. Panzer-Division* at Kirowograd. In a bold night attack—tanks protecting the unarmored vehicles to all sides—*General* Bayerlein broke out of the encirclement, moved right through the middle of the enemy forces and reached Wladimirowka early on the eighth. The magnificently led division immediately turned around and took Ossikowata that same morning in a counterattack to the east. A rare example of the still unbroken fighting morale of the troops.

Following that, the reconnaissance battalion, along with the attached *6./Panzer-Regiment 6* of *Leutnant* Theimer, received the mission to eliminate the enemy battle group from the Soviet 67th Tank brigade, which had broken through as far as the command post of the *XXXXVII. Panzer-Korps* at Mal. Wiski. Because the tanks, which were coming from another mission, had to be resupplied, the force was delayed in moving out until the afternoon. The small battle group then took off and reached the area directly around Mal. Wiski after the onset of darkness, moving along poor roads that were iced-over in places.

The armored reconnaissance patrols that were sent ahead reported that the enemy force, which had thrust far ahead of its main body, was apparently cut off from its supplies. It was receiving neither supplies nor reinforcements from the rear, since the gap that had been created initially was then being over-watched by German forces. The airfield south of Mal. Wiski was being held by *Luftwaffe* ground forces. *Stukas* and other formations under the command of *Oberst* Rudel had attacked the village all day and apparently destroyed a number of tanks there. Since darkness in unfamiliar territory promised little success for an attack, the commander decided after thoroughly analyzing the situation to set up his battle group east of Mal. Wiski in such a manner that it would be able to attack at first light following thorough reconnaissance. The warning order was issued for an attack in the morning and standing patrols were established so that all movement into and out of the village could be monitored. Dismounted patrols were sent to ascertain the situation in the village proper.

During the night of 10–11 January, the armored reconnaissance patrols reported the sounds of tracked vehicles and noticeable movement in Mal. Wiski. A short while later, the closest patrol reported that a column of tanks and trucks with mounted riflemen were moving eastward. That report was the clarion call for the battle group. The companies, which had already been alerted, were ready to move in an amazingly short period of time. Based on the continuous reports concerning the direction of movement of the enemy column, the battle group was formed up in such a manner that the tank company and the *SPW* company (*Oberleutnant* Kleffel) could attack south in a wedge as a mixed formation, while the motorcycle infantry company under *Oberleutnant* Möller followed in a refuse right formation echeloned towards the rear. In the first light of the new day, the lead fighting vehicles suddenly spotted the enemy column about 1,500 meters in front of it and heading east. There were approximately fourteen to sixteen T-34's, along with a few trucks and other vehicles. A few seconds later, fighting vehicles and *SPW's* closed up along a wide front, opened fire and hit the Russians by surprise in the flank. In the blink of an eye, a few T-34's were burning, and the riflemen fled into the nearby thickets. A wild hunt followed, in which practically all of the enemy tanks were destroyed or rendered combat ineffective. A large amount of equipment was captured, as well as a fairly large number of prisoners taken.

By then, the motorcycle infantry company was being employed against Mal. Wiski, where remnants of the enemy forces were still located. After a short fight in the village, their resistance was broken. Contact was established with the *Luftwaffe* strongpoint, and a large portion of the corps documents could be secured. The village showed signs of the previous fighting, when the Russian tank elements arrived there. Among the unburied dead was the corps adjutant, *Major* Hasse, who had won the Gold Medal in the 1936 Olympics.

The reconnaissance battalion was able to report the same day to the commanding general, *General der Panzertruppen* Vormann, at his provisional corps headquarters at Nowij Mirgorod that its mission had been accomplished.

On 10 January, the division was far ahead of the rest of the German front. Soviet tank wedges had moved past the division to both the north and south. In accordance with orders, the division evacuated its positions at Ossikowata during the night of 10–11 January. *Panzergrenadier-Regiment 3* and the *II./Panzer-Regiment 6* pulled back to a line running Petrowka–Alexandrowka–Point 231.4. Enemy tanks and riflemen pursued, and antitank elements knocked out two T-34's. *Leutnant* Puchta's *2./Panzergrenadier-Regiment 3* conducted an immediate counterattack and took 200 prisoners.

At noon on 10 January, the division received another sector, where the situation had deteriorated: Enemy tanks had broken through the front lines of the *320. Infanterie-Division* and advanced as far as Kanish. Accordingly, elements of the division were pushed into the area around Gruskoje to restore the situation. The tactical assembly had to be cleared ahead of time by means of individual engagements. *Leutnant* Leuthardt's *5./Panzer-Regiment 6* then conducted a classical tank attack, during which fifteen 7.62-centimeter antitank guns in Andrejewka were destroyed. The *2./Panzergrenadier-Regiment 3*, fighting at another location, turned back a Russian tank attack. In close combat, *Leutnant* Puchta and *Leutnant* Schneck each knocked out a T-34. An additional T-34 was destroyed late in the evening by means of close combat, after the tank had broken through the German front as far as the division command post at Kowaljewka.

The division was fighting on practically all sides. It not only had to defend against the enemy to the north, east and south, but it also had to establish a front oriented to the west against the tanks that had originally broken through at Mal. Wiski that were then trying to escape to the east. The losses in vehicles were enormous. For example, the *I./Panzergrenadier-Regiment 3* no longer had any radio vehicles. Its maintenance section in Lipjanka had its hands full. The two medical companies had each established a main clearing station in Pantschewo and Nowij Mirgorod; they had also established a forward clearing station at Fedorowka. The division logistics officer had a support point established in Tarnowka, where engineer materiel was stored. The *3./Panzer-Pionier-Bataillon 39* constructed a temporary bridge at Matussowka.

Generalmajor Bayerlein ordered the *II./Panzer-Regiment 6* and the reconnaissance battalion to the right wing of the division during the night of 10–11 January in order to take a collective farm the next day and block the retreat route for the Soviets out of Mal. Wiski. Starting at 1000 hours, the attack made good progress. There were no strong enemy forces found anywhere. It was not until the force reached the vicinity of Marjanowka that the enemy put up a stubborn defense. Additional enemy tanks gathered at Wladimirowka, where *Panzergrenadier-Regiment 394* was defending. The *282. Infanterie-Division*, rolling down from the north in trucks, was attached to the division in the evening.

The Armed Forces Daily Report of 11 January reported the successful efforts of the division: "In the fighting around Kirowograd, the Brandenburg *3. Panzer-Division* particularly distinguished itself under the command of *Generalmajor* Bayerlein."

While the soldiers of the division heard those words on their radios, they also read a Russian leaflet that had just been dropped at the same time. The text: "German officers and soldiers! Everywhere the forces of the German military attempt to check the Russian attack, they themselves are encircled and eliminated! The German military is as impotent in the defense as it is in the attack. If you do not wish to fall victim to Hitler's strategy of defeat, then set out for home or surrender. All further resistance assures a certain death!"

On 11 January, the Soviets moved out north of Gruskoje again after a strong artillery preparation. The front was pushed back. The German artillery, including the divisional artillery, helped hold up the Russian tanks. The *3. Panzer-Division*, reinforced by two regiments from the *282. Infanterie-Division*, conducted an immediate counterattack on 12 January. The 2nd Battalion of the armor regiment and the reconnaissance battalion formed the spearhead. The reconnaissance battalion succeeded in taking Marjanowka in its first effort. The tanks moved into the wooded area south of Alexandrowka with mounted infantry. *Leutnant* Langendorff's 6th Company attacked enemy antitank-gun position along the wood-line, while the mechanized infantry assaulted the enemy rifle positions within the woods. The enemy was surprised and pulled back. The German force destroyed eight assault guns, two tanks, and ten antitank guns. The fighting vehicles were positioned on Hill 220.7, having reached the attack objective. Contact was established with the *10. Panzergrenadier-Division*, which had been fighting its way out of Kirowograd for the last three days, along with the two other divisions.

For their part, the Soviets achieved a complete success along the boundary between the *XI. Armee-Korps* and the *XXXXVII. Panzer-Korps*. The *106.* and *389. Infanterie-Divisionen* were unable to hold out against the enemy and had to give ground. Correspondingly, the *3. Panzer-Division* received orders on 13 January to be pulled out of its sector and sent to the area around Pantschewo to straighten up the situation. The division moved to the new sector on 14 January. The combat elements moved into tactical assembly areas right behind the *106.* and *389. Infanterie-Divisionen* during the night. Both the infantry divisions were attached to *Generalmajor* Bayerlein. The division commander, who celebrated his forty-fifth birthday that day, worked out an attack plan with his terrific operations officer, *Oberstleutnant i.G.* Voss. The intent was to hit the enemy in the flank. The attack objective was Reimentarowka, which was to be enveloped and taken from the rear. A company of *Panthers* from *Panzer-Regiment 15* of the *11. Panzer-Division* was attached to the division for that purpose.

The attack started at 0900 on 15 January. Initially, it headed from Ossitnjashka to the southeast. By noon, it succeeded in taking the high ground south of Burtki and the villages of Wassiljewka and Nowaja Ossitnjashka. The Russians were overrun in their positions. Elements pulled back, leaving behind a lot of weapons and materiel in the process. When the assault continued, contact was lost between the tanks, which had roamed far ahead, and the grenadiers that were following, with the result that it was not possible to take Reimentarowka.

The division continued its attack on 16 January. This time, the battalions had more success,

and the enemy pulled back. Reimentarowka was taken at noon by *Panzergrenadier-Regiment 3*. *Panzergrenadier-Regiment 394* took up security east of the locality. It was intended to clear the terrain the next day, but the Russians launched an attack on Jamki that same day. *Hauptmann* König's *II./Panzer-Regiment 6* straightened out the dangerous situation.

The fighting around Kirowograd had been decided. The German divisions were able to maintain their sectors, with the *3. Panzer-Division* bearing the main burden. The formations of the *8. Armee* were able to register the following spoils-of-war in the week of fighting:

Destroyed: 490 tanks: 100 artillery pieces; 564 antitank guns; and 15 antiaircraft guns. Captured: 3,871 prisoners. The attack by thirty-one Russian divisions was stopped. The front was stabilized in such a manner that the *11.* and *14. Panzer-Divisionen* could be pulled out of the line to be used elsewhere. The *3. Panzer-Division* remained around Krassnossilka and Reimentarowka as the only armored formation. It was there that the enemy's focal point had been over the previous few days. The field army concentrated its artillery assets behind the *3. Panzer-Division*.

The Soviet 5th Guards Army gave up any further attempts to break through on 17 January. The *3. Panzer-Division* found itself with some time to regroup. The heavy fighting of the previous few weeks had taken their toll on personnel and equipment. The battalions had shrunken greatly in size. *Major* Deichen, the commander of the reconnaissance battalion, had been wounded and *Oberleutnant* Motz, the commander of the *2./Panzergrenadier-Regiment 394*, had been killed. Those are but two names out of many.

The trench strength of *Panzergrenadier-Regiment 3* had diminished in numbers to that of a battalion. The 1st Battalion, which *Hauptmann* Jobst started commanding on 19 January, had only enough personnel to form an *ad hoc* company. It took up positions in Reimentarowka. *Oberleutnant Freiherr* von Eckardtstein assumed command of the regiment's headquarters company. The *II./Panzer-Regiment 6* had lost a number of tanks. It consolidated its assets into a single tank company under the command of *Oberleutnant* Hossfeld. *Leutnant* Aschermann commanded the battalion's remaining forces. *Hauptmann* Fiehl was placed in charge of the maintenance company. *Heeres-Flak-Abteilung 314* was reorganized under *Major* Fleischer. Its heavy self-propelled *Flak* proved to be an invaluable asset to the division. The reconnaissance battalion was sent to Pissarewka to be the division reserve.

Generalmajor Bayerlein left the division on 18 January to assume his new duties as commander of the *Panzer-Lehr-Division*. In the months that he commanded the division, he had earned the respect and admiration of all of its soldiers.

Oberst Lang succeeded him. The acting division commander had been a Bavarian alpine officer. At the start of the war, he had been the commander of *Gebirgs-Panzer-Abwehr-Abteilung 44*.[5] Prior to his assignment as acting commander of the division, Lang had fought in Tunisia.

Over the next week, the forces that were not employed in the front lines were busy establishing a new defensive line. From 22 to 24 January, the division's bridging section constructed two antitank-gun, three heavy machine-gun, and thirteen light machine-gun positions and forty-eight dugouts, as well as digging 250 meters of trench line.

The offensive of the 1st Ukrainian Front started on 24 January. Its eight field armies were directed into the Tscherkassy area. It only remained quiet in front of the positions of the *3. Panzer-Division* for a day, although patrols and aerial reconnaissance had indicated Soviet build-ups. The friendly forces to the left, the *389. Infanterie-Division*, were overrun by the enemy and lost Burki, despite the employment of *Stukas*. There was thick fog spread across the countryside on 25 January when heavy Russian artillery fire was heard from around Burtki and suddenly started impacting around Reimentarowka. Tanks and riflemen of the 5th Guards Army started charging the main line of resistance in the sector of *Panzergrenadier-Regiment 394*. The mechanized infantry, combat engineers, antitank elements and cannoneers defended with all their power against the enemy. The Soviets understood how to exploit their superiority in numbers in the fog and penetrated into the German positions. The fighting raged back and forth, increasing both in intensity and casualties by the hour. Contact had long since been lost with the *389. Infanterie-Division*. There were almost thirty Soviet tanks on fire in front of the German main line of resistance. But the enemy's pressure did not let up and, as it turned dark, Reimentarowka had to be evacuated. The division moved its left wing back and occupied a new position southwest of the locality.

The Soviets continued through breakthrough the next day, which was marked by a thaw. Despite that, the *3. Panzer-Division* was able to retain a cohesive front. Unfortunately, it was no longer in a position to maintain contact with the friendly forces on the left. Groups of enemy tanks were thrusting past the division to the north and heading west. They reached the Smela–Slatopol rail line, swung southwest and fired at the rear-area services in Jusefowka.

Oberstleutnant Beuermann's *Panzergrenadier-Regiment 394* served as the bulwark of the entire front! The day passed with a lot of heavy fighting. There was no quiet spell during the night, either. Enemy artillery fires caused continuous casualties. The friendly batteries fired in kind, as well as they could. The counterattack of the *11.* and *14. Panzer-Divisionen* started to make itself felt. Both of the battle groups from those divisions took Tischkowka and Pissarewka on 27 January.

---

5. The mountain antitank battalion was organic to the *1. Gebirgs-Division*. As the commander of that battalion, Lang was awarded the Knight's Cross on 23 August 1941.

On that day, the wedges of Soviet armor were far to the rear of the division. The enemy's plan—to encircle the German salient extending far to the front at Tscherkassy—slowly started to be discernible. The positions of the division were not charged that day; instead, they were kept under continuous fire. The enemy kept sending reinforcements north of Rossoschowatka. Since that was developing into a threat to the *3. Panzer-Division*, *Hauptmann* König and his tanks were sent there on 28 January to conduct an immediate counterattack. The tank attack the next day gained considerable ground. By 1000 hours, seven Russian fighting vehicles had been knocked out. An enemy antitank-gun belt prevented any further advance, however, and the attack was stopped. The Soviets then attacked from out of Saschita. The clearing station there had to be evacuated in the face of approaching T-34's. At noon, *Panthers* from the *11. Panzer-Division* started advancing out of Slatopol, where *Panzergrenadier-Regiment 3* and *Panzer-Aufklärungs-Abteilung 3* were defending. The *Panthers* pushed the enemy back somewhat, creating some breathing room for the defenders.

On the evening of 28 January, a new major danger emerged for the German Army in the East. The spearheads of the 5th and 6th Guards Tank Armies established contact at Swenigorodka, to the east of Uman. That created a pocket around Korsun, which contained two corps: *General der Artillerie* Stemmermann's *XI. Armee-Korps* and *Generalleutnant* Lieb's *XXXXII. Armee-Korps*. The two corps, totaling around 50,000 men, had the following divisions attached to them: *57., 72., 88.,* and *389. Infanterie-Division, SS-Panzergrenadier-Division "Wiking,"* and *SS-Freiwilligen-Strum-Brigade "Wallonien."*[6]

Strangely enough, it was quiet in the sector of the *3. Panzer-Division* on 29 January. To rein-force its main line of resistance, the division received the *320. Infanterie-Division* in attachment that day, later followed by *Oberstleutnant d.R.* Mummert's *Panzergrenadier-Regiment 103.*[7] Despite many efforts, it was not possible to establish contact with the elements of the *XI. Armee-Korps* that were cut off to the north. The Russian pocket was hermetically sealed. Based on the threatening situation, the field-army group directed immediate countermeasures. According to the higher command, an attack was to be launched during the night of 2–3 February to relieve the two corps. The *III. Panzer-Korps* of *General der Panzertruppen* Breith positioned itself north of Uman behind the eastern wing of the *1. Panzer-Armee* with its *1., 16.,* and *17. Panzer-Divisionen* and *SS-Panzer-Grenadier-Division "Leibstandarte SS Adolf Hitler."* At the same time, *Generalleutnant* Vormann's *XXXXVII. Panzer-Korps* staged along the western wing of the *8. Armee* south of Swenigorodka with its *3., 11., 13., 14.,* and *24. Panzer-Divisionen.*

For the next two days, the *3. Panzer-Division* held its frontage against every attempt to break through it. Although there were considerable casualties, especially those caused by heavy artillery—*Oberarzt* Dr. Lippold of the armored regiment was badly wounded, for instance—the Russians were unable to shake the division's battalions anywhere along the front. The division received orders to turn over its positions to the *376. Infanterie-Division* on 1 February. The divisional engineers, led by *Hauptmann* Sedlaczek, who had replaced the wounded *Major* Schwing, had finished constructing a rearward line by that time.

The division moved to the west, with the command post being established in Korotschino. The march columns followed over the course of the next two days and collected in the area north of Korotschino–Rubanyi Most–Antonowka–

---

6. The Walloon SS Volunteer Storm Brigade, recruited from the French-speaking minority in Belgium.
7. One of the mechanized infantry regiments of the *14. Panzer-Division*. Werner Mummert became one of the most highly decorated and ranking reserve officers of the war.

Lipjanka. *Oberleutnant* Mertens and his bridging section moved out of Lekarewo in a downpour during the night of 1 February. *Leutnant* Gäbel's *3./Panzer-Pionier-Bataillon 39* constructed a 19.2-meter sixteen-ton provisional bridge north of Lekarewo the same night between 0130 and 0530 hours. The troop movements suffered as a result of the muddy routes, because it rained without interruption. The weather did not change the next day, with the result that the columns became widely separated. There were time-consuming delays, especially at the entrances to bridges. They were magnified by the fact that the *11. Panzer-Division* had to use the same routes.

By then, the Soviets had moved west via Tolmatsch. At noon on 2 February, they attacked south in Lipjanka Valley. *Panzergrenadier-Regiment 394* was the first formation to reach Nitschajewka after moving through Nowo-Mirgorod. It defended along the northern edges of the locality. *Oberstleutnant* Beuermann and his regimental headquarters fought in the front lines. Just as the situation was turning critical, the fighting vehicles of the *II./Panzer-Regiment 6* arrived. They had been held up by the construction of the bridge at Marslowka. The tanks of the armor battalion advanced across the outpost lines of *Panzergrenadier-Regiment 394* and ejected the enemy from Hill 187.8. They then turned west, assaulted Hills 211 and 190.9 and established contact with the men of the divisional reconnaissance battalion. The division had wrested control of its designated outpost line from the enemy. *Panzergrenadier-Regiment 394* established its positions in Nitschajewka, followed by the armor battalion and the divisional engineers. *Panzergrenadier-Regiment 3* screened between Hills 211 and 190.9, while the divisional reconnaissance battalion positioned itself along the eastern edge of Antonowka. The battle-weary and tired soldiers set up in provisional quarters and waited for further fighting.

The weather increasingly worsened. The rain and slush continued. In places, the muck appeared to be bottomless. The approaches to most of the bridges were flooded. It was almost impossible to make forward progress in that morass. The tanks were only able to move at a maximum speed of five kilometers an hour; the trucks, staff cars and motorcycles became hopelessly stuck. The 2nd Medical Company was stuck in its entirety and unable to move. The wounded had to be loaded onto panje carts. The bridging section, which had been directed to the supply point at Wintel-Nikolajewka, got stuck at Korotschino and had to establish an all-round defense there.

Despite the rigors of the weather, the division still had to attack on 3 February. *Oberstleutnant* Fleischauer's *Panzergrenadier-Regiment 394* formed the main effort. The men of *Hauptmann* Jobst's and *Major* Dietrich's battalions advanced determinedly against the enemy. The mechanized infantry moved in their *SPW's* and drove back the enemy. Hill 190.9 was taken in an assault. At noon, the men of *Panzergrenadier-Regiment 3* and *Panzer-Aufklärungs-Abteilung 3* advanced on Kamunowka and occupied it. They did not stop there. The soldiers, magnificently supported by the artillery and the antitank elements, penetrated into Bratskije in the evening and established a blocking position there against Russian forces moving to the southwest. At 1930 hours, the division submitted the following daily report: "In Kamunowka, 21 3.7-centimeter antitank guns, 14 7.62-centimeter antitank guns, 10 trucks, 10 mortars, 4 guns, and at least 100 limbers captured. 200 to 300 enemy dead. Approximately 4 battalions wiped out. Mission accomplished!"

As soon as it turned first light on the morning of 4 February, the batteries of the divisional artillery opened fire on the enemy positions in the area around Tolmatsch. *Panzergrenadier-Regiment 3* and *Panzer-Aufklärungs-Abteilung 3* moved out to assault again along the left wing. Despite the strong defense put up by the Russians, the mechanized infantry worked their way forward to Wodjanoje and entered the village. They were unable to move farther, since the expected tanks from the *11. Panzer-Division* did not show up. That division, under the command of *Generalmajor* Wiethersheim, the former adjutant for officer affairs of the *3. Panzer-Division*, was only able to progress slowly as a result of the thick mud. It was able to drive the enemy back from Tolmatsch, however. *Panzer-Aufklärungs-Abteilung 3*, which had moved out from Bratskije at 1100 hours, participated in the latter attack.

The *II./Panzer-Regiment 6* had followed behind its neighbor on the left. At 1300 hours, it made a surprise move and turned east. The Russians pulled back to Lipjanka. *Oberleutnant* Taulien's tank elements did not let go of the enemy and followed him. *Panzergrenadier-Regiment 394* exploited the opportunity and attacked Lipjanka from the south. As a result, the entire division was on the attack, despite the rain and the mud. The mechanized infantry took Lipjanka and captured thirty antitank guns. On the east bank of the river, the antitank elements knocked out five T-34's. It seemed that a big success was soon to be had.

Then there was a huge rushing sound from the west bank of the Lipjanka. The Soviets had concentrated a lot of artillery there, and it was starting to take the area under systematic fire. The German forces had to stop their advance and set up in the burned-down houses or provisional bunkers. The extremely heavy artillery fire continued to rain down on the German positions for the next few days and nights.

The division took pains to improve the positions it had won and hold on to them. As a consequence of the enemy's superiority in numbers and the terrible ground conditions it was impossible to continue the attack. *Hauptmann* Schwarzenberger, the commander of the *1./Panzer-Nachrichten-Abteilung 39*, made the following laconic entry in his diary on 5 February: "Dreary, bad weather. All movement dies in the mud; even motorized vehicles get stuck." Contact with both the *11.* and the *14. Panzer-Division* could only be maintained sporadically. The Soviets plastered the German positions with immense amounts of ammuni-

tion, and the casualties mounted. *Panzergrenadier-Regiment 394* had a trench strength of only 80 to 100 men at one point. The forward clearing stations at Sobelewka and Antonowka could barely keep up with the influx of wounded. The weather negatively influenced every movement; fuel and supply vehicles could only come forward sporadically. The messengers abandoned their motorcycles and switched to horses.

The *8. Armee* radioed orders on 7 February:

To relieve the *XI.* and *XXXXII. Armee-Korps*, the following [formations] attack: *XXXXVII. Panzer-Korps* after regrouping with a strong west wing from the vicinity of Jeriki through Kasazkoje on to Olschana; *III. Panzer-Korps* from the area around Winograd with right wing [advancing] via Lissjanka to Morenzy. *Gruppe Stemmermann* forces a breakthrough through the encirclement and advances with an armored wedge along a line running Schanderowka–Kwitki toward Morenzy, while massing its forces along its inner wings and covering its flank and rear.

The movement of the *3. Panzer-Division* to the area around Jeriki was set for 11 February. The movement was a fiasco, despite constant work on the roads, routes and vehicles. The mud was worse than the enemy. The daily logs of the bridging section noted on 11 February:

The vehicles are only able to advance by meters. The vehicles that only have rear drives have to be towed from the onset by two vehicles with all-wheel drive in order to cover even 100 meters. Despite that, the driver and assistant driver have to push, throw bundles of sticks and brush under the tires and also remove clumps of mud with shovels. . . . The march speed is also slowed by the overworking of the vehicles. For instance, the vehicles used to tow burn up their motor oil.

The movement continued despite the hardships caused by the weather. The command staff of the division moved out of its quarters on 12 February to Mokraja-Kaligorka, where it arrived in the evening. The remaining formations followed in fits and spurts. The 1st Medical Company established a clearing station in Korotino. The Ukrainian countryside at the time was a single puddle of mud, in which two armored corps prepared to attack to relieve two encircled corps.

The final fighting for the Tscherkassy Pocket started on 13 February under a driving snow. The German front had slowly closed up between Uman and Pantschewo. The forces still holding out west of Tscherkassy were pressed together in an area defined by Schanderowka–Chilki–Komarowka. They staged for a breakout to the southwest. The encircled divisions had been supplied since 28 January by *Generalleutnant* Seidemann's *VIII. Flieger-Korps*. The transporters flew in 2,026 tons of supplies weekly and 2,188 wounded out. Despite the deprivations, the morale of the encircled forces was good. Several offers to capitulate were turned down. It should be noted that officers of the "Committee for a Free Germany" (for example, Seydlitz-Korbach, Korfes, Hadermann, Steidle, Lewerenz, Büchler, and *Graf* von Einsiedel) were calling out for soldiers to desert via loudspeakers. It was the first large-scale, front-line employment of the "National Committee" and also its last. It turned out to be a disaster, and Stalin forbade any further propaganda exercises of the type.

The breakout attempt and the relief effort were set for 2300 hours on 16 February. The encircled forces were to break out along a front fifty kilometers wide to the southwest. *General der Artillerie* Stemmermann was killed while with the spearhead of one of his divisions. The Soviets had inserted strong formations between Lissjanka and Komarowka, which pushed the Tscherkassy forces farther south.

By then, the *III. Panzer-Korps* had reached Lissjanka. *Oberst* Frank, the commander of *Panzer-Regiment 1* (*1. Panzer-Division*) and for-mer commander of the *II./Panzer-Regiment 6*, led the spearhead of the corps. Enemy divisions placed themselves in the path of the attacking fighting vehicles and slowly gained the upper hand. The tanks of the *III. Panzer-Korps* were unable to advance any farther. The *XXXXVII. Panzer-Korps* also had to admit defeat outside of Swenigorodka. The closest formation to reach the encircled soldiers was the spearhead of the *11. Panzer-Division* (*Generalmajor* Wietersheim), which worked its way to within twenty-five kilometers of the pocket. But then it was also halted.

The German armored forces were forced to go on the defensive due to the overwhelming numbers of the Soviets and the mud. The formations of the *III. Panzer-Korps* that were positioned around Lissjanka passed through the lines the elements of the four infantry divisions and the two SS formations that made it through. They were at the end of their rope: filthy, lice infested, starving, frozen, clothed in rags, and, in some cases, without weapons. There were about 30,000 men that reached the German lines as human wrecks. Although the Armed Forces Daily Report announced a victory at Tscherkassy, in reality, the two corps—*XI. Armee-Korps* and *XXXXII. Armee-Korps*—no longer existed.

The fighting for the *3. Panzer-Division* was not over. The Soviets knew that several thousand soldiers had escaped and proceeded to attack the divisions that were holding the passage lines with overwhelming numbers. A violent snowstorm had swept over the steppes for the past two days and created snowdrifts everywhere. The resilient muck had not frozen, however, and vehicles continued to get stuck everywhere. The division surgeon, *Oberstabsarzt* Dr. Stribny noted on 17 February: "Considerable signs of exhaustion within the 394th and 3rd as a result of the uninterrupted winter fighting without permanent quarters." There was a large Russian attack on 18 February. *Panzergrenadier-Regiment 394* braced itself against the enemy and the snow in its six-kilometer-wide position at

Skoterowo. The divisional artillery supported the hard-fighting mechanized infantry as best it could. Officers and cannoneers loaded guns, fired, hauled ammunition, and defended in close combat. Frequently, they were the final measure of defense whenever enemy tanks attacked. The battery commander of the 2nd Battery, *Hauptmann* Lempp, later received the Knight's Cross for his actions.

The next few days did not see any change in the situation. The losses within the division rose to alarming levels. The orders to pull back arrived on 23 February. The forces were unable to take all of their vehicles with them, since many were still stuck in the mud. A vehicle recovery detail was formed under the direction of *Major* Rütt. The 2nd Medical Company was attached to Rütt's command to ensure medical attention for personnel on the vehicles was achieved.

The division command staff moved to Nowo Ukrainka on 24 February. The troop elements of the division followed in a road march. The movement was sheer torture for the men and the materiel. The division established its command post in Bobrinez on 26 February. The troop elements arrived in fits and spurts. The thaw, which had arrived by then, caused additional difficulties. Many vehicles and the majority of the heavy weapons could not be brought back fast enough as a result of the poor road network. Within the *II./Panzer-Regiment 6*, twenty fighting vehicles were stuck. The recovery details of the maintenance company were able to retrieve all but four of them. The remainder were no longer combat operational and were blown up. The maintenance personnel of the *3. Panzer-Division* received special recognition for their achievements during this period. The Knight's Cross of the War Service Cross with Swords—a rare award—was presented to *Oberfunkmeister* Hock of the armored regiment on 21 February.

The personnel end strength of the division had shrunk dramatically. Both of the mechanized infantry regiments were consolidated into a single battle group, which *Oberstleutnant* Beuermann and the headquarters of *Panzer-*

grenadier-Regiment 394 commanded. The vehicle situation dictated the formation of an *Einsatz-Bataillon* under *Hauptmann* Müller-Röhlich. The *II./Panzer-Regiment 6* consisted of a single combat company under *Oberleutnant* Hossfeld, with the rest of the battalion under *Oberleutnant* Raupp and the maintenance company under *Hauptmann* Fiehl.

The *3. Panzer-Division* was attached to the *LVI. Panzer-Korps*, which belonged to the *6. Armee*. The division command post was located in Schewschtschenkowo on 28 February. The division remained a reserve of the corps. It was directed for the medical companies to establish clearing stations in Wodjana and Bratoljubowka. But there were already medical facilities of the *76. Infanterie-Division* there, so that the individual companies were only employed in transporting the sick and the wounded. A battle group from *Panzergrenadier-Regiment 3* had to rush to Bukowo on 1 March, when Russian riflemen broke through there.

There were not too many days available for rest and refitting. The Soviets had moved out for a major offensive against Kriwoi Rog and had already ripped open the German front. The *Einsatz-Bataillon* and the *II./Panzer-Regiment 6* were quickly rail loaded and transported to the threatened area. *Oberstleutnant* Lühl formed a small battle group out of both of the battalions, which had to undergo hard fighting in the next few weeks, away from the division, under extremely difficult circumstances and under inhumane conditions. Operations in the deep mud northwest of Kriwoi Rog was a singular difficulty. Initially, the tanks and *SPW's* could only move in first gear. A number of vehicles were not brought back as the result of a lack of spare parts or recovery means. *Gepanzerte Gruppe Lühl* was employed as a "fire brigade" and inserted into the line between weak infantry elements. It served as the "backbone" for divisions falling back from one blocking position to the next.

The muddy roads made it impossible to move quickly so that most of the vehicles used the railway tracks as a roadway. Russian fighter-bombers constantly attacked the columns. Instead of the directed 100 kilometers, the bridging section was only able to cover 35. The troop units of the division reached the Ingul on 11 March. Moving there was no better. The roads still appeared to be bottomless seas of mud. Numerous *balkas* and valleys led to constant march stoppages by hundreds of vehicles. Whenever the forces finally crossed such an obstacle, they were frequently greeted by the report that the Soviets had already crossed the same obstacle to the north or the south and were already cruising in front of the columns. The different columns were widely dispersed. It was impossible to establish a unified command.

Most of the division, which was road marching by either motorized vehicle or horse-drawn conveyance, reached Rostoschachowka on 13 March. A newly arrived snowstorm and the hard-pressing enemy made the last leg of the movement to the Bug difficult.

The columns churned their way forward meter by meter from Bratskoje. Whenever a vehicle was stranded as a result of engine problems or a broken axle, it was blown up, since there were no replacement parts. The 1st Medical Company had to destroy seven vehicles and the bridging section four. Between Kriwoi Rog and the Bug, the recovery section from *Panzer-Regiment 6* of *Leutnant* Aschermann and *Oberschirrmeister* Heller blew up more than forty fighting vehicles.

On 17 March, the division arrived in Wosnessensk. Hitler had declared that the city was a *Fester Platz*, a fortified area. As a result, the battle groups were immediately incorporated into the defensive plans. The individual formations of the division had to provide alert units. The situation was unclear, and no one knew what was happening. The columns of the division closed into the city over the next two days and occupied designated areas. On 18 March, the Red Army succeeded in establishing its first bridgehead over the Bug to the north of Wosnessensk. Based on the situation, the Army High Command ordered the city evacuated. The very next day, the division started moving westward across the Bug.

The burial of *Major* Dittmer in Stepani in November 1943. The officers of *Panzergrenadier-Regiment 3* take their leave.

Generalmajor Bayerlein shakes hands with the division surgeon, Dr. Stribny. Next to him is *Hauptmann* Schulze, the division adjutant (officer affairs), who later went on to command the *I./Panzergrenadier-Regiment 3*.

Generalmajor Bayerlein, commander of the division from October 1943 until January 1944.

The "backbone" of the army: the corporals of *Heeres-Flak-Abteilung 314.*

Major Schwing, commander of *Panzer-Pionier-Bataillon 39.*

Unteroffizier Görlich, a squad leader in
the *1./Panzergrenadier-Regiment 394*.

Crew of an *Sd.Kfz. 250* of *Panzer-Aufklärungs-
Abteilung 3*. Despite the withdrawals,
humor and comradeship remained.

Unteroffizier Eggers, a gunner in the *7./Panzer-Regiment 7.*

Oberleutnant Kleffel, commander of the *4./Panzer-Aufklärungs-Abteilung 3.*

Hauptmann Lempp, battery commander of the *2./Panzer-Artillerie-Regiment 75.*

Hauptmann Dietrich, commander of the *II./Panzergrenadier-Regiment 3.*

CHAPTER 9

From the Bug to the Narew: A Fighting Retreat in Romania and Poland

Effective 21 March 1944, the division was attached to the *LII. Armee-Korps*. Once across the Bug, the formations marched through the abandoned villages of German settlers. Munich . . . Lichterfelde . . . Rastatt . . . those were a few of the names. The battle-weary men were only granted a few days before they had to move again. The sunny weather gave way to rain, which once again softened up the roads.

The command staff of the division moved to Zaredavowka on 23 March. From there, the columns were directed to march westward at a rate of twenty-five to thirty kilometers a day. The movements moved like molasses, however, since the forces were only partially motorized. *Panje* horses were often the last hope, whenever the heavily laden vehicles became stuck. On 26 March, the news arrived that the Soviets had advanced to the west of the road and taken Balta. Because of that, the direction of march was changed to the southwest. The movement was conducted in stages, with the Russians following closely behind. The T-34's frequently passed the columns, which then had to detour through the muddy terrain. The few roads were hopelessly jammed. The *II./Panzer-Regiment 6* marched along a different road and could not help the division.

Despite the hardships, the withdrawal movements were accomplished. Nowo Pawlowka was reached on 27 March, where hundreds of vehicles were stacked up waiting to cross the Tschitscheklija. Frost arrived the next day, when the formations moved through Troitzkoje. The Tiligul was crossed. The movements then led across steep hills and deep valleys as far as Andrejewka and Walegizulowo. The division was then attached to *General der Panzertruppen* Knobelsdorff's *XXXX. Panzer-Korps*.

The columns of the division marched in a pouring rain on 1 April, arriving in Dubossary. The large bridge over the Dnjestr was crossed there early in the afternoon. That meant that the division had finally left Russia after almost three years of continuous fighting. The area the division was entering was Romania. The names of the towns were already completely different: Crioleni, Duska, Onitcani, Boscana, and Karantin.

The command post was established in Branesti. Fortunately, replacements, weapons and equipment had arrived there, with the results that the battalions and battle groups could go back into battle somewhat stronger than they had been in the previous weeks. The *II./Panzer-Regiment 6* had also arrived; it had been in enemy contact since 31 March.

The divisional reconnaissance battalion was sent north soon after it had crossed the Dnjestr. It received the mission of reconnoitering the area around Susleni west of the river and to the north. On the way there through the mountainous terrain that was filled with valleys, it began to snow. Soon, any non-wooded areas had a blanket of snow on them. By the onset of darkness on 2 April, Susleni had been reached without any enemy contact. Standing patrols were dispatched in the direction of Burdasi for the night, while the battalion set up an all-round defense in the village. During the following night, the temperature dipped further and heavy snowstorms commenced. They led to snowdrifts, which made the already bad road network almost impassable. In the narrow valleys that were more like defiles, the patrols could barely make any progress along the iced-over and precipitous routes. By the same token, the enemy had the same difficulties. In the areas north of Susleni, only occasional foot patrols and outposts could be identified of the Soviet forces that were advancing west and southwest farther

north along an apparently improved road. While the supply company was able to take the battalion fuel and rations with a great deal of difficulty on 2 April from its support point established at Furceni on the far side of the Rautul, it proved impossible to deliver supplies the next day in the face of the increasingly violent snowstorms. By then, the enemy had advanced to Orhei and had his lead elements to the rear of the battalion. On 4 April, orders were finally received to pull back and move to Orhei, where other orders were to be anticipated.

Although the march route was only fourteen kilometers, it took hour upon hour for the battalion to work its way through the high snow, which often topped out at several meters. The vehicles had to halt again and again to clear snow. After extraordinary physical effort, the battalion reached the Rautal at Paharniceni around noon and received the report there that enemy tanks had already penetrated into Orhei. Since no anti-armor weaponry was available, it made no sense to attempt to do anything at Orhei. The next crossing point over the river was several kilometers farther to the southeast; to reach it based on the road conditions and the low fuel situation was impossible. The only option remaining was to search for a ford and attempt to cross the men and vehicles by that method. The Rautal is a sixty-to-eighty-meter-wide, rapidly flowing but not all-too-deep stream. The bed was generally rocky. Reconnaissance indicated a possible crossing point across from Paharniceni. After the crossing point was secured against any possible surprises from the enemy, preparations started for the crossing. Beams and other materials were hauled in from the village, mostly to guard the unprotected engines of the wheeled vehicles while fording. The work extended into the night, but it was successful. In the end, all the vehicles and soldiers were able to get to the south bank and escape the clutches of the enemy.

The bled-white *Panzergrenadier-Regiment 394* received replacements during these weeks. It formed two battalions, each with three line companies. *Hauptmann* Steinmüller was entrusted with the 1st Battalion, while *Hauptmann* Müller-Röhlich commanded the 2nd Battalion. Since the heavy companies were no longer capable of being employed, they were consolidated into a single command under *Hauptmann* Gappel (later: *Oberleutnant* Urban). On 23 March, *Oberstleutnant* Lühl was designated as the acting commander of the regiment. As a result of the loss of so many vehicles, all of the line companies were dismounted. Only the headquarters and the trains elements had motorized transport.

Heavy snowstorms negatively affected the march movements. The combat elements moved into the Orhei area as soon as possible and established defensive positions oriented north. The rear-area services were ordered to Kischinew. The German forces had to brace themselves one more time against the snowdrifts and horrific ice storms. Most of the *panje* horses were up to their necks in snow. There was no forward movement, and the Russians were attacking.

Both of the mechanized infantry regiments occupied their provisional positions on 4 April. In the afternoon, several waves of Soviet riflemen advanced. The *II./Panzergrenadier-Regiment 394* had difficulty in fending off the dangerous attack, since the high snow took away almost all observation and made the maintenance of contact with neighboring elements almost impossible. The men of the 2nd Medical Company, who had set up a main clearing station in Hartopul, were barely able to evacuate the wounded.

The enemy repeated his assault the next day. On that occasion, he advanced from the north and northwest with fourteen tanks and two rifle battalions. The enemy pushed back the extremely weakened companies, which evacuated Orhei. The Soviets immediately pursued. One of the enemy tanks succeeded in getting across the bridge over the Rautul faster than the German soldiers. A critical situation developed for *Panzergrenadier-Regiment 394*.

The crew of an immobilized *Panther* on the north bank of the river did not lose its nerves. It allowed the Russian tank to approach closely and then knocked it out at pointblank range. A German antitank gun prevented a second Russian tank from crossing, and it also caught fire. That gave the enemy pause. The remaining twelve tanks turned around and pulled back. The Russian foot soldiers left the city in a wild panic. When they got to the northern edge of the locality, they started receiving Soviet antitank-gun fire, which caused even more confusion.

The situation was skillfully exploited by *Major* Dietrich, the commander of the *II./Panzergrenadier-Regiment 3*. He pursued the fleeing Russians in a bold immediate counterattack. The mechanized infantry ejected the Russians from Orhei and took back their main line of resistance. It was only on the western side of the city that a few Russian strong-points continued to hold out, since it was not possible to assault them at the time. The bold attack by the mechanized infantry gave the division some breathing room. The soldiers started talking about the "Miracle of Orhei." *Major* Dietrich later received the Knight's cross for his actions that day.

Hauptmann Fiehl, the acting commander of the *II./Panzer-Regiment 6*, ordered the tank section of *Oberleutnant* Veltheim forward during the night to clear out the last remaining pockets of resistance of the enemy. Thick snow flurries kept them from doing that, however. Shortly after midnight, the enemy launched his own immediate counterattack and entered Orhei for the second time. Orhei had to be evacuated again. The few vehicles left became a hindrance, inasmuch as they slid off the roads numerous times and got stuck. *Oberleutnant* de Voss lost his orientation in the snowstorm and moved right into a Russian column, which took him prisoner.

The Soviets were being reinforced constantly. Over the next four days, they attacked the thin German lines again and again. The mechanized infantry, motorcycle infantry and combat engineers up front had a difficult time of it. They defended with their last reserves of strength against a foe who greatly outnumbered them and who was also being supported by heavy artillery and the Red Air Force, neither of which the Germans had. The casualties mounted each day. *Hauptmann* Steinmüller, the commander of the *I./Panzergrenadier-Regiment 394*, was killed during that round of fighting. *Oberleutnant* Arndt assumed acting command of the shrunken battalion. The tank section lost one *Panzer IV* after the other in a series of immediate counterattacks.

Easter Sunday, 9 April 1944, arrived. The logistics personnel were able to bring up personal demand items in time. In some of the units, each man received a *Frontkämpferpäckchen* ("Front Fighter's Package"), four bars of chocolate, two Schoka-Colas, one roll of hard candy, and one pouch of tobacco.

The bakery company baked cakes and the division logistics officer made wine available. For the first time in a while, the weather was good. The sun shone and brought a thaw with it.

The Soviets didn't observe the holiday, however. When it started to turn dark, they attacked. Using superior numbers, they crossed the Rautul east of Orhei and west of Paharniceni with armor and infantry forces and established two small bridgeheads. The immediate counterattacks launched by the two mechanized infantry regiments and the armored reconnaissance battalion failed. *Hauptmann* Fiehl employed his last five fighting vehicles. The tanks did not even reach the front lines, when two of them were knocked out by Russian antitank guns. The remaining three under the command of *Oberleutnant* Veltheim turned around, only to get stuck in the muck and the snow. The heavy fighting lasted the entire night, without any visible results. *Panzergrenadier-Regiment 394* evacuated its positions and pulled back to Furceni in a delaying action.

The Armed Forces Daily Report announced the fighting for Orhei on 10 April. It still wasn't over on that day. *Panzergrenadier-Regiment 110* of the *11. Panzer-Division* was attached to the *3. Panzer-Division* that day in order to firm up the front. It came none too soon, as the Soviets wanted to advance on Kischinew at all costs. Russian aircraft were constantly bombing the city and the bridges there. *Heeres-Flak-Abteilung 314* was committed to the area around Kischinew

in an air-dense role. During the night, its 4th Battery succeeded in shooting down a nuisance bomber. The number of wounded at the main clearing station in Hartopul climbed steadily. It was thanks to the efforts of *Oberstabsarzt* Dr. Stribny and the *Luftwaffe* air-ground liaison officer to locate a Fieseler *Storch*, which was used to evacuate the severely wounded. On just 10 April alone, the aircraft accomplished the amazing feat of evacuating eighteen badly wounded. Forty-one slightly wounded men were sent to the rear on foot in order to make room for new patients.

When the sun set in the west on that clear day, the Soviets attacked. This time, they directed their efforts against *Panzergrenadier-Regiment 3* and *Panzergrenadier-Regiment 110* west of Paharniceni. Both of the regiments turned back all of the enemy's efforts during the night. The *7./Panzergrenadier-Regiment 110* did the best, with the result that it was directly mentioned in the Armed Forces Daily Report of 16 April: "Numerous enemy attacks along the lower Dnjestr and at Orhei failed at the hands of our forces, which were magnificently supported by the Luftwaffe. Local penetrations were sealed off and eliminated. Over the last few days, the *7./Panzergrenadier-Regiment 110* of *Oberleutnant* Henk especially distinguished itself."

The command post of the command staff was moved to Ivancea as a result of the unfavorable developments at the front. On 11 April, the headquarters of the regiments and the division troops also arrived there. The locality was already under enemy artillery fire. Since the Soviet presence was being increased, the main clearing station was moved, with the 2nd Medical Company being sent to Kischinew. By then, the 1st Medical Company of *Stabsarzt* Dr. Douglas had established a main clearing station in Peresecina. In order to better manage the evacuation of the wounded, the three ambulance platoons were consolidated to form *Krankenkraftwagen-Kompanie 83*, which was led by *Oberfeldwebel* Winzker.

Panzergrenadier-Regiment 110 was released from its attachment to the division on 11 April. *Panzergrenadier-Regiment 394* relieved it on the line. The Soviets exploited the relief and immediately pressed into the thick woods along the river. But the lines had solidified to such an extent by then that the neighboring regiments of the *11. Panzer-Division* were able to interdict most of the Soviets, with the exception of those in the wooded area outside of Ivancea.

On 13 April, the Soviets once more attacked from the wooded area along the river to the east of Orhei. They succeeded in penetrating in regimental strength into a defile that led into a large wooded tract. From the eastern portion of the woods, the company commander of the *4./Panzer-Aufklärungs-Abteilung 3, Oberleutnant* Kleffel, observed the advance of the enemy riflemen. Kleffel's reconnaissance company had been positioned there. He realized that if the enemy were to establish himself in the broad expanse of woods, it would mean a serious threat to the entire defensive position south of Orhei.

Without waiting for orders, he moved out to attack with his eight light *SPW's*. As soon as he reached the high ground from which he intended to advance against the flanks of the Soviets, he was greeted by antitank-gun fire. The enemy had established a belt of antitank guns on the high ground south of Orhei that dominated the terrain with its fires.

Agilely led and using every swell in the ground, the small and fast *SPW's* eluded the enemy's antitank guns and reached the cover and concealment offered by the defile. The machine guns then opened up on the surprised Soviet infantrymen, who fled back in wild disarray after a short firefight. At the head of his company, Kleffel pursued the fleeing enemy forces, crossed a bridge that was within the effective firing range of the enemy's antitank guns and continued to inflict heavy casualties on the enemy rifle regiment. Before the Soviets had time to take countermeasures, the company commander had pulled his *SPW's* back across the bridge. In

short order, he and his brave men were ready to participate in operations elsewhere.

Oberleutnant Kleffel was later awarded the Knight's Cross for his decisiveness and personal bravery in mastering a critical situation.

Starting at 1000 hours on 16 April, heavy artillery fire was placed on the German positions. The anticipated Russian offensive had started. The fighting was terribly hard. The enemy was able to penetrate into the front lines of *Panzergrenadier-Regiment 394* in battalion strength at the whistle stop two kilometers west of Furceni. The officers quickly rallied their battle groups and were able to seal off and contain the dangerous penetration by noon. *Oberst* Wellmann assumed command of the two mechanized infantry regiments, as well as the reattached *Panzergrenadier-Regiment 110*, in an effort to ensure unified command. The mechanized infantry were able to hold on to their positions and prevent the Soviets from achieving any other breakthroughs. *Unteroffizier* Görlich, a squad leader in the *1./Panzergrenadier-Regiment 3*, distinguished himself in such a manner that he was later awarded the Knight's Cross for his bravery. Starting at 1900 hours, *Oberst* Wellmann initiated an immediate counterattack with his battalions and threw the Russians back, with the result that all of the original main line of resistance was reestablished by the evening.

Despite the division being able to maintain the positions around Orhei, the threatening situation and fighting had shown that they were quite poor. The field army instructed the division to begin preparations to conduct a retrograde movement. In the fighting along the Dnjestr up to that point, the *3. Panzer-Division* had suffered the loss of 960 men. The *II./Panzer-Regiment 6* had only six operational tanks. Its acting commander, *Hauptmann* Fiehl, became the first member of the division to be awarded the German Cross in Silver.[1]

---

1. Although instituted at the same time as the German Cross in Gold (17 November 1941), the German Cross in Silver is less well known and was presented far less frequently than its counterpart. The silver version was presented for distinguished service in the war effort, as opposed to bravery.

The movement of the division that had been planned for 19 April was called off, since the neighboring corps had reduced the enemy's bridgehead at Dubossary in a counterattack, thus considerably improving the over-all position of the *8. Armee*. Only the division trains and elements not employed were sent back to Zamosi. The maintenance services were also located there, where they took pains to gradually return motorized vehicles to the divisional formations and eliminate the need for the ubiquitous *panje* carts.

But two days later, the stay on the movement proved short lived. The positions were transferred to the *11. Panzer-Division*. Starting on 21 April, the headquarters and troop elements started moving back, occupying quarters around Kischinew. After the command staff had established its headquarters in Kischinew, orders arrived that the division was to move to the area around Vorniceni on 22 April. The division was still administratively attached to the *XXXXVII. Panzer-Korps*, but it reported directly to the headquarters of the *8. Armee*.

The sun was beneficent on 24 April, with the result that all of the movements proceeded without a hitch. By evening, the main bodies of the formations reached the new quartering area 30 kilometers northwest of Kischinew. The division headquarters moved to Vorniceni and discovered that the division was to be the reserve of *Heeresgruppe Nordukraine* effective 25 April. The field-army group had come about through a consolidation of the former *Heeresgruppe A* and *Heeresgruppe Süd*. Under the command of *Generaloberst* Schörner, the field-army group was responsible for defending the front between Dnjestr through Kischinew and Jassy as far as the Carpathians.

The troop elements set up in the small Romanian settlements. No one knew how long that quiet period would last, but it had certainly been earned. It was imperative to reorganize the companies, clean the weapons and maintain the vehicles. Moreover, it was vitally important to allow the forces in the field time to recover from physical and mental exertions and deprivations.

The division surgeon and his medical personnel contributed greatly to helping the soldiers recover. On 24 April, he wrote in his diary: "Danger of epidemic typhus after the soldiers had been employed during the winter without a break and were completely infested with lice. Delousing urgent. Moreover, summer illnesses, such as dysentery and typhus, can be counted on in Bessarabia. It is critical to ensure that measures are taken against flies and discipline is maintained in the latrines. Moreover, there is an increased danger of venereal disease in Romania. Troops need to be briefed on it. Need to procure protection . . ."

The 2nd Medical Company established an aid station in Straseni, while the 1st Medical Company set up a clearing station and a dental clinic in Vorniceni.

The time was used to conduct a battlefield reconstitution of the troop elements and integrate replacements. *Panzergrenadier-Regiment 394* had shrunk the most in headcount. Its 1st Battalion was attached to the sister regiment as a fighting battalion. The 2nd Battalion was dissolved and an alert battalion consisting of specialists formed over the next few days. Since there still weren't enough weapons and materiel, only one heavy company could be formed, the 4th. The divisional replacement battalion under the command of *Oberstleutnant* Feldhuß was located in Sascut and prepared the replacements and convalescents arriving from the homeland on trains for operations at the front. *Panzergrenadier-Regiment 3*, which had established its quarters at La Pusna along the Pruth River, had emerged from the last round of fighting in better shape. The divisional artillery, the 2nd Battalion of the armor regiment and the divisional engineers were able to be filled up with materiel and manpower enough over the next two weeks that they could be considered fully operational.

The health situation among the forces improved markedly. The danger of a typhus epidemic was avoided, although the first illnesses of that type were observed within the *I./Panzergrenadier-Regiment 394*, which had miserable quarters, on 30 April. A few cases of dysentery were soon isolated, so that no units had to suffer through that epidemic.

The days of rest afforded opportunity for reflection on the recent past and on fallen comrades. The performance of the division was recognized through the presentation of awards. In addition to the Knight's Cross recipient already mention, there were a number of recipients of the German Cross in Gold since the start of the New Year: *Oberstleutnant* Beuermann (commander of *Panzergrenadier-Regiment 394*); *Hauptmann* Brandt (I./Panzergrenadier-Regiment 3); *Hauptmann* König (*II./Panzer-Regiment 6*); *Hauptmann* Lempp (*2./Panzer-Artillerie-Regiment 75*); *Hauptmann* Zeise, *Hauptmann* Golze, and *Unteroffizier* Otte (all from *Panzer-Aufklärungs-Abteilung 3*); *Oberleutnant* Geis (*10./Panzergrenadier-Regiment 3*); *Oberleutnant* Veltheim, *Oberfeldwebel* Jäckle, and *Feldwebel* Voigt (all *Panzer-Regiment 6*).

There were also some changes in duty positions. The former adjutant for officer affairs, *Major Graf* Pilati, was transferred out of the division on 20 April. *Major* Alvensleben took his place. *Oberst* Wellmann was transferred to the offices of the Inspector General of the Armored Force, where he assumed responsibility for the mechanized infantry directorate. *Oberstleutnant* Haberland assumed command of *Panzergrenadier-Regiment 3*.

The operations were planned for the *3. Panzer-Division*. On 6 May, the commander in chief of the field-army group, *Generaloberst* Schörner landed next to the quarters of the division logistics officer and announced this intention. Since the landing did not go well, and the Fieseler *Storch* sank halfway in mud, the mood of the commander in chief was not exactly the best. When Schörner discovered a prepared "coffee and cake" arrangement at the location of the division logistics officer, *Major i.G.* Bülow, he confiscated the cake on the spot. From that point forward, the officer of the headquarters called Schörner the "cake thief." Since it could be proven that the ingredients for the cake were

purchased on the private market, Schörner later paid for the costs.

While he was present, Schörner intimated that "something could happen" soon.

General der Artillerie de Angelis's *6. Armee* intended to eliminate the Soviet bridgehead over the Dnjestr at Butor-Tighina that had been established by the Soviet 8th Guards Army of Colonel General Tschuikow, the defender of Stalingrad. The field army stripped its front of all reserves at the beginning of May and formed two corps groups under *General der Panzertruppen* Knobelsdorff, with the *13.* and *14. Panzer-Divisionen* and the *294.* and *320. Infanterie-Divisionen*, and *General der Infanterie* Buschenhagen, with the *3. Panzer-Division*, the *17. Infanterie-Division*, the *2. Gebirgs-Division*, and the *2. Fallschirmjäger-Division*. The reserves for these two forces were formed by the *97. Infanterie-Division*.

The operations order arrived at noon on 7 May. The formations of the division prepared for the road march the same day. As a deception measure, the marching was only to be conducted at night. The commanders were summoned to Kischinew on 8 May for a conference. The attack plan was announced, while the formation assembled in the woods around Vadului Voda. The 2nd Medical Company had already established a field hospital in Kischinew, while the 1st Medical Company established a forward clearing station at Malaesti.

The division moved into the Nazareni Woods on the evening of 9 May. The division formed four battle groups with its organic formations and attached forces: *Major* Deichen commanded the *II./Panzer-Regiment 6*, *Panzer-Aufklärungs-Abteilung 3*, and *Sturmgeschütz-Brigade 911*; *Oberstleutnant* Lühl commanded his own *Panzergrenadier-Regiment 110 (11. Panzer-Division)*; *Oberst* Wellmann continued to command *Panzergrenadier-Regiment 3*, as he had not yet relinquished command of the regiment; and *Major* Hartmann's *Gebirgsjäger-Regiment 13 (4. Gebirgs-Division)*. The divisional engineers of *Hauptmann* Sedlaczek were designated as the reserve.

Major Deichen's battle group, with a battery of the divisional artillery in direct support, had the mission of advancing deep into the bridge-head under cover of darkness after overrunning the enemy positions at Balabauesti. It was then to occupy the so-called "Helmet Hill," a domi-nant piece of terrain, from the east.

This was to be the first major night engage-ment of the division. It marked the development of a style of fighting that had been forced upon it by the constantly increasing firepower of the enemy and especially by the strength of the anti-tank-gun belts that he employed. It was necessary to carefully plan and prepare for the attack and the following thrust into the depths of the enemy.

The battle group moved into its tactical assembly area in a patch of woods about three kilometers southwest of Balabauesti during the night of 8–9 May. Artillery fires provided cover for the sounds of the movement. The assembly area was not far from the enemy positions so as to preserve some element of surprise with the short approach. During the last conference, the timelines and the flow of the individual phases were discussed one more time. The importance of the operations for the overall success of the attack operations against the Butor Bridgehead was stressed.

A powerful artillery preparation by all of the participating German batteries shredded the quiet of the night at 0200 hours on 10 May. The attack started across the entire front. The *2. Fallschirmjäger-Division* succeeded in breaking through the enemy lines at Balabauesti, which were echeloned three deep, in a spirited attack. The armored battle group then advanced through the gap that had been formed to the south in the direction of the Dnjestr. The night was relatively dark, but it was light enough that visual contact could be maintained between the fighting vehi-cles. The tanks, which advanced in a wedge, formed the core of the battle group, while the assault guns and the light *SPW's* assumed responsibility for guarding the flanks. Artillery observers, a medical section, and some supply vehicles were incorporated into the middle of the wedge. With a muffled roar, the armored vehicles moved slowly through the night. Off to the left, the villages of Corjeva and Dubossary could be made out in the shadows.

The nighttime fighting raged across the entire front. It proved possible to take the initial enemy positions on the first try. The success garnered that first hour fired up the forces, but the resist-ance soon increased in front of the battle groups and progress was slow and measured in terms of a walking pace.

Apparently, however, the Soviets did not realize that a breakthrough had occurred along a narrow sector that could lead to an advance to the rear of their bridgehead by an armored force. In order not to prematurely alert the enemy to what was happening, the men were only allowed to fire in case of serious resist-ance. There were eighteen kilometers to be cov-ered before the objective was reached, and the road seemed to stretch on forever in that direc-tion. Short halts to be oriented were constantly needed. First light soon made its appearance to the east, without the main part of "Helmet Hill" having been reached. Far to the rear, the fight-ing was raging with intensity on both sides. The rolling meadow- and farmlands offered only isolated small groups of trees or patches of woods, but it also provided the opportunity by means of the depressions and reverse slopes to temporarily hide from the enemy's view. Once the sun came up, it was no longer possible to hide the location of the battle group.

Further ahead, the enemy's forces had been alerted, and a number of well-emplaced and excellently camouflaged antitank gun positions had been established in the high-ground posi-tions in the depths of the rear area.

Between Delacheu, a narrow village along the riverbank and a small patch of woods in front of the northern tip of "Helmet Hill," the tanks and assault guns encountered serious resistance. It was only with difficulty that the enemy's pock-ets of resistance were eliminated and the forces advanced to the plains north of the objective. At that point, the ridgeline was about 1,500 meters in front of the battle group. The division constantly asked when it was thought the high ground would be taken.

While the battle group turned to the south in an effort to take the flatter eastern slope, which was more suitable for the attack, enemy fighter-bombers attacked, dropping light bombs and strafing. They caused some casualties. The attack churned its way forward with difficulty. On the east banks of the Dnjestr, enemy guns were openly moved up to engage the German vehicles over open sights.

The Soviets fought for every dugout and constantly inflicted casualties with their well-emplaced antitank guns and antitank rifles. The battalion surgeon, Dr. Bittner, who was responsible for the initial treatment of the wounded, was in his medic *SPW* when it received a direct hit. He was mortally wounded.

The battle group was wedged between the Dnjestr and the high ground and was unable to advance another step in the defensive fires of the enemy. The attack of the other battle group of the division from the west was only gaining ground slowly and was not bringing the necessary relief. In order to get out of the unpromising situation and still complete the mission, all of the forces had to be concentrated. *Oberleutnant* Veltheim's tanks and the assault guns and light *SPW's* of *Oberleutnant* Kleffel were pulled back, reorganized and then took off in a dash towards the high-ground positions. The lead elements were able to advance as far as the plateau, which stretched out for more than a kilometer. But then the brave men were received by a murderous defensive fire. Although the enemy had also suffered considerable losses, the battle group was unable to take the high ground.

The armored vehicles pulled back in such a manner that they were able to take up positions in the dead zone halfway down the slope. From there, they were always able to force the enemy to take cover with fire from their machine guns. A final attempt was then made. The tanks and the other armored vehicles were gradually moved to the steeper north slope in an effort to

use the slope to their advantage in approaching the crest. Finally—it was around 1000 hours—the enemy softened. Along the western edges of the crest, the tanks and riflemen of *Oberst* Wellmann and *Oberstleutnant* Lühl finally appeared, while the artillery covered "Helmet Hill" one more time with fire. Together with the other battle groups, the hill was finally taken, thus eliminating the bulwark of the enemy's defenses in the bridgehead. During the last phase of that fighting, *Oberleutnant* von Veltheim was once again badly wounded. Of the twenty-four tanks that had started the fight, only six were still operational. The spoils of war included numerous antitank guns and artillery pieces, some trucks and a number of prisoners.

The division's casualties during the heavy fighting were high. *Hauptmann* Fiehl, the circumspect and capable commander of the *II./Panzer-Regiment 6*, had two tanks knocked out from under him that day. *Leutnant* Stabenow was wounded and *Leutnant* Leuthardt of the *5./Panzer-Regiment 6*, was killed shortly before his promotion could be announced.

Starting at 1700 hours, the division was directed to the south by the *LII. Armee-Korps*, so that it could advance to the right of the Saxon *14. Panzer-Division* in the direction of Scherpeni. It was intended to finally eliminate the Russian bridgehead at that place. The orders were issued during the night and the battle groups reorganized. The command post moved into the "Bear Defile" south of "Box Woods."

The command of the 3rd Ukrainian front recognized the dangerous situation its forces were facing and dictated decisive countermeasures. Stalin personally signed orders on the evening of 10 May that said:

> Enemy formations—the 14th, 13th, and 3rd Tank Divisions—are in the Dnjestr bridgehead. They can cut off the logistics lines of communication of the 3rd Ukrainian front at any time. The objective of the 3rd Ukrainian Front is to safeguard the logistics. I therefore order the 135th Tank

Brigade of the XXIII Tank Corps, in conjunction with the infantry, to eliminate the bridgehead and establish a straight-line front. The 2nd Ukrainian Front in the north and the 3rd Ukrainian Front in the south will attack with the objective of crossing the Dnjestr and taking the city of Kischinew. I wish the formations good success.

/signed/ Stalin

On 11 May, the *3. Panzer-Division* was attached to the *14. Panzer-Division* of *Generalmajor* Unrein. It was directed that the open left flank be closed. The division's formations initially remained in the positions they had taken on "Helmet Hill" to firm up the friendly front, which ran all along the bend in the Dnjestr. It was only *Panzergrenadier-Regiment 110*, still attached to the *3. Panzer-Division*, that supported the attack of the *14. Panzer-Division* on Voinowo, which was unsuccessful. It was directed for the advance to be continued the following day.

On 12 May, the Armed Forced Daily report announced: "In the destruction of the enemy bridgehead reported yesterday, the forces reporting to *General der Infanterie* Buschenhagen destroyed seven enemy rifle divisions. The Bolsheviks lost 2,600 prisoners, more than 600 guns and mortars, 334 machine guns and large amounts of weapons and war materiel."

On 12 May, the *3. Panzer-Division* was still unable to advance. It had only seven operational tanks, which were given to *Leutnant* Aschermann to command. He was the last available officer of the battalion after *Oberleutnant* Raupp was wounded the previous day. The fighting vehicles were attached to the armored reconnaissance battalion , which conducted a night attack to reach the banks of the Dnjestr. But the Soviets proved stronger; only five tanks returned. *Oberleutnant* Kleffel was wounded.

The next day saw summery, hot weather. *Stukas* from the *VIII. Flieger-Korps* attacked the enemy positions. But as soon as the soldiers moved out of their trenches, they received such strong defensive fire that the division was unable to take a single meter of ground. That led to tension between the corps and *Oberst* Lang. Contrary to expectations, the night of 13–14 May passed quietly. To the west, at 0130 hours, however, a powerful barrage was placed on Koschnitza on the bend in the Dnjestr. That signaled the start of the counteroffensive ordered by Stalin.

Soviet tanks penetrated the positions at Koschnitza and reached the banks of the river across from the *3. Panzer-Division*. They fired madly with their main guns into the surrounding terrain and across the river. It was an impressive display of firepower, especially since no one really knew what was going on. The clearing station at Malaesti, which was endangered, was evacuated. Fortunately, that was accomplished without taking any casualties with the exception of *Assistenzarzt* Dr. Pirwitz, who was slightly wounded.

Although the Soviets did not cross the river, they positioned themselves in such a manner that they could not be identified by our observers. In contrast, the enemy artillery had registered its guns on the German side of the river and stopped all movement. In addition, fighter-bombers were constantly in the air, monitoring the entire sector. There was no protection from above for the German forces.

The division headquarters moved out of the bend in the Dnjestr to the area around Budesti; only the command staff remained up front in "Bear Defile." The situation was tense, since the Soviet superiority in numbers grew larger day-by-day. By 15 May, the division had suffered some 700 losses since it had started operations in the sector.

The division's battle groups remained in the position they had originally taken and did not participate in any further operations against the Butor bridgehead.

Oberstleutnant i.G. Voss, the highly capable Division Operations Officer, was transferred on 15 May. He was replaced by *Major i.G.* Schwerdtfeger.

The weather had turned cool and rainy. Despite that, the Russian bomber and close-support aircraft bombed and strafed the terrain between the German lines. Rumors started to filter in slowly that the division was going to be pulled out of the bridgehead. As early as 18 May, *Panzerjäger-Abteilung 543* was relieved. The *II./Panzer-Regiment 6*, which had suffered enormously, was pulled back for a few days and refitted with new crews and tanks.

The fighting was still not over, however. It raged back and forth to the right and the left of the division. *Panzergrenadier-Regiment 103* and *Panzergrenadier-Regiment 110* were released from attachment to the division. Elements from the *320. Infanterie-Division* assumed their sectors. *Oberstleutnant* Haberland, the commander of *Panzergrenadier-Regiment 3*, assumed command of all of the forces of the division in the bridgehead. After *Panzergrenadier-Regiment 3* and the *I./Panzergrenadier-Regiment 394*—it had a trench strength of 100 men at the time—were pulled out by 22 May, only the 2nd Battalion of the latter regiment and *Panzer-Aufklärungs-Abteilung 3* remained in the bridgehead.

On 23 May, the *LII. Armee-Korps* ordered a new attack to clear out the remaining portions of the Dnjestr bridgehead still held by the Soviets once and for all. The *3. Panzer-Division* was given the locality of Scherpeni as its objective. Once again, the shells of the divisional artillery hammered the Russian positions before *Hauptmann* Müller-Röhlich's *II./Panzergrenadier-Regiment 394*, *Major* Deichen's *Panzer-Aufklärungs-Abteilung 3*, and the combat section of *Hauptmann* Fiehl's *II./Panzer-Regiment 6* moved out to attack.

The attack succeeded on the first attempt, and the village was quickly occupied. The men had barely reached the outskirts on the far side of the village, when the Soviets replied with an immediate counterattack, which the German forces were in no position to contain. *Leutnant* Kossel of the armored battalion was killed and *Hauptmann* Müller-Röhlich was badly wounded. In addition to him, all of the company commanders

and acting commanders of the battalion became casualties as well. The forces yielded to the superiority of the Russians and gave up Scherpeni. The badly battered battalions and sections of the battle groups were passed through the lines of the *294. Infanterie-Division*, which was pulling into the sector of the *3. Panzer-Division*.

By then, orders had arrived directing the division to be pulled out of the front on 24 May in order to become the reserve of the *6. Armee*. The advance parties had already departed during the evening of the previous day to the area southwest of Kischinew. The division headquarters moved into the city, while the divisional forces took up quarters in the small villages of the surrounding area over the next few days. *Panzergrenadier-Regiment 394* and *Panzer-Regiment 6* took up quarters in Durlesti.

A training period lasting several weeks for the division was announced. The acting division commander, *Oberst* Lang, was reassigned on 25 May. His successor was *Generalleutnant Dipl.-Ing.* Phillips, who had started the war as the commander of *Panzer-Regiment 11* and had most recently been a directorate head within the Army Procurement Office. That meant that a tanker was once again at the helm of the division. The new commander gave an indication of his personality when he closed his first commander's conference with the words: "The pessimist suffers time, the optimist experiences it."

The various formations of the division prepared appropriate training plans for the upcoming training. The training had barely commenced, when orders were received to move again. On 5 June, the Red Air Force attacked the city of Kischinew. Since that was seen as a sign of an expected offensive, all of the forces had to evacuate the city. The division received a new quartering area around Zahaicana. The first battalions started departing their quartering areas at 1900 hours and reached the new staging area under a bright moon. There were already elements of the *282. Infanterie-Division* there, meaning that questions about quarters were initially met with resistance. It took hours for the vehicles to be positioned and the soldiers could get some sleep.

The division headquarters established itself in Zahaicana, with *Panzer-Artillerie-Regiment 75* in Futuro, *Panzergrenadier-Regiment 3* in Boscana, *Panzer-Aufklärungs-Abteilung 3* in Ciopleni (in Cut. Ciorobata after 10 July), and *Panzer-Pionier-Bataillon 39* in Fauresti. The armored regiment and *Panzergrenadier-Regiment 394* remained in Durlesti for the time being, only moving to Ciopleni (East) on 21 June. The same was true of *Heeres-Flak-Abteilung 314*, which pulled into Zahaicana on 12 June.

The training program was restarted by the division after it moved into its new assembly area. Field training and gunnery were the priorities. In addition, poison gas courses were conducted as well as junior noncommissioned officer courses. Map exercises and nighttime exercises alternated with sports competitions. The cabaret of *Panzer-Regiment 6, "Die Panzersprenggranate,"* even enjoyed a rebirth. It goes without saying that work to construct field fortifications was not neglected. A tank ditch, fifteen kilometers northeast of Zahaicana, was shoveled out by the men of the *3. Panzer-Division*. At the same time, the vehicles received long-neglected maintenance and repair, with the result that the formations started to be come fully motorized again. In the summer of 1944, temperatures in that sector reached up to 40 degrees [104 Fahrenheit] in the shade.

A few personnel changes occurred during the "quiet" time. *Oberst* Thunert, the former chief of staff of the *LVIII. Panzer-Korps* assumed command of *Panzergrenadier-Regiment 394*. The regiment, which celebrated its fourth anniversary in a worthy manner in Cojusna on 1 August, had suffered 1,500 dead up to that point. The 1st Battalion received a new commander in the form of *Hauptmann* Möller. *Oberstleutnant* Lühl, who had been acting commander of the regiment over the previous few weeks, was designated commander of *Panzer-Regiment 6*, relieving *Oberstleutnant* Goecke. *Oberstleutnant*

Freiherr Rüdt von Collenberg became the new commander of the divisional artillery. *Hauptmann* Seifert assumed command of the *II./Panzergrenadier-Regiment 3*.

The officer roster for *Panzer-Regiment 6* during the period had the following duty positions filled:

Regimental Headquarters
Commander—*Oberstleutnant* Lühl
Adjutant—*Oberleutnant Freiherr* Funck
Maintenance Officer—*Hauptmann* Stähr
Weapons Officer—*Leutnant* Lindenbeck
Headquarters Company Commander—
Oberleutnant Lippoldt

Headquarters, *II./Panzer-Regiment 6*
Commander—*Hauptmann* Voigts
Adjutant—*Oberleutnant* Rodde
Liaison Officers—*Leutnant* Diest-Koerber,
Leutnant Wrede, and *Leutnant* Theimer
Signals Officer—*Leutnant* Schoch
Battalion Surgeon—Dr. Schwedt
Paymaster—*Zahlmeister* Christiansen.

Company Officers, *II./Panzer-Regiment 6*
Headquarters Company: *Oberleutnant* Sorge,
Oberleutnant Knebel, and *Leutnant* Klinck
5th Company: *Oberleutnant* Aschermann,
Oberleutnant Brümmer, *Leutnant* Starck, and
Leutnant Bernuth
6th Company: *Oberleutnant* Seyfried,
Oberleutnant Raupp, and *Leutnant* Korff
7th Company: *Oberleutnant* Hossfeld and then
Oberleutnant Veltheim, *Leutnant* Rieger, and
Leutnant Rosen
8th Company: *Hauptmann* Zobel, *Oberleutnant*
Schirp, *Leutnant* Langendorff, and *Leutnant*
Luttitz
Maintenance Company: *Hauptmann* Fiehl and
Hauptmann Schramm

Hauptmann Sedlaczek, the commander of the divisional engineers, was badly wounded on 20 June. Replacing him was the leader of the division's bridging section, *Oberleutnant* Mertens.

The commander of *Panzer-Nachrichten-Abteilung 39* was also transferred, and he was replaced by *Hauptmann* Talkenberg. *Hauptmann* Schulze assumed command of the *I./Panzergrenadier-Regiment 3*. *Hauptmann* Jobst, the former commander, was dispatched to the *Führer* Headquarters in East Prussia for discussions with the Inspector General of the Armored Forces. The future of the *I./Panzergrenadier-Regiment 3* was the topic at hand there. Upon Jobst's return, he was assigned as the commandant of the division headquarters.

On 1 June, the *I./Panzergrenadier-Regiment 3* had been loaded on trains at Husi for reconstitution in the homeland. The rail movement took the grenadiers through Hungary and Austria to Fallingbostel in the Lüneburg heath. Six days later, after a trip that seemed like a long-forgotten fairy tale to the men, the soldiers arrived at their new garrison. Over the next two months, after all of the soldiers had also been granted home leave, the soldiers were trained on new *SPW's*.

The equipment situation for the remaining troop elements of the division was not exactly "rosy." The medical sections, which hardly had any vehicles left, had to help themselves for a long time, despite repeated requests through the field army and the field-army group. For example, when the field-army group dispatched five medical vehicles from Klausenburg on 24 June, only two of them reached the division. The other three got stranded somewhere in the Carpathians. *Oberstabsarzt* Dr. Stribny traveled to the *Führer* headquarters and the commander in chief of the Replacement Army in Berlin in an effort to get some relief. With the assistance of the Military District Physician in the General Government of Poland, whose vehicular inventory was being dispersed, thirty-four operational medical vehicles could finally be provided to the division in August.

The reconstitution period for the division took place at the exact moment as the efforts of *Gen-*

eraloberst Guderian, the Inspector General of the Armored Force began to be decisively felt, albeit too late. He had initiated a general restructuring of the armored force.

Panzer-Regiment 6, the most powerful combat force of the division, was equipped as follows in the summer of 1944:

* Headquarters Company: *Panzer IV's* and a *Flak* platoon with three self-propelled *Flak*, with each vehicle mounting a quad 2-centimeter gun.
* 5th Company: 17 *Sturmgeschütz III's* (with long 7.5-centimeter main guns).
* 6th, 7th, and 8th Companies: 17 *Panzer IV's* with long 7.5-centimeter main guns.

It should be noted that the 8th Company received seventeen *Sturmgeschütz IV's*[2] with the long 7.5-centimeter main gun (same as on the *Panther*) in November. *Oberleutnant* Hossfeld's *7./Panzer-Regiment 6* was sent on special assignment as a training company to the Romanian Army, where it instructed Romanian tankers on the *Panzer IV*. The company never returned to the division and met its end when the Red Army rolled over Romania like a tidal wave.

As part of the overall reorganization directed by the Inspector General of the Armored Forces, the equipment for the armored reconnaissance battalions was ordered changed. The remaining motorcycle infantry companies were reequipped with light *SPW's*, and a second armored reconnaissance company was added to the battalion, albeit equipped with light *SPW's*. That resulted in an extremely maneuverable and armor-protected motorized formation. As early as March and April, elements of the divisional reconnaissance battalion had been dispatched to the training areas at Wildflecken and Stahnsdorf to both reconstitute and reorganize.

In the first half of July, one of the companies equipped with the brand-new light *SPW's* arrived in Kischinew under the command of *Oberleutnant* Möller. On its way to the quartering area of the battalion, it was stopped by *Gen-*

---

2. These vehicles would be *Jagdpanzer IV/70's*, officially the *Panzer IV/70(A)* based on the *Panzer IV* chassis.

eraloberst Schörner, who landed next to it in a Fieseler *Storch*, who ordered it to operations along the Dnjestr. Unfortunately, the division was not informed. It was only after some effort on the part of the division headquarters that the company could be pulled out of the line of the infantry division it had been attached to and returned to *Panzer-Aufklärungs-Abteilung 3*.

During those weeks of training, a number of personnel finally received the high awards they had earned. At the end of August, the German Cross in Gold was awarded to the following officers and noncommissioned officers: *Oberstleutnant* Voss, division operations officer; *Oberleutnant* Westerman, *Oberfeldwebel* Borghard, and *Oberfeldwebel* Schönfeld, all from *Panzergrenadier-Regiment 3*; *Oberstleutnant* Lühl and *Oberleutnant* Leuthardt, both from *Panzer-Regiment 6*; *Unteroffizier* Hofner and *Unteroffizier* Hinz from *Panzer-Aufklärungs-Abteilung 3*; *Hauptmann* Buchmann, battery commander of the *3./Panzer-Artillerie-Regiment 75*; and *Oberleutnant* Kunze, commander of the *2./Panzer-Pionier-Bataillon 39*. Receiving the German Cross in Silver were *Feldwebel* Graupner, the maintenance NCO for *Panzergrenadier-Regiment 394* and *Oberfeldwebel* Landsberg, a maintenance section leader within the *II./Panzer-Regiment 6*.

On 22 July, movement orders were received. The *10. Panzergrenadier-Division* had been badly battered and was being pulled out of sector, and the 3. Panzer-Division was directed to take its quartering area. The command staff moved out during the evening of 23 July and established a new command post in Ghidighici. The march serials moved that night. By the morning, the division had reached all of its assigned bivouac areas. The command posts of the division forces were located as follows: *Panzergrenadier-Regiment 3* in Gratiesti; *Panzergrenadier-Regiment 394* in Cojusna; *Panzer-Artillerie-Regiment 75* in Sireti; *Panzer-Aufklärungs-Abteilung 3* in Truseni; and *Panzer-Pionier-Bataillon 39* in Ululbvaca. Only *Panzer-Regiment 6* remained in Durlesti. Two days later, a warning order was received that another movement of the division could be expected shortly. Initially, the date was set as either 3 or 5 August. But during the evening of 28 July, new orders were received: "The rail movement is taking place tomorrow!" It was directed that the division be rail loaded in Kischinew for transport to Poland. The forces received the appropriate instructions during the night.

The first units departed at 0600 hours on 29 July. *Major* Fleischer, the commander of *Heeres-Flak-Abteilung 314*, was at the rail station in Kischinew as the division movement officer. The Romanian railway officials took their own time, even though various German headquarters had informed them of the urgency of the rail movement. The first trains did not arrive until 1300 hours, but the necessary locomotives for the departure were not on hand. It was midnight before the command staff of the division left Kischinew along with the operations sections of *Panzer-Nachrichten-Abteilung 39*. Enemy aircraft disrupted the loading, but their bombs did not hit the tracks. The movement became a hardship for all of the formations. The trains were fully loaded and the quarters too confining, with the result that most of the soldiers slept on their vehicles. On top of all that, the summertime heat beat down from the heavens, sometimes reaching 50 degrees [122 Fahrenheit]. The movements were conducted at a snail's pace. For most of the time, the trains remained stationary on open stretches of track or on some waiting track. Every Romanian train, whether official or civilian, enjoyed priority.

The operations officer of the division, *Major i.G.* Schwerdtfeger, went ahead of the troops with his section in their staff cars so that he could get operations orders as soon as possible. When he arrived at the main headquarters of the field-army group in Cracow, he was informed that the division would be transported to East Prussia. At that point, Schwerdtfeger and his section went to the Army High Command in Rastenburg. But when the officer arrived there, he was informed that the division was to detrain in Cracow. Schwerdtfeger was able to fly back in a courier aircraft.

The division was still actually in the trains that were taking it across the Carpathians (Gyimes Pass) and into Hungary. All of a sudden, the movement was faster and with less interruption. Transylvania was rapidly crossed, before reaching a small section of Romania, where it reverted back to more "sitting than moving." The Hungarian border was crossed one more time. Klausenburg, Großwardein, Szolnok, and Budapest were the next waypoints on the journey, although the stations proper were transited quickly. The trains were then rolling through Slovakia and towards the Beskid Range by way of Sillein. The men cross the Jablunka pass and arrived in Cracow at 0600 hours on 7 August. The first formations to detrain were the reconnaissance battalion and the *II./Panzergrenadier-Regiment 394*; all of the remaining division formations were still in bound.

The *3. Panzer-Division* reported directly to *Heeresgruppe Nordukraine*. The formations were immediately sent to the area around Slomniki, north of Cracow, to screen. Up to then, there had only been three construction battalions positioned there. The engineers were attached to the division. That same afternoon, the division established its command post in Prandocin. The remaining combat elements of the division reached their designated staging areas over the course of the next two days. The division command staff moved forward through Laczyn and on to Lipnik. Effective 9 August, the division was allocated to the *4. Panzer-Armee* of *General der Panzertruppen* Balck and attached to *General der Panzertruppen* Breith's *III. Panzer-Korps*. As a welcome reinforcement, the division received two *Tiger* battalions in attachment, *schwere Panzer-Abteilungen 501* and *503*.

Ever since it launched its major offensive against *Heeresgruppe Mitte* on 22 June 1944, the Red Army had continued to advance to the west, occupying considerable portions of White Russia and Poland. South of Sandomir, the 1st Ukrainian Front of Field Marshal Koniev had crossed the Vistula along thirty kilometers of front at the end of July and formed the Baranow bridgehead. The right wing of the Russian field-army group was able to expand its militarily decisive bridgehead by 4 August to a depth of thirty kilometers and a width of fifty kilometers.

The Army High Command planned to reduce the bridgehead by means of armor forces. The corps order for the attack arrived at the division command post shortly after midnight on 11 August. According to the order: "The *III. Panzer-Korps* eliminates the enemy that has broken across the Vistula. The *19. Panzer-Division* (right) advances along the Vistula in the direction of Baranow and takes the crossing point. The *3. Panzer-Division* (left) covers the flank, advancing simultaneously into the deep flank of the enemy, and thus prevents further enemy attacks to the north. After reaching Chmielnik, both *Tiger* battalions are to turn southeast to support the *16. Panzer-Division*."

For those that had already arrived, the formations were sent marching the same hour. *Generalleutnant* Philipps moved forward with his battle staff at 0300 hours. The armored elements of the division were consolidated under the command of *Oberst* Bernuth, who had assumed command of *Panzer-Regiment 6* for the second time on 1 August. The movement proceeded in fits and spurts, with the *Tigers* getting stuck several times in the darkness and causing road blockages. The routes were very sandy, and the woods were very dark, with the result that orientation was very difficult. The armored group, which had been joined by the command staff of the division, did not reach the village of Potok until 0600 hours. The Russians were already in the neighboring village.

A short artillery preparation opened the attack of the division. The reconnaissance battalion, attached to the armored regiment, eliminated enemy combat outposts in the patches of woods west of Rakow and then advanced on the village with both of its light *SPW* companies and the tanks of the armor regiment. The attack transpired as if on a training exercise. But the initial success was then greeted by concentrated fires from enemy antitank guns, which had been emplaced east of the Czarna in excellently camouflaged positions. Two fighting vehicles from the *6./Panzer-Regiment 6* were immediately knocked out, and the *SPW* of *Leutnant* Kühn received a direct hit, killing all on board. A sharp fight for the bridge developed, but it was taken in the end after an aggressive attack by the *SPW's* and tanks. The resistance in the village flared up again, and heavy fighting ensued. With some difficulty, it was possible to advance to the far side of the village.

The division then ordered the *II./Panzergrenadier-Regiment 3* forward. The mechanized infantry crossed the river and pressed eastward. The companies then turned on Rakow from the rear. The enemy put up a desperate defense. Correspondingly, the German attack only made step-by-step progress. It was not until evening that Rakow was completely in German hands. By then, the Soviets had brought forward heavy artillery and Stalin organs, which constantly plowed up the terrain. There were a lot of casualties. Since there were no medical forces forward yet, the evacuation of the wounded also meant a race against death. A field-army medical company was placed at the disposal of the division; the division's own 1st Medical Company was unable to reach the battlefield until 12 August.

In the evening, the formations of the division remained in the positions they had taken. During the night, the *II./Panzer-Regiment 6* was withdrawn from Rakow and pushed further south. The *16. Panzer-Division* had made better progress and taken Czarna. The next day, 12 August, represented no significant change. Since the Soviets had no tanks in front of the German sector, it was only their numerical superiority in artillery that made life difficult for the German forces. Whenever a T-34 appeared to conduct some reconnaissance, it was soon eliminated by the division's fighting vehicles. In place of the enemy tanks, however, the enemy's antitank guns had become a dangerous opponent. The guns had been well emplaced behind stacks of grain and allowed the German tanks to roll past, only to engage them from the rear.

On the second day of fighting, the corps ordered the *3. Panzer-Division* to pivot south. The enemy had attacked the German forces from within the bridgehead and put the *16. Panzer-Division* in a precarious position at Szydlow. The division was directed to assist the *20. Panzergrenadier-Division* south of Szydlow as soon as possible. *Pionier-Bataillon 70* (a field-army asset) was attached to *Panzergrenadier-Regiment 3*. Together, they were directed to hold the positions around Rakow until elements of the *16. Panzer-Division* could arrive to relieve them. That same night, *Panzergrenadier-Regiment 394* was sent south, followed closely by the *II./ Panzer-Regiment 6*.

The Red Air Force dominated the air space. Several low-level attacks on 13 August forced the division command post to be moved into the woods at Osowka. Considerable losses were reported by the battalions. The 1st Medical Company, which had set up a main clearing station in Rudki, was no longer able to properly treat all the wounded.

The German attack did not succeed that day. The corps then planned to reduce the Soviet blocking position in front of the Vistula the next day. But that effort on 14 August did not meet with success, either.

In the evening, the division was surprised by an order directing it to new operations sixty kilometers to the south. The elements started moving that night at 02000 hours and proceeded via Chmejelnik and Busko-Zdvoj, where the main clearing station had been established, to the area around Bronina. The command staff quartered in Topola. *Oberst* Thunert's *Panzergrenadier-Regiment 394* bore the brunt of the fighting on 15 August. Both of his battalions advanced along the road to the east and made good progress, capturing good jumping-off positions for the next day.

At 0600 hours on 16 August, the division attacked again. The divisional artillery of *Oberst Freiherr Rüdt* von Collenberg fired one preparation after the other. The mechanized infantry exploited the powerful support and broke into the enemy positions. The *II./Panzer-Regiment 6* also arrived and started rolling against the Russians at 0900 hours. The enemy force was large and knew how to defend. A few of the fighting vehicles were knocked out, and the attack started to waver. At that point, the Soviets launched an immediate counterattack. Their heavy artillery tore up the lead elements, while close-air-support aircraft attacked the rearward columns at the same time. The *II./Panzergrenadier-Regiment 3* was hit on two sides and ran into the danger of being encircled. The battalion had to evacuate the terrain it had taken and pull back.

Both of the *Tiger* battalions arrived in the nick of time and interdicted the Russians. Also by surprise, a liaison officer from *Werfer-Regiment 81* (a field-army asset) reported to the division. *Oberstleutnant* Collenberg immediately employed these and his own divisional artillery against the oncoming Russians. The batteries fired a final protective fire to rival that of the first year of the war and saved the division that day. By evening, the front was once again cohesive, and *Major* Deichen's reconnaissance battalion established contact with the *1. Panzer-Division* at Mosmodzienice.

Since enemy outnumbered the friendly forces in both men and materiel, the *II./Panzer-grenadier-Regiment 394* transitioned to the defense on 17 August and was left in its positions. The *II./Panzergrenadier-Regiment 3* was pulled out of the line, however, in order to conduct an enveloping move on Olesnica to the left. Despite good artillery support, the attack progressed slowly. When the Soviets launched an immediate counterattack in the afternoon, the mechanized infantry bogged down again.

The next day was overshadowed by enemy initiative as well. The Red Air Force became the decisive factor on the battle for the Baranow bridgehead. A warning order was received at the division command post on the evening of 17 August, which indicated the division was to be pulled out of the line and moved. On the previous day, *Major i.G.* Bülow took the place of *Major i.G.* Schwerdtfeger, who had contracted hepatitis.

The elements employed up front were relieved during the night and moved back to a staging area between Topola and Suchowola. The columns marched to the west and reached Pinozow around midnight. From there, they moved along improved roads (asphalt) to the north. Since a lot of formations were on the move, whose paths crossed or approached one another, the movement cost a lot of time. At Kielce, which was transited at first light, the division turned east. Around 1000 hours, it bivouacked in the woods at Boksyce, to the west of Ostrowiec. The *XXXXVIII. Panzer-Korps* of *General der Panzertruppen* Gräser held this sector.

The elements of the *3. Panzer-Division* were able to remain in that area for several days and used the time to maintain and replace weapons and materiel. The *I./Panzergrenadier-Regiment 3*, returned back to the division from the homeland on 22 August.

On 22 August, the reconnaissance battalion was attached to the *24. Panzer-Division*, which was getting ready to seal off enemy penetrations by means of a counterattack east of the Vistula and northeast of Tarnow. The battalion crossed the Vistula at Tarnow, advanced to Lisia Góra and reported to the command of *Kampfgruppe Waldeck*. Working closely with the tanks of the battle group, the battalion was able to retake the positions in the Zarowka–Roza–Jazwiny area on 24 and 25 August. Once again, the two light *SPW* companies of *Hauptmann* Kleffel and *Hauptmann* Möller distinguished themselves.

The period of quiet did not last long. During the afternoon of 24 August, the division moved into the sector of the *88. Infanterie-Division* north of Opatow. The command staff moved to Kornacice, *Panzergrenadier-Regiment 3* to Szczucice, *Panzergrenadier-Regiment 394* to Drzenkowice, and *Panzer-Regiment 6* to Glinka-Opatow, where a forward clearing station was also established. The divisional artillery was in Zocheinek, the divisional engineers in Rzukow and *Heeres-Flak-Abteilung 314* in Boguslawice. The forces moved into the tactical assembly areas on 25 August, and a commander's conference was held at noon at the command post, where the attack order was issued. According to it, the *XXXXVII. Panzer-Korps* was to attack at Zarowka on 28 August with the *1.*, *3.*, and *23. Panzer-Divisionen*. In the sector of the *3. Panzer-Division*, *Panzergrenadier-Regiment 3* was to attack on the right and *Panzergrenadier-Regiment 394* on the left, which was also the division's main effort. The direction of attack was Iwanowka, where contact was to be established with the *III. Panzer-Korps*.

The forward assembly areas were occupied during the night. The division command moved to the forward command post in the eastern portion of Kochowek. A short while later, the batteries of the corps' artillery hammered away at the Russian positions along the northern edge of the Baranow bridgehead. The two mechanized infantry regiments attacked along a broad front. The *II./Panzer-Regiment 6* was to follow closely behind to be able to exploit the opportunity once the mechanized infantry penetrated the Russian defenses. The attack never did really unfold properly, however. The Soviet fire, especially that of the heavy artillery, was so powerful that the companies could barely deploy. Instead, they had to struggle for every meter of ground. As a result, the fighting vehicles were pushed forward sooner than had been planned.

By noon, *Oberstleutnant* Haberland's *Panzergrenadier-Regiment 3* had taken the village of Brotkow in hard fighting. It then slowly turned in the direction of Rudniki, to the southwest. *Oberst* Thunert's *Panzergrenadier-Regiment 394* was west and northwest of Kobylany at the same time, where his men were maintaining contact with the *1. Panzer-Division*. The operations were equally harsh and bloody for all of the participating formations. *Hauptmann* Gaebler, the commander of the *II./Panzer-Artillerie-Regiment 75*, contributed greatly to the attack with the fires of his batteries. *Stabsgefreiter* Nöske of the *3./Panzer-Aufklärungs-Abteilung 3* distinguished himself through his personal bravery at Zarowka and was later inducted into the Army Honor Roll. The armored regiment lost its commander:

Oberst von Bernuth, who had distinguished himself in every theater of war, died on the battlefield along with many of his officers and men. The armor regiment lost a great number of experienced tank commanders in the fighting for the Baranow bridgehead. It was only the 5th Company of *Leutnant* Starck that did not take as many casualties; its assault guns, with their low silhouettes, offered a more difficult target for the Russian antitank guns.

The forces set up all-round defenses for the night so as to be able to continue the attack in the morning. The remaining elements of the armor regiment moved to Opatow, where a forward clearing station had been established. *Oberst* Friedrich assumed command of the regiment. When it turned first light on the morning of 27 August, German shells started to pound the Russian positions again. The mechanized infantry, combat engineers, and scouts raised up out of their positions at 0600 hours and formed up to attack. The weather was very hot and made life difficult for the soldiers. The Russian resistance proved no less tough the next day. The attack was only able to chew its way forward slowly. The casualties were high. The 2nd Medical Company was pushed forward to establish a main clearing station at Lipowa. The casualties among the medical personnel rose daily as well. *Unterarzt* Dr. Rettig was killed and *Unterarzt* Kreuzer was wounded.

That evening, the division set up for the defense in the positions it had reached. The attack was taken up again at first light on 28 August. The enemy's resistance had become even stronger. At many locations, there was bitter close combat. Towards noon, the Soviets even launched a counterattack from the northwest, threatening Rudniki. By concentrating all available forces, the enemy's thrust could be turned back. As the lead element, *Panzergrenadier-Regiment 394* reached Iwaniska. At that point, it's attack stalled out. The Russians were placing barrage fires in front of the bridgehead that could not be broken through or outrun. *Generalleutnant* Philipps ordered the division on the defense. Towards midnight, the positions around Iwaniska had to be evacuated. The Soviets immediately pursued, but they met with no success. It was even possible to pull the *II./Panzergrenadier-Regiment 394* out of the line and move it to Marcinkowice, where the division command post was located. It was designated as the division's ready reserve.

The twenty-ninth of August passed without any serious incident. The command staff of the division moved back to Zochcinek. During the night it rained, with the result that the attack planned for 30 August was called off. Other orders arrived in its place calling for the *3. Panzer-Division*, together with the *1. Panzer-Division*, to attack west the next day. The main effort was to be with the sister division, with the result that what was left of the *II./Panzer-Regiment 6* was attached to it. *Panzergrenadier-Regiment 394* remained in its previous positions and screened the attack.

The division moved out on 31 August. Over the next few days, *Panzergrenadier-Regiment 3* was in the thick of the fighting. Its 1st Battalion suffered a lot of losses, including the commander, *Major* Schulze, and his adjutant, *Leutnant* Kallert. The battalion had only one *SPW* left that was operational. All of the line companies had become "leg" infantry. They fought tirelessly against a toughly defending enemy in their effort to reduce the enemy lines in front of the Vistula.

The *XXXXVII. Panzer-Korps* continued its attack. Once again, the *II./Panzer-Regiment 6* formed the sharp end of the stick for the *3. Panzer-Division*. Casualties among the personnel and losses among the equipment continued to climb, since the Soviets had emplaced large minefields that caused damage to many fighting vehicles. *Oberst* Friedrich, the armor regiment commander, was badly wounded on 2 September. The brave officer passed away three days later from his wounds at the main clearing station in Lipowa. Other officers of the regiment who were killed during this period: *Leutnant* Luttitz, *Leutnant* Lehmann, *Leutnant* Lippoldt,

and *Leutnant* Wilhelm. The following capable noncommissioned officers also died on the field of battle: *Oberfeldwebel* Sydow (German Cross in Gold) and *Feldwebel* Zierath. Among the wounded officers: *Hauptmann* Zobel, *Oberleutnant* Rodde, and *Oberleutnant* Raupp. On 5 September, the commander of the divisional engineers, *Major* Sedlaczek, was badly wounded.

For the first eight months of 1944, the division's reconnaissance battalion reported the following personnel losses: killed—ten noncommissioned officers and thirty-four enlisted personnel; wounded—thirty-seven noncommissioned officers and ninety-four enlisted personnel. Since the start of the war through the fighting for the Baranow bridgehead, the battalion had suffered a total of twenty-two officers killed.

The *3. Panzer-Division* paid for its operations along the Vistula with a deep cut to its veins. Nonetheless, the division's soldiers proved that they still knew how to fight and to die at the beginning of the fifth year of war. For the German divisions employed, the offensive against the Baranow bridgehead had brought an average ground gain of seventy to eighty kilometers. At that point, the Germans had reached the end of their strength. The lead tank elements got stuck twenty kilometers from the bridges over the Vistula at Baranow. Although infantry divisions were brought forward to take over the positions and establish a cohesive defensive line, it would not be possible to break through the Soviet position and eliminate the bridgehead. Fate would have it that five months later the last enemy offensive would start from there, cross the Oder and end in the Battle for Berlin.

On 7 September, the division received orders to turn over its positions and be pulled out of the line. The advance parties for the new assembly area departed that same day. The march serials of the division started moving out on 8 September. The route took the division's elements through Ostrowiec, Skarzysko, Kamienna, Sydlowiec, and on into an area about fifteen kilometers southwest of Radom. The division established its quarters in the Oronsco Palace. While the soldiers got their first rest in the new assembly area they heard the following supplement to the Armed Forces Daily Report on 9 September:

In the Vistula bridgehead west of Baranow, the forces reporting to the Supreme Command of *General der Panzertruppen* Balck and the corps commands of *General der Panzertruppen* Breith and *General der Panzertruppen* Gräser, as well as *General der Infanterie* Recknagel, have thwarted the efforts of massed Soviet forces to break through during the past month and have reduced the bridgehead after a series of successful counterattacks. The enemy has suffered heavy losses in men and materiel. From 3 August to 7 September, 650 tanks and assault guns and 942 artillery pieces of all calibers were destroyed or captured and 3,000 prisoners taken in.

The *3. Panzer-Division* remained for about a week in the area around Radom. The days devoted to recovery and maintenance—all under continuous nice weather—quickly came to an end. The new chief of staff of the German Army, *Generaloberst* Guderian, feared that the Soviets would launch a major offensive in central Poland. A large portion of the armored divisions were withdrawn from the front at his request and made available to *Heeresgruppe Mitte*. The *3. Panzer-Division* was part of that and loaded on trains at the Rozki rail station on 16 September. The long transport trains rolled in a huge arc to the south and the west through Kamienna, Tomaszow Maz., Litzmannstadt, Kutno, and Plock to Nasielsk, southwest of the Serock Fortress. The first unit left its train at 2100 hours on 17 September. Russian bombers were there and precisely dropped their bombs on the detaining operations. There were some casualties, especially among personnel of *Panzer-Nachrichten-Abteilung 39*.

The battalions moved on the good asphalt roads starting at midnight and reached the assembly areas during the morning of 18 September. The command staff of the division established itself at the edge of Nowe Miasto (Neustadt). The division logistics officer and his section moved to Zichenau. The division's replacement battalion remained behind in Nasielsk. The combat elements moved as far as the Mielau Training Area and set up bivouac there.

The division set up reconstituting its forces and reorganizing them. Replacements and weapons arrived. The *II./Panzer-Regiment 6* once more became a powerful combat formation. The 8th Company of the armor regiment received *Sturmgeschütze IV's* with the main gun also found on the *Panther*.[3] *Heeres-Flak-Abteilung 314* disbanded its 5th Battery and consolidated the quad gun platoon in to the 3rd Battery. The mechanized infantry battalions received *SPW's*.

A few of the command positions changed. On 12 September, *Oberstleutnant* Weymann assumed command of *Panzergrenadier-Regiment 3*. Shortly thereafter, *Oberst* Thunert left command of *Panzergrenadier-Regiment 394* to assume acting command of the *1. Panzer-Division*. *Oberst* Schacke was named to replace him. *Oberstleutnant* Rohrbeck was put in command of the armored regiment. *Hauptmann* Golze, the commander of the *1./Panzer-Aufklärungs-Abteilung 3*, replaced *Major* Deichen in command of the battalion. *Major* Medicus took command of *Panzerjäger-Abteilung 543*. The division logistics officer, *Major i.G.* Bülow, was transferred and replaced by *Major i.G.* Willich.

The divisional artillery commander, *Oberstleutnant* Freiherr Rüdt von Collenberg, received the German Cross in Gold, while *Stabsfeldwebel* Krioß of the divisional artillery received the German Cross in Silver. *Heereshauptwerkmeister* Bartsch of the *II./Panzergrenadier-Regiment 3* also received the same award.

On 1 October, the division received orders from *Generaloberst* Reinhardt's *Heeresgruppe Mitte* to immediately become the field army

---

3. *Jagdpanzer IV/70*, officially designated *Panzer IV/70(A)*.

group's reserve. Further, the division was to be employed against the Soviet bridgehead along the Narew at Serock, north of Warsaw. The combat elements were to occupy a staging area at Wiesniany as soon as possible. They departed that afternoon in a pouring rain. The trains elements remained in the previous assembly areas.

The night of 3–4 October slowly came to an end. At that point, the sound of hundreds of German artillery pieces could be heard barking. The soldiers in the trenches jumped up with a fright. They hadn't experienced anything like that in years. There was a howling and screeching headed over towards the enemy's side. The unmistakable sound of rockets from the *Nebelwerfer* could be heard above the rest as they churned up the ground. A short while later, the divisions moved out.

Once again, the *3. Panzer-Division* was the wing division. It was clear from the outset that the flanks would become longer and more exposed as the attack proceeded. The terrain consisted of hillocks that were covered in vegetation and deep woods. Two Tiger battalions were attached to the division, and they formed the spearhead. *Hauptmann* Voigts's *II./Panzer-Regiment 6* followed in the second wave. The Russians were so shaken up by the preparatory fires that he proved incapable of offering any serious resistance. The fighting vehicles moved right through the enemy's front lines and soon found themselves among his artillery before the enemy started to regain his composure. The resistance grew more stubborn by the hour. The mechanized infantry lost contact with the tanks, since they were attacked several times in the flanks.

The farther the tanks advanced, the tougher the Russian resistance became. The enemy riflemen had established themselves in well-constructed field fortifications that were terrifically camouflaged. By early afternoon, the *Tigers* stalled in front of the enemy's antitank-gun fires. The 5th, 6th, and 8th Companies of the armored regiment were then called forward. Two assault guns from the 5th Company were lost during the

approach through mines. But *Oberleutnant* Aschermann was soon there with his vehicles and extended the front the *Tigers* had created to the right. The assault guns maneuvered to find good firing positions from which to engage the Russian antitank guns. The assault guns of Feldwebel Beckenfelder and Inter were hit.

By then, the 6th Company of *Oberleutnant* Weh and the 8th Company of *Oberleutnant* Lope had also arrived. Both of the companies enveloped from the right, hit the Soviets in the flank and overran approximately twenty enemy antitank guns. The 8th Company lost three tanks and had to pull back. *Oberleutnant* Lope's tank was knocked out. He was captured but was able to escape two hours later and make his way back to German lines.

The two *Tiger* battalions then attempted the third run at the enemy positions. They wanted to exploit the path that had been created by the division's armored vehicles and cover the last few kilometers to the Narew. It had become late afternoon by then and time was pressing, if the Germans wanted to eject the enemy before the onset of darkness. The *Tigers* advanced in a death-defying manner into the enemy positions, but the Russian resistance only seemed to intensify. Artillery shells were also coming in from the far bank of the Narew and landing among the steel animals. The men of the armor regiment were amazed as to how much punishment a *Tiger* could take and then continue to move. But, in the end, the effort was futile. And it was only two kilometers to the Narew. It could not be done. The Russians did not waver, and they used their advantage in artillery.

Despite everything, the division tried one more time. *Panzergrenadier-Regiment 3* was sent forward during the night, the *II./Panzer-Regiment 6* regrouped and the *Tiger* battalions concentrated once more. The Tigers exploited the success garnered by the 8th Company during the afternoon and attacked at that location. They were closely followed by the mechanized infantry. The *5./Panzer-Regiment 6* provided flank protection against the broken-up and vegetated terrain to the left. The nighttime thrust appeared to do the trick. The Soviets started to flee from their trenches.

The *Tigers* had the dangerous depression behind them and rolled towards the high ground. Their silhouettes rose up against the light nighttime skies. Then there was a rattle, as three Russian "Stalin" tanks approached. They attacked from the flank. When they were about 150 meters from the *Tigers*, they opened fire. One German vehicle flew into the air. The *5./Panzer-Regiment 6* saw the danger and rolled forward. The lead assault gun of *Oberleutnant* Aschermann took up the fight. The gunner, *Obergefreiter* Wörl, essentially aimed and fired at the same time. The first round hit; the second one decisively. A "Stalin" exploded. By then, the *Tigers* had turned, knocking out a second "Stalin." The third one escaped in the darkness.

The battlefield was illuminated by the burning fighting vehicles of both sides and offered good targets for the enemy's artillery. As a result, the attack had to be called off. *Panzergrenadier-Regiment 3* dug in 300 meters from the river road along the Narew. The front lines of the division jutted like a wedge into the Russian positions. The *II./Panzer-Regiment 6*, cut by losses down to the size of a company, provided security along the open flank. When it dawned on 5 October, Russian tanks could be identified. The *Panzer IV's* and assault guns immediately took up the fight, with *Leutnant* Korff's platoon being particularly successful. The enemy tanks were not even able to attack.

When the situation turned critical a second time, the sound of tank engines could be heard coming from the rear. Seventeen *Panzer IV's* approached. *Oberleutnant* Hossfeld jumped down from the first tank and reported to *Oberleutnant* Aschermann. Aschermann looked like he had lost his senses, when the long-absent commander of the *7./Panzer-Regiment 6* appeared in front of him. What was the story? The 7th Company had long since been written off, after it had been detailed to the Romanian Army to serve as an instruction and training company

and the Soviets had taken Romania. All of the tanks were lost, but the officers and men were able to make their way back with relatively few casualties. They got to Germany and assembled at Neuruppin. They were issued tanks there and then returned to the division, which suddenly had a 7th Company again.

The 7th Company immediately relieved the other companies, which moved back across the high ground, with smoke grenades concealing their move. The companies had expended all of their ammunition and reached the trains with their last liters of fuel. After they had rearmed and refueled, and the men had had a chance to sleep a bit, they were sent forward again. The division remained in the positions it had taken. The main effort of the German attack had taken place at the southern end of the bridgehead. It was also able to significantly reduce the bridgehead, if not totally eliminate it.

The division made plans to attack that night in an effort to finally clear the terrain in front of it of the enemy. The attack was to take place in the early morning hours, while it was still dark, in an effort to prevent the enemy from offering a disciplined defense. *Panzergrenadier-Regiment 3*, supported by the *7./Panzer-Regiment 6*, attacked frontally, while *Panzergrenadier-Regiment 395*, supported by the *5./Panzer-Regiment 6*, screened to the right and, if possible, advanced on the cemetery at Serock. But the Soviets did not allow themselves to be shaken. As soon as the German attack started, they employed all available weapons and placed a murderous fire on the advancing forces. *Panzergrenadier-Regiment 3* was turned back after 100 meters. There was no progress on the wing, either, when the Soviets opened fire with their antitank guns and knocked out the first few *Panzer IV's*. The division pulled back to its jumping-off positions early in the morning.

The situation did not change the next day, and it also did not allow for any major reorganizations. The mechanized infantry, engineers and reconnaissance soldiers could barely lift their heads. The tanks, which had pulled up right behind the forward positions, could only be considered "moral support." During that round of fighting, *Unteroffizier* Pollack, a squad leader in the 3rd Company of the reconnaissance battalion, distinguished himself through his personal bravery.

On 7 October, a neighboring division reported an enemy penetration. The division immediately formed a battle group consisting of the reconnaissance battalion and the 5th and 7th Companies of the armor regiment to help out. But by the time the companies arrived, the situation had stabilized. All of the 2nd Battalion of the armor regiment was pulled out of the front and moved to the rear so as to be able to commit it as a "fire brigade" in threatened sectors.

The fighting for the bridgehead on the Narew near Serock slowly ebbed. The division was pulled out of the lines on 10 and 11 October in order to be moved further north. Forced to move far to the west, the columns moved through Neustadt, Plonsk, Zichenau, and Golymin en route to Karniewo. The forces spent the night there; it was already fairly cold. The march continued the next day and proceeded through Macheim (Makow) to Retka Nowe. The command staff established itself in earthen bunkers, since the villages had been heavily damaged and the front was by no means quiet.

The units were committed to the fighting as soon as they arrived, since the Soviet divisions were already attacking. The Soviets owed a great deal of thanks for their previously achieved successes to the tireless efforts of the Red Air Force. Fighter-bombers were constantly above the columns. Since the regiments and battalions could not properly deploy, many a success was denied to the German forces. The battered formations had great difficulty in maintaining a cohesive front and not allowing contact with neighboring elements to be lost. It was possible to contain smaller penetrations and, generally speaking, clear them up during the night.

The *II./Panzer-Regiment 6* had reorganized into two combat sections under the commands of *Oberleutnant*s Hossfeld and Lope. Both were

constantly on the go as "fire brigades" in an effort to stabilize critical situations. For the men of the armor battalion, the next few days were bloody. There were a number of losses, with the ones suffered by the "old hands" weighing the heaviest, since the new replacements had not even been completely integrated into the units. Those killed that week were *Oberleutnant* Lope, *Feldwebel* Hennings (6th Company) *Unteroffizier* Wollboldt (7th Company), and *Stabsgefreiter* Krullack (who had fought in Spain as part of the *Legion Condor*). The losses were such that the battalion eventually had to be removed completely from the front lines and placed in ready reserve in a small patch of woods in the vicinity of the division command post.

The division was ordered out of the fight on 18 October and road marched the next day to a new mission. This time, the division's columns steered towards Nasielsk again. They moved along familiar roads and through familiar villages, until they reached the Mogowo in the vicinity of Nasielsk on 20 October. The Soviets had attacked east of the locality and expanded their bridgehead to the same size it had previously been weeks ago. It was not intended to employ the division as a whole. Instead, it reported directly to the *2. Armee* of *Generaloberst* Weiß, whose adjutant was the former officer personnel officer for the division, *Oberst* Oppen.

The *II./Panzer-Regiment 6*, *Panzer-Aufklärungs-Abteilung 3*, and *Panzerjäger-Abteilung 543* formed three battle groups that were committed by the field army at especially threatened sectors when the situation demanded it. As a result, *Major* Medicus's antitank battalion had to move to the area around Modlin, when an enemy offensive started there. The self-propelled antitank guns arrived in the nick of time to be effectively employed against the Russian attacks. Later on, tank sections under *Oberleutnant* Aschermann and *Leutnant* Junckermann were also sent there, but they were no longer needed when they arrived.

At the same time, another tank section under *Oberleutnant* Hossfeld was alerted. The enemy had launched an attack along the northern portion of the bridgehead. The *Panzer IV's* were able to turn back the enemy forces and stabilize the situation. *Leutnant* Rosen, a Swede who had volunteered for service in the German Army, was the "hero of the day." He entered the Russian tactical assembly area unnoticed at night and knocked out seven T-34's in the space of a few minutes from a distance of only twenty meters.

November had arrived. The division remained the ready reserve of the *2. Armee* in the area around Nasielsk. The division headquarters was located in Glodowo. The forces found time to reorganize and get new equipment. In Zichenau, *Panzergrenadier-Regiment 3* received ninety-six new *SPW's*. The *II./Panzer-Regiment 6* formed a combat section and a supply company. All of the battalion trains were consolidated into the latter company under *Hauptmann* Poerch. The two medical companies were in Zichenau and Golozysna. *Oberstabsarzt* Dr. Stribny was able to register a personal success in getting a "soldiers' home" established in Zichenau during this time period. The so-called "Bear Home" was visited by officers and enlisted personnel of the division on a rotating schedule.

Awards were also presented to deserving soldiers. In the last quarter of 1944, the German Cross in Gold was presented to *Generalleutnant* Philipps; *Hauptmann* Seifert (commander of the *II./Panzergrenadier-Regiment 3*); *Leutnant* von dem Osten, *Leutnant* Schröder, *Oberfeldwebel* Kerstan, *Unteroffizier* Lüchtefeld, and *Oberge-*

freiter Schenk (*Panzer-Aufklärungs-Abteilung 3*); *Oberleutnant* Rosemeyer, *Oberleutnant* Minzlaff, and *Feldwebel* Hoppe (*Panzergrenadier-Regiment 394*); *Oberleutnant* Zedlitz and *Oberfeldwebel* Schmuths (*Panzer-Pionier-Bataillon 39*); *Hauptmann* Milstrey (commander of the *1./Heeres-Flak-Abteilung 314*); and *Oberwachtmeister* Künkel (*5./Panzer-Artillerie-Regiment 75*). Receiving the German Cross in Silver was *Heereswerkmeister* Laukötter of *Panzer-Regiment 6*.

As the month of November came to a close, the division received new marching orders. *Generalleutnant* Philipps and his new operations officer, *Major i.G. Freiherr* Posten, worked out the movement order. *Major i.G.* Schwerdtfeger had been relieved of his post as operations officer, since he was no longer allowed to perform General Staff duties because of his so-called "international ties" (his mother was English). *Major* Gerhardt assumed command of the divisional artillery after *Oberst Rüdt* von Collenberg was transferred. The division was rail loaded under Russian long-range artillery fire in Nasielsk on 29 November. The trains left Poland the next day and rolled through Soldau and Neidenburg on their way to Willenberg. The division, along with the *20. Panzer-Division* and the *Führer-Grenadier-Brigade*,[4] formed the ready reserve of *Heeresgruppe Mitte*. The soldiers of the division were starting to believe they would spend Christmas in beautiful East Prussia, when they received movement orders on 10 December causing them to take leave of Germany.

---

4. One of several formations formed from the original *Panzergrenadier-Division "Großdeutschland"* and the guard elements that were posted at the Rastenburg *Führer* headquarters. Although designated a brigade, it had at least as much firepower as the *3. Panzer-Division* at the time, with an armored regiment, a mechanized infantry regiment, an assault-gun "brigade" (a battalion), a *Flak* detachment, and an armored reconnaissance company.

In Romania in March 1944: *Leutnant* Schneck and *Leutnant* Henze, both of the *I./Panzergrenadier-Regiment 3*, with locals.

The Romanian frontier as seen from a transport train.

Rail transport of armored elements from Romania to Poland in August 1944. Based on the vehicles, they are probably from *Panzer-Aufklärungs-Abteilung 3*.

Along the Narew in Poland in
August 1944, track repair is
being conducted.

Detraining in Poland.

Interrogating a prisoner in the Narew bridgehead.

Generalleutnant Dipl.-Ing. Phillips, the division
commander from 25 May 1944 to 19 January 1945.

CHAPTER 10

From the Danube to the Raab: The Battle for Hungary

In August 1944, the Red Army conquered all of Romania and pressed forward through Kronstadt, Hermannsburg, and Neumarkt with the 2nd Ukrainian Front of Marshal Malinkowski. Hungary was the enemy's next objective. The fighting continued there through the end of September, when the *1. Panzer-Armee* was pushed back through the Dukla Pass. On his own initiative, *Generaloberst* Guderian directed the front be pulled back to behind the Theiß. That turned Hungary into a war zone.

The 2nd Ukrainian Front started the second phase of its offensive on 6 October to the rear of *Generaloberst* Frießner's *Heeresgruppe Süd*. The German formations braced themselves against the Russians and were able to prevent the collapse of the field-army group, even though they no longer had the strength to operate offensively anywhere. The enemy then turned his main effort against the Hungarian 3rd Army, which was scattered at Kecskemet on 30 October. On 4 November, Soviet armored spearheads were already outside of Budapest. At that point, in harsh and bloody fighting, German and Hungarian formations temporarily prevented the Soviets from gaining any more ground.

The 3rd Ukrainian Front of Marshal Tolbuchin, which was then brought forward, advanced west of the Danube on 1 December. The enemy divisions were then interdicted by heroically fighting German forces in the so-called Margarethe Position between Budapest and Lake Balaton through 8 December.

The Soviet field armies had reached the Danube to both sides of Waitzen and turned from the north in the direction of Budapest. The forces reporting to *General der Panzertruppen* Breith's armored group—the *13. Panzer-Division, Panzer-Division "Feldherrnhalle"* (*Generalmajor* Pape) and the Hungarian 10th and 12th Infantry Divisions—conducted a tough fight, but they were unable to prevent the Soviets from taking the outlying suburbs of Budapest. Rain and snow delayed the movements of the German armor, in addition to the already short supplies of fuel.

Starting on 10 December, the *3. Panzer-Division* found itself on trains headed from East Prussia to Hungary. The advance parties of the division had been loaded at Willenberg that day; the division's elements followed at short intervals. The route took the soldiers through western Poland and Silesia, followed by Moravian Ostrau and Trentschen (Trencin) in Slovakia. During the night of 11–12 December, the lead elements crossed the Hungarian frontier. The detraining took place in a broad area on both sides of the Danube. Since the German railway officials had no control over the Hungarian railway administration, the individual elements of the division were detrained split up and at a wide assortment of rail stations. Despite that, it was possible to reorganize relatively quickly. The division's replacement battalion, which was the last formation to leave East Prussia, did not arrive in Hungary until the Christmas period, where it was quartered in the area around Papa-Tete.

On 16 December, the division received orders to assemble in the Mór area. Only weaker elements were to remain north of the Danube, since the situation there was completely uncertain and the appearance of the enemy could be expected at any time. The command staff of the division moved from Mocsa (south of Komárom) to Mór that afternoon. Shortly after it arrived in that ethnic German enclave, directives were received to move all of the division's elements there.

Over the next few days the division's regiments and battalions found some time to reorganize somewhat and prepare for their upcoming missions. A reconnaissance detachment under the command of *Oberst* Schacke, the commander of *Panzergrenadier-Regiment 394*, was sent to Budapest of 17 December to explore options for the planned attack. The attack order arrived at 0400 hours on 18 December. The operation was directed to commence on 20 December, but by the same afternoon the start time had been delayed by forty-eight hours.

The Soviets seized the initiative prior to that. They moved out at Kismaros, north of the Danube, on 18 December. They ripped open the German front at Ipolyság as the result of the failure of *SS-Sonder-Brigade "Dirlewanger."* An immediate counterattack launched by the *8. Panzer-Division* did not meet with success.

Based on the situation, the Army High Command ordered an immediate attack by the mechanized infantry regiments of the *3., 6.,* and *8. Panzer-Divisionen* under the command of *General der Panzertruppen* Kirchner's *LVII. Panzer-Korps*. The corps had the mission of reestablishing contact with the *8. Armee*. The armored regiments initially remained as immediate reserves in the area around Stuhlweißenburg.

The *3. Panzer-Division*, which positioned the *I./Panzergrenadier-Regiment 3* and the *II./Panzer-Artillerie-Regiment 75* near Stuhlweißenburg in addition to *Panzer-Regiment 6*, received orders for the mechanized infantry attack on the evening of 19 December. The operation was called Spätlese ("Late Vintage"). Command and control of the area around Stuhlweißenburg was assumed by *General der Panzertruppen* Breith's *III. Panzer-Korps*, to which the *1.* and *23. Panzer-Divisionen, Panzer-Regiment 11* of the *6. Panzer-Division*, and the armored group of the *3. Panzer-Division* were attached.

This meant that the division was split in two for the next few weeks. The main body of the division, which was directed to participate in the attack being conducted by the *LVII. Panzer-Korps*, had only a few armored vehicles, all located within *Panzer-Jäger-Abteilung 543* and *Panzer-Aufklärungs-Abteilung 3*. The same held true for the *6.* and *8. Panzer-Divisionen*, even though the attack was being conducted in terrain entirely suitable for armored vehicles. For its part, the armored group, which was attached to the *III. Panzer-Korps*, lacked grenadiers, as was soon found out.

The command staff of the division moved to the area north of Esztergom and the command post of the *LVII. Panzer-Korps* during the night of 19–20 December. The division logistics section moved to Köbbelkut and then Beny. The *3. Panzer-Division* was directed to assemble north of Vamosmikola and then attack Kistompa, together with the *6. Panzer-Division*. The attack was intended to close the gap existing with the *8. Armee*. The departure of the division proceeded slowly, since the fuel sections had not closed up. In the meantime, enemy tank forces had succeeded in blocking the logistics lines of communications east of the Ipoly. As a result, the columns had to take detours that took them many kilometers out of the way.

That same day, the 2nd and 3rd Ukrainian fronts moved out on both sides of Budapest for their decisive offensive. Hitler decided to change the leading commanders. At that critical juncture, *General der Infanterie* Wöhler assumed command of *Heeresgruppe Süd* and *General der Panzertruppen* Balck became the commander in chief of the *6. Armee*. Twenty Soviet divisions attacked a single German corps that day.

Panzer-Regiment 6, which under the command of *Oberstleutnant Graf* von der Schulenburg at that point, was alerted on the evening of 20 December. The regiment was at full strength. The *I./Panzer-Regiment 6*, which had been separated for nearly two years from the division and had been employed with the *Panzer-Lehr-Division* in the west after being trained on and issued *Panthers*, had returned to the regiment. It was the 1st Battalion that was to be the first one alerted. It left its quartering area around Mór that same night. Soviet tanks had approached to within striking distance of Stuhlweißenburg. It was directed that *Panzer-Regiment 6* defend the beautiful city.

Major Fiehl's 1st Battalion moved through Stuhlweißenburg and took up positions along the edge of the city at first light. The Soviets started attacking. Enemy artillery fire caused the first losses. The *Panthers* that threw down the gauntlet against the Soviet T-34's and Stalins. The 2nd Company commander, *Oberleutnant* Seyfried, and another officer from the company, *Leutnant* König, were knocked out. *Leutnant* Blaich, a Knight's Cross recipient, who had only received his officer's commission a few days previously, assumed acting command of the company. The 2nd Battalion was also committed. Both of the battalions were employed far apart from one another and conducted a separate fight. The 1st battalion was positioned forward of Stuhlweißenburg. The 6th and 7th Companies of the 2nd Battalion were employed along Lake Velence under the command of *Oberleutnant* Hossfeld, they were the only two companies of the 2nd Battalion immediately available.

Oberleutnant Aschermann was sent to Stuhlweißenburg with the 5th and 9th Companies. When the assault guns and the *Panzer IV's* were about 250 meters out of the city, they started receiving antitank-gun fire. The regiment insisted that the attack be continued, however, and dispatched *Oberleutnant* Brümmer's *Panther* company to assist. By then, it was broad daylight. Aschermann's platoons attacked. The *Panzer IV's* of *Unteroffizier* Schulze advanced to the left of the road, while the assault guns of *Leutnant* Lohringer and *Oberfeldwebel* Hampel took up the attack from a depression to the right of the road. The fighting vehicles had barely advanced another 500 meters, when they started receiving a blizzard of defensive fire. *Oberfeldwebel* Hampel's assault gun flew into the air. T-34's started advancing; they were taken under fire by the *Panthers*.

The German attack was postponed at that point; it was to be renewed that afternoon. *Hauptmann* Gaebler's *II./Panzer-Artillerie-Regiment 75* opened the attack with an artillery preparation. The 2nd and 3rd Companies attacked on the left through the tree-covered terrain, while the 5th and

6th Companies provided covering fire. *Unteroffizier* Schulze's platoon was able to knock out three T-34's. After taking 2,000 meters of terrain, the attack stalemated. Two *Panthers* were alight in the vineyards.

Hauptmann Voigts's 6th and 7th Companies had an even harder time of it. The Soviet tanks did not allow themselves to be intimidated by the numerically weak German forces. They went around the pockets of resistance and continued advancing inexorably westward. As a result, the 2nd Battalion was practically encircled by the enemy on 22 December, but both companies eventually broke out and regrouped. As a result of the enemy's penetration, the two tank battalions were twenty kilometers apart.

Oberstleutnant Graf von der Schulenburg ordered the 1st Battalion, which had also been bypassed, to pull back. The *Panthers* formed the spearhead, while the assault guns and the *Panzer IV's* followed in the second wave. They were, in turn, followed by the trains under *Oberleutnant* Knebel and the self-propelled guns of the artillery. Functioning as rearguard were a few Panthers. The Soviets were unable to stop that group. The *Panthers* overran everything that got in their way. A few antitank guns were crushed, and 200 prisoners were taken; some enemy trucks were set alight and *Unteroffizier* Grünhage knocked out a T-34. At first light, the battle group reached the combat outposts of the *I./Panzergrenadier-Regiment 3*.

The mechanized infantry battalion of *Major* Schulze had also been involved in the fighting in and around Stuhlweißenburg. *Oberleutnant* Schirp's *4./Panzer-Regiment 6*, attached to the mechanized infantry, had particularly distinguished itself and allowed the mechanized infantry's retrograde movement through its own counterattacks.

During the night of 22–23 December, Stuhlweißenburg was evacuated. The battle groups pulled back through the vineyards. The *I./Panz-*

ergrenadier-Regiment 3 set up for the defense the following morning at the Iskasentiörgy Palace. The Soviets pursued through Stuhlweißenburg with tanks and motorized infantry. The sun illuminated the battlefield in brilliant beauty. That same morning, the armor regiment had initiated preparations to launch a counterattack to hold up the enemy advance. The 5th and 6th Companies of the armor regiment, joined by two troops from *Kavallerie-Regiment 5*,[1] moved out to attack. The objective was the road to Stuhlweißenburg, five kilometers distant. The advance was successful. *Feldwebel* Engels and his platoon from the 6th Company tackled the enemy resistance head on and then hit the Russian tanks in the flank, driving them in front of the guns of the assault guns of *Leutnant* Lohringer and *Feldwebel* Knorre. The two armored companies and the cavalrymen continued the assault. After five kilometers, the advance came to a standstill in the Russian defensive fires, however. The fighting vehicles and the cavalry had to work their way back, section-by-section.

The enemy then launched an immediate counterattack with ten T-34's, employed in pairs. The German force had collected itself and set up on a slight rise. When the T-34's had closed to within 500 meters, *Oberleutnant* Aschermann issued the order to fire. Two Soviet tanks flew into the air; the gunner of the company commander, *Gefreiter* Rickert, set another two alight. Since the German fighting vehicles had expended their ammunition by that point, they pulled back. *Oberleutnant* Aschermann, *Leutnant* Lohringer, *Leutnant* Dahme and *Feldwebel* Engels brought up the rear, knocking out another T-34. The Russians then gave up their efforts to pursue. The armored regiment had held its position and was relieved late in the afternoon of Christmas Eve.

Most of the *3. Panzer-Division* was unaware of the heavy fighting around Stuhlweißenburg. It

---

1. Part of the *4. Kavallerie-Brigade*, which had this regiment as well as another primarily horse-mounted regiment and separate brigade troops (artillery regiment and armored reconnaissance battalion).

was positioned considerably farther north. The events there unfolded in a manner similar to that of the armored group. It had been directed for the division, together with the *6. Panzer-Division*, to attack on the evening of 21 December in the effort to close the gap in the front. The overall situation had developed to the point where the IV, V, and XXV Guards Corps of the 6th Guards Army had expanded their breakthrough at Ipolysag in the direction of Lewa. The *IV. Panzer-Korps*, with its *24. Panzer-Division*, *46. Infanterie-Division*, and *SS-Sonder-Brigade "Dirlewanger,"* continued to hold its front with some difficulty in the northern portion of the point of penetration. While the *357. Infanterie-Division* stood its ground to the southwest and the *LVII. Panzer-Korps*, with the *3., 6.,* and *8. Panzer-Divisionen*, prepared for its attack. There were no other German forces in that area north of the Danube. The *3. Panzer-Division* started conducting intensive reconnaissance for the upcoming attack during the morning of 21 December. *Oberst* Schacke, the commander of *Panzergrenadier-Regiment 394*, and his adjutant, *Hauptmann* Reinders, were badly wounded in the process. The acting commander of the *II./Panzergrenadier-Regiment 394, Hauptmann* Schmidt, was also badly wounded, later dying of his wounds. *Major* Siebenhüner, who had only recently arrived in the division, assumed acting command of the regiment. *Oberleutnant* Gohle, the commander of the 2nd Company of the reconnaissance battalion, and *Feldwebel* Friedrich of the reconnaissance battalion headquarters distinguished themselves that day in the course of conducting reconnaissance.

The corps moved out to attack with the battle groups of the *3.* and *6. Panzer-Divisionen* that evening. The mechanized infantry, engineers and scouts had a tough opponent in front of them this time, who could not be ejected. Correspondingly, the *3. Panzer-Division* could not take its objective, the Russian main supply route at Kistompa. Elements of the *6. Panzer-Division* had more luck and temporarily entered Kistompa. The Soviets moved reinforcements forward dur-

ing the night, since they realized the dangers inherent in a German attack from the south. Large concentrations of tanks moved against the thin German lines from the northwest on the morning of 22 December. The mechanized infantry did not have the strength any more to turn them back. A few T-34's succeeded in reaching the area around the division command post at Lonto. Three of the T-34's were knocked out at close range by men of the *1./Panzer-Nachrichten-Abteilung 39*, who employed the *Panzerfaust* antitank rocket.

The division headquarters moved to Ipoly-Szakallos, where the command posts of the *6.* and *8. Panzer-Divisionen* were already located. Based on the enemy's numerical superiority, the corps called off its attack and transitioned to the defense. The *3. Panzer-Division* received orders to guard the flank of the neighboring *6. Panzer-Division* on the right. In order to improve the defensive capabilities of the main line of resistance, Szaczd was evacuated. The enemy skillfully exploited the situation and moved against Ipoly-Szakallos from the west with his tanks. Hastily formed battle groups from all sorts of units rallied immediately against the Russians. A few wildly firing T-34's succeeded in temporarily entering the locality, but they pulled back just as quickly.

Hauptmann Seifert's *II./Panzergrenadier-Regiment 394* had just arrived from Szaczd and was committed against the attacking enemy. *Hauptmann* Benthien's *1./Panzerjäger-Abteilung 543* supported the attack and was primarily responsible for the Russians giving up so quickly. The success could not be exploited, however, since *Panzergrenadier-Regiment 394* was attacked in the rear at the same time. The Soviets had broken through between the *3.* and *6. Panzer-Divisionen*.

Despite all that, the corps was of the opinion that a German attack to the north would force the enemy to turn around. To that end, the corps had formed a battle group formed out of an assortment of reserve elements and placed it under the command of *Oberst* Quentin. The battle group was inserted into the line next to the *3. Panzer-Division*. The counterattack could not develop properly on 24 December, since the enemy pressure continued to increase. The enemy succeeded in penetrating deeply into the Ipolyvisk Bridgehead along the right flank of the division, which was only weakly covered. A battle group under *Hauptmann* Glaubitz, the commander of the *3./Heeres-Flak-Abteilung 314*, was dispatched against the enemy force in the morning. Its self-propelled guns were joined by a few armored cars from the reconnaissance battalion. The force encountered four enemy self-propelled guns. One of the Russian guns was destroyed, while the crews abandoned the three other ones. *Wachtmeister* Albers booked the most success in that engagement. The battle group was unable to advance any farther, however, since enemy artillery kept the terrain under fire. Russian formations pushed the outposts around Ipolyvisk back.

The last Christmas of the war was marked by frost and continuous snowfall. For most of the men, there was no time for quiet or reflection or the ability to enjoy messages of love from the homeland or personal demand items. There was little time to read letters or gaze reflectively into candles. Officers and soldiers were on alert in their bunkers. Only those who were lucky enough to spend Christmas Eve in a permanent structure had a bit of time to unpack packages received in the field post and perhaps enjoy the sight and scent of a pine branch or two. Worse than the direct physical threat was the emotional weight of the night.

Once again, the Soviets paid no attention to the Christmas feast. As it started to dawn on the morning of 25 December, enemy guns started to bark all across Hungary. The fighting started at 0400 hours on both sides of Budapest. The joyful capital of Hungary underwent its first day of a painful death. Budapest was encircled by the Red Army. *General der Waffen-SS* Pfeffer-Wildenbruch, the commander of the "fortress," led the German and Hungarian forces that were tossed together by fate. On Hitler's orders, it was to be held to the last round. It would hold

out for two months against the Soviet superiority and, in the end, most of the defenders would be murdered in a bestial manner.

The men of the *3. Panzer-Division* felt the harshness and barbarism of the war on that first day of Christmas. The armored group reporting to the *III. Panzer-Korps* had already encountered probing Russian tanks during the night. Although *Kavallerie-Regiment 5* was able to prevent a breakthrough, the front was wavering. *Panzer-Regiment 6* and the *I./Panzergrenadier-Regiment 3* were employed in an immediate counterattack at first light. The battle group formed by the *II./Panzer-Regiment 6* conducted a successful attack, along with one of the cavalry battalions, which was commanded by *Major* Schwerdtfeger, the former operations officer of the division. The assault guns and *Panzer IV's* created a gap in the Soviet lines, through which the cavalrymen charged the enemy positions. The Soviets wavered and pulled back.

At the same time, the *I./Panzergrenadier-Regiment 3* cleared up a penetration in the front that occurred in the sector of the Hungarians in front of it. A Russian battalion had broken through there at first light and ejected the Hungarian companies from their positions.

By the time the orders came for an immediate counterattack, the mechanized infantrymen had long since been wide awake, since one of the battalion's ammunition carriers had gone up in the air during the preparatory fires of the Soviets. As a result of the explosion, all of the windows in the palace courtyard had been shattered.

When the battalion returned to its strongpoint, the commander of the *1./Panzergrenadier-Regiment 3* saw that the driver of his *SPW* had made the attack in his underwear. That was just one of several signs that the men had moved out in a hurry.

The speed of the mechanized infantrymen had paid off: there were no casualties. This, despite the fact that Christmas Eve had been spent with considerable imbibing.

That signaled the end of the fighting for the armored group that morning. A section under

Leutnant Kleffel remained forward with the cavalrymen, while the rest of the companies returned to their previous quarters. The Soviets attacked several more times during the day, but they were always turned back.

During the night, the *III. Panzer-Korps* pulled its front back. The Russians followed immediately. Since there was a thick fog over the front lines, Russian forces temporarily penetrated into Chakbereny. *Major* Schulze interdicted the Russian forces with his mechanized infantry, guaranteeing that the remaining forces could pull back to Söred and Magyaralmas the next night according to plan. The front ran north in the direction of the Bakony Woods, where the enemy had good observation into the German rear area. The corps remained in that sector for the next few days with the attached battle groups of *Oberstleutnant* Weymann and *Oberstleutnant Graf* von der Schulenburg. Although the Soviets constantly attempted to force the lines, they were always turned back with bloody casualties. During that period, the *III. Panzer-Korps* destroyed sixty-eight tanks. The situation at the front remained unchanged through 31 December.

The forces of the division that were employed in the north were also attacked by the Soviets on the first day of Christmas. Russian tanks ejected the men of *Kampfgruppe Quentin* from their positions and soon penetrated through the withdrawing companies to the division command post. Various elements of the corps were used to try to stop the Soviet advance. The fighting raged back and forth for hours. Whenever the enemy succeeded in advancing a few hundred meters, he was pushed back in an immediate counterattack. The bravery and endurance of the soldiers were admirable. *Oberleutnant* Winter and his men of *Heeres-Flak-Abteilung 314* especially distinguished themselves. Russian tanks had blown apart his prime movers, with the result that the gunners had to manhandle their 2- and 8.8-centimeter *Flak* into position. The German forces succeeded in halting the enemy and establishing a blocking position north of Ipolypasto, where the command staff of the division moved in the course of the night.

The fighting did not ratchet down in intensity on 26 December, either. The battle groups continued to turn back the enemy again and again. *Hauptmann* Sedlaczek, the commander of the divisional engineers, was badly wounded. His engineers knew what was at stake. Ipolypasto was held, since it was the linchpin of the entire corps defensive position. The loss of it would mean that the formations of the 6. and 8. *Panzer-Divisionen* fighting farther to the east and northeast would be cut off. The Soviets were attacking everywhere. Their tanks and riflemen were advancing south along the Garam River. By doing so, they were cutting off the three German armor divisions. But the defensive sector north of Ipolypasto did not waver. During the morning hours of 27 December, the Soviets attacked the town from the north. The mechanized infantry, combat engineers and antitank elements defended stubbornly. It was only a matter of time, however, before the German lines would collapse under the onslaught.

The division's command staff had absolutely no communication with the corps. *Generalleutnant* Philipps and the commander of the 8. *Panzer-Division* reached a decision that morning to advance via Beny to the Garam and cross it to the west. The 6. *Panzer-Division* was moving west via Kövesd. The division's formation slowly disengaged from the enemy. The Russians followed and reached Ipolypasto. The 8. *Panzer-Division* turned to the south to avoid being cut off again. The 3. *Panzer-Division* pulled back via Vilmosmir. The enemy's artillery hammered down on the German columns incessantly. They finally made it to the Garam late in the afternoon. The mechanized infantry and the reconnaissance elements succeeded in establishing a bridgehead at Beny during the night. The divisional engineers immediately started constructing a bridge. *Heeres-Flak-Abteilung 314* was pulled forward to protect the bridge site. At the same time, the engineers were ferrying wounded and ammunition across the river. The division headquarters established itself in Kis Gyarmat.

The crossing of the German forces on ferries continued without interruption during the night. The engineers took no breaks while constructing their bridge. *Major i.G.* Willich, the division logistics officer, reported the completion of the sixteen-ton bridge at 0900 hours on 28 December. Soviet long-range artillery and Stalin organs attempted to hold up the division. At the same time, enemy tanks attacked from the north. *Major* Medicus's *Panzerjäger-Abteilung 543* and *Hauptmann* Golze's *Panzer-Aufklärungs-Abteilung 3* interdicted the attacks and held them off. *Unteroffizier* Paul of the 2nd Company of the reconnaissance battalion particularly distinguished himself around Kis Gyarmat. The self-propelled guns of the antitank battalion were able to book an unforgettable score over the next few days: seventy Russian tanks were set alight in front of the German lines.

On that day, the *3.* and *8. Panzer-Divisionen* were able to cross around 1,400 vehicles over the river. That included all of the tanks and guns, including two 21-centimeter cannon. While the last elements were crossing the Garam, an order arrived from the *LVII. Panzer-Korps* to eliminate a Russian bridgehead at Kövesd. The division commander protested and indicated there would be heavy losses, but orders remained orders.

The command staff moved that night to Bela. Advance parties reconnoitered the tactical assembly areas during the morning of 29 December. During the day, the division assembled its forces. An assault group under Major Medicus was formed. The attack started at evening twilight. *Major* Medicus advanced rapidly forward in his *SPW* and with his self-propelled guns. The battle group took the bridge northeast of nana. When the soldiers approached the village, they started to receive murderous defensive fires. The Soviets had skillfully hidden their tanks in barns and farmers' houses. The attack bogged down outside of the village.

The corps ordered the continuation of the attack on the morning of 29 December. But the division was at the end of its strength. In addition, a successful conduct of the attack would lead to the division having to occupy positions that were directly in front of the dominant high ground on the east bank of the Garam and the south bank of the Danube. Defending those positions later on would only have been possible, if at all, at the cost of continued high casualties. *Generalleutnant* Philipps and *Major i.G. Freiherr* Rotberg expressed those concerns to the commanding general, who finally rescinded the attack order. The division transitioned to the defense in the areas it had taken west of the Garam. The men of the 2nd Medical Company at the main clearing station at Köbbelkut were granted no respite. The number of casualties was high. The next days were spent defending against Russian attacks. The New Year saw no change in the situation. The soldiers of the division greeted the New Year with the consumption of higher quantities of signal flares.

The enemy's superiority in numbers continued unchanged with the New Year. The Army High Command took measures to help prevent the Red Army from breaking through again and, at the same time, launching offensive operations. The *III. Panzer-Korps* and the *IV. SS-Panzer-Korps* were directed to advance on Budapest from Komorn. The entire *6. SS-Panzer-Armee* of *SS-Oberstgruppenführer* "Sepp" Dietrich was pulled out of the Ardennes offensive and moved to Hungary. The German offensive started on 2 January. Both of the aforementioned corps made only slow progress against extremely tough resistance. On 3 January, the *5. SS-Panzer-Division "Wiking"* assaulted Tarjan. The *6. Panzer-Division*, the *96.* and *711. Infanterie-Divisionen*, and *Kampfgruppe Pape* fought against a numerically superior enemy and the icy winter storms. On 12 January, the Vikings were only twenty-one kilometers from Budapest. That attack, as well as the second one that followed to free the Hungarian capital, turned into a sacrificial offering on the part of the recently reconstituted German armored forces.

Kampfgruppe Weymann—Panzer-Regiment 6, Panzergrenadier-Regiment 3, the *II./Panzer-Artillerie-Regiment 75*—experienced the start of the New Year away from the division in the area around Stuhlweißenburg. On 1 January 1945, *Panzergrenadier-Regiment 3* moved from Söred to Magyaralmas. Local reconnaissance was conducted from there. On 7 January, the armored group participated in an attack on Zamoly by *General der Kavallerie* Harteneck's *I. Kavallerie-Korps*. The first objective was the Guylamayor estate. The fighting vehicles of the *I./Panzer-Regiment 6* took the lead. *Hauptmann* Schramm, the new battalion commander, who had been a *Hauptfeldwebel* at the start of the war, was knocked out after reaching the objective. Making a snap decision, *Oberleutnant* Schirp, the commander of the 4th Company, assumed acting command of the battalion. The tanks broke through Russian field positions, overran enemy antitank guns and knocked out a few T-34's and American-built tanks. *Leutnant* Schenk of the 2nd Company, who had only recently arrived at the battalion, knocked out three Russian tanks with his crew. The rapid onset of darkness and a snowstorm brought the attack to a standstill. The estate was attacked and taken on 8 January. The battle group set up for the defense there.

By then, most of the *3. Panzer-Division* had arrived in the Lake Balaton–Stuhlweißenburg area. The movement orders had reached the division on 4 January. The Hungarian "Lazlo" Armored Division relieved the division's forces the next day; around 2100 hours on 5 January, they crossed the Danube. On the first day of movement, the first elements had just reached the area around Bakonycsernye, when a cease movement order arrived. The Soviets had figured out that the division had been relieved and broken through the lines of the Hungarian armor division. The last elements of the division got mixed up in that fight. The main clearing station in Köbbelkut was temporarily closed. Fortunately, all of the wounded were able to be evacuated. Only the 2nd Medical Company suffered some losses. Since November 1943, the medical elements of the division had suffered the following officer losses: two dead, six wounded, and one missing in action.

After halting for four hours, the division continued its movements on 6 January. In the evening, it arrived in the area northwest of the positions of the *I. Kavallerie-Korps*. It was intended to employ the division on the left wing of the corps next to the *4. Kavallerie-Brigade*. When the corps attacked on 7 January, the division did not have any artillery in support, since the guns had become stranded due to a lack of fuel. The advance on the dominant high ground around Csakbereny made no decent progress at all. The completely exhausted mechanized infantry got stuck in the deep snow. The only armored vehicles on hand at the time—three self-propelled guns from *Panzerjäger-Abteilung 543*—could not accomplish much. For that reason, the division regrouped in the evening. *Kampfgruppe Weymann* was directed farther south. While it was still dark, the *II./Panzergrenadier-Regiment 3* took an important hill southwest of Csakbereny.

The attack continued the next day. The *I./Panzergrenadier-Regiment 394* encountered an extremely strong enemy force and was unable to break through. The sister battalion of the regiment was able to take Hill 280, a dominant terrain feature, however. The division's reconnaissance battalion was able to break through the initial Russian positions, but then it was unable to advance any farther against a Russian antitank-gun belt. The corps regrouped, since it was intended to conduct the attack of the armored formations farther to the south. The Hungarian 2nd Armored Division was attached to the *3. Panzer-Division*. The first battalions of the Hungarians to arrive were employed immediately. The *3. Panzer-Division* remained in its positions initially, throwing back intense enemy attacks that focused primarily on the *II./Panzergrenadier-Regiment 3* on Hill 225. The hill was lost twice and recaptured twice. One time, it was by the *II./Panzergrenadier-Regiment 3*. The second time, it was by the *II./Panzergrenadier-Regiment 394*. The casualties were considerable and were even more painful due to the fact that the Hungarian comrades-in-arms were unreliable and deserted by the company. The reconnaissance battalion received orders to monitor the Hungarian positions. On 11 January, the armored cars encountered a previously undetected enemy antitank-gun position. The reconnaissance forces attacked the enemy by surprise and eliminated fourteen guns.

Kavallerie-Regiment 5, an assault-gun battalion, and the *I./Panzergrenadier-Regiment 3* booked a similar success that day. The object of their attack was the important transportation hub of Zamoly. Despite considerable losses, the cavalrymen, and mechanized infantry remained unflappable in their advance and assaulted the locality. *Rittmeister Graf* von Plettenberg, the commander of the assault-gun brigade, was mortally wounded.[2] Plettenberg ordered the timely withdrawal of the force, since it started to be bombed in waves by the Red Air Force, which was attacking Zamoly. The battle group pulled back to the nearby woods and moved further back to Magyaralmas in the evening.

The *3. Panzer-Division* remained three days in that sector. Contrary to the norm, the enemy remained relatively quiet. The weather turned warmer, and the snow started to melt. The forces set up for the defense. On 14 January, the division commander and the operations officer attended a conference in Öskü concerning a new offensive. On 11 January, Hitler had ordered another powerful advance on Budapest from Stuhlweißenburg. It was intended for the attack to advance to the Danube and then turn north so as to relieve the encircled forces from the south. To that end, the *3. Panzer-Division* was attached to the *IV. SS-Panzer-Korps* and received *Kampfgruppe Weymann* back into its fold. Weymann was later awarded the Knight's Cross to the Iron Cross for his actions around Stuhlweißenburg.

The *IV. SS-Panzer-Korps* staged in the area between the Bakony Woods and Lake Balaton. The following divisions were arrayed from left to right: the *1. Panzer-Division* (*Generalmajor* Thunert); the *3. SS-Panzer-Division "Totenkopf"* (*SS-Brigadeführer* Becker); the *5. SS-Panzer-Division "Wiking"* (*SS-Brigadeführer* Ullrich); the *3. Panzer-Division*; and *Kampfgruppe Pape*. The friendly forces to the left were the *23. Panzer-Division* of the *III. Panzer-Korps* and, on the right, the *I. Kavallerie-Korps* (which was not participating in the attack). On 15 January, the *3. Panzer-Division* moved into its new assembly area. The command post was located in the magnificent spa at Balatonkenese on the northeast bank of Lake Balaton. The *6. Armee* of *General der Panzertruppen* Balck directed the attack to start on 18 January. The order from the field army stated, in part: "Strong artillery, rocket launcher, armored, and aviation assets are prepared to support you. The objective of the attack is Budapest."

The last major offensive of the *3. Panzer-Division* started at 0530 hours on 18 January 1945. An artillery preparation by guns and rocket launchers of the *Waffen-SS* opened the attack. The mechanized infantry jumped out of their positions and followed the *Panthers* of the *I./Panzer-Regiment 6*. But the Soviets were prepared to defend. They had brought a lot of antitank guns forward, whose fires caused the first casualties. One minefield after the other—four in all—prevented a rapid advance. The Russians were true masters at emplacing those types of obstacles, and the gaps were covered with high-power lines. The engineers had to be called forward. The tanks and the artillery batteries held the enemy down, while the men of the divisional engineers created a breach by dint of tiresome effort.

Finally, after five hours, they did it. The *Panthers* rolled out, followed closely by the *Panzer IV's* of the 2nd Battalion and the *SPW's* of the mechanized infantry.

The force encountered an antitank-gun belt that attempted to hold it up. Under the covering

---

2. Georg *Graf* von Plettenberg actually commanded *schwere Kavallerie-Abteilung 4* of the *4. Kavallerie-Brigade*. He received the Knight's Cross to the Iron Cross on 12 August 1944 as the commander of that battalion. He later became the 730th recipient of the Oak Leaves to the Knight's Cross for the actions described above.

fires provided by the armored regiment, the *I./Panzergrenadier-Regiment 3*, echeloned somewhat to the rear, was able to envelop, moving far out to the left. The lead company, under the terrific leadership of its commander, *Oberleutnant* Bürger, was able to move on line with the antitank guns, turn inwards and overrun the enemy position from the flank, shooting up its guns and firing at the crews.

The attack finally came into its own. The Russian main line of resistance had been broken through. The division advanced across the road east of Lake Balaton and took the extended village of Enying. The Hungarian population, which had suffered for weeks under the plundering, rapes and murders of the Russians, greeted the German soldiers enthusiastically. The women made pancakes and bakes pastries. But there wasn't a lot of time available for resting. Elements of *Panzergrenadier-Regiment 394*, together with Hungarian elements, took up the flank guard mission on the right, while the armor regiment and *Panzergrenadier-Regiment 3* advanced another 40 kilometers past Enying and took the Sáviz Canal at Káloz.

The division regrouped during the night and brought up supplies and fuel in a timely manner. Unfortunately, only the tanks of *Oberleutnant* Schirp's 4th Company, which had been attached to the *I./Panzergrenadier-Regiment 3*, could be refueled. *Generalleutnant* Philipps decided to move out without the main body of the armored regiment. At 0515 hours, without any artillery preparation, *Major* Medicus's *Panzerjäger-Abteilung 543* and *Major* Schulze's reinforced *I./Panzergrenadier-Regiment 3* advanced out of the bridgehead. That initiated a tank raid, the likes of which the soldiers had not seen since the days of the Caucasus. The *SPW's* and self-propelled guns thundered through the ranks of the enemy forces without stopping. The force moved through the villages of Deg, Sarbogard and Hercefalva. The Russians fled helter-skelter. They abandoned their vehicles, including twenty-five brand-new tracked prime movers and American fuel trucks. The *SPW's* had to

push the many vehicles out of the way in order to create room to move. The "wild hunt" continued. When it turned 0800 hours, the vehicles rolled into the large industrial city of Dunapentele. They had reached the Danube.

The populace of the city was overwhelmed with joy and greeted the soldiers as liberators. The tanks of the armored regiment closed up and took positions along the riverbank. The Soviets had left the city in a panic. Their last formations boarded watercraft while taking fire from the German fighting vehicles. A few watercraft caught fire and drifted downstream. In a unique engagement, the tanks of the *I./Panzer-Regiment 6* took on a Russian cannon boat, setting it alight. They also destroyed a mine ship.

To the east of the Danube, long columns of enemy armor and trucks moved south in the direction of the next bridge over the Danube at Dunaföldvár. Reconnaissance conducted by a *SPW* company indicated only weak enemy forces on the German side of the Danube. It was thought that it might be possible to make the bridge there unusable for the enemy forces. Elements of the *I./Panzergrenadier-Regiment 3* immediately headed south. They quickly made headway, but they were stopped on radio orders from the division and ordered back to Dunapentele.

The armored group was so far in front of the rest of the division that no fuel or ammunition made it forward to Dunapentale that day. The main body of the division was about half way there. The southern flank grew longer by the hour. Enemy reconnaissance efforts were turned back. The command staff moved to Deg.

Oberstleutnant Graf von der Schulenburg assumed command of the forces in Dunapentale. Fortunately, the supply vehicles made it there by noon on 20 January. *Panzer-Regiment 6*, the *I./Panzergrenadier-Regiment 3* and *Panzerjäger-Abteilung 543* attacked north along the road to Budapest at 1330 hours. The forces were attacked several times by Soviet fighter-bombers. The fighting vehicles and the *SPW's* paid them no heed and continued to march north, entering Rácz-Almas and Perkáta. It was not until a minefield was encountered that the continued advance was halted outside of Adony.

The winter's night set in. All of a sudden, the situation changed dramatically. The Soviet XVIII Corps with its 21st, 104th and 122nd Rifle Divisions broke through the front of the *5. SS-Panzer-Division "Wiking"* to the left and headed south. Before the division recognized the danger to its own forces, the Russians had reached the road on both sides of Hercefalva. *Hauptmann* Golze's *Panzer-Aufklärungs-Abteilung 3*, which was screening there, was unable to brake the Soviet onslaught and evacuated the village, which the enemy promptly occupied.

The armored group knew nothing of all that yet and advanced on Adony on the morning of 21 January. *Oberleutnant* Bürger's *1./Panzergrenadier-Regiment 3* was the first unit to break the enemy's resistance, and his men stormed Adony, taking it. Later on, *Major* Schulze, *Oberleutnant* Bürger and *Oberleutnant* Schirp received the Knight's Cross to the Iron Cross for their actions and leadership over the last three days. They would be the last three officer recipients of that high award within the division.

Generalleutnant Philipps called off any further attempt to advance north. The battle group was turned around 180 degrees in order to hit the Russian forces that had broken through in the flanks. The *I./Panzergrenadier-Regiment 3* pulled back to Perkáta and set up security in the area around a nuns' cloister. The battalion translator, *Obergefreiter* Eitel, formerly a teacher in Hungary, encountered a Hungarian soldier that night, who turned out to be one of his former students.

The attack by the armored group came too late to hit the enemy forces that had broken through in the flank. Most of them had already crossed the road to the south. Deep snowdrifts forced the German fighting vehicles and *SPW's* to remain on the few available roads. Friendly aerial reconnaissance reported that the enemy was taking additional strong forces across the Danube at Dunaföldvár and that they were turning to the northwest. As was later determined,

these were forces of the Soviet XXX Corps, which had three to four rifle divisions. The division assumed that the forces that had broken through would turn around and, together with the forces being brought up from the south, attack north. At that point, it was imperative to establish a defensive front that was oriented south along the road, thus protecting the right flank of the corps against the considerable threat. To that end, Hercegfalva had to be taken. Together with the armored group, the *I./Panzergrenadier-Regiment 394* moved out to take the locality.

The Soviets had established themselves in Hercegfalva with strong armor and rifle formations. The staging for the German attack took the entire day, since the division was already having to defend to all sides. The attack by the *6. Armee* had not really made much progress anywhere. Stuhlweißenburg, which was considered the linchpin of the entire offensive, was stubbornly defended by the Soviet I Corps (Mechanized). The enemy corps was a thorn in the side of the German divisions. On 21 January, the commanding general of the *IV. SS-Panzer-Korps*, *SS-Gruppenführer* Gille, who was a recipient of the Diamond to the Oak Leaves to the Knight's Cross of the Iron Cross, ordered Stuhlweißenburg to be taken in a night attack. The *23. Panzer-Division* attacked the city from the west, while elements of the *5. SS-Panzer-Division "Wiking"* came in from the east. At the same time, the two mechanized infantry regiments of the *1. Panzer-Division* attacked from the south. An assault detachment of Hungarian volunteers under *SS-Obersturmführer* Ney, himself a Hungarian, finally entered the city. The fighting continued for another two days, however, before the city was firmly in German hands. The main line of resistance was established just east of the city and ran from there to the southern corner of Lake Valencze. *Generalmajor* Thunert's *1. Panzer-Division* advanced past the lake and got as far as Martonvásár and Vál on 26 January. It was only sixteen kilometers from there to Budapest.

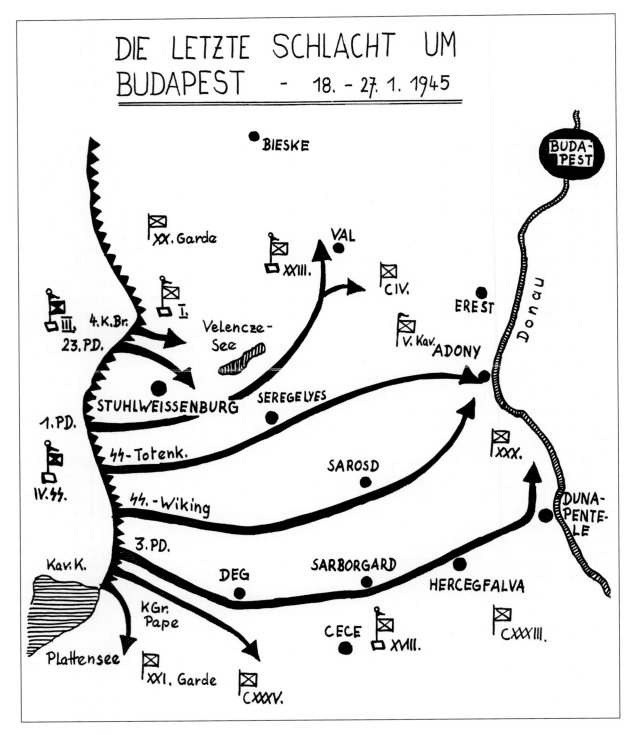

The Final Battle: Budapest

18–27 January 1945

KavK = *Kavallerie-Korps*; *Plattensee* = Lake Balaton.

On 23 January, the *3. Panzer-Division* was involved in heavy fighting at Hercegfalva. The Russians were putting up a tough defense and were not giving up a single step of ground. Soviet tanks formed the backbone of the defense. Since their fighting vehicles had good concealment opportunities from within the city, they were difficult to identify. In addition, thick snow flurries prevented a rapid advance. The *I./Panzer-Regiment 6* was the first battalion to enter the city. Enemy tanks and antitank guns knocked out four *Panthers*. After overcoming the initial shock, the tankers collected themselves. They were soon joined by antitank elements and mechanized infantry. The first T-34 flew into the air, followed by a second and then a third. The companies advanced slowly from house to house. The battalion commander of the *II./Panzergrenadier-Regiment 394*, *Hauptmann* Berg, was mortally wounded in his *SPW* right at the start of the attack. That afternoon, the Company Commander of the 5th Company of that battalion, *Leutnant* Deckwerth, was killed; he and his company had distinguished themselves in the fighting. The battalion took heavy losses, and the 5th Company was disbanded. The trench strength of the remaining companies averaged twenty men. The enemy put up an especially stiff defense around the church. In the end, however, the tanks and mechanized infantry became the masters of Hercegfalva.

On 24 January, the division was allocated to the Hungarian 3rd Army. With that transfer of command authority, the division no longer participated in the offensive to relieve Budapest. The division headquarters moved to Kis Hantos, not too far from Sárosd. *Hauptmann* Schubert's *Panzer-Nachrichten-Abteilung 39* had already laid wire to all of the subordinate command posts.

An advance south by the armored group of the division—consisting of the armored regiment and the antitank battalion—ended successfully, with ten enemy tanks and numerous antitank guns being knocked out.

The anticipated attack by the enemy against the new sector of the division had not yet started in force. Apparently, the enemy's intent was to probe the German lines with weaker forces in an effort to find a good jumping-off point for his attack. During the night of 23–24 January, Russian tanks attacked Sar-Szt. Miklos, which was only being defended by a weak engineer company. The reconnaissance battalion was directed to take back the locality. The attack conducted on 25 January east of the village destroyed a Russian battalion. Without suffering any losses, the scouts took in seventy-two prisoners.

The attack was continued the next day by the *I./Panzergrenadier-Regiment 3*, which had been reinforced by tanks. By then, the enemy had considerably reinforced his presence there. Rocket launchers and T-34's only allowed a slow advance by the companies. The *SPW* of *Oberstleutnant* Weymann was knocked out. The commander of the 1st Company, *Oberleutnant* Bürger, was wounded. The German losses were heavy, and the attack was called off. The forces transitioned to the defense.

On the morning of 26 January, *Generalleutnant* Philipps left the division. With an effective date of 1 January 1945, he had been transferred back to the Army Procurement Agency. *Oberst* Söth, the former commander of *Panzer-Artillerie-Regiment 73* of the *1. Panzer-Division* and a separate mechanized infantry brigade, arrived to take his place. The new acting commander was immediately faced with a difficult mission. The higher levels of the German command admitted that day that the encircled "Budapest Fortress" could not be relieved. The brave men defending the city would hold out for another twenty days, before von Pfeffer-Wildenbruch issued orders to break out. In all, 1,800 officers and enlisted personnel were able to make their way back to German lines, while 14,200 remained behind in the city, dead or wounded.

At 0830 hours on 27 January, the Soviets opened their offensive against the entire sector of the *3. Panzer-Division* with a mighty barrage. The assigned sector of the division ran for more than forty-five kilometers from the Sarviz Canal to the Danube. The fact that the weak forces of the division had to hold that extended sector was made all the more difficult by the fact that the deep snow barely allowed for a mobile defense. Large groups of enemy tanks initially advanced against the right flank of the division, which was being held by the reconnaissance battalion and the divisional engineers. The attack then spread a short while later to the positions of *Panzer-grenadier-Regiment 394*. The first to break through was a group of six T-34's that advanced straight to the regimental command post without stopping. *Major* Siebenhüner and his headquarters were able to get out in the nick of time. The neighboring communications section of *Leutnant* Griessenbeck had to defend itself with *Panzerfäuste* in close combat. The regiment's two battalions put up a stubborn defense, but eventually had to yield. The casualties were high. Hercegfalva was lost once again.

Hauptmann Seifert's *II./Panzergrenadier-Regiment 394* defended Dunapentale. The enemy was singularly unsuccessful in his efforts there. It was not until night that Russian tanks crossed the Perkáta–Dunapentale road to the northeast. *Panzer-Aufklärungs-Abteilung 23* of the *23. Panzer-Division*, which was screening Perkáta, was pushed back and had to evacuate the town. Based on the threatening situation, the division headquarters moved to Sárosd.

On the left wing of the division, the armored group found itself in the middle of the axis of advance of the Soviet fighting vehicles. *Panzer-Regiment 6* and *Panzergrenadier-Regiment 3* put up a stubborn defense. Many T-34's and Shermans were knocked out. In the end, however, the battle group had to pull back to the north on 28 January. Fortunately, a counterattack conducted by the *1. Panzer-Division*, which retook Perkáta, improved the situation. The Russians were already pushing north of Sárosd toward Seregé-

lyes. The division command post was only one kilometer behind the main line of resistance.

During the evening, the division issued a report concerning the fighting between 20 December 1944 and 28 January 1945. According to it, the division had destroyed 515 tanks, 430 trucks, 461 horse-drawn conveyances, 28 armored personnel carriers, 17 assault guns, 5 armored cars, 13 motorcycles, 639 guns and antitank guns, 60 mortars, 123 antitank rifles, 116 machine guns, 69 submachine guns, 477 rifles, 11 antiaircraft guns, 3 antiaircraft, and 6 watercraft on the Danube. In addition, 1,500 Russian soldiers had been taken prisoner.

Hauptmann Seifert's *II./Panzergrenadier-Regiment 3* remained encircled in Dunapentele. Since the division was unable to free up its own forces to relieve Seifert and his men, battle groups from the *1. Panzer-Division* under *Oberstleutnant* Huppert and *Major* Marcks attacked. On 29 January, the two groups advanced to the Danube, seven kilometers north of the city. The enemy resistance increased. *Major* Marcks and his soldiers did not give up. The *I./Panzergrenadier-Regiment 1* and the *10./Panzergrenadier-Regiment 113* pressed south the next day. At the same time, other elements of *Panzergrenadier-Regiment 1* under *Major* Ritz encountered combat outposts of the *II./Panzergrenadier-Regiment 3* in Galambos. The battalion was saved.

At 0700 hours on 29 January, most of the division attacked south. Despite an intense snowstorm, the reconnaissance battalion took Kis Venyim. The battalion suffered many losses to frostbite and attacks by fighter-bombers. During the night, the village had to be evacuated. The advance of the armored regiment and *Panzergrenadier-Regiment 394* on Nagylók did not succeed. *Major* Siebenhüner was wounded. The *II./Panzergrenadier-Regiment 394* was disbanded. A ready-reaction company under the command of Leutnant Halboth screened the road in Kishantos with the rest of the 2nd Battalion (eight men). The corps ordered the division to go over to the defensive. The enemy was attacking without interruption. On 31 January, the *I./Panzergrenadier-Regiment 3*, which was on the left wing, turned back several armored attacks. The next night, the *II./Panzergrenadier-Regiment 3* fought its way out of Dunapentele, breaking through to Perkáta. The exhausted battalion was immediately committed again.

On 1 February, the division received orders to pull back about twelve to fifteen kilometers and establish a new main line of resistance. The positions ran in a straight line from Sárosd to the northeast. The movements proceeded without major incident. The division command post moved to Seregélyes, and *Panzergrenadier-Regiment 3* was positioned in the vicinity of the Andomayor estate. The two companies of *Panzer-Nachrichten-Abteilung 39* under *Hauptmann* Schwarzenberger and *Oberleutnant* Eckelmann pulled off the impossible by establishing landlines that night and maintaining radio contact with all stations. Just to *Panzergrenadier-Regiment 3* alone there were fourteen lines. The rear-area services had a difficult time of it. The division had only one serviceable supply route. For a while, the quartermaster section was in danger of being overrun by Russian tanks. The Hungarian populace was horrified at the sight of the German withdrawal. It had unbelievable fear concerning its future.

The Soviets immediately pursued behind the withdrawing German formations. Their tanks broke through in the sector of the *5. SS-Panzer-Division "Wiking."* The left wing of the *3. Panzer-Division* got involved in that fight. By first light, the sector of *Panzergrenadier-Regiment 3* was also torn apart. The enemy fighting vehicles were outside of Seregélyes a short while later. Soviet artillery fire impacted in the town. The eastern part of the locality, where the command post of the Vikings was located, had to be evacuated. Complete darkness and thick fog made the fighting even more difficult. There

was fire from tanks, antitank guns and machine guns coming from all sides, even though the targets could not be made out. All of the landlines were destroyed. The division escort company of *Leutnant* Poincilit prepared to defend the command post.

The bedlam continued the next day (3 February). The Russians had already advanced past Seregélyes and blocked the road to Sárosd. The armored regiment launched an immediate counterattack east of Sárosd. The attack made it to about the middle of the road, where the tanks established a blocking position. *Panzergrenadier-Regiment 3* had to yield to the enemy pressure and pulled back towards Sárosd. The fighting increased in its harshness during the night.

The division recommended to the corps that its front be shortened. The request was denied. Since the situation continued to grew ever more critical, *Generalmajor* Söth—promoted on 30 January—made a decision, together with the commander of the Vikings, to conduct a local withdrawal. The command post moved to the Belsöbarand Palace. The Soviets remained on the heels of the division's elements. During the morning of 4 February, Russian tanks and riflemen advanced on Sárosd. *Oberleutnant* Rhinow's *4./Panzergrenadier-Regiment 3*, which was holding there, sent out but a single radio message: "Russians everywhere." Then the company was silent forever. The immediate counterattack that was launched failed. The rest of the battalion was pushed out of the city. *Oberleutnant* Kallert's *1./Panzergrenadier-Regiment 3* was able to collect itself in a cornfield. *Oberstleutnant* Weymann organized the continued defense of his regiment from there.

The division dug in around Sárosd. The enemy attacked again in the evening and assaulted Csillagmayor with strong forces. *Panzergrenadier-Regiment 394* took heavy casualties and yielded to the enemy. Portions of the regiment were temporarily encircled, but they were able to make it back to the German lines, albeit leaving behind much of their heavy equipment and weapons. The signals platoon of *Oberwachtmeister* Carstensen, which was attached to the regiment, was able to escape only by destroying all of its equipment. Twelve enemy tanks continued to advance and showed up three kilometers from the command post. *Panzerjäger-Abteilung 543* knocked out eight T-34's. *Panzergrenadier-Regiment 3* was pulled back to Belsöbarand.

During the night of 4–5 February, the division received orders to pull back to the so-called Margarete Position. The division's forces disengaged from the enemy at 0430 hours. The command staff moved eight kilometers to the west. The enemy pursued immediately. Six tanks and about 1,000 men attacked the withdrawing formations. The concentrated fires of *Hauptmann* Gaebler's *II./Panzer-Artillerie-Regiment 75* held back the attackers. The trench strength of the units was horrific. *Oberstleutnant* Frevert's *Panzergrenadier-Regiment 394* had thirty to forty men capable of combat. Within the armored regiment, only six fighting vehicles were mobile. The trains were combed through once more in an effort to close the gaps at the front.

The Russians penetrated into the sector of the *5. SS-Panzer-Division "Wiking." Panzergrenadier-Regiment 3* was pushed to the left to relieve *SS-Panzer-Grenadier-Regiment "Westland."* Elements of the *23. Panzer-Division* took over portions of the regiment's former sector. Since the SS units were unable to hold the following night, the relief proved illusory. Because of that, *Oberstleutnant* Weymann had his regiment occupy high ground to the rear. On 6 February, the division's reconnaissance battalion was attached to the Vikings.

On 7 February, the Vikings and the *1. Panzer-Division* attacked the enemy forces that had penetrated to the left of the *3. Panzer-Division*. It proved impossible to occupy the Margarete

Position, since all of it was under water. Correspondingly, the division remained in its positions along the high ground. The corps agreed to those measures.

The *1./Panzer-Nachrichten-Abteilung 39* took pains to lay landlines in the trees. The 1st Medical Company tore down the main clearing station it had established only a few days previously at the Polgardi Palace and transported its wounded and materiel to Veczprem. The division remained in its positions for two days, until movement orders arrived on 9 February, and the divisional formations left their positions during the night. Only the armored group and the 2nd Battalion of the divisional artillery remained in sector for another twenty-four hours.

The division marched to the area around Polgardi. The command post was established in Mezöszentgyörgy. Since the Hungarian forces that had been positioned there were too weak and had yielded ground, it was intended to reinforce and restore the main line of resistance. The division formed a battle group under *Oberstleutnant Graf* von der Schulenburg, which consisted of *Panzer-Regiment 6*, the *I./Panzergrenadier-Regiment 3*, the *II./Panzer-Artillerie-Regiment 75*, and *Panzerjäger-Abteilung 543*. The battle group moved out at 1430 hours on 11 February. The thick fog, the numerous irrigation ditches and the completely muddy terrain were a worse enemy than the Russians. The mechanized infantry were only able to advance as far as the Ercsimayor estate, where they literally bogged down in the mud. The fighting vehicles made it to Kislang, but they were unable to take the locality because of the heavy antitank defenses there.

The Soviets started 12 February with a heavy artillery barrage. The casualties of the new day were heavy. *Stabsfeldwebel* Ziegler of the *I./Panzergrenadier-Regiment 3* was among the dead. Around 0700 hours, after the mechanized infantry had closed up, *Kampfgruppe Schulenburg* attacked Kislang. The enemy put up a stubborn defense. The fighting vehicles overcame two antitank-gun belts and occupied the town.

Unteroffizier Wietersheim, an officer candidate and the gunner on the tank of *Leutnant* Bernuth, who would later be killed, entered the following in his diary for 12 February:

> In action all day without interruption. Around 1000 hours, we pushed up to the locality of Kislang, without firing. Then— be prepared to fire. A Sherman in a cornfield. Fire when ready. One round. The turret lifted and it was all over. Additional tanks appeared, T-34's. A wild firefight on both sides. We had a good position, and I was able to take out two more tanks by direct hits. We approached closer to the locality. There was an assault gun between the houses. Fired . . . hit . . . crew bailed out. But a short while later, the same Ivan was firing again. Put another one in him. Another hit, but a ricochet. Was unable to penetrate the frontal armor. We then placed aimed fires with some other vehicles on the assault gun until it was taken care of. The "kill" counted for the 5th Company.

Working together with the *1. Panzer-Division*, Nagylang was taken. The tanks of the division advanced as far as the Sárviz Canal. The enemy had fortified himself so well there that there were no crossing points to be found. *Generalmajor* Söth called off any further advance and assembled the division around Kislang, screening to the southeast. The Armed Forces Daily Report of 15 February, announced the successes of the German forces in the Lake Balaton–Budapest area from 1 January to 15 February. According to it, the enemy lost 2,045 tanks, 2,727 artillery pieces and much more. In addition, 5,100 prisoners were taken.

The situation did not change over the next few days. It was impossible to conduct a mobile defense due to the muddy roads. The only road available for supplies was unusable. The field messes were unable to come forward. Only tracked vehicles and *panje* wagons were up to the task. The soldiers set up in the houses that had been abandoned by the locals as best they could. Since the evacuation of the farmsteads often took place without much notice, there was livestock and foodstuffs aplenty. The front-line units hardly needed the field kitchens.

Movement orders arrived during the afternoon of 16 February. The division was directed to relieve *Generalmajor* Roden's *286. Sicherungs-Division* east of Lake Balaton. The sector of the *3. Panzer-Division* was assumed by Hungarian formations. The intent of the field army was to have the division undergo a battlefield reconstitution and, at the same time, act as a "corset stay" for the unreliable Hungarians. The division departed for its new area of operations on 17 February. The reconnaissance battalion formed the rearguard and left combat-capable patrols at intervals to secure behind the Hungarian front.

The division command post moved to Csajag. The village was four kilometers east of Balatonkenese, where the division's offensive had started on 18 January. The weather was sunny and warm, almost spring-like. The division's units were able to establish themselves comfortably in their new quarters. The headquarters occupied abandoned estate buildings and palaces. The regiments and battalions reconstituted as replacements arrived and new tanks, *SPW's* and artillery pieces were issued. The weapons were maintained, exercises conducted and courses held for noncommissioned officers and poison gas training. The corps surgeon of the *III. Panzer-Korps*, *Oberfeldarzt* de Freese, held lectures for the medical officers at the Lovasz-Patona Palace. The division was directed to provide a detail of one officer and eighty men daily to assist in the improvement of the "Maragarete" Position. The twenty-sixth of February was designated as the division's "dig day," with all of its units participating. The result: The creation of 416 meters of continuous trench line, including machine-gun positions.

The rest period also brought the soldiers some opportunity to relax and enjoy less taxing pursuits. Films were shown, even though most were years old. There were daily lectures about politics. The beautiful countryside practically invited the soldiers to take walks. The efforts of the division surgeon, *Oberfeldarzt* Dr. Stribny, to establish a "soldiers' home" paid off. The "Bears' Home," with its large, open outdoor stairs and beautiful veranda was located in the middle of the woods not far from the small and quiet town of Zirc on the southeast edge of the Bakony Woods. The wounded, the convalescing and those detailed away from their units could spend a few days there in a full-fledged vacation. The beds were clean. The hearts of the soldiers were gladdened by the good rooms, the abundant food, the female staff and the theatrical presentations. The "Bears' Home" was a home-away-from-home for the soldiers of the division during that February.

A special occasion for the division was the award of the Knight's Cross to the Iron Cross to *Oberstleutnant* Weymann on 20 February. All of the formations of the division sent representatives to participate in the honor at Balatonkenese. The division commander also celebrated his birthday that day. The division operations officer, *Major i.G. Freiherr* von Rotberg was detailed to the *6. Panzer-Division* from 26 February to 17 March to serve as an acting battalion commander. In his stead, *Major i.G.* Willich served as the acting division operations officer. *Major* Wiese, who hailed from Kaiserswaldau, assumed duties as the division logistics officer.

The security for the assembly area was provided by the reconnaissance battalion and an *SPW* company from each of the battalions. The

enemy remained quiet, with the exception of 26 February, when broken-through Russian forces had to be ejected by the *2./Panzergrenadier-Regiment 3*. By contrast, the Red Air Force attacked the quartering area several times. An especially severe attack was conducted against Veczprem on 21 February, where the main clearing station was located. The dead were buried at the military cemetery at Balatonkenese.

In February, Hitler had ordered a counteroffensive in Hungary, without listening to the counterarguments of his army chief of staff, *Generaloberst* Guderian. The *6. SS-Panzer-Armee* had arrived from the west by then and detrained. The plan envisioned *General der Infanterie* Wöhler's *Heeresgruppe Süd*, consisting of the *6. SS-Panzer-Armee*, the *6. Armee*, the *8. Armee*, and the Hungarian 3rd Army, breaking out of the bottleneck between Lakes Balaton and Velencze, while *General der Artillerie* de Angelis's *2. Panzer-Armee* attacked due east from south of Lake Balaton. The objective was the Danube.

On 1 March 1945, *Heeresgruppe Süd* had the largest concentration of armor the German Army still had. At the disposal of the field-army group were five Army armored divisions (1st, 3rd, 6th, 13th, and 23rd), three SS armored divisions ("*Wiking*," "*Totenkopf*," and "*Frundsberg*")[3] and one Hungarian (2nd). The remaining field-army groups on the Eastern Front had considerably fewer armor formations. There was no question that the main effort on the German side was in Hungary. The divisions moved during the first days of March to the jumping-off points for the last German offensive of the Second World War. During the evening of 4 March, the *3. Panzer-Division* moved from its quartering area around Balatonkenese, reaching its staging area the next morning. The columns moved via Polgardi and Szabadbattyan to Stuhlweißenburg. The soldiers were astonished to see German for-

---

3. Three other SS armored divisions were in theater: *"Leibstandarte SS Adolf Hitler," "Das Reich,"* and *"Hohenstaufen."*

mations on all the roads around them. Field army–level artillery moved forward and rocket-launcher batteries were in position. Heavy tank battalions with the *Königstiger*, the last and most heavily armed and armored main battle tank to be fielded by the German Army, were to be seen. No one knew exactly what was happening. Rumors flew. Soldiers started talking about breaking through to the Romanian oil fields and similar nonsense.

The sixth of March dawned cold and windy. It was 0400 hours. An ear-deafening din from artillery disrupted the stillness of the morning. Guns of all calibers flung their shells towards the Russian main battle area. The guns of the divisional artillery remained silent. This time, the *3. Panzer-Division* was not in the first wave. Instead, it was to follow after the lead divisions had broken through the enemy front. The division's soldiers could observe the hurricane of fire from their quarters southwest of Stuhl-weißenburg. The medical personnel established a temporary clearing station in Falu-Battyan. The next few days were spent in a slow wait, waiting for the word to move out. On 9 March, the command post moved to Szabadbattyan, and *Panzergrenadier-Regiment 3* moved to Stuhl-weißenburg, where the regimental headquarters was set up in the building of the radio station.

The offensive moved slowly. *Generalleutnant* Thunert's *1. Panzer-Division*, which formed the spearhead of the *III. Panzer-Korps*, attacked in the direction of Belsö-Bar from Föveny. Its regiments churned their way through the muck and the Russian antitank-gun belts. The enemy was prepared for the offensive and employed his superior air power, including U.S. bombers. The aerial attacks were directed against the quartering area, with the result that the formations suffered casualties even before their actual commitment.

Finally, on 9 March, orders arrived: "Get ready to move out." The division moved out the next day. The columns departed during the night and

reached the area around Felsö-Zeresceny, moving via Seregélyes. The *6. Panzer-Division* had been inserted into the line to the left of the *3. Panzer-Division*, while the *1. Panzer-Division* moved farther north in an effort to cut off the enemy forces west of Lake Velencze from the south.

Starting at 0900 hours, the divisional artillery fired a preparation, with the vehicles moving forward. The enemy had expected the attack and immediately employed his airpower. Soviet bombers and fighter-bombers bombed and strafed without interruption. The air was filled with a continuous din. The losses sustained the first hour were large. Within a short period, the *3./Panzergrenadier-Regiment 3* lost all of its *SPW's*. The *SPW* of the battalion commander of the *II./Panzergrenadier-Regiment 3*, *Hauptmann* Seifert, received a direct hit. The commander was badly wounded and two of his personnel in the vehicle, *Feldwebel* Stülcken and *Obergefreiter* Nowack, were killed.

The attack of the *3. Panzer-Division* could not develop, even after a battle group under *Oberst* Bradel of the *1. Panzer-Division* came to its aid. Supplies were no longer getting forward. Enemy bombers made it impossible to move. In addition, the gigantic marshland between lake Velencze and Seregélyes blocked the terrain. As a result, *Kampfgruppe Medicus* lagged far to the rear. The main effort of the offensive had shifted to the south, where most of the enemy formations were positioned. *General der Panzertruppen* Breith's *III. Panzer-Korps* was literally stuck in the mud on 12 March. Only *General der Kavallerie* Harteneck's *I. Kavallerie-Korps* gained some ground that day—in the direction of Fünfkirchen—with its *3.* and *4. Kavallerie-Divisionen* and the *44. Reichsgrenadier-Division "Hoch- und Deutschmeister."*

The mud and the Red Air Force hampered the continuation of the offensive over the next few days. The two tank battalions of *Hauptmann* Schramm and *Hauptmann* Voigts were only able to crawl their way forward by the meter. The mechanized infantry were at least able to hold on to the ground already gained, while the combat engineers attempted to clear movement routes. Movement during the day was barely possible, since the Red Air Force was almost always in the sky. The division was unable to make any more progress and had to content itself with straightening out the front lines. On 13 March, *Major* Schulze's *I./Panzergrenadier-Regiment 3*, supported by the *2./Panzer-Regiment 6* (*Oberleutnant* Blaich), attacked Juliamayor. Despite extremely heavy antitank defenses, the attack succeeded. That night, however, the battle group had to pull back. The night was as unsettled as always. It was not until the following morning that all of the companies had reassembled. At 1100 hours, the mechanized infantry prepared to attack again. But two hours passed, before the necessary artillery support could be obtained. *Leutnant* Heydebreck's *2./Panzergrenadier-Regiment 3* was the spearhead. The *SPW's* moved out of the woods at 1300 hours, raced down the slope, broke through the surprised Russians in their main line of resistance, entered Juliamayor and took the city in a *coup de main.*

The regimental commander and the battalion commander observed the dashing attack from the high ground. The enemy remained quiet, with the exception of individual machine-gun and small-arms fire coming from the right. All of a sudden, *Oberstleutnant* Weymann collapsed. He had been shot in the head. His *SPW* immediately rolled to the rear with the badly wounded man, but the division surgeons were unable to help him. The regimental commander was taken to the head trauma unit of the SS hospital in Haimaskar and then on to Steinamanger. The battle-tested and brave commander of the regiment died there of his wound. *Major* Schulze assumed acting command of the regiment, while *Hauptmann* Treppe took over the 1st Battalion. Another regimental commander of the division was wounded that dreary day as well. *Major*

Bösang, the new acting commander of *Panzergrenadier-Regiment 394*, was also wounded, but he remained with his troops.

On 14 March, the *3. Panzer-Division* joined the rest of the divisions in the *III. Panzer-Korps*—*1.* and *6. Panzer-Divisionen*—in the general attack south of Lake Velencze. The Soviets defended stubbornly. German artillery, tanks and mechanized infantry pounded the Soviet positions. That operation was praised in the official Soviet history of the war as follows: "They were the very last German attacks that forced the Red Army into the defense." Even if that statement is a bit disturbing, it also fills those surviving veterans of the *3. Panzer-Division* with some satisfaction that they were among the last German forces that showed themselves superior to the Soviets.

The two mechanized infantry regiments and the armored regiment continued to fight on, from farmstead to farmstead, from one patch of woods to the next and from one piece of high ground to another. The *I./Panzer-Regiment 6* supported *Panzergrenadier-Regiment 3* in its attack on Orekegi. The *SPW's* of both battalions suffered terribly under the mortar fire. The companies were able to take the railway embankment in front of the city. They were unable to proceed any further; a Russian antitank-gun belt could not be broken. The *SPW's* halted and waited for the first *Panthers*. Then the mechanized infantry heard armor rolling up from behind. It was the 2nd Company. The tanks went into position on a rise and took identified Russian positions under fire. The first fighting vehicle that attempted to cross the railway embankment was knocked out by antitank guns. The second vehicle suffered the same fate. It was taken out by tank rounds. Stalin tanks rolled slowly towards the railway embankment, where the mechanized infantry were defenseless against them.

Oberleutnant Blaich, the commander of the 2nd Company and a Knight's Cross recipient, recognized the threat that was posed. He ordered: *"Panzer marsch."* The remaining vehicles of his company churned their way forward with howling engines. They stopped to fire and then rolled on again. The first Stalin went up in the air, but a *Panther* was also knocked out. A tough tank engagement followed.

No one wanted to yield ground. A flame shot out of the tank of the company commander. *Hauptmann* Treppe, who was nearby in his *SPW*, raced over to the stricken tank. The mechanized infantry took the wounded crew on board. The brave company commander, who had once been a member of the *Legion Condor*, remained behind in his tank; he was dead.

Hauptmann Treppe ordered the force back. The Soviets fired at the withdrawing forces with 17.2- and 7.62-centimeter guns. The edge of the woods northeast of Juliamayor was reached hours later, but there was no quiet to be found there. Russian artillery fired on the force with uncanny precision. A direct hit impacted on the command post. *Funk-Unteroffizier* Thom and *Gefreiter* Grathwohl were killed; the 1st Battalion adjutant, *Oberleutnant* Grotefend, and *Unteroffizier* Drews were badly wounded. Slightly wounded were the signals officer, *Leutnant* Stoellen, and *Funk-Unteroffizier* Tenning.

After taking twelve kilometers of ground slowly over the course of two days, the *3. Panzer-Division* could advance no farther. Forty percent of all of the tanks were lost or disabled. *Generalmajor* Söth therefore decided to call off the attack. The regiments set up for the defense.

The Soviets were being reinforced by the hour. Barrage fire broke out along the entire front in Hungary at first light on 16 March. The vastly superior divisions of the 2nd and 3rd Ukrainian Fronts moved out on their offensive to the west that morning. The main line of resistance of the Hungarian 3rd Army and the *IV. SS-Panzer-Korps* was broken through. Russian tanks pressed on toward Tes and took the high ground of the Bakony Woods. By doing so, the enemy was already far to the rear of the *6. SS-Panzer-Armee*,

the *I. Kavallerie-Korps*, and the *III. Panzer-Korps* on the first day of his offensive. All of those major formations were still southeast of lakes Balaton and Velencze. On 16 March, the *5. SS-Panzer-Division "Wiking"* turned back a frontal attack against Stuhlweißenburg. At that point, the field army group issued orders to pull back.

The forces of the *III. Panzer-Korps* remained in their positions along the main line of resistance on 17 March. The *6. SS-Panzer-Armee*, positioned farther to the south, as already pulling back to the rear between Lakes Balaton and Velencze to establish a front oriented north. The Soviet artillery fire in front of the sector of the *3. Panzer-Division* grew more intense. The corps pulled back during the night. During the morning of 18 March, the *1. Panzer-Division*, the *44. Grenadier-Division "Hoch- und Deutschmeister,"* the *3. Panzer-Division*, and the *356. Infanterie-Division* (from left to right) reached the area southeast of Polgardi, where contact was established with the *I. Kavallerie-Korps*. Most of the *3. Panzer-Division* was still holding out in a small bridgehead around Seregélyes. The situation was completely confused. The divisional artillery fired to three sides. The only way open was to the west. The Soviets were already south of Stuhlweißenburg, however, and were threatening the one escape route. The division command post moved to Külsörbarand, south of the Stuhlweißenburg airfield, on 19 March.

The Russians moved into the beautiful Hungarian metropolis on that day and, on 20 March, advanced south. The *3. Panzer-Division* was the last division to remain in position. The *1.* and *6. Panzer-Divisionen* and the *5. SS-Panzer-Division "Wiking"* had already pulled back to the west. Russian armored forces broke through in the sector of the *I. Kavallerie-Korps* south of Lake Balaton, advancing to the north banks of the lake. New Soviet forces staged between Lepseny and Polgardi. The two Soviet attack wedges were only ten kilometers apart. If the pincers closed, the *III. Panzer-Korps* would be lost.

Farther east of the pincers were the *3. Panzer-Division* and the *44. Reichsgrenadier-Division "Hoch- und Deutschmeister."*

The confusing state of affairs during that time and, indeed, during the final weeks of the war, is demonstrated in the diary entries of *Unteroffizier* Wietersheim, who vividly describes the daily routine of a tank crew:

> 20 March. It was directed to evacuate Seregélyes. Our assault gun received orders to blow up a bridge and a mill with a few people from a recently formed *Luftwaffe* field division. Around 1700 hours, we moved forward. The *Luftwaffe* people were all newcomers. For example, where a rifle shot was heard at some distance, they all thought it was an artillery impact.— Well, then. We executed the order and moved back into the village. All of a sudden, the report came in that the Russians were at one end of the one-street village with tanks. Before we could comprehend, a lot of wild firing started. The roofs of a few farm buildings immediately caught fire. I could not fire, since I could not see anything. We were radioed orders to pull back to the west. Just outside of the village, we got stuck in marshland. A *Panther* hooked up in front of us. Since we had to use our flashlights a bit in order to see anything, a "hooded crow" spotted us and started dropping his "eggs,"[4] which started going off about forty to fifty meters away. All of us were on our bellies underneath the vehicle. The *Panther* then also got stuck in the muck and was unable to free itself. It was only with the help of another *Panther* that we got out several hours later.
>
> 21 March. Around first light, we were positioned a few kilometers west of Seregélyes, prepared to support a battalion from *Panzergrenadier-Regiment 394*—two *Panzer IV's* and our assault gun (vehicle commander: *Unteroffizier* Grünhagen). We checked our weapons. Visibility was especially good. All of a sudden, I saw artillery impacts and clouds of smoke on the horizon, about two kilometers distant. That was our grenadiers, who had to pull back in the face of Russian tanks. Eleven were reported. The three of us immediately moved forward, occupied a good reverse-slope position and waited. Each vehicle had a specific sector to observe Through the gun optics, I could make out a row of trees, a flat field and a small rise about 1,000 meters away. The infantry was already far behind us. A turret edged its way above the crest. I took aim and waited, until I had the bottom of the turret in sight, and fired.
>
> Hit. The crew bailed out. The crate was already starting to burn along the rear deck. Even so, the vehicle moved backwards. I gave it another round. A shot of flame. It was all over. The turret lifted itself off its race and landed next to the chassis.
>
> Another T-34 pushed its way forward close to the stricken tank. Once again, I put the aiming point at the base of the turret and fired. The second tank was no more. By then, there was a wild firefight going on. *Leutnant* Schoch was able to knock out another T-34. The terrain had turned hazy from the smoke. I was able to knock out an enemy assault gun. All the way to the right, about 1,700 meters away, was a Stalin. They were dangerous. All three vehicles took it under fire, but all the rounds ricocheted. Another three rounds. It turned away. We breathed a sigh of relief. The six hits must have really shaken them up.

---

4. Soldier slang for the nuisance bombers that constantly flew over the German lines at night, with the metaphor extended to include the bombs as "eggs."

A *Panther* from the 1st Battalion came to support us. It was just in time, as another two T-34's appeared, racing like crazy towards the vehicle of *Leutnant* Schoch. Schoch knocked out one of them, while the *Panther* took care of the other one. It only took a matter of seconds.

That same day, our small group had to turn back seven attacks by Russian infantry, with a 2-centimeter *Flak* coming in especially handy. The Russians came with their sleeves rolled up, helmets on their heads and rifles in their hands. The commissars drove the people in front of them with shovels and other types of blunt instruments. About thirty meters in front of us, they got into the tangle of trench line and fired like crazy at us with their rifles. In addition, there was some nasty mortar fire.

All of a sudden, there was an impact. Smoke in the vehicle; the rear deck had been hit. Looking through the rear vision block, I saw that it was starting to catch fire. But a few water canisters that had been hit and were emptying their contents put out the flames right away. Our clothes were a mess, though.

The Russians came again after 1400 hours. In the second attack, a few of them made it all the way to us and climbed up on our vehicle. I drew the neighboring tank's attention to them, and it placed some well-aimed fires on the Russians, sending them to heaven or someplace else. Nonetheless, it was an uncomfortable situation for us. My gun optics had been shattered. The order to pull back and cover the other vehicles pulling back came at just the right time . . .

The situation grew increasingly worse. The German batteries east of lake Balaton fired the last of their ammunition. Most of the *I. Kavallerie-Korps* and the *6. SS-Panzer-Armee* had got-ten out through Veczprem. Only the *1.*, *3.*, and *23. Panzer-Divisionen*, the *44. Reichsgrenadier-Division "Hoch- und Deutschmeister"*, and the remnants of differing units were south of Stuhlweißenburg. On 21 March, the corps ordered a withdrawal to the Sárviz Canal. *Hauptmann* Schubert's *Panzer-Nachrichten-Abteilung 39* was able to manage to maintain communications with all of the formations. The medical personnel evacuated the clearing stations in Berhida, Zirc and Veczprem. The last clearing station to be evacuated was the one in Polgardi, which was run by *Leutnant* Fritzsche's 2nd Platoon (1st Medical Company). It had treated 840 wounded. The evacuation of the wounded to the rear got caught up in a bombing raid on Varaslöd, which caused even more wounded and dead.

Starting at midnight on 22 March, the *3. Panzer-Division* started pulling back with its initial elements. *Oberstleutnant* Schulenburg's *Panzer-Regiment 6* had already been sent to the northwest. The enemy had already occupied Polgardi with about eighty tanks and was threatening the last retreat route. The armored regiment had been directed to attack that enemy force and hold open a narrow escape route. The reconnaissance battalion formed the lead element of the division. *Heeres-Flak-Abteilung 314* formed the rearguard. At 0230 hours, *Leutnant* Griessenbeck of the 1st Company of the signals battalion removed the last lateral landline to the neighboring division, the *44. Reichsgrenadier-Division "Hoch- und Deutschmeister."* The latter division, under the command of *Generalleutnant* Rost, was completely exhausted and burned out; it barely had any weapons or horses left. The remnants of the brave Austrian division established contact with the *1. Panzer-Division*, which was temporarily encircled at Jenö. Both of the divisions fought their way westward with difficulty. In that final round of fighting, Rost and many of his officers were killed.

That signaled the start of a terrible retrograde movement. Those that experienced it would never forget. A sampling of some firsthand accounts:

> Departure of the division headquarters to break through the pocket. Moved via Falubattyan and Polgardi, then cross-country as far as Csajag, and then on to Balatonkenese. We just made it through and got there by noon. A *Tiger*, which was providing cover for us to the north of Polgardi, was knocked out right at the moment we were passing by. Extremely intense artillery, mortar and machine-gun fire at five different places. At Polgardi, we moved on the hill, which was under fire, and then down the other side, also under fire. All of the heavy weapons, most of which had no ammunition, moved along in the trek as long as there was enough fuel and the terrain was not too marshy. Many simply remained behind.
>
> To the left of us was Lake Balaton, then the vegetation along the banks, our road and, to the right, the upward slopes of the hills. It was impossible to get off the road. We asked the driver of the ammunition truck how much he had on board. At that point, the column was attacked from the air. We were able to make it to cover with our last jump. The ammo truck burned. Large quantities of small-arms ammunition burned out. We had to wait a long time before the truck finally exploded. While that was happening, Russian fighter-bombers attacked us. Just get out of here. We crawled past the burning truck and reached our field mess. But there was no movement; the road was jammed. Finally, we started rolling again.
>
> Our Horch moved across the softened-up field paths, meadowlands, and creeks. Another trench that had only been flattened out to a bare minimum. The vehicle lurched forward; the front wheels buried deeply. No getting out under our own power. Russian riflemen were getting ever closer. Time was of the essence. Since the front axle was broken, it was all over. Continue on by foot. It was difficult, since we frequently had to seek cover. Finally did it. I ran into a crazy mix of soldiers. Horse-drawn and motorized. Many wounded . . . vehicles of all types . . . a few tanks, *SPW's*, and trucks. We set up an all-round defense.
>
> Fighter-bomber and bomber attacks increased. The roads and trails were jammed. It was only by dint of great effort that those in charge were able to keep traffic moving. While most of the division rolled back, other elements provided cover. Ivan surprised us just outside a patch of woods outside of Balatonkenese. He had us in his pincers, approaching our column from both the left and right. Rounds rang out, and machine guns rattled in between. Antitank guns barked. Gasping, we reached the woods, which offered us concealment. But even there many comrades were killed or others started the long road to captivity.

As the night of 23 March came to a close, most of the *3. Panzer-Division* had gotten around the northern corner of Lake Balaton and reached the area around Veczprem. The division command staff, which had just managed to escape being attacked at its command post in the gunpowder factory at Balaton-Füzfö, moved to Vilmos mjr. The divisions was attached to the *IV. SS-Panzer-Korps* and received orders to defend Veczprem. Up to then, elements of the *1. SS-Panzer-Division "Leibstandarte SS Adolf Hitler"* had been employed there, but they soon took off. The *3. Panzer-Division* was all by itself in that sector without any heavy weapons.

The division did not have to wait long for the Soviets. Starting at 0300 hours, heavy artillery fire was placed on the city, which had already been bombed to pieces. Enemy tanks appeared in the northeast. Since there were insufficient armor-defeating weapons on hand, the city was evacuated of all rear-area-service personnel, the trains and the wounded. The civilian populace sought protection in the large air-raid shelter at the cloister. The groups of enemy tanks slowly approached the city. Fifty T-34's then raced as fast as lightning down the outer streets. They overran the weak outposts and ejected the rearguard of the division from the city around 1400 hours. The division pulled back expeditiously to the west. Patrols reported large groups of armor attacking from all sides. It became apparent that the enemy wanted to cut off the division while it was still at Lake Balaton.

Since there was a lack of fuel, a lot of vehicles had to be blown up. It was no longer possible to command intact units and formations. Every commander attempted to get his force to the west on his own initiative. During the afternoon of 24 March, the signals battalion was able to establish a link between the division operations officer and the commander of the neighboring *1. Panzer-Division*. *Major i.G.* Rotberg and *Generalleutnant* Thunert discussed ways the divisions could operate together, since no superior headquarters could be reached. The momentary strength of the two divisions was about that of a mechanized infantry regiment.

All of a sudden, patrols of the *Waffen-SS* and the military police appeared at all of the street corners to check vehicles and papers. A corps order was brought forward by liaison officers, which stated that no tanks were to pull back as long as they had ammunition. This type of order had long since been overcome by events.

On 24 March, the *3. Panzer-Division* evacuated Kövesgyür and moved in the direction of Leanyfalu. The command post was established there, and a main clearing station rapidly set up.

The Russians were already there by night and engaged the division sector at first light on Palm Sunday. Although the outposts were able to turn back the first attack, they could not hold out for long. The main enemy forces had closed up by noon and broke through to Nemes-Nagyvascono with several T-34's. A planned defense was impossible. *Panzergrenadier-Regiment 3* was only able to escape encirclement by marching out on foot. The regiment had only four *SPW's* left. The prime movers were employed in towing the supply trucks and the medical vehicles in an effort to bring good essential for the sustenance of life to the rear. The division pulled back further to the southwest. *Hauptmann* Treppe, the commander of the *I./Panzergrenadier-Regiment 3*, was killed during that action by an antitank rifle round. *Hauptmann* Koblitz assumed acting command of the battalion.

Since the Soviets continued in their efforts to envelop the German forces from the north and press them against Lake Balaton, the *3. Panzer-Division* received orders on 26 March to disengage from the front towards the east and guard the corps from the north. The formations pushed forward once more towards the outskirts of the Bakony Woods. It was not possible to occupy the designated positions everywhere, since the Red Air Force attacked the division's formations in waves. The command staff moved to Zalahalápz. The divisional signals battalion also arrived there and established landlines with all of the division's battle groups during the night. *Panzergrenadier-Regiment 3* screened at Sümeg. The first few Stalin tanks that appeared there could be stopped, allowing elements of the *5. SS-Panzer-Division "Wiking"* and the *1. Gebirgs-Division* to pull back to the west.

On 27 March, the *3. Panzer-Division* was not in a position to stop the Russian advance. There was a lack of all types of ammunition for the weapons, fuel for the vehicles, and personnel for the fight. The Russian tanks often got to a crossroads faster than the division's forces, which had been ordered to occupy them. *Leutnant* Griessenbeck of the 1st Company of the signals battalion wrote the following in his diary on 27 March:

> A short while later, Russian tanks in front of the village. I wanted to take down the lines and saw the tanks that had broken through and the attacking infantry when I looked down the road in the direction of the headquarters. Turned around immediately with the section and headed off in the direction of Sümeg. Everyone was fleeing back down the road. . . . It was mostly soldiers, who had no idea of the general situation, who abandoned their vehicles. A panic ensued. All of a sudden, T-34's also appeared off in the woods to the right, about 800 meters away. Horses bolted; tack was ripped off. In front of us was a heavy vehicle, a radio vehicle from the artillery, and an ambulance in front of it. Most of the vehicles got stuck in the mud, including the ambulance. We went to Sümeg with four vehicles that made it through. Elements of *Panzer-Aufklärungs-Abteilung 3* were in position along the left side of the road. They yelled at us: "The Russians are coming.

The movement back became a long, continuous torture. The soldiers were hungry, tired and apathetic. They had only one desire: To get as quickly as possible to the west. Sümeg, which was defended by elements from all of the division, had to be evacuated in the afternoon. The headquarters moved to Zalazentgrot, but it was pushed out during the night by Russian tanks. The forces were pulling back everywhere. The remnants of *Panzergrenadier-Regiment 394* were the last forces to leave Baltavar early in the morning of 28 March. The corps had ordered the front to be held. *Generalmajor* Söth issued his own orders and directed his division to the Raab, to establish a bridgehead at Eisenburg.

The *IV. SS-Panzer-Korps* arrived at the Raab in the course of 28 March with its divisions, the *1.* and *3. Panzer-Divisionen* and the *5. SS-Panzer-Division "Wiking."* The enemy immediately pursued and penetrated in the sector of the *1. Panzer-Division*. The battle groups of the *3. Panzer-Division* were able to hold their positions. Behind them, the various units and formations were flooding across the broad river in the direction of Steirmark in Austria. Some trains elements, maintenance services and supply columns were already within the Reich. The Soviets attacked from Steinamanger to the southwest and pressed towards Körmend. Once again, the danger arose that the *3. Panzer-Division* could be encircled. All non-essential vehicles were rapidly sent through Körmend on the road to Graz. There were crazy scenes on display. At one place, oxen were used to tow a few trucks; at another, one prime mover was towing twenty different vehicles.

The Russians advanced again on 30 March. The *I./Panzergrenadier-Regiment 3* temporarily defended the palace at Körmend. Every unit commander was completely responsible for the forces entrusted to him, since he was often the only command authority for some distance. The corps was no longer in control. It had pulled back without notifying the division. *Generalleutnant* Thunert, as the senior officer, assumed command of the *3. Panzer-Division* in addition to his own *1. Panzer-Division*. He directed the bridgehead at Eisenburg be evacuated. To that end, he received permission from the commander in chief of the *6. Armee*, *General der Panzertruppen* Balck, while discussing the option with the commanding general of the *III. Panzer-Korps*. The enemy had already passed through Körmend to the west and was establishing a bridgehead on the Raab.

The first elements of the division crossed the borders of the Reich at Heiligenkreuz that day. The rear-area services moved through Fürstenfeld to Altenmarkt. The 1st Medical Company set up a main clearing station in Heiligenkreuz.

The 2nd Medical Company was still on Hungarian soil, where it tended to the casualties occurring there. While the trains of the division found themselves back on German soil after three and one-half years of operations at the front, the men of the two mechanized infantry regiments, the antitank battalion, the antiaircraft battalion, the artillery and the engineers were still fighting around Körmend.

Since the Soviets were already advancing on Güssing on 31 March, the *3. Panzer-Division* received orders to evacuate Hungary and pull back to the so-called Reich Protective Position. The clearing stations were pulled back to Fürstenfeld. The division headquarters moved to St. Nikolaus, near Güssing. The command post of *Panzergrenadier-Regiment 3* was established in Reinersdorf. With that, the soldiers of the division left foreign territory on 31 March 1945. The division had returned to the Reich, albeit in a manner much different than they had imagined when they moved out in the East in 1941.

CHAPTER 11

From the Raab to the Enns: The Fateful End of the Division

Easter, 1945. It was the last Christian holiday of that unchristian war. The German Armed Forces had been beaten on all fronts. The Allied field-army groups were in Germany. The Soviet armored wedges were driving on Berlin. The Red Army had reached the borders of the Reich on the southeast. The *6. Armee* of *General der Panzertruppen* Balck saved its field divisions by moving into the Steiermark. Most of the fighting and other vehicles, as well as the heavy guns, had been blown up or abandoned in Hungary . . .

After conquering Hungary, the 2nd and 3rd Ukrainian fronts prepared for their last attack into the territory of the Reich. The 2nd Ukrainian Front advanced in the direction of Vienna. Its armor and rifle formations reached the outskirts of the Austrian capital in the first days of April and, effective 6 April, entered the city proper. The 3rd Ukrainian Front advanced into the Steiermark. Its divisions were given the mission of taking Graz. The Armed Forces Daily Report of 1 April commented laconically on that fighting: "To the south of Steinamanger, our forces are involved in intense defensive fighting against the Bolsheviks pressing on the borders of the Reich."

The *1.* and *3. Panzer-Divisionen* and the *1. Gebirgs-Division* took up hasty positions behind the German border. The populace living there knew nothing yet of the horror of war. It was only when the first Hungarian refugees, arriving on Easter after having made it through the woods, told them about the horrific scenes in their homeland that the people of the

Steiermark knew for the first time what it meant when it was said that the Russians were coming. The communications center of the *3. Panzer-Division* intercepted a message from the *Führer* Headquarters during the afternoon of 1 April, which stated that "not a single meter of ground was permitted to be given up any more."

The two armored divisions formed battle groups that Sunday, which advanced into the Raab Valley and attempted to hold up the advancing enemy tanks. In the process, the strength of the enemy forces was supposed to be determined, as well as enabling any potential German formations to pass through the lines. *Major* Medicus, the commander of *Panzerjäger-Abteilung 543*, led the battle group of the division, which was composed of the last remaining tanks, self-propelled guns and *SPW's*. The armored element of the *1. Panzer-Division*, as well as its *Panzergrenadier-Regiment 113*, staged to the right of Medicus's group. On the morning of 1 April, the two battle groups rolled out and into the Raab Valley. The elements of the *1. Panzer-Division* entered Feldbach and drove the Russians out. The battle group of *Major* Medicus took Vasszentmihály at 1030 hours and occupied the important road hub. But because the formations had to be stingy with every liter of fuel, they pulled back again in the evening. The success of the operation was evidenced by the fact that the enemy was prevented from making a surprise penetration into the Reich Protective Position.

The division regrouped and formed new battle groups. Reserves were created, and the maintenance sections repaired the damaged vehicles as quickly as they could. The weapons were cleaned and maintained and the wounded are taken care of. Elements of the *Volkssturm* and the *Hitlerjugend*[1] were employed securing crossroads and closing gaps in the front.

The morning of 2 April belonged to the enemy air forces. American bombers—268 in all—approached from the north and dropped

their bombs on the division's forces. There was nothing that could be done against them, and the soldiers were forced to endure the punishment. As a counterbalance, an armor raid into the Raab Valley was planned for the afternoon. This time, it was executed by *Panzergrenadier-Regiment 3*, the *1./Panzergrenadier-Regiment 394*, and *Panzer-Aufklärungs-Abteilung 3*. The *SPW's* advanced in a bold approach from out of the wooded mountains down into the valley. Russian truck and panje columns were moving along the road, unaware of what was about to happen. The machine guns rattled, and the Soviets fled. The mechanized infantry and reconnaissance personnel rolled on. Vasszentmihály, Rátot, Gastony, Renck and Alsö were reoccupied. The enemy forces in those villages were ejected and fled to the rear. Numerous trucks and mortars were captured. In addition to finding a lot of civilian clothing on one truck, 7,000 cigarettes were found. The Hungarians were happy that the German soldiers were there. The soldiers released fifty young women and girls that the Soviets had barricaded in the basement of a house and had wanted to haul off that evening.

The battle group set up an all-round defense that night in Vasszentmihály. When it dawned on 3 April, enemy trucks approached again. The mechanized infantry positioned themselves at the outskirts of the town in concealed positions in their *SPW's*. "Fire at will." The first enemy vehicle flew into the air with a monstrous detonation. It had had mines on board. The explosion was so intense, that many houses were destroyed. The remaining trucks halted, turned and took off. German machine-gun fire chased them down the road. The battle group was able to refuel with many canisters of captured Russian fuel, which was worth more than gold at that point.

The division ordered the battle group back behind the border on 4 April. Since strong Russian forces had succeeded in breaking through the front farther north, the division had to be

---

1. The *Volkssturm* was a "people's" militia consisting largely of those either too old or otherwise unfit for normal military service. The *Hitlerjugend* was the "Hitler Youth."

prepared for any eventuality. The division regrouped again, so that it could be prepared to defend.

At the beginning of April, the division had only six operational tanks. There were an additional thirty at the maintenance companies that were in an "incurable" condition. Since there were hardly any tanks left and most of the artillery had been lost, the armored elements had to be greatly reduced in personnel. New units were formed for infantry duties. The divisional signals battalion provided the guard company for the division command post, since it no longer had any vehicles. The company consisted of one officer and seventy-five men, who were armed with five submachine guns, fifty rifles, and eleven *Panzerfäuste*. In addition, it had five *panje* wagons. The reconnaissance battalion formed a so-called alert company out of all of its assets; the company was attached to *Panzergrenadier-Regiment 3*.

On 4 April, *Panzerjäger-Abteilung 543* suffered a heavy loss. *Major* Medicus was killed in a fighter-bomber attack. The brave commander was buried the next day at the main clearing station in Walkersdorf. The antitank battalion was dissolved.

The situation at the front quieted down somewhat over the next few days. Either the Soviets had not yet closed up with their main body or they had turned off in the direction of Vienna. The first T-34's and Stalins turned up on the far side of the road to Graz, but they did not bother the divisional elements for the time being. The division was able to complete its regrouping at a relatively slow pace. *Major* Bösang's *Panzergrenadier-Regiment 394* conducted a reconnaissance-in-force in the direction of Heiligenkreuz. The locality was taken and held until 10 April. *Hauptmann* Seifert's *II./Panzergrenadier-Regiment 3* also remained forward of the Reich border and established a blocking position between Raab and the mountains of the Steiermark.

Rations at the time were extraordinarily good. The district leader of Fürstenfeld had provided the division with foodstuffs and smoking prod-

ucts, including 30,000 cigarettes. A second source was two supply trains that had been stranded at Güssing, since the Russians were already at the next train station. Chocolate, canned meat and other delights tickled the palate.

The Armed Forces Daily Report of the time: "In the German-Hungarian border area, formations of the Army and the *Waffen-SS* have brought the enemy advance in the direction of Graz to a standstill in days of hard offensive and defensive fighting."

The situation could not stay that way for long. Enemy fires increased by the day. Since the *3. Panzer-Division* and the neighboring forces had long since been outflanked to the north, it was planned to move the division back during the evening of 9 April. But before the columns could roll out, orders were received from the field-army group, which *Generaloberst* Rendulic had commanded since 25 March: "The *3. Panzer-Division* is to remain in the front salient."

Spring air wafted over the slopes of the Steiermark countryside on 10 April. In the morning, the Russian guns and rocket-launcher batteries roared up. The earth around Heiligenkreuz shook. The Soviets were attacking. Tank engines roared, machine guns rattled. The Soviet battle cry echoed: Urräh. The mechanized infantry fired for as long as they had ammunition. The losses sustained by *Panzergrenadierregiment 394*, which was in the center of the fighting, climbed. Casualties were also taken within the ranks of the tankers, antitank gunners and artillery gunners, who had been reassigned as infantry. They were less the results of battle and more along the lines of broken limbs and sprains. The tattered companies were in no position to stand up to the enemy's numerical superiority. The Russians entered Heiligenkreuz and took the important town from the regiment, which moved back through Poppendorf.

The *I./Panzergrenadier-Regiment 3*, positioned around Groß Mürbisch and Strem, was alerted at 1000 hours. The wounded collection point was in the *Gasthof Miklos*. There were twenty-six wounded German soldiers in the large hall. Miklos, the owner of the inn, transported the wounded men individually in his wagon to the main clearing station in Güssing, since there were no ambulances up front. The battalion attacked in the wooded terrain. The few *SPW's* rattled along the narrow road. The mountains climbed off to the left; off to the right, there was a sharp drop. The enemy's observers identified the attack, and the first artillery rounds started impacting. The commander's *SPW* was hit, as was the following vehicle. The burning vehicles blocked the route. Since the battalion could not properly deploy, the *SPW's* turned around and moved back. Fortunately, there were no further casualties.

Moving the long way around, the *I./Panzergrenadier-Regiment 3* was able to link up with *Panzergrenadier-Regiment 394*, where it was attached to *Major* Bösang. The enemy force was already so strong that the German elements were in a critical situation. The situation took on threatening dimensions. The division alerted all of its elements, since there was a danger it could be enveloped. The civilian populace was very nervous and prepared for the arrival of the Russians. In the end, however, the division was able to maintain its positions during the day.

The enemy pressure continued during the night. The division headquarters moved that morning to Tobaj. Only the landline section remained in St. Nikolaus until noon, in an effort to maintain communications with the battle groups. The situation grew ever more intense. The Russians had already advanced past the division on both the left and the right. Usually, penetrations in the lines could be temporarily sealed off and eliminated, but the arrival of the weak ready reserve was frequently too late.

Panzergrenadier-Regiment 3 was hastily committed at Rosenberg. A short while later, the *SPW's* made a hellish journey back to Güssing. The Soviet artillery of all calibers was firing at everything that moved. It was only possible to move through the streets of Güssing at eighty

kilometers an hour. The Güssing Palace was under artillery fire. Since the situation was becoming untenable, the division ordered a withdrawal for the coming night. At 2100 hours, the command staff moved to Kaltenbrunn.

Most of the division was able to disengage from the enemy in a disciplined manner, but it was no longer possible to conduct the retrograde movements under a tight rein. The few remaining Hungarian forces fled, causing the neighboring German companies to waver. *Hauptmann* Seifert's *II./Panzergrenadier-Regiment 3* was once again encircled during the night by the Russians. It took the mechanized infantry three hours to fight their way through. The last remaining platoons of the battalion reached the Austrian border at Moschendorf and Eberau at 0230 hours. It was later determined that Seifert's men represented the last battalion of the German Armed Forces to leave Hungarian soil.

During the day, *Panzergrenadier-Regiment 3* pulled back to the Kaltenbrunn area. The 1st Battalion of the regiment occupied positions along the 361-meter-high Himlerberg south of the village. The lead Soviet armored elements felt their way forward as far as this area by evening. *Volkssturm* elements from Steiermark attempted to put up resistance, but they were overrun. The older men of the *Volkssturm* and the teens of the *Hitlerjugend* took many casualties. The 1st Battalion pulled back to Dietersdorf to prepare for an immediate counterattack during the night. The morale from the division headquarters on down to the simplest *Landser* was not rosy. The placards pasted to the walls of the houses everywhere did not do much to lift spirits: "The *Panzerfaust* and the *Landser* are stronger then Red tanks."[2]

During the evening hours, the division pulled back again. The command staff moved to Altenmarkt. The main clearing station in Walkersdorf was taken down. The most important materiel was already on the road to the northwest. Both of the weak mechanized infantry regiments

---

2. It rhymes in the original German: *Panzerfaust und deutscher Landsers sind stärker als rote Panzer.*

remained in their positions. During the morning of 13 April, the *I./Panzergrenadier-Regiment 3* launched a mounted attack. It failed less as a result of enemy antitank measures and more to the terrain, which was ill suited for *SPW's*.

Since the Russians were pressing relentlessly, the battle groups engaged with the enemy could not hold. They yielded additional terrain on 14 April. Both of the mechanized infantry regiments pulled back to the Fürstenfeld area. The regiments established a new main line of resistance along the last remaining high ground of the Burgenland region, two kilometers in front of the city. The enemy did not relent anywhere. Russian tanks rolled against the clearing station in Rudersdorf. It was only by dint of great effort that the wounded could be evacuated in time. The reconnaissance company, which was employed on the left wing, evacuated Rudersdorf.

The division took precautions for a continued movement to the rear. The division's advance party departed at 1400 hours, in order to establish a new command post at the Kalsdorf Palace, near Ilz. The palace was abandoned; in some places, it had been plundered. The commander of the *1./Panzer-Nachrichten-Abteilung 39*, *Hauptmann* Schwarzenberger, was transferred. His replacement, *Leutnant* Neubauer, established landlines with the different command posts during the day. The command staff occupied the palace, located between Ilz and Sinabelkirchen, during the morning of 15 April.

There was nothing peaceful about that Sunday. The Soviets had pursued the divisional forces and had closed up during the night all around the high ground around Fürstenfeld. It was only quiet for a few hours on 15 April. All of a sudden, there was a howling and a hissing in the air, which signaled the start of a large attack. Heavy rounds from howitzers and rockets rained down on the pretty city. A hurricane of fire descended on the city that drove its citizenry into the deepest hiding places of its burning houses. Many of the buildings were in flames. In between the breaks in the firing, the rattling of tracked-vehicle movement could be heard. The Russians were coming.

Enemy tanks and rifle formations broke through the main line of resistance and threw the battalions back to Fürstenfeld. The mechanized infantry, combat engineers and cannoneers, joined by men of the *Volkssturm*, offered resistance to the Soviets at every street corner and building complex. Wild street fighting ensued. The many fleeing civilians made the fighting more difficult. Others implored, begged or even threatened the soldiers to spare their house or street. They were "full of it" and preferred an "ending in terror" that a "terror without end."

The *3./Panzergrenadier-Regiment 3* put up a stiff defense at the freight rail yard, but it was enveloped. The acting commander of *Panzergrenadier-Regiment 394*, *Major* Bösang, was badly wounded. Although he was evacuated from under fire by his people, he succumbed to his wounds the following day. *Major* Schulze, the acting commander of *Panzergrenadier-Regiment 3*, was slightly wounded and remained with his troops. Years later, 338 dead, including many soldiers of the *3. Panzer-Division*, would find their eternal resting place at the military cemetery there. It was only with great difficulty that the wounded could be evacuated to the temporary clearing stations that had been established at Wetzawinkel and Laßnitzhöhe. The most seriously wounded of the men were taken to the hospital in Fürstenfeld. Dr. Feischl, the terrific administrator of the hospital, took care of them, even when the Russians dwelled like wild animals in Fürstenfeld and the hospital later on.

All of the bravery of the soldiers was in vain. The enemy was stronger. After ten hours of heroic fighting, the meager forces of the division were pushed out of the city. The last German vehicle to leave Fürstenfeld was a captured T-34 that was manned by tankers of the armor regiment. It moved in reverse and fired at the Soviets as it departed. The battle groups put up a stubborn defense and established positions just outside the city along the road to Graz. Although Fürstenfeld had been lost, the front had remained cohesive. The Armed Forces Daily Report announced on 18 April: "In the

Austrian border area . . . repeated attacks by the Soviets . . . to both sides of Fürstenfeld . . . were turned back."

A restless night for the division came to a close. The division was badly battered. On the morning of 16 April, it had only two *Panthers*, twelve guns, two mortars, and four antitank guns with prime movers. That was all that remained of the division, which had once conducted a bold raid from the Bug to the Caucasus. The men set up in their positions in front of Altenmarkt. In some cases, the positions had been built by the local civilian populace over the last few weeks in a very professional manner. Unfortunately, there were no plans or sketches, so the units had to figure everything out for themselves. *Gefreiter* Laubach of the reconnaissance battalion has provided a vivid firsthand account of this period:

> The tankers and radio operators had become grenadiers. Armored car and tank commanders became section and platoon leaders in the infantry. It was a different type of fighting; different than the years of the victorious advances. The past few years had torn large gaps in the ranks. Many old comrades had to be left behind in foreign soil. Even more were no longer with the division as a result of their wounds. New, young faces were there, faces that had to endure the final fury of the war along with the old and proven men. The superiority of the Soviets was great. Our own combat power had sunk to a minimum; but our willpower to hold out. Companies of only twenty men held sectors that were not inconsequential.

The mechanized infantry, combat engineers and gunners could look into Fürstenfeld from their positions at Altenmarkt. Russian tanks, infantry and guns were closing in. The division could anticipate the Russian tank force to advance at any time. The forces quickly occupied their new main line of resistance. The rear-

area services primarily set up in Ilz. The first Soviet tanks and riflemen felt their way forward on 17 April. But they were not as strong as had been anticipated. Their attack could be turned back. Only the reconnaissance company employed on the left wing of *Panzergrenadier-Regiment 3* was pushed back. It was driven out of Stadtbergen, but it was able to collect itself 500 meters to the rear along the edge of the greening Buchenwald and establish itself there.

In a duel, the *SPW's* of the *I./Panzergrenadier-Regiment 3* eliminated two Russian antitank guns. Another example of the fighting of those days is offered by that of an unknown soldier. A forester by trade and a local to the area, he took two *Panzerfäuste* one night and snuck off to an inn, where two tanks and a self-propelled gone were located. He fired the first *Panzerfaust* through a window and into the room, where a battalion headquarters had established itself. Using the second antitank rocket, he eliminated the self-propelled gun. It exploded in a mighty blast that also took the T-34 next to it with it. He had truly earned his Iron Cross, First Class. The actions of the men of the *Volkssturm* should also not be forgotten. They became loyal helpers to the division's soldiers. For instance, the Siegel brothers cleared Russian minefields at night and collected unexploded ordnance during the day. *Volkssturmmann* Pappel served as a messenger for *Heeres-Flak-Abteilung 314*. These were but a few of many.

The division was able to maintain its positions for the next few days. The Soviets did not attack for some reason. They remained behind Fürstenfeld. The civilian populace, which had lost its houses or had fled, lived in dug-outs next to the livestock that had been saved. The Soviets were apparently diverting their tanks to Vienna. The soldiers found some time to take a breather and adjust to positional warfare. Higher levels of command attempted to maintain discipline by the issuance of drastic orders, which threatened executions. It was during this period that Hitler issued his last general order to the soldiers of the Eastern Front (16 April). It stated, among other things:

If, in the coming days and weeks, every soldier on the Eastern Front does his duty, then the last assault of Asia will be shattered, just like, in the end, the appearance of our enemy in the west will fail, despite everything.

Berlin will remain German, Vienna will be German again and Europe will never be Russian.

Form a band of brothers to defend. Not to defend an empty concept like the fatherland, but to defend your homeland, your wives and your children and, by doing so, our future.

At this hour, the entire German people look towards you, my warriors in the east, and only hope that the Bolshevik assault will drown in a bloodbath thanks to your steadfastness, your fanaticism, your weapons and your leadership.

In this moment, when fate took the greatest war criminal of all times [Franklin D. Roosevelt] from this earth, the war has reached a turning point.

The quiet days saw personnel changes. *Major* Rausche assumed command of *Panzergrenadier-Regiment 394*, which was in position in the Burgau area. The commander of *Heeres-Flak-Abteilung 314*, *Major* Fleischer, was transferred to a new duty position on 14 April. The *I./Panzergrenadier-Regiment 3* received its last commander in the person of *Hauptmann* Bürger. A few days later, on 21 April, the news arrived that *Generalmajor* Söth would be assuming a new duty position.

During this time, the division also presented high-level awards to deserving officers and enlisted personnel. Among them were Knight's Crosses for *Major* Schulze, *Oberleutnant* Bürger, and *Oberleutnant* Schirp. The final German Crosses in Gold were presented to *Oberleutnant* Aschermann and *Oberfeldwebel* Oehler of *Panzer-Regiment 6* and *Feldwebel* Potthoff of *Panzer-Aufklärungs-Abteilung 3*. In March, the same award had been presented to *Oberst* Fleis-

cher (*Panzergrenadier-Regiment 3*); *Hauptmann* Schramm and *Hauptmann* Voigts (battalion commanders in *Panzer-Regiment 6*); *Hauptmann* Schmidt (commander of the *II./Panzergrenadier-Regiment 394*); *Oberleutnant* Brümmer and *Oberleutnant* Blaich (*Panzer-Regiment 6*); *Feldwebel* Voutta (*Panzergrenadier-Regiment 394*); *Obergefreiter* Dickfoss (*Panzer-Aufklärungs-Abteilung 3*); and two deserving individuals of the rear-area services, *Major* Riessberger (division engineer) and *Inspektor* Sonnek (*Panzer-Nachrichten-Abteilung 39*).

The overall situation did not change much over the next few days. The Soviets brought up vehicles with loudspeakers on them, with which they initiated psychological warfare. Among other things, it was stated that an attack was to be expected on 23 April. The mechanized infantry prepared for it, but the attack never materialized. There were a few skirmishes between combat and reconnaissance patrols and an occasional artillery duel.

The medical personnel established a main clearing station in Ilz; it was to be the last one of the war. The men, who succumbed to their wounds, were buried at a nearby military cemetery. By the end of the war, there were seventy-nine graves there that belonged to the last fallen of the *3. Panzer-Division*. The 2nd Medical Company set up a secondary clearing station in Eggersdorf. The comrades who died there were laid to eternal rest at Gleisdorf. The ambulance company set up in Edelsbach. By order of the field army surgeon, *Generalarzt* Baumeister, the 2nd Medical Company was detached from the division in order to report directly to the field army.

Spring arrived in all its radiance and beauty in the hilly countryside of the Steiermark. All who experienced it stated that it was the nicest one in a long time. The soldiers "enjoyed" those days, as long as they were not in the main line of resistance or had to pull guard. In the rear-area quarters, there was even time for training, so as not to allow boredom to set in. On 24 April, the *6. Armee* ordered the formation of an anti-partisan detail, whose mission was to look for

Russians, who had broken through, downed aviators and deserters. The anti-partisan detail from the division was formed from the personnel of the signals battalion and consisted of *Leutnant* Griessenbeck, three noncommissioned officers, and ten enlisted personnel. It was outfitted with bicycles to make it mobile. A large-scale operation conducted by all the details from the divisions of the *6. Armee* on 28 April between Neudorf and Ilz yielded fourteen English prisoners of war and one soldier from *Panzergrenadier-Regiment 394* from out of the woods, where they had been hiding for days. Unfortunately, the number of cases of long-serving noncommissioned officers and enlisted soldiers who left their units increased during this time. They wanted to try to make their way home to distant Berlin or the Brandenburg province, which were undergoing their tragic end that week.

The situation in the sector of the *3. Panzer-Division* did not change. Even though there was no large-scale fighting, the news heard on the radio did nothing to lift spirits. Some of the men heard that the region they called home had already been overrun by Russian tanks. They knew that the Russians were already deep in Austria and that the Americans were approaching from their rear. They found out that some divisions, field armies and even field-army groups were capitulating on their own. It was learned on 1 May that Hitler was dead. The oath of allegiance to his successor, *Großadmiral* Dönitz, was only done in a mechanical fashion by most.

Oberst Schöne, previously assigned as a staff officer to the military delegation to the Reich Protectorate of Bohemia and Moravia, arrived on 2 May to assume acting command of the division. *Generalmajor* Söth left the division on 5 May. Acting on behalf of the *6. Armee*, he was sent to act as an emissary to the American forces. He was directed to try to bring about a ceasefire with the Allied commanders in chief or other commanders. If that did not succeed, he was then to establish a blocking position with motorized elements. To that end, he was given

Panzergrenadier-Regiment 3, *Panzer-Aufklärungs-Abteilung 3*, and what was left of *Panzer-Regiment 6*. Those formations were to move the same day to Gleisdorf.

They were greeted by a train there and rattled off on 7 May through Graz to Bruck an der Mur. The soldiers experienced a nice movement though wonderful countryside. The train stopped on open track in the evening. *Major* Schulze had his *Kübelwagen* off loaded in order to move forward to *Generalmajor* Söth. The battalion's soldiers jumped off the train to stretch their legs. Not too far from the railway embankment was a *Flak* position. The gunner got a big laugh and said that the war was already over. The men did not want to believe that. *Feldwebel* Simon of the *1./Panzergrenadier-Regiment 3* blew up and shouted: "If you don't want to fight any more, the 3rd will still remain solid." The men remained unfazed. When the train started to take off again, they jumped back on the cars, but not without first having "procured" some 2-centimeter *Flak* rounds for their own *SPW's*.

The train rolled through the next night and finally stopped at Liezen. The battalion detrained there and took up positions. *Hauptmann* Bürger had the men paid and their military identity books distributed. The paymaster and supply sergeant opened their stores and brought out the last of their rations. *Assistenzarzt* Dr. Moldenhauer reported on the health status of the force one last time. *Hauptmann* Bürger assembled the officers of his staff and had the troops march past. There were officers who openly wept. *Leutnant* Starke, the liaison officer of the battalion, moved ahead in a *Kübelwagen* in order to determine whether there were any additional orders. It was directed that the battalion move to the demarcation line at Rastadt an der Enns and screen the crossing of the division.

The commander in chief of the *6. Armee*, *General der Panzertruppen* Balck, held a commanders' conference in Gleisdorf on 7 May, in which all of the division commanders and commanding generals participated. The commander in chief issued the order that upon hearing the code word *Stabsauflösung* ("Headquarters Disbandment"), the field army was to disengage from the Russians and pull back to the American sector. The retrograde movement was planned in such a way that the formations of the field army were to continue to occupy lines of resistance and not give up the Steiermark for about two weeks.

Most of the *3. Panzer-Division* was in the Altenmarkt area at the time. The command staff and the initial elements moved back to Sinabelkirchen toward evening. The next morning, around 0630 hours, a message was radioed to the division in the clear that it was to evacuate the Steiermark in a single move and that it needed to reach the Enns River near Liezen and cross it no later than 0700 hours on 9 May. The formations that had not crossed the demarcation line by then would belong to the Soviets.

Oberst Schöne and his operations officer, *Major i.G.* Rotberg, issued appropriate orders that same hour. Starting at 0800 hours on 8 May, the division moved out in several serials. The *1. Gebirgs-Division* was to the left and the *1. Panzer-Division* to the right. *Panzer-Pionier-Bataillon 39* and elements of *Panzergrenadier-Regiment 394* were to remain in their positions another twenty-four hours to safeguard the rearward movement.

The departure of the force was blessed by magnificent sunshine. The Austrian civilian populace took down the tank obstacles everywhere and unfurled red-white-red banners.[3] Occasionally, armed civilians were encountered, who glumly allowed the columns to pass. There were scenes witnessed that were worse than those which could have been composed by a painter. *Leutnant* Griessenbeck has provided a firsthand account:

> In a small village after Bruck, Nicklasdorf, the locals had raised a red flag in addition to the flag of the Austrian Freedom Movement. I immediately ordered my men to fire on the red flag with signal flares.

Behind us, a 2-centimeter quad *Flak* of the railways opened fire on the red flag. Within a few minutes, it was like a firing range out of control. Result: The red flag was taken down. The retreat route was a crazy sight. All of the damaged vehicles or those without fuel were abandoned. "Get out and hitchhike." The vehicles were either pushed into the Mur or down slopes or burned. There were all types there: From Mercedes luxury cars to the Volkswagen. There were *Landser* items littering the way on both sides. In addition, there were all sorts of destroyed weaponry: Antitank guns, artillery pieces, machine guns, submachine guns, rifles, pistols etc. The last signal flares were fired off.

There was no more keeping the news about the capitulation under wraps. The troops knew it and, since they also knew the Soviets, they all wanted to get to the demarcation line on the Enns. The *I./Panzergrenadier-Regiment 3*, the field-army group reserve at the time, was disbanded and "sent home" by its commander. The men then tried to cover as much ground as possible in their *SPW's*. They passed through Mitterndorf, Bad Assee and Bad Ischl. They kept moving until American patrols put an end to their movements.

Most of the division was on the move all through the night of 9 May. The roads were hopelessly blocked. The civilian populace was reserved, if not already at arm's length. The discipline of the division did not suffer; no one removed the national insignia from his uniform. It was not until morning dawned that the effects of the news of the capitulation could be seen. Vehicles were abandoned or tipped over on the side of the road. In between them were mountains of personal belongings, weapons and rations. Any *Landser* was able to serve himself to whatever he wanted. The first units of the division were across the Enns at Liezen around

---

3. The traditional Austrian colors, as a sign of distancing themselves from the Third Reich.

0900 hours. There were only a few American soldiers there; they stood guard, chewing gum.

All of a sudden, at 1200 hours, the crossing point was blocked. *Generalmajor* Söth, who was at Liezen, was able to arrange with the Americans after exhausting discussions that the barriers be lifted for several more hours. The flood of German military continued to pour towards the river. Thousands of soldiers and fleeing civilians were jammed up at the bridge. In two and one-half hours, the line of traffic extended back twenty kilometers. Many of the soldiers attempted to get to the far bank by swimming. A few had to pay for that attempt in the cold and rapid waters with their lives. Finally, around noon, the crossing point was open again. Everything started streaming across the river.

Under the glaring heat of that 10 May, the soldiers of the *3. Panzer-Division* waited along the roads, open spaces and meadowlands of Liezen. All non-essential items had to be discarded, since the few vehicles were only there to transport people. The departure of the columns started that night and moved via the Pyhrn Pass, Windisch-Garsten, St. Pankraz, Micheldorf, St. Konrad, Gmunden, and Vöcklabruck. The troops were warmly received and greeted with wine and bouquets of flowers. The men's spirits started to lift. The morning of 11 May was marked with the most beautiful May weather imaginable. The columns rolled on, passing through Frankenmarkt, Straßwalchen, Mattighofen and Uttendorf (south of Braunau am Inn).

Frontline operations for the division had ended. Many, who had started the war in its ranks, were to be found buried somewhere on European battlefields. *Panzer-Regiment 6*, once the "Guards" armored regiment of the German Army, had suffered 92 officers and 581 enlisted personnel killed. The division found itself in the last assembly area of the *6. Armee*. That encompassed the area between Mattighofen and Braunau and consisted of ten individual camps. Twenty-thousand soldiers from all combat arms and about 3,000 vehicles flowed into those camps in the next few days. Later on, a total of 180,000 German soldiers were held there. The U.S. forces left the organization of the camps up to the *6. Armee. General der Panzertruppen* Balck commanded the camps just as he had commanded in wartime. He gathered capable officers in his staff. Since the quartermaster section of the field army was not in the camps, a new section was established, for which the *3. Panzer-Division* provided the responsible officers. The over-all administrator was the former administrative officer of the division, *Oberfeldintendant* Angermann, who had most recently held the same function in a *Waffen-SS* field army. The medical services were entrusted to *Oberfeldarzt* Dr. Stribny and vehicle matters to *Major* Riessberger. *Generalmajor* Söth assumed command of the camp for the *3. Panzer-Division*.

Since the weather was very nice then and the soldiers still had sufficient rations, life was not too difficult to take there initially. The Americans took very little interest on what was going on in the camps. Since the medical units had saved their materiel, it was also possible to provide medical services. The 1st Medical Company provided a source of drinking water for those parts of the camp that did not have access to wells or water lines. The troops kept as busy as they could. Sports competitions were held. The team fielded by the *I./Panzergrenadier-Regiment 394* won the final handball game of the camp tournament against a combined team from *Panzerjäger-Abteilung 543* and the division support command with a score of 3:2.

The American command authorities made their presence known starting on 14 May. U.S. officers and translators tried to determine branches, troop elements, and officers by means of deceptive measures. The elements of the *Waffen-SS* were transferred to Altheim, to the east of Braunau. It should be mentioned that the conditions there were not good, and the treatment by the camp personnel left a lot to be desired. The signals personnel were transported to Weng. *Oberst* Schöne and *Major i.G.* Rotberg took their leave of the signals personnel on 14 May.

The *3. Panzer-Division* ceased to exist without much fanfare after ten years. The first personnel to be discharged were on 17 May. Initially, it was only enlisted personnel originally from Austria. Rations grew more Spartan by the day, with morale sinking correspondingly. The nice weather passed, and it was replaced by rain and storms. It was fertile ground for rumors, mistrust and displeasure. The release of the enlisted personnel continued. Soon, the native Germans were in line. On 27 May, the signals camp in Weng was practically disbanded. Only the officers, the mess personnel, and a few drivers had to remain behind. The personnel there from the *3. Panzer-Division* included *Oberleutnant* Eckelmann, *Oberleutnant* Spieckermann, *Oberleutnant* Schmarsow, *Leutnant* Fischer, *Leutnant* Griessenbeck, and *Zahlmeister* Jache from the signals battalion and *Leutnant* Schaeffers from the armored regiment.

General der Panzertruppen Balck was led away by the Americans under degrading circumstances on 26 May. On 6 June, the officers started to be released, with the exception of the staff officers and the medical personnel. The first 800 officers were assembled on 7 June and had to endure the following procedures: remove all awards; undergo a political interrogation; receive a medical examination; and have their personal belongings inspected. After that, there were issued discharge papers. Staff officers and medical personnel were released at the end of June. Only the general officers and the general staff officers remained. *Generaloberst* Rendulic had been sent to the camps in the meantime and became the senior officer. Life was drab and dreary. Weeks passed. One camp after the other was closed and, in the end, only Mauerkirchen remained. The American authorities finally closed that camp at the end of August.

The journey of the *3. Panzer-Division* was over. Most of the soldiers returned to their homeland, destroyed by bombs and occupied by the victors. A few men of the *I./Panzergrenadier-Regiment 3* were picked up by the French and did not come home until 1947.

Many members of the division never saw Germany again. They lay there where they gave their lives in fulfillment of their duty. They left home in the belief they had to protect it. The greatness of their sacrifice cannot be diminished by the fact that an unscrupulous leadership had deceived them. Some of the members of the divisions died in Russian camps, by themselves and quietly.

The majority of those who survived lived in the Soviet Zone of Occupation, separated from their comrades in West Berlin and the Federal Republic. Thus, the division from Berlin and Brandenburg is also a reflection of a divided fatherland.

All of the terrible sacrifices, the superhuman efforts and the bravery did not suffice to change the end result. Despite that, the virtues of self-sacrifice and comradeship demonstrated in the years of warfare justify the hope that the spiritual strength of our people on both sides of the Iron Curtain is strong enough that it may one day lead to a reunification though peaceful means.

Award of the Knight's Cross to *Oberstleutnant* Weymann, commander of *Panzergrenadier-Regiment 3* on 20 February 1945 (from left to right): *Generalmajor* Söth, *Oberstleutnant* Weymann, and *General der Panzertruppen* Breith.

Großmürbisch in Burgenland, the easternmost region of Austria. The men of the division were there for a short while in 1945.

Steiermark, Austria, in April 1945: *Generalmajor* Söth presents awards to tankers after the recent fighting.

Last area of operations in 1945.
(Image taken in 1965.)

Stadtbergen near Fürstenfeld was
evacuated on 17 April 1945.

Oberleutnant Schirp, commander of the *4./Panzer-Regiment 6*. Schirp wears a unit badge on his cap. The unit badges were frequently seen toward the end of the war in a variety of formations. They were unofficial but generally tolerated as a sign of *esprit de corps*.

City Hall in Fürstenfeld. The last remaining vehicles of the division moved through the medieval gate of the town on 15 April 1945.

Major Schulze, commander of the *I./Panzergrenadier-Regiment 3*. He became the last commander of the regiment.

Oberleutnant Bürger, commander of the *1./Panzergrenadier-Regiment 3*. The Knight's Cross was added in the photo studio, a common practice late in the war, when there was no time for a formal sitting.

Oberfunkmeister Hölck. He was the signals sergeant of *Panzer-Regiment 6* and the only member of the division to be awarded the Knight's Cross to the War Service Cross with Swords.

Military cemetery in Ilz.

Newly arranged cemetery in Fürstenfeld. Many members of the division are buried at both of these cemeteries.

Movement to turn over weapons to the Americans in May 1945.

At the American prisoner-collection point.

Generalmajor Munzel (*Panzer-Regiment 6*).

Generalmajor Gorn (*Kradschützen-Bataillon 3*).

Oberstleutnant i.G. Plato (*Schützen-Regiment 3*).

Oberst Burmeister (*Panzer-Regiment 6*).

Oberst Wechmar (*Aufklärungs-Abteilung 3*).

Hauptmann Kageneck.

Hauptmann Oskar Eysser (*Panzer-Regiment 6*).

Hauptmann Rolf Rochell (*Panzer-Regiment 5*), who later received the Oak Leaves.

Memorial Grove for the fallen comrades of the armored divisions at Munster-Lager in the Lüneburg Heath.

The memorial stone for the *3. Panzer-Division* in the Memorial Grove.

The former garrison cemetery in Berlin on Lilienthalstraße with the division's memorial tablet.

A close-up of the memorial tablet: "To the Fallen of the *3. Panzer-Division* of Berlin-Brandenburg in grateful comradeship, 1935/1945."

APPENDIX 1

Rank Table

U.S. Army	German Army	Waffen-SS	English Equivalent
Enlisted			
Private	*Schütze*	*SS-Schütze*[1]	Private
Private First Class	*Oberschütze*	*SS-Oberschütze*[2]	Private First Class
Corporal	*Gefreiter*	*SS-Sturmmann*	Acting Corporal
(Senior Corporal)	*Obergefreiter*	*SS-Rottenführer*	Corporal
(Staff Corporal)	*Stabsgefreiter*	*SS-Stabsrottenführer*[3]	
Noncommissioned Officers			
Sergeant	*Unteroffizier*	*SS-Unterscharführer*	Sergeant
(None)	*Unterfeldwebel*	*SS-Scharführer*	Staff Sergeant
Staff Sergeant	*Feldwebel*	*SS-Oberscharführer*	Technical Sergeant
Sergeant First Class	*Oberfeldwebel*	*SS-Hauptscharführer*	Master Sergeant
Master Sergeant	*Hauptfeldwebel*	*SS-Sturmscharführer*	Sergeant Major
Sergeant Major	*Stabsfeldwebel*		
Officers			
2nd Lieutenant	*Leutnant*	*SS-Untersturmführer*	2nd Lieutenant
1st Lieutenant	*Oberleutnant*	*SS-Obersturmführer*	1st Lieutenant
Captain	*Hauptmann*	*SS-Hauptsturmführer*	Captain
Major	*Major*	*SS-Sturmbannführer*	Major
Lieutenant Colonel	*Oberstleutnant*	*SS-Obersturmbannführer*	Lieutenant Colonel
Colonel	*Oberst*	*SS-Standartenführer*	Colonel
(None)	(None)	*SS-Oberführer*	(None)
Brigadier General	*Generalmajor*	*SS-Brigadeführer*	Brigadier General
Major General	*Generalleutnant*	*SS-Gruppenführer*	Major General
Lieutenant General	*General der Panzertruppen*, etc.	*SS-Obergruppenführer*	Lieutenant General
General	*Generaloberst*	*SS-Oberstgruppenführer*	General
General of the Army	*Feldmarschall*	*Reichsführer-SS*	Field Marshal

1. *SS-Mann* before 1942.
2. Not used before 1942.
3. Rank did not officially exist but has been seen in written records.

APPENDIX 2

Major Command and Duty Positions, 1942–45

The Division Headquarters

Division Commander

Breith	*Generalleutnant*	1 October 1941–30 September 1942
Westhoven	*Generalleutnant*	1 October 1942–14 October 1943
Bayerlein	*Generalmajor*	15 October 1943–9 January 1944
Lang (acting)	*Oberst*	10 January 1944–24 May 1944
Philipps	*Generalleutnant*	25 May 1944–19 January 1945
Söth	*Generalmajor*	20 January–30 April 1945
Schöne	*Oberst*	1–8 May 1945

Division Operations Officer (Ia)

Voss	*Oberstleutnant i.G.*
Schwerdtfeger	*Major i.G.*
Rotberg	*Major i.G.*

Division Logistics Officer (Ib)

Dankworth	*Hauptmann*
Borne	*Major i.G.*
Bülow	*Major i.G.*
Willich	*Major i.G.*

Division Intelligence Officer (Ic)

Knesebeck	*Hauptmann*
Twardowski	*Hauptmann*
Pauck	*Leutnant*
Wiemer	*Oberleutnant*

Adjutant General (Officers) (IIa)

Necker	*Rittmeister*
Wietersheim	*Major*
Oppen	*Major*

Adjutant General (Officers) (IIa) *continued*

Düwel	*Hauptmann*
Menard	*Oberleutnant*
Pilati	*Major*
Alvensleben	*Major*
Brauchitsch	*Hauptmann*
Markowski	*Hauptmann*

Administrative Officer (IVa)

Neiden	*Stabsintendant*
Angermann	*Oberstabsintendant*
Blümel	*Indentanturrat*
Falk	*Oberstabsintendant*

Division Surgeon (IVb)

Muntsch	*Oberstabsarzt*
Böhm	*Oberstabsarzt*
Zinsser	*Oberfeldarzt*
Stribny	*Oberfeldarzt*

Division Chaplains (IVd)

Heidland	Protestant
Sieburg	Protestant
Drews	Protestant
Laub	Catholic
Ruzek	Catholic

Division Transportation Officer (V)

Brätsch	*Regierungs-Baurat*
Rein	*Hauptmann (Ing.)*
Lanig	*Major (Ing.)*
Riessberger	*Major (Ing.)*

Schützen-Brigade 3

Westhoven	*Oberst*	1 February 1942–30 September 1942

Panzer-Regiment 6

Munzel	*Oberst*
Schmidt-Ott	*Oberstleutnant*
Liebenstein	*Oberst*
Munzel	*Oberst*
Schmidt-Ott	*Oberstleutnant*
Goecke (acting)	*Oberstleutnant*
Lühl	*Oberstleutnant*
Bernuth	*Oberst*
Friedrich	*Oberst*
Rohrbeck	*Oberstleutnant*
Schulenburg	*Oberstleutnant*

Schützen-Regiment 3 / Panzergrenadier-Regiment 3

Wellmann	*Oberst*

Schützen-Regiment 3 / Panzergrenadier-Regiment 3 *continued*

Fleischauer	*Oberstleutnant*
Haberland	*Oberstleutnant*
Weymann	*Oberstleutnant*
Schulze	*Major*

Schützen-Regiment 394 / Panzergrenadier-Regiment 394

Chales de Beaulieu	*Oberst*
Pape	*Major*
Beuermann	*Oberst*
Peschke	*Major*
Lühl	*Oberstleutnant*
Thunert	*Oberst*
Schacke	*Oberst*
Siebenhüner	*Major*
Frevert	*Oberstleutnant*
Bösang	*Major*
Rausche	*Major*

Artillerie-Regiment 75 / Panzer-Artillerie-Regiment 75

Lattmann	*Oberst*
Weymann	*Oberstleutnant*
Collenberg	*Oberstleutnant*
Gerhardt	*Oberstleutnant*

Kradschützen-Bataillon 3 / Panzer-Aufklärungs-Abteilung 3

Pape	*Major*
Cochenhausen	*Major*
Deichen	*Hauptmann*
Golze	*Hauptmann*

Aufklärungs-Abteilung 1

Ziervogel	*Major*

Panzerjäger-Abteilung 543

Hoffmann	*Hauptmann*
Medicus	*Major*

Pionier-Bataillon 39 / Panzer-Pionier-Bataillon 39

Petzsch	*Major*
Groeneveld	*Major*
Schwing	*Major*
Sedlaczek	*Hauptmann*

Heeres-Flak-Abteilung 314

Fleischer	*Major*

Feld-Ersatz-Bataillon 83

Biegon	*Hauptmann*
Feldhuß	*Oberstleutnant*
Schaumburg-Lippe	*Major*

Nachrichten-Abteilung 39

Böttge	*Major*
Helfritz	*Major*
Poersch	*Major*
Talkenberg	*Hauptmann*
Schubert	*Hauptmann*

Division Support Command

Feldhuß	*Oberstleutnant*

APPENDIX 3

Winners of the Knight's Cross while Assigned to the Division

OAK LEAVES				
Kruse	*Oberfeldwebel*	Platoon Leader	7./Panzergrenadier-Regiment 3	17 May 1943
Pape	*Oberst*	Regiment Commander	Panzergrenadier-Regiment 394	15 September 1943
Wellmann	*Oberstleutnant*	Regiment Commander	Panzergrenadier-Regiment 3	30 November 1943

KNIGHT'S CROSS				
Brandt	*Oberleutnant*	Company Commander	3./Pionier-Bataillon 39	20 August 1942
Wellmann	*Oberstleutnant*	Battalion Commander	I./Panzergrenadier-Regiment 3	2 September 1942
Tank	*Oberleutnant*	Company Commander	6./Panzergrenadier-Regiment 3	24 September 1942
Kruse	*Oberfeldwebel*	Platoon Leader	7./Panzergrenadier-Regiment 3	6 October 1942
Schmidt-Ott	*Oberstleutnant*	Acting Commander	Panzer-Regiment 6	7 October 1942
Erdmann	*Hauptmann*	Battalion Commander	I./Panzergrenadier-Regiment 3	10 December 1942
Volckens	*Hauptmann*	Company Commander	7./Panzer-Regiment 6	17 December 1942
Dittmer	*Hauptmann*	Battalion Commander	I./Panzergrenadier-Regiment 3	3 April 1943
Steinführer	*Oberfeldwebel*	Platoon Leader	2./Panzergrenadier-Regiment 394	8 May 1943
Deichen	*Hauptmann*	Battalion Commander	Panzer-Aufklärungs-Abteilung 3	10 September 1943
Taulien	*Oberleutnant*	Company Commander	7./Panzer-Regiment 6	18 October 1943
Westhoven	*Generalleutnant*	Division Commander	3. Panzer-Division	25 October 1943
Eggers	*Unteroffizier*	Gunner	7./Panzer-Regiment 6	14 December 1943
Schwing	*Major*	Battalion Commander	Panzer-Pionier-Bataillon 39	30 December 1943
Peschke	*Major*	Battalion Commander	II./Panzergrenadier-Regiment 394	15 January 1944
Sorge	*Oberleutnant*	Company Commander	5./Panzer-Regiment 6	7 February 1944
Kleffel	*Oberleutnant*	Company Commander	4./Panzer-Aufklärungs-Abteilung 3	14 May 1944
Lempp	*Hauptmann*	Company Commander	2./Panzer-Artillerie-Regiment 75	14 May 1944
Dietrich	*Hauptmann*	Battalion Commander	II./Panzergrenadier-Regiment 3	26 June 1944
Görlich	*Unteroffizier*	Squad Leader	1./Panzergrenadier-Regiment 394	4 July 1944
Weymann	*Oberstleutnant*	Regiment Commander	Panzergrenadier-Regiment 3	10 February 1945

KNIGHT'S CROSS *continued*

Phillips	*Generalleutnant*	Division Commander	3. Panzer-Division	5 March 1945
Schirp	*Oberleutnant*	Company Commander	4./Panzer-Regiment 6	28 March 1945
Schulze	*Major*	Battalion Commander	I./Panzergrenadier-Regiment 3	14 April 1945
Bürger	*Oberleutnant*	Company Commander	1./Panzergrenadier-Regiment 3	14 April 1945

KNIGHT'S CROSS TO THE WAR SERVICE CROSS

Hoelck	*Oberfunkmeister*	Regimental Signals NCO	Panzer-Regiment 6	21 February 1944

APPENDIX 4

Winners of the Knight's Cross Assigned to the *3. Panzer-Division* at One Time

OAK LEAVES WITH SWORDS AND DIAMONDS TO THE KNIGHT'S CROSS					
Model	*Generalfeldmarschall*	Commander-in-Chief, Heeresgruppe Mitte	Division Commander, 3. Panzer-Division	17 August 1944	17[1]

OAK LEAVES WITH SWORDS TO THE KNIGHT'S CROSS					
Model	*Generaloberst*	Commander-in-Chief, 9. Armee	Division Commander, 3. Panzer-Division	3 April 1943	28
Gorn	*Oberst*	Regiment Commander, Panzergrenadier-Regiment 10	5./Kradschützen-Bataillon 3	23 July 1943	30
Breith	*General der Panzertruppen*	Commanding General, III. Panzer-Korps	Division Commander, 3. Panzer-Division	21 February 1944	48
Wietersheim	*Generalmajor*	Division Commander, 11. Panzer-Division	Adjutant General (Officers), 3. Panzer-Division	26 March 1944	58
Bayerlein	*Generalleutnant*	Division Commander, Panzer-Lehr-Division	Division Commander, 3. Panzer-Division	20 July 1944	81
Weidling	*General der Artillerie*	Commanding General, XXXXI. Panzer-Korps	Regiment Commander, Artillerie-Regiment 75	23 November 1944	115
Nehring	*General der Panzertruppen*	Commanding General, XXIV. Panzer-Korps	Regiment Commander, Panzer-Regiment 5	22 January 1945	124

1. Indicates sequencing number of the award.

OAK LEAVES

Gorn	Oberstleutnant	Battalion Commander, Kradschützen-Bataillon 59	5./Kradschützen-Bataillon 3	17 August 1942	113
Wietersheim	Oberst	Regiment Commander, Schützen-Regiment 113	Adjutant General (Officers), 3. Panzer-Division	15 January 1943	176
Bayerlein	Generalmajor	Chief-of-Staff, Italian 1st Army	Division Commander, 3. Panzer-Division	6 July 1943	258
Funck	Generalleutnant	Division Commander, 7. Panzer-Division	Regiment Commander, Panzer-Regiment 5	22 August 1943	278
Rocholl	Hauptmann	Battalion Commander, III./Grenadier-Regiment 569	Panzer-Regiment 5	31 August 1943	287
Kleemann	Generalleutnant	Division Commander, Sturm-Division Rhodos	Brigade Commander, Schützen-Brigade 3	16 September 1943	304
Nehring	General der Panzertruppen	Commanding General, XXIV. Panzer-Korps	Regiment Commander, Panzer-Regiment 5	8 February 1944	513
Kageneck	Hauptmann	Battalion Commander, schwere Panzer-Abteilung 503	Panzer-Regiment 6	26 June 1944	513
Behr	Oberst	Acting Commander, 90. Panzergrenadier-Division	Battalion Commander, Nachrichten-Abteilung 39	9 January 1945	689
Engelien	Oberstleutnant	Regiment Commander, Panzergrenadier-Regiment 25	Company Commander, 6./Schützen-Regiment 3	27 March 1945	788

KNIGHT'S CROSS

Burmeister	Generalmajor	Division Commander, 25. Panzergrenadier-Division	II./Panzer-Regiment 6	14 January 1945	
Diest-Koerber	Hauptmann	Battalion Commander, schwere Panzer-Abteilung 503	Panzer-Regiment 6	1 May 1945	
Engelien	Major	Battalion Commander, Panzer-Aufklärungs-Abteilung 12	Company Commander, 6./Schützen-Regiment 3	25 August 1944	
Everth	Hauptmann	Company Commander, Aufklärungs-Abteilung 3	1./Aufklärungs-Abteilung 3	11 July 1942	
Eysser	Hauptmann	Company Commander, Panzer-Regiment 31	5./Panzer-Regiment 6	15 November 1944	
Fechner	Major	Battalion Commander, III./Panzer-Regiment 23	Panzer-Regiment 6	7 October 1943	
Fischer	Oberleutnant	Company Commander, 8./Panzer-Regiment 23	1./Panzer-Regiment 5	28 December 1943	
Friebe	Oberst	Acting Commander, 8. Panzer-Division		5 May 1944	
Grün	Hauptmann	Acting Commander, I./Panzer-Regiment 5		8 February 1943	
Hoehno	Leutnant	Platoon Leader, Schwere Panzer-Abteilung 510	Panzer-Regiment 6	31 December 1944	
Kageneck	Hauptmann	Battalion Commander, schwere Panzer-Abteilung 503	Panzer-Regiment 6	4 August 1943	
Knauth	Leutnant der Reserve	Acting Commander, 1./schwere Panzer-Abteilung 503	III./Panzer-Regiment 6	17 November 1943	
Liebenstein	Generalmajor	Division Commander, 164. leichte Division	Panzer-Regiment 6	15 May 1943	
Munzel	Oberst	Acting Commander, 14. Panzer-Division	Panzer-Regiment 6	25 October 1944	
Plato	Oberstleutnant i.G.	Operations Officer, 5. Panzer-Division	Schützen-Regiment 3	5 September 1944	

KNIGHT'S CROSS *continued*

Rocholl	*Oberleutnant*	Company Commander, Panzer-Regiment 5		3 August 1942
Thunert	*Generalmajor*	Division Commander, 1. Panzer-Division	Regiment Commander, Panzergrenadier-Regiment 394	9 February 1945
Tröger	*Generalmajor*	Division Commander, 17. Panzer-Division	Battalion Commander, Kradschützen-Bataillon 3	15 May 1944
Weidling	*Generalmajor*	Division Commander, 86. Infanterie-Division	Regiment Commander, Artillerie-Regiment 75	15 January 1943
Ziegler	*SS-Brigadeführer*	Division Commander, SS-Freiwilligen-Panzer-Grenadier-Division "Nordland"	Panzer-Brigade 3	15 September 1944

APPENDIX 5

Recipients of the German Cross in Gold

Markowski	*Oberleutnant*	Company Commander	8./Panzer-Regiment 6	16 March 1942
Ziervogel	*Major*	Battalion Commander	Panzer-Aufklärungs-Abteilung 1	25 March 1942
Sorge	*Oberfeldwebel*		7./Panzer-Regiment 6	25 March 1942
Mente	*Oberleutnant*	Company Commander	7./Schützen-Regiment 3	11 April 1942
Schiller	*Leutnant der Reserve*	Acting Company Commander	II./Schützen-Regiment 394	14 April 1942
Wacker	*Oberfeldwebel*		8./Panzer-Regiment 6	14 April 1942
Peschke	*Hauptmann*	Acting Commander	II./Schützen-Regiment 3	30 May 1942
Arndt	*Oberfeldwebel*		5./Schützen-Regiment 394	30 May 1942
Pfeiffer	*Oberfeldwebel*		4./Schützen-Regiment 3	30 May 1942
Frank	*Major*	Battalion Commander	II./Panzer-Regiment 6	30 May 1942
Heyden-Rynsch	*Hauptmann*	Battalion Commander	I./Schützen-Regiment 394	8 June 1942
Wellmann	*Major*	Battalion Commander	I./Schützen-Regiment 3	8 June 1942
Lange	*Oberleutnant*		5./Artillerie-Regiment 75	29 August 1942
Pomtow	*Oberstleutnant i.G.*	Operations Officer	3. Panzer-Division	12 September 1942
Kersten	*Hauptmann*	Battalion Commander	III./Artillerie-Regiment 75	13 September 1942
Lingk	*Hauptmann*	Company Commander	3./Panzerjäger-Abteilung 521	13 September 1942
Streger	*Major*	Battalion Commander	Panzerjäger-Abteilung 521	18 October 1942
Kanthak	*Oberfeldwebel*	Platoon Leader	1./Panzergrenadier-Regiment 394	23 October 1942
Rodenhauser	*Hauptmann*	Company Commander	1./Panzer-Regiment 6	31 October 1942
Harbeck	*Leutnant*	Acting Company Commander	Kradschützen-Bataillon 3	31 October 1942
Kageneck	*Oberleutnant*	Company Commander	4./Panzer-Regiment 6	28 November 1942
Becker	*Leutnant der Reserve*	Acting Commander	8./Panzer-Regiment 6	24 December 1942
Weigel	*Oberleutnant der Reserve*	Acting Commander	2./Panzer-Pionier-Bataillon 39	20 January 1943
Busch	*Oberleutnant*	Company Commander	1./Panzergrenadier-Regiment 3	29 January 1943
Munzel	*Oberst*	Regiment Commander	Panzer-Regiment 6	14 February 1943
Wiedenhöft	*Feldwebel*		2./Panzer-Regiment 6	14 February 1943
Berg	*Oberleutnant*	Company Commander	7./Panzergrenadier-Regiment 3	6 March 1943
Lindemann	*Unteroffizier*		4./Kradschützen-Bataillon 3	14 March 1943
Reiss	*Oberfeldwebel*	Platoon Leader	1./Panzergrenadier-Regiment 394	14 March 1943
Lesch	*Oberfeldwebel*		6./Panzergrenadier-Regiment 3	14 March 1943
Müller-Röhlich	*Hauptmann*	Battalion Commander	II./Panzergrenadier-Regiment 394	2 April 1943
Hagenguth	*Hauptmann*	Company Commander	1./Panzerjäger-Abteilung 543	2 April 1943
Schulze	*Oberleutnant der Reserve*		II./Panzergrenadier-Regiment 394	2 April 1943

Audörsch	*Oberstleutnant*	Regiment Commander	Panzergrenadier-Regiment 394	21 April 1943
Dentler	*Feldwebel*		7./Panzergrenadier-Regiment 394	21 April 1943
Rüdenburg	*Oberfeldwebel*		1./Kradschützen-Bataillon 3	8 May 1943
Deichen	*Hauptmann*	Company Commander	2./Kradschützen-Bataillon 3	8 May 1943
Blass	*Unteroffizier*		3./Kradschützen-Bataillon 3	8 May 1943
Voutta	*Oberleutnant*	Company Commander	Kradschützen-Bataillon 3	8 May 1943
Huhn	*Oberleutnant*	Acting Commander	8./Panzer-Regiment 6	13 May 1943
Möllhoff	*Oberleutnant*	Company Commander	3./Panzer-Pionier-Bataillon 39	3 June 1943
Zimmermann	*Oberst*	Regiment Commander	Panzergrenadier-Regiment 3	28 July 1943
Weymann	*Major der Reserve*	Regiment Commander	Panzer-Artillerie-Regiment 75	7 August 1943
Sydow	*Oberfeldwebel*		8./Panzer-Regiment 6	7 August 1943
Krotke	*Fahnenjunker-Oberfeldwebel*		8./Panzer-Regiment 6	7 August 1943
Stockmann	*Major*	Battalion Commander	II./Panzer-Regiment 6	7 August 1943
Von Krenzki	*Oberfeldwebel*		5./Panzergrenadier-Regiment 394	8 September 1943
Schroeder	*Oberfeldwebel*	Platoon Leader	1./Panzergrenadier-Regiment 394	8 September 1943
Strucken	*Feldwebel*		5./Panzergrenadier-Regiment 394	8 September 1943
Ossenbühn	*Leutnant*		I./Panzergrenadier-Regiment 394	8 September 1943
Haase	*Feldwebel*		2./Panzer-Aufklärungs-Abteilung 3	8 September 1943
Comberg	*Hauptmann der Reserve*	Company Commander	9./Panzergrenadier-Regiment 3	14 September 1943
Adamek	*Oberleutnant der Reserve*	Company Commander	8./Panzer-Regiment 6	14 September 1943
Wykopal	*Hauptmann*	Battalion Commander	I./Panzer-Artillerie-Regiment 75	15 September 1943
Arnoldt	*Hauptmann*	Acting Commander	II./Panzergrenadier-Regiment 394	15 September 1943
Eggert	*Hauptmann*	Acting Commander	I./Panzergrenadier-Regiment 394	15 September 1943
Dietrich	*Hauptmann*	Company Commander	5./Panzergrenadier-Regiment 3	15 September 1943
Motz	*Oberleutnant*	Company Commander	I./Panzergrenadier-Regiment 394	15 September 1943
Kölle	*Oberleutnant*	Adjutant	II./Panzer-Regiment 6	22 September 1943
Paschek	*Oberfeldwebel*		1./Panzergrenadier-Regiment 3	12 October 1943
Klingbeil	*Oberfeldwebel*		4./Panzergrenadier-Regiment 3	12 October 1943
Gaebler	*Hauptmann*	Battery Commander	4./Panzer-Artillerie-Regiment 75	25 October 1943
Kleffel	*Oberleutnant*	Company Commander	4./Panzer-Aufklärungs-Abteilung	16 November 1943
Oelrich	*Hauptmann*	Adjutant	Panzer-Regiment 6	17 November 1943
Lattmann	*Oberst*	Regiment Commander	Panzer-Artillerie-Regiment 75	21 November 1943
Biegon	*Hauptmann*	Acting Commander	Feld-Ersatz-Bataillon 75	21 November 1943
Schmidt	*Hauptmann*	Company Commander	5./Panzer-Artillerie-Regiment 75	21 November 1943
Harzer	*Oberleutnant*	Company Commander	1./Panzer-Pionier-Bataillon 39	21 November 1943
Tiemann	*Oberfeldwebel*		6./Panzergrenadier-Regiment 394	21 November 1943
Ostwald	*Oberwachtmeister*		5./Panzer-Artillerie-Regiment 75	1 December 1943
Koczula	*Oberfeldwebel*		6./Panzergrenadier-Regiment 3	26 December 1943
Jäckle	*Oberfeldwebel*		6./Panzer-Regiment 6	13 January 1944
Beuermann	*Oberstleutnant*	Regiment Commander	Panzergrenadier-Regiment 394	4 February 1944
Golze	*Hauptmann*	Company Commander	1./Panzer-Aufklärungs-Abteilung	4 February 1944
Voigt	*Feldwebel*		Panzer-Regiment 6	4 February 1944
Brandt	*Hauptmann*	Acting Commander	I./Panzergrenadier-Regiment 3	13 February 1944
Geis	*Oberleutnant*	Company Commander	10./Panzergrenadier-Regiment 3	21 February 1944
Zeise	*Hauptmann der Reserve*	Company Commander	2./Panzer-Aufklärungs-Abteilung	21 February 1944
Von Veltheim	*Oberleutnant*	Acting Commander	6./Panzer-Regiment 6	17 March 1944

Lempp	*Oberleutnant*	Battery Commander	2./Panzer-Artillerie-Regiment 75	24 April 1944
Otte	*Unteroffizier*		2./Panzer-Aufklärungs-Abteilung 3	24 April 1944
König	*Hauptmann*	Acting Commander	II./Panzer-Regiment 6	28 April 1944
Westerman	*Oberleutnant der Reserve*	Company Commander	7./Panzergrenadier-Regiment 3	11 May 1944
Kunze	*Oberleutnant*	Company Commander	2./Panzer-Pionier-Bataillon 39	14 May 1944
Hofner	*Unteroffizier*		4./Panzer-Aufklärungs-Abteilung 3	14 May 1944
Goedecke	*Unteroffizier*		2./Panzergrenadier-Regiment 394	23 May 1944
Von Borcke	*Leutnant*	Acting Company Commander	I./Panzergrenadier-Regiment 394	23 May 1944
Lühl	*Oberstleutnant*	Battalion Commander	II./Panzer-Regiment 6	1 June 1944
Voss	*Oberstleutnant i.G.*	Division Operations officer	3. Panzer-Division	4 June 1944
Borghard	*Oberfeldwebel*		3./Panzergrenadier-Regiment 3	15 June 1944
Buchmann	*Hauptmann*	Battery Commander	3./Panzer-Artillerie-Regiment 75	20 June 1944
Hinz	*Unteroffizier der Reserve*	Squad leader	4./Panzer-Aufklärungs-Abteilung 3	8 July 1944
Schönfeld	*Oberfeldwebel*	Platoon Leader	7./Panzergrenadier-Regiment 3	21 July 1944
Leuthardt	*Oberleutnant der Reserve*	Acting Company Commander	5./Panzer-Regiment 6	17 August 1944
Collenberg	*Oberstleutnant*	Regiment Commander	Panzer-Artillerie-Regiment 75	30 September 1944
Zedlitz	*Oberleutnant*	Company Commander	1./Panzer-Pionier-Bataillon 39	9 October 1944
Minzlaff	*Oberleutnant der Reserve*	Company Commander	4./Panzergrenadier-Regiment 394	9 October 1944
Milstrey	*Hauptmann*	Battery Commander	1./Heeres-Flak-Abteilung 314	10 October 1944
Rosemeyer	*Oberleutnant der Reserve*	Company Commander	5./Panzergrenadier-Regiment 394	10 October 1944
Kerstan	*Oberfeldwebel*		4./Panzer-Aufklärungs-Abteilung 3	12 October 1944
Lüchtefeld	*Unteroffizier*		4./Panzer-Aufklärungs-Abteilung 3	21 October 1944
Schenk	*Obergefreiter*		3./Panzer-Aufklärungs-Abteilung 3	27 October 1944
Schröder	*Leutnant*	Liaison Officer	Headquarters, Panzer-Aufklärungs-Abteilung 3	27 October 1944
Hoppe	*Feldwebel*	Company Headquarters Section Leader	7./Panzergrenadier-Regiment 394	14 November 1944
Osten	*Leutnant der Reserve*		4./Panzer-Aufklärungs-Abteilung 3	14 November 1944
Schmuths	*Oberfeldwebel*		1./Panzer-Pionier-Bataillon 39	27 November 1944
Künkel	*Oberwachtmeister*		5./Panzer-Artillerie-Regiment 75	27 November 1944
Seifert	*Hauptmann*	Acting Commander	II./Panzergrenadier-Regiment 3	15 December 1944
Phillips	*Generalleutnant*	Commander	3. Panzer-Division	30 December 1944
Brümmer	*Oberleutnant der Reserve*	Company Commander	I./Panzer-Regiment 6	8 March 1945
Blaich	*Leutnant*	Acting Commander	I./Panzer-Regiment 6	8 March 1945
Voigts	*Hauptmann*	Battalion Commander	II./Panzer-Regiment 6	9 March 1945
Schmidt	*Hauptmann*	Acting Commander	II./Panzergrenadier-Regiment 394	22 March 1945
Dickfoss	*Obergefreiter*		3./Panzer-Aufklärungs-Abteilung 3	22 March 1945
Voutta	*Feldwebel*		Panzergrenadier-Regiment 394	22 March 1945
Fleischauer	*Oberst*	Acting Commander	Panzergrenadier-Regiment 3	24 March 1944
Schramm	*Hauptmann*		I./Panzer-Regiment 6	30 March 1945
Potthoff	*Feldwebel der Reserve*		Headquarters Company, Panzer-Aufklärungs-Abteilung 3	14 April 1945
Aschermann	*Oberleutnant der Reserve*		5./Panzer-Regiment 6	27 April 1945
Oehler	*Oberfeldwebel*		7./Panzer-Regiment 6	27 April 1945

APPENDIX 6

Recipients of the German Cross in Silver

Fiehl	*Hauptmann*	Company Commander	Armor Maintenance Company, Panzer-Regiment 6	21 April 1944
Graupner	*Feldwebel*	Maintenance Sergeant	Panzergrenadier-Regiment 394	21 June 1944
Landsberg	*Oberfeldwebel*	Maintenance Section Leader	II./Panzer-Regiment 6	21 June 1944
Kroiss	*Stabsfeldwebel*	Armaments NCO	Panzer-Artillerie-Regiment 75	9 September 1944
Bartsch	*Heereshauptwerkmeister*	Leader of the Maintenance Section	II./Panzergrenadier-Regiment 3	22 September 1944
Laukötter	*Heereshauptwerkmeister*		Armor Maintenance Company, Panzer-Regiment 6	5 November 1944
Riessberger	*Major*	Division Engineer	3. Panzer-Division	20 April 1945
Sonnek	*Technischer Inspektor Nachrichten*		Panzer-Nachrichten-Abteilung 39	20 April 1945

APPENDIX 7

Induction in the Army Honor Roll

Name	Rank	Unit	Date	Location	Induction Date
Müller-Hauff	*Oberleutnant*	Company Commander, 3./Panzer-Regiment 6	1–3 January 1942	Trudy	1 March 1942
Cochenhausen	*Hauptmann*	Company Commander, 1./Kradschützen-Bataillon 3	19 January 1942	Maschnino	18 March 1942
Boehm	*Major*	Battalion Commander, II./Panzergrenadier-Regiment 3	30–31 July 1942	Proletarskaja	5 September 1942
Hess	*Leutnant*	Acting Commander, 4./Kradschützen-Bataillon 3	14 September 1942	Ischerskaja	19 November 1942
Rohrbeck	*Hauptmann*	Battalion Commander, I./Panzer-Regiment 6	9 November 1942	Artaschikoff	7 January 1943
Rode	*Major*	Battalion Commander, I./Panzergrenadier-Regiment 394	15 January 1943	Brjanskij	7 May 1943
Steinführer	*Fahnenjunker-Oberfeldwebel*	Platoon Leader, 2./Panzergrenadier-Regiment 394	4 July 1943	Gerzowka	27 September 1943
Veltheim	*Oberleutnant*	Platoon leader, Light Platoon of the II./Panzer-Regiment 6	5 July 1943	Krassnyj-Potschink	19 September 1943
Mente	*Hauptmann*	Battalion Commander, II./Panzergrenadier-Regiment 3	8 July 1943	Luchanino	7 October 1943
König	*Leutnant*	Liaison Officer, II./Panzergrenadier-Regiment 394	11 July 1943	Ssyrzewo	19 September 1943
Rövekamp	*Oberleutnant*	Company Commander, 5./Panzergrenadier-Regiment 394	12 July 1943	Werchopenje	19 September 1943
Sorge	*Leutnant*	Acting Commander, 7./Panzer-Regiment 6	19–21 July 1943	Luchanino	5 November 1943
Peschke	*Major*	Panzergrenadier-Regiment 394	20 July 1943	Gremutschij-Ssyrzewo	7 March 1944
Steinmüller	*Hauptmann*	Adjutant, Panzergrenadier-Regiment 394	16 August 1943	Polewaja	21 December 1943
Brandt	*Hauptmann*	Adjutant, Panzergrenadier-Regiment 3	22 August 1943	Star. Ljubotin	27 October 1943
Romeike	*Leutnant*	Armored Car Platoon Leader, 1./Panzer-Aufklärungs-Abteilung 3	1 October 1943	Kretschatschik	17 November 9143
Gäbel	*Leutnant*	Platoon Leader, 3./Panzer-Pionier-Bataillon 39	7–15 October 1943	Butschak	7 December 1943
Kunze	*Oberleutnant*	Company Commander, 2./Panzer-Pionier-Bataillon 39	8–13 October 1943	Butschak	5 December 1943
Nöske	*Stabsgefreiter*	3./Panzer-Aufklärungs-Abteilung 3	23 August 1944	Zarowka	17 October 1944
Gaebler	*Hauptmann*	II./Panzer-Artillerie-Regiment 75	23 August 1944	Lisow	25 October 1944
Brümmer	*Leutnant*	1./Panzer-Regiment 6	21 September 1944	Biesdorf	27 October 1944
Pollack	*Unteroffizier*	Squad Leader, 3./Panzer-Aufklärungs-Abteilung 3	11 October 1944	Wiersbitz	27 November 1944

Name	Rank	Unit	Date	Location	Induction Date
Army High Command: Paperwork submitted but decision never published					
Friedrich	*Oberfeldwebel*	Headquarters, Panzer-Aufklärungs-Abteilung 3	20 December 1944	Forestry Offices, Leledhidi	
Gohle	*Oberleutnant*	2./Panzer-Aufklärungs-Abteilung 3	21–29 December 1944	Tergenye	
Winter	*Oberleutnant*	Heeres-Flak-Abteilung 314		North of Ipoly-Szakallos	
Benthien	*Hauptmann*	1./Panzerjäger-Abteilung 543	25–26 December 1944	Tergenye	
Paul	*Unteroffizier*	2./Panzer-Aufklärungs-Abteilung 3	27–28 December 1944	Kis-Gyarmat	

APPENDIX 8

Accredited Skirmishes, Engagements, and Battles of the *3. Panzer-Division*, 1942–45

5 February 1942–8 May 1945	Campaign in the East
5 February–8 March 1942	Defensive fighting for Kursk
9 March–11 May 1942	Fighting along the Upper Donez and along the Son and the Ssemina
9 March–11 May 1942	Defensive fighting north of Charkow
12 May–26 June 1942	Battle for Charkow
22–27 May 1942	Pocket battle southwest of Charkow
28 May–21 June 1942	Defensive fighting along the Donez
22–25 June 1942	Battle of Isjum–Kupjansk
27 June–18 November 1942	1942 Offensive in the East
27 June–8 July 1942	Breakthrough and pursuit towards the Upper Don; capture of Woronesch
9–24 July 1942	Breakthrough and pursuit in the Donez Basin and towards the Lower Don
20 July–13 August 1942	Pursuit across the Lower Don
14 August–18 November 1942	Fighting in the Terek area
31 December 1942–28 January 1943	Withdrawal from the Central Caucasus to the Lower Don
29 January–13 February 1943	Defensive fighting in the Donez area
14 February–4 March 1943	Battle between the Donez and the Dnjepr
5–31 March 1943	Defensive fighting in the Mius–Donez Position
1 April–3 July 1943	Defensive fighting along the Middle Donez
4 July–31 December 1943	Defensive fighting in the east in 1943
4–12 July 1943	Offensive in the Kursk area

5 February 1942–8 May 1945	Campaign in the East
13–22 July 1943	Defensive fighting in the Kursk area
23–27 July 1943	Employment in the rear area of *Heeresgruppe Mitte*
28 July–3 August 1943	Staging for the counterattack along the Mius and retaking of the Mius Line
4 August–27 September 1943	Defensive fighting in southern Russia and withdrawal to the Dnjepr: 6–23 August: Defensive fighting for Charkow 24 August–14 September: Defensive fighting in the area west of Charkow
28 September–31 December 1943	Defensive fighting along the Dnjepr: 29 November–13 December: Defensive fighting at Tscherkassy 14–30 December: Defensive fighting in the Kirowograd area
1 January–20 May 1944	Defensive fighting in the southern Ukraine.
1–5 January 1944	Fighting in the Kirowograd area
5–26 January 1944	Fighting south of Schpola
27 January–24 February 1944	Defensive fighting at Jampol
25 February–1 March 1944	Employment in the rear area of *Heeresgruppe Südukraine*
2–6 March 1944	Defensive fighting along the Dnjepr and the Ingulez
7–26 March 1944	Defensive fighting north of Nikolajew and fighting retreat to the Bug
27 March–2 April 1944	Fighting retreat through Transistrien to the lower Dnjepr
3–22 April 1944	Defensive fighting in northern Bessarabia
23 April–9 May 1944	Employment in the rear area of *Heeresgruppe Südukraine*
10–12 May 1944	Offensive operations south of Grigoriopol
13–20 May 1944	Positional fighting in the sector of *Heeresgruppe Südukraine*
21 May–29 July 1944	Employment in the rear area of *Heeresgruppe Südukraine*
30 July–19 August 1944	Information missing
20 August–21 December 1944	Offensive and defensive operations in the Baranow Bridgehead and southeastern Prussia
21 December–15 March 1945	Offensive and defensive operations in the area around Stuhlweißenburg–Budapest
16 March–2 April 1945	Defensive fighting in western Hungary; fighting retreat to the borders of the Reich
3 April–8 May 1945	Defense of the Steirmark (Austria)